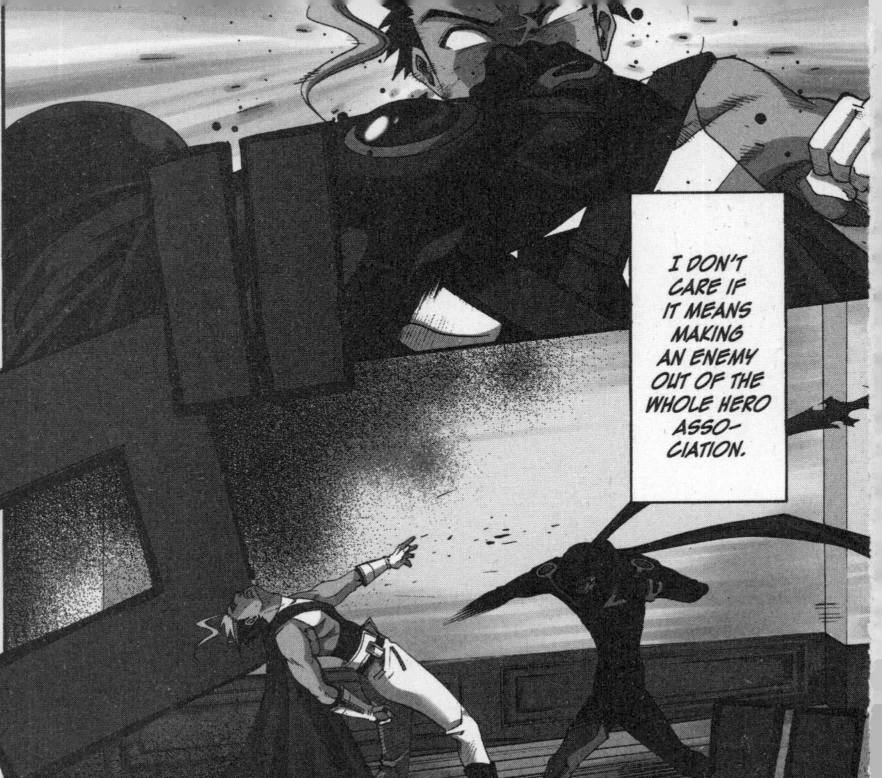
I DON'T CARE IF IT MEANS MAKING AN ENEMY OUT OF THE WHOLE HERO ASSO-CIATION.
THE SMALLEST HERO!?
RATMAN

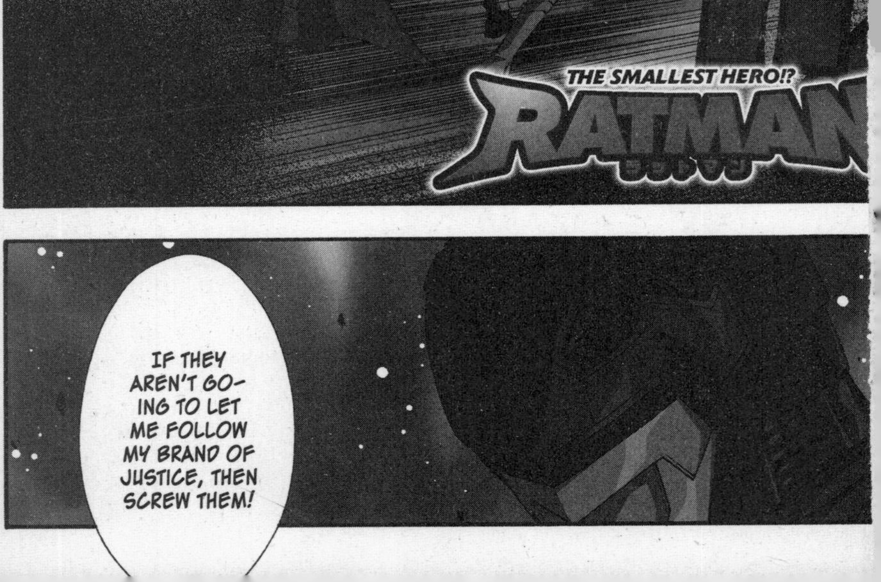
IF THEY AREN'T GO-ING TO LET ME FOLLOW MY BRAND OF JUSTICE, THEN SCREW THEM!

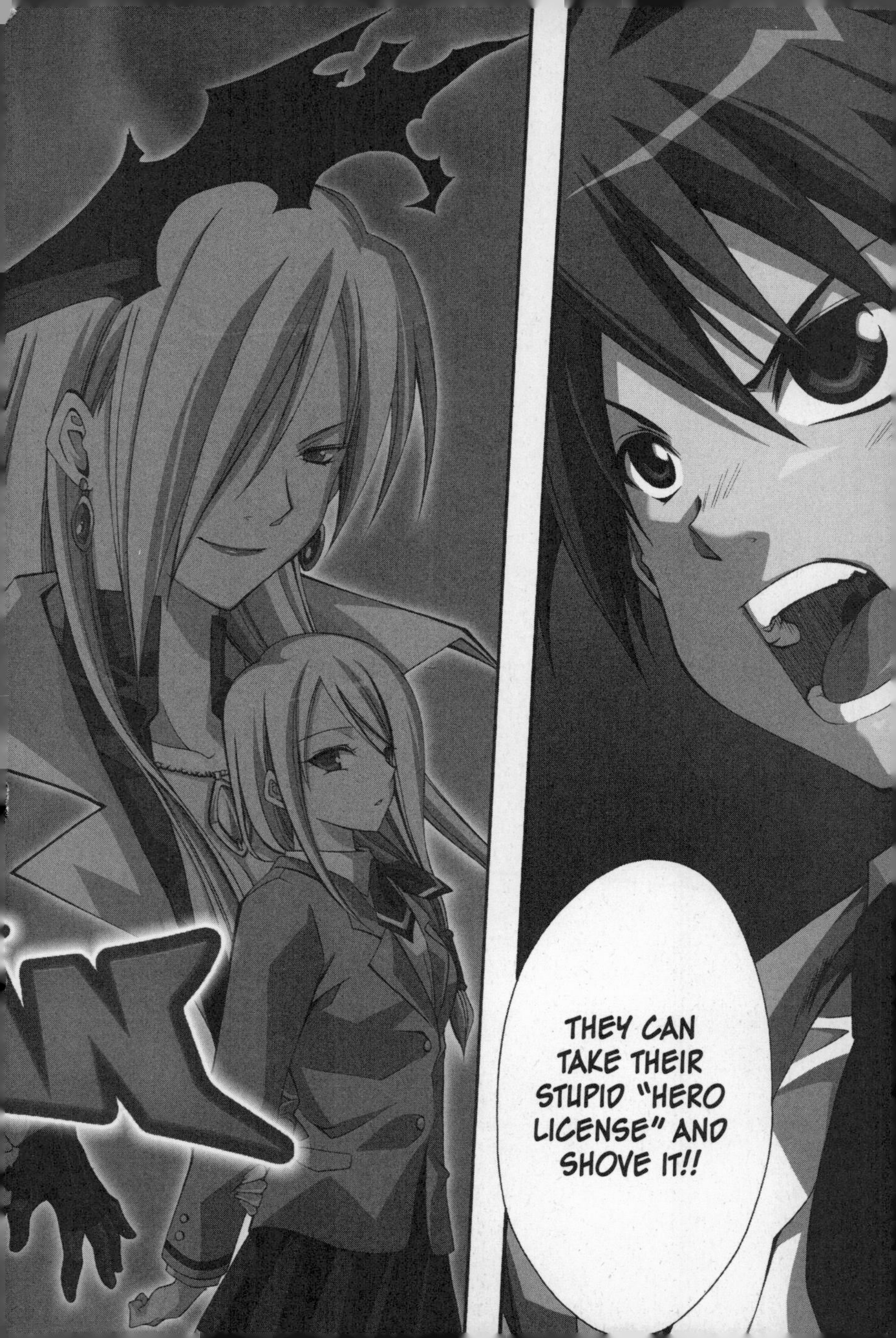
THEY CAN TAKE THEIR STUPID "HERO LICENSE" AND SHOVE IT!!

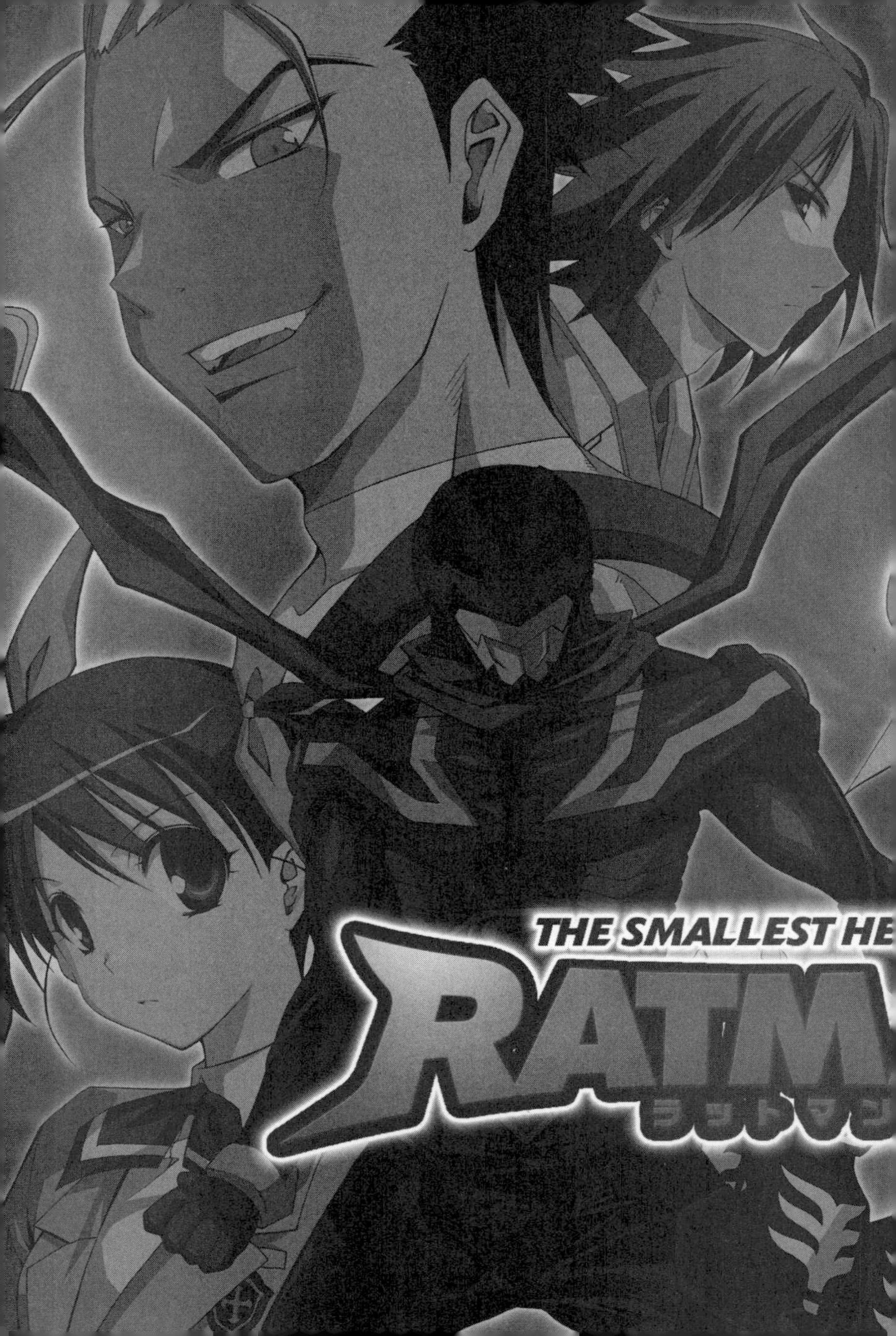
THE SMALLEST HE
RATM

Ratman Volume 3
Created by Sekihiko Inui

Translation - Adrienne Beck
English Adaptation - Bryce P. Coleman
Retouch and Lettering - Star Print Brokers
Production Artist - Rui Kyo
Graphic Designer - Louis Csontos

Editor - Cindy Suzuki
Print Production Manager - Lucas Rivera
Managing Editor - Vy Nguyen
Senior Designer - Louis Csontos
Art Director - Al-Insan Lashley
Director of Sales and Manufacturing - Allyson De Simone
President and C.O.O. - John Parker
C.E.O. and Chief Creative Officer - Stu Levy

A **TOKYOPOP** Manga

TOKYOPOP and are trademarks or registered trademarks of TOKYOPOP Inc.

TOKYOPOP Inc.
5900 Wilshire Blvd. Suite 2000
Los Angeles, CA 90036

E-mail: info@TOKYOPOP.com
Come visit us online at www.TOKYOPOP.com

ISBN: 978-1-4278-1747-1

First TOKYOPOP printing: January 2011
10 9 8 7 6 5 4 3 2 1
Printed in the USA

THE SMALLEST HERO!?
RATMAN

by Sekihiko Inui

HAMBURG // LONDON // LOS ANGELES // TOKYO

THE SMALLEST HERO!?

RATMAN

ラットマン

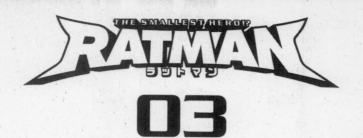

03

Sekihiko Inui PRESENTS

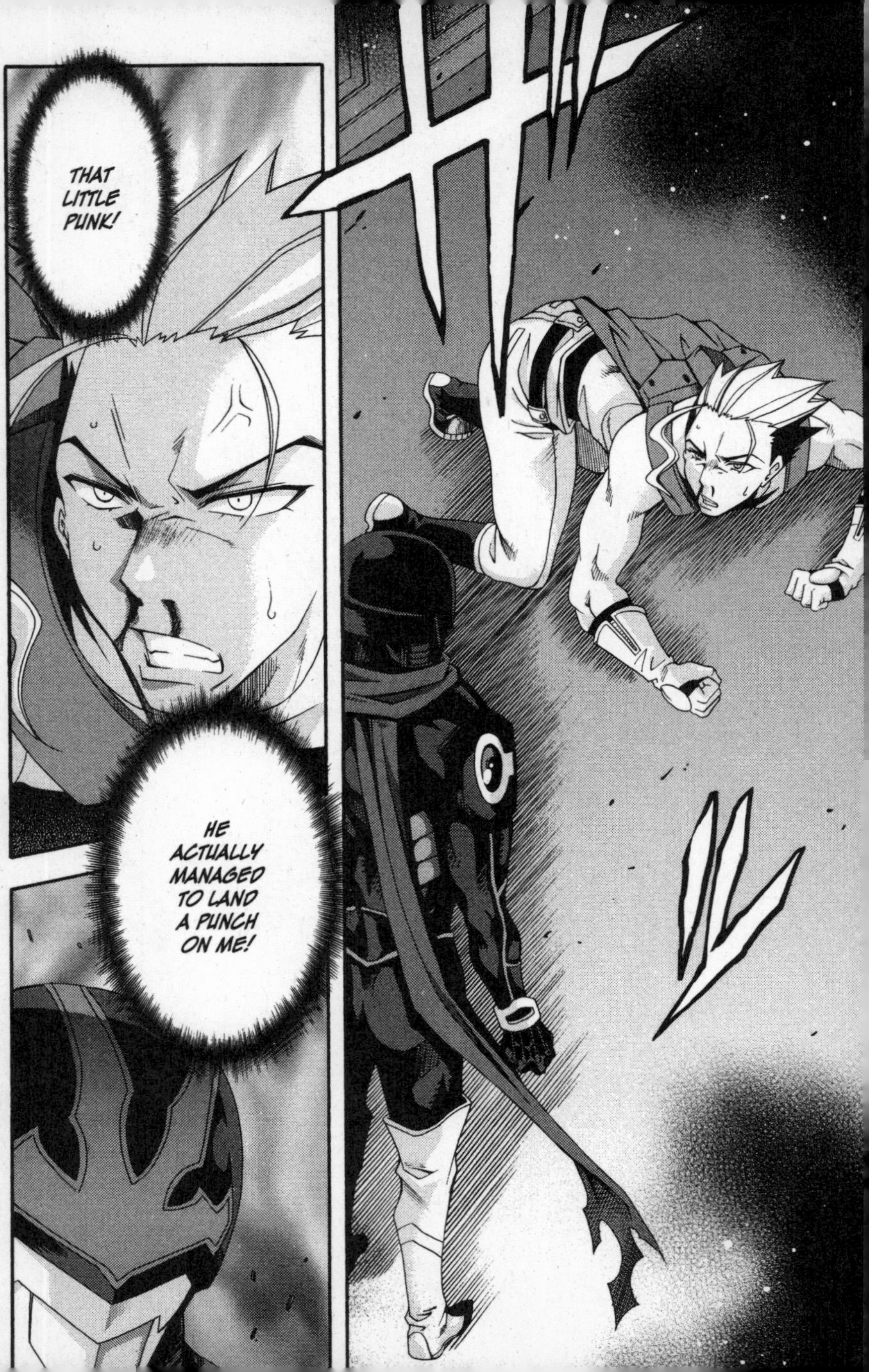
THAT LITTLE PUNK!
HE ACTUALLY MANAGED TO LAND A PUNCH ON ME!

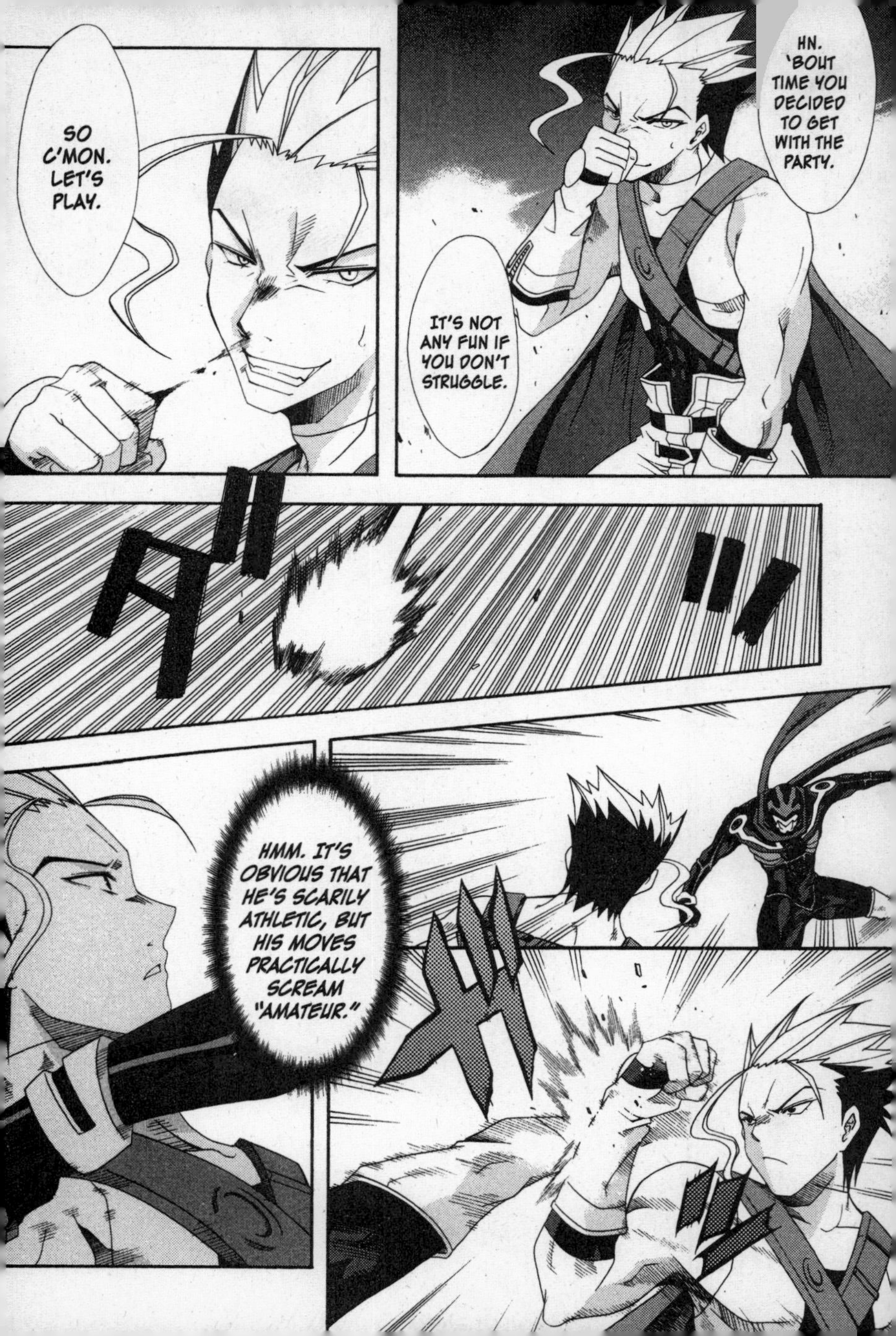
HN. 'BOUT TIME YOU DECIDED TO GET WITH THE PARTY.
IT'S NOT ANY FUN IF YOU DON'T STRUGGLE.
SO C'MON. LET'S PLAY.
HMM. IT'S OBVIOUS THAT HE'S SCARILY ATHLETIC, BUT HIS MOVES PRACTICALLY SCREAM "AMATEUR."

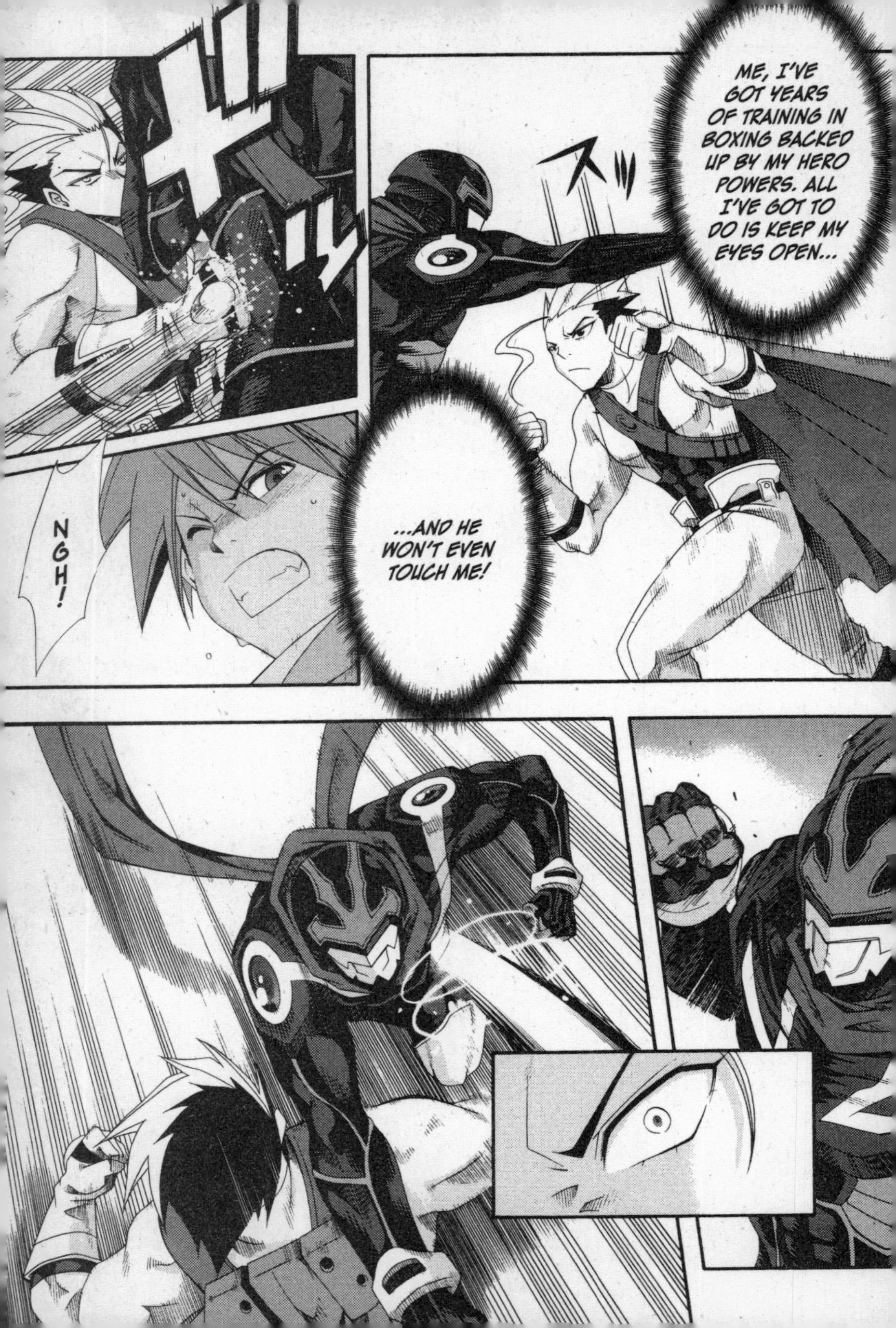
ME, I'VE GOT YEARS OF TRAINING IN BOXING BACKED UP BY MY HERO POWERS. ALL I'VE GOT TO DO IS KEEP MY EYES OPEN...
...AND HE WON'T EVEN TOUCH ME!
NGH!

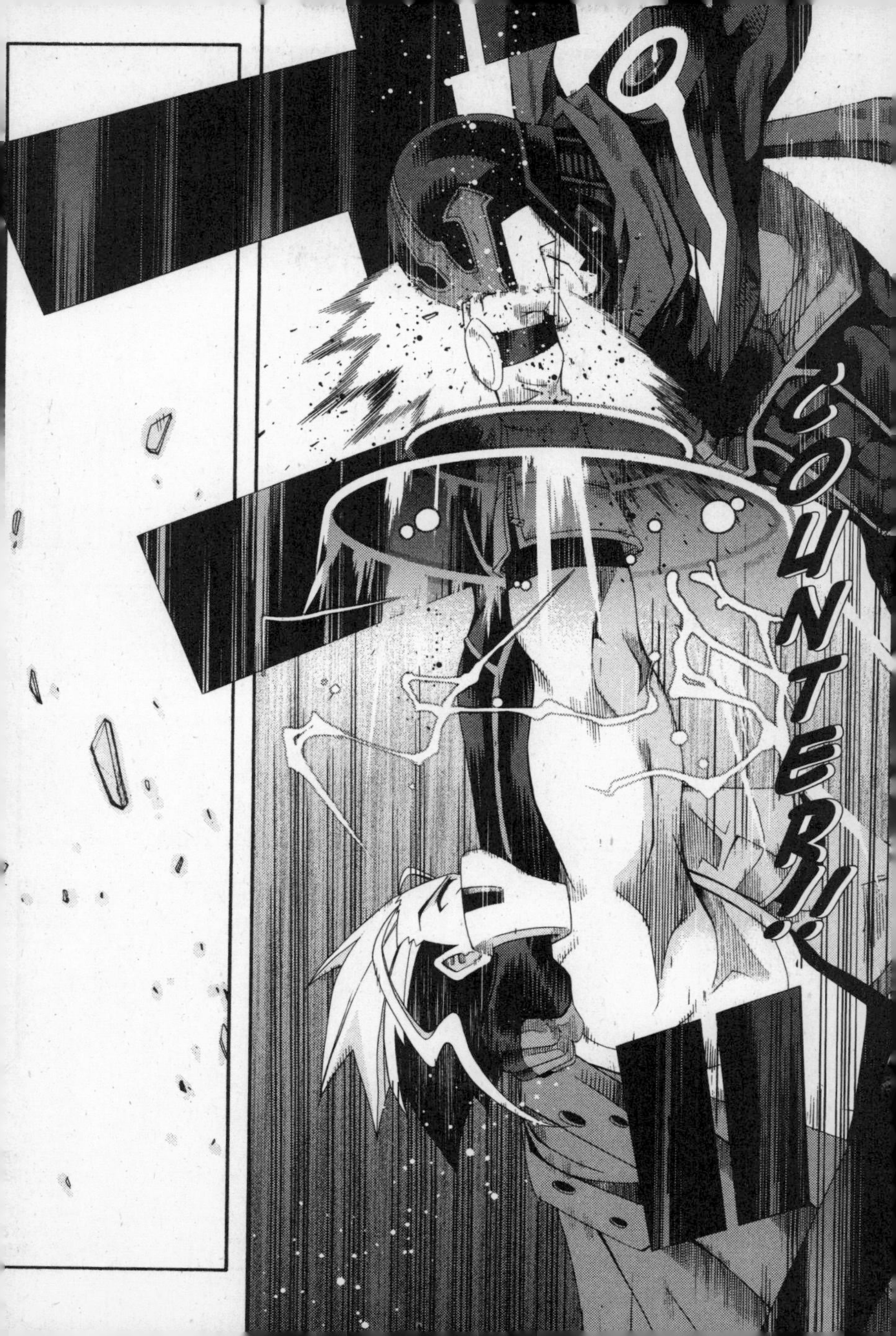
COUNTER!!

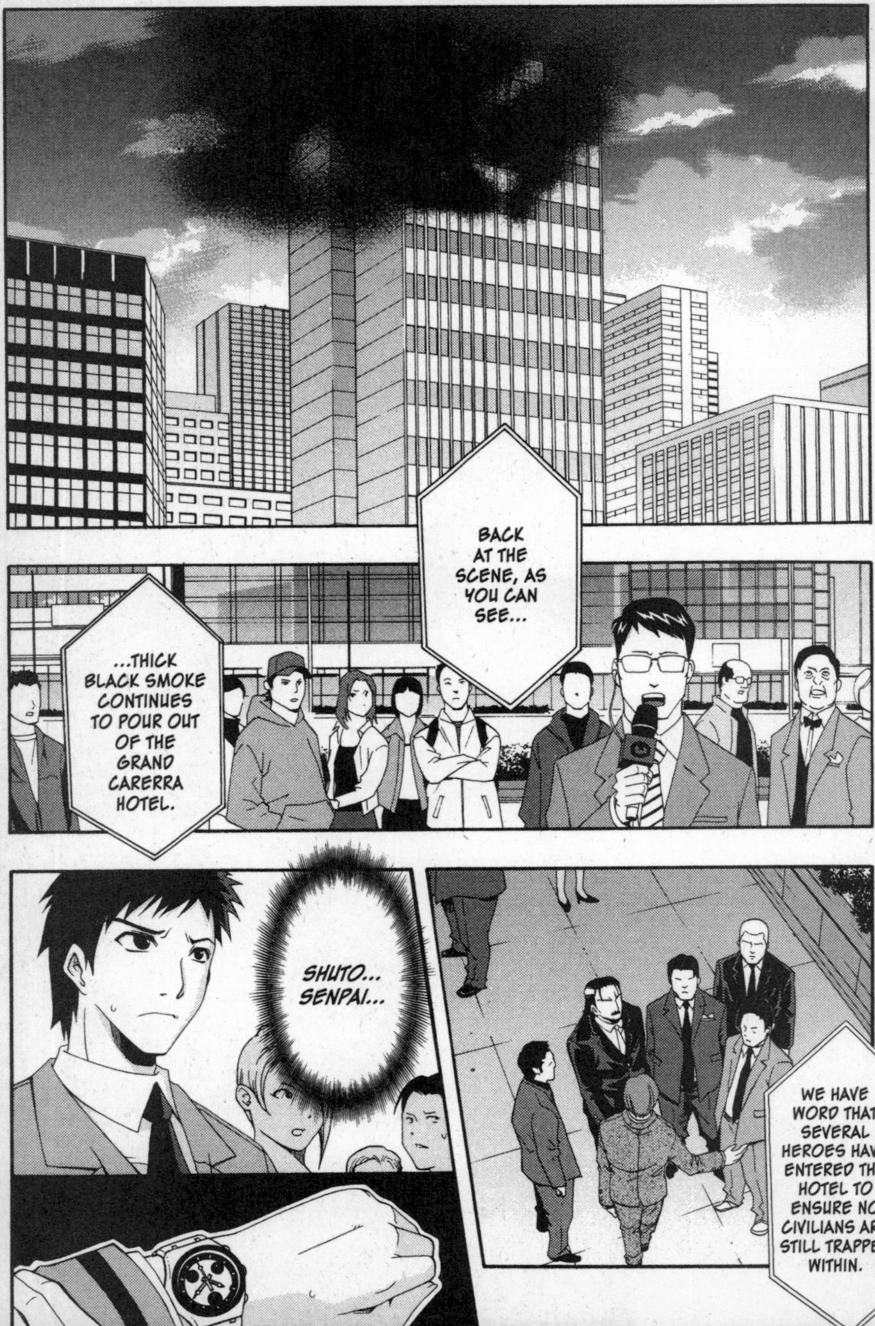
BACK AT THE SCENE, AS YOU CAN SEE...
...THICK BLACK SMOKE CONTINUES TO POUR OUT OF THE GRAND CARERRA HOTEL.
WE HAVE WORD THAT SEVERAL HEROES HAVE ENTERED THE HOTEL TO ENSURE NO CIVILIANS ARE STILL TRAPPED WITHIN.
SHUTO... SENPAI...

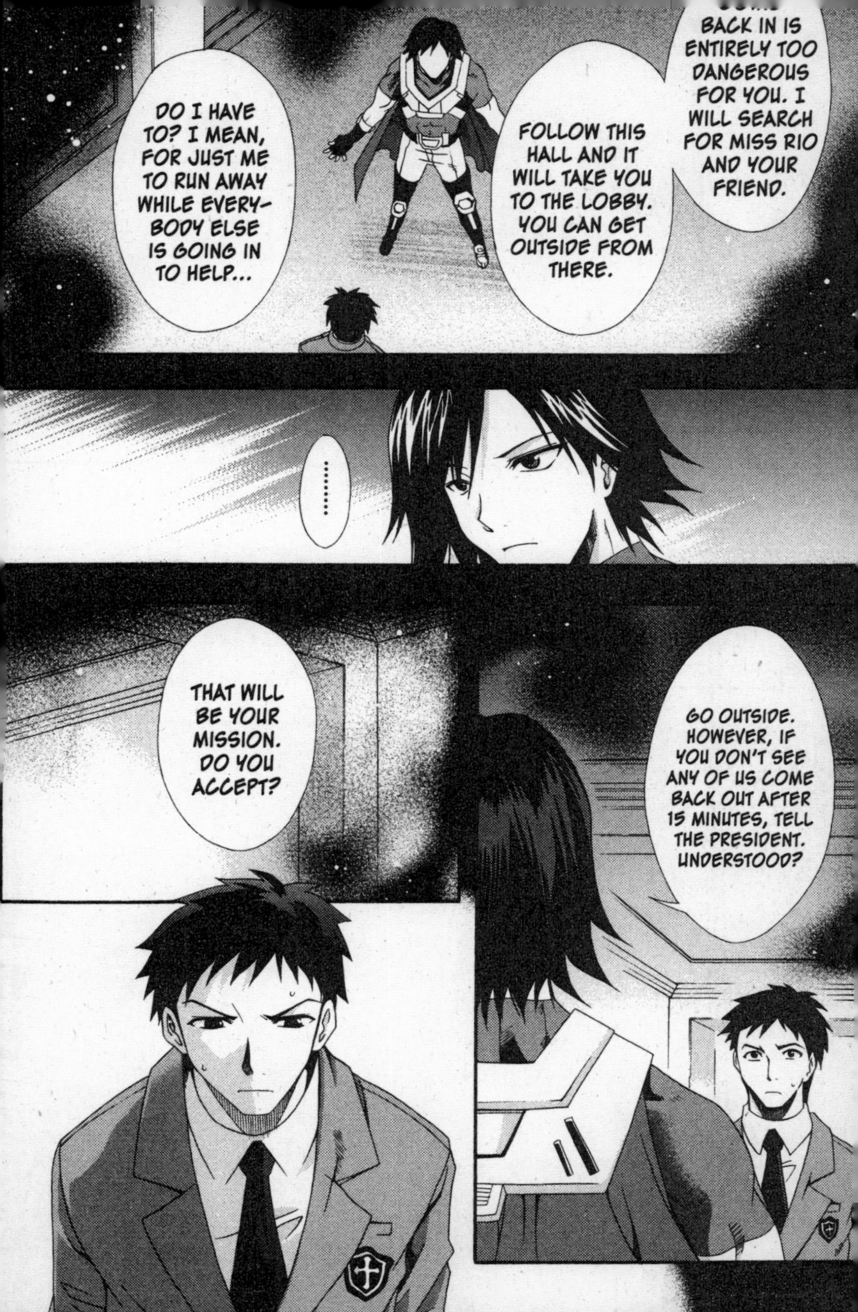
BACK IN IS ENTIRELY TOO DANGEROUS FOR YOU. I WILL SEARCH FOR MISS RIO AND YOUR FRIEND.
FOLLOW THIS HALL AND IT WILL TAKE YOU TO THE LOBBY. YOU CAN GET OUTSIDE FROM THERE.
DO I HAVE TO? I MEAN, FOR JUST ME TO RUN AWAY WHILE EVERY-BODY ELSE IS GOING IN TO HELP...
....
GO OUTSIDE. HOWEVER, IF YOU DON'T SEE ANY OF US COME BACK OUT AFTER 15 MINUTES, TELL THE PRESIDENT. UNDERSTOOD?
THAT WILL BE YOUR MISSION. DO YOU ACCEPT?

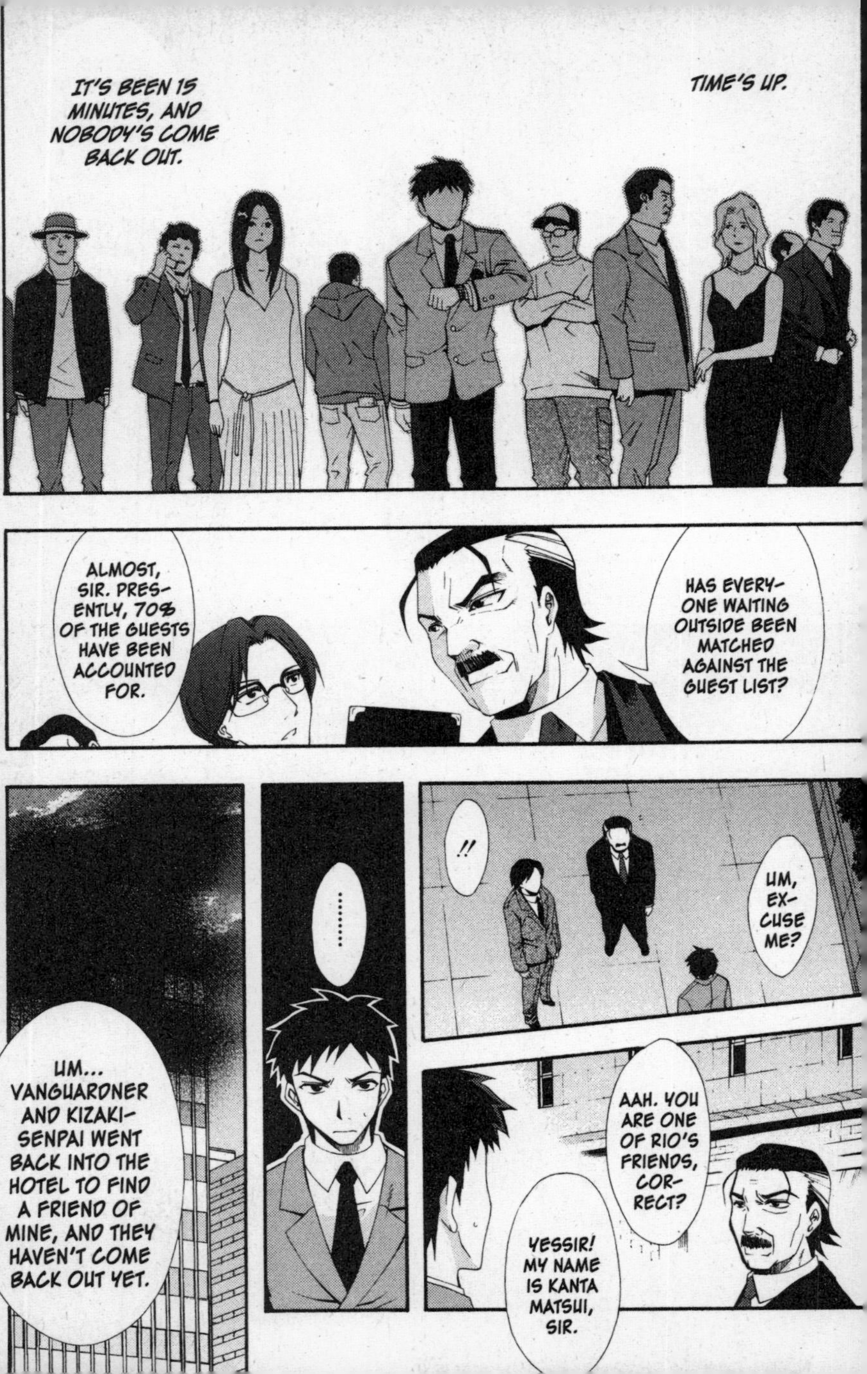
TIME'S UP.
IT'S BEEN 15 MINUTES, AND NOBODY'S COME BACK OUT.
HAS EVERY-ONE WAITING OUTSIDE BEEN MATCHED AGAINST THE GUEST LIST?
ALMOST, SIR. PRES-ENTLY, 70% OF THE GUESTS HAVE BEEN ACCOUNTED FOR.
UM, EX-CUSE ME?
!!
AAH. YOU ARE ONE OF RIO'S FRIENDS, COR-RECT?
YESSIR! MY NAME IS KANTA MATSUI, SIR.
....
UM... VANGUARDNER AND KIZAKI-SENPAI WENT BACK INTO THE HOTEL TO FIND A FRIEND OF MINE, AND THEY HAVEN'T COME BACK OUT YET.

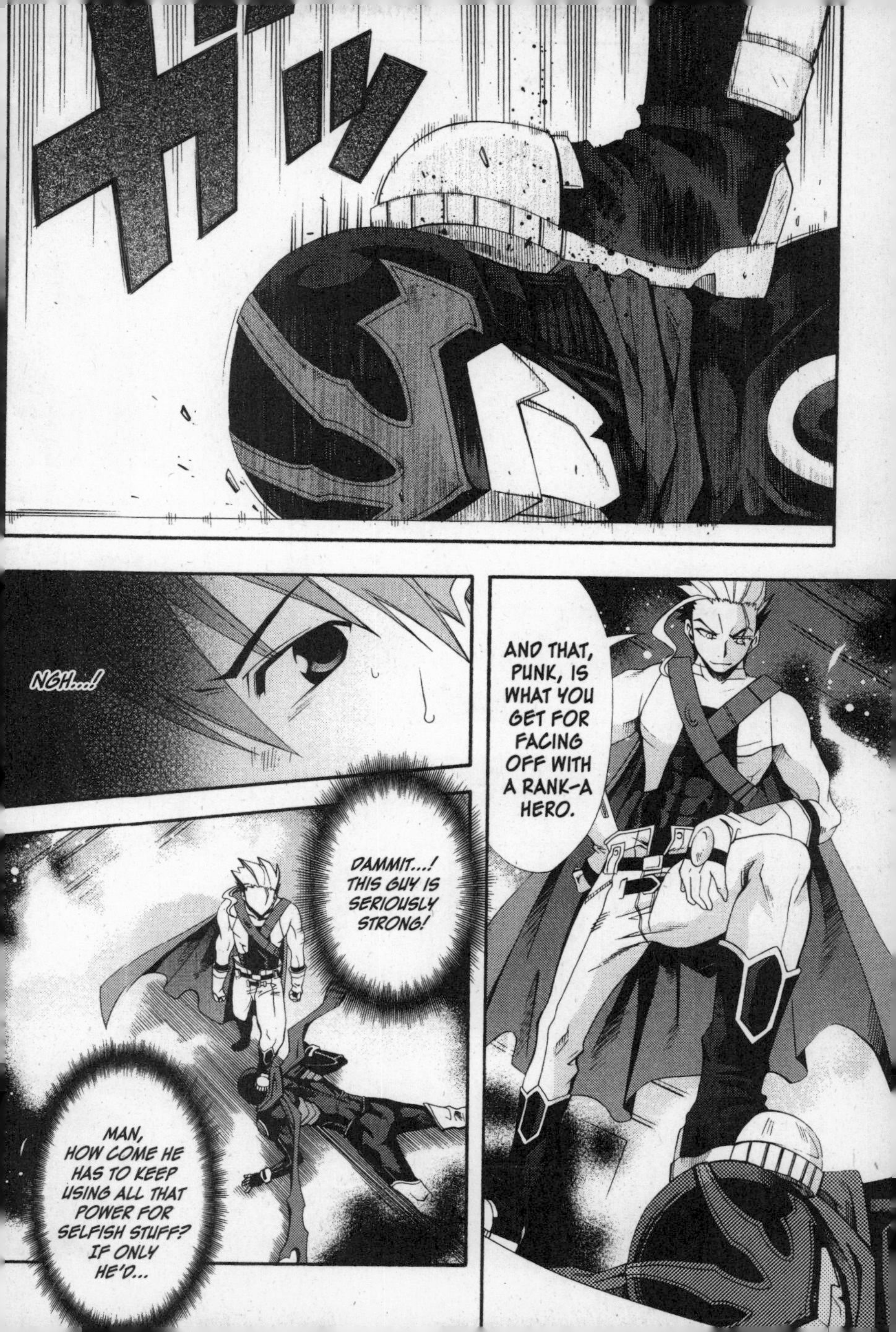
ガッ
AND THAT, PUNK, IS WHAT YOU GET FOR FACING OFF WITH A RANK-A HERO.
NGH...!
DAMMIT...! THIS GUY IS SERIOUSLY STRONG!
MAN, HOW COME HE HAS TO KEEP USING ALL THAT POWER FOR SELFISH STUFF? IF ONLY HE'D...

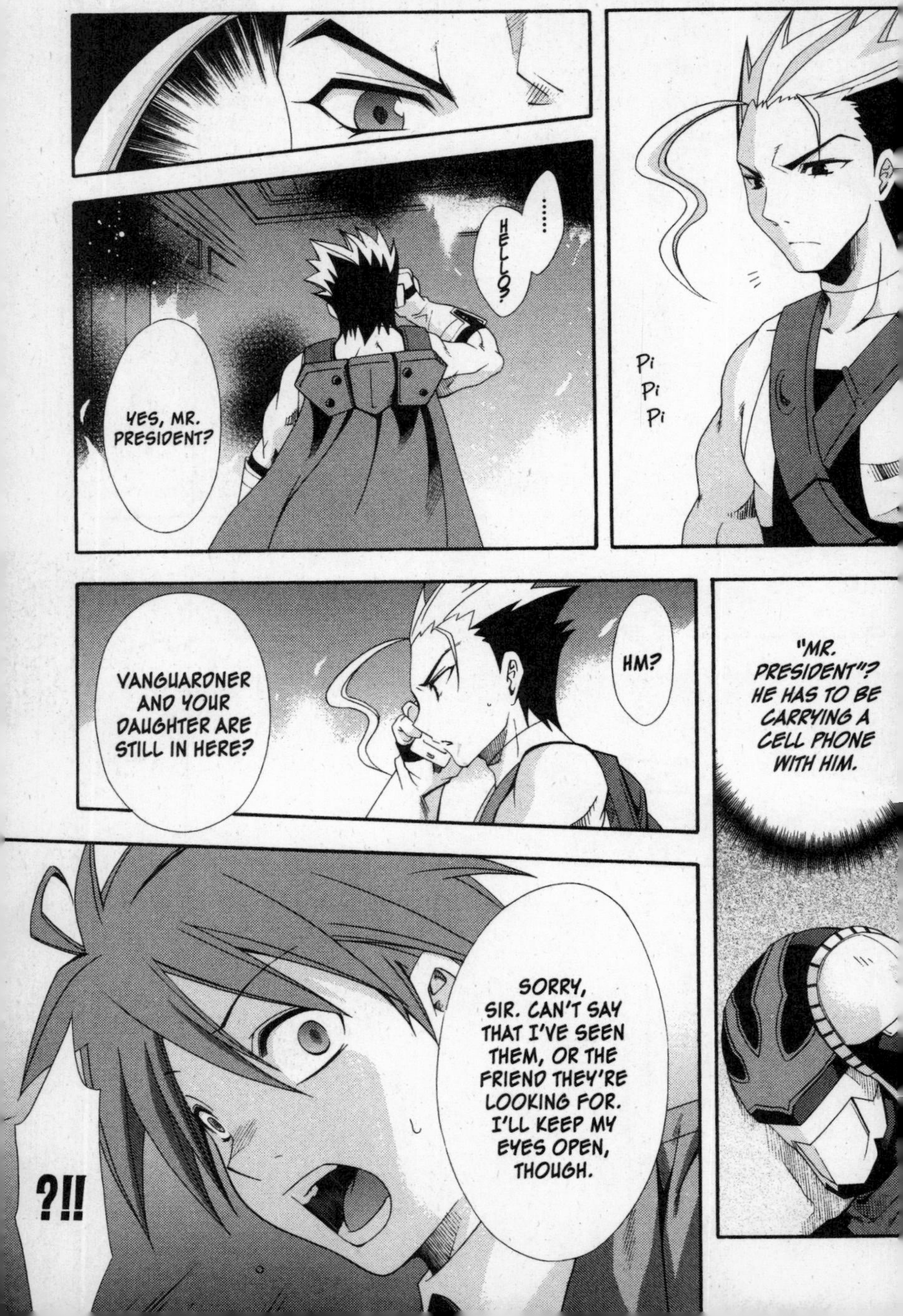

Pi
Pi
Pi
......
HELLO?
YES, MR. PRESIDENT?
"MR. PRESIDENT"? HE HAS TO BE CARRYING A CELL PHONE WITH HIM.
HM?
VANGUARDNER AND YOUR DAUGHTER ARE STILL IN HERE?
SORRY, SIR. CAN'T SAY THAT I'VE SEEN THEM, OR THE FRIEND THEY'RE LOOKING FOR. I'LL KEEP MY EYES OPEN, THOUGH.
?!!

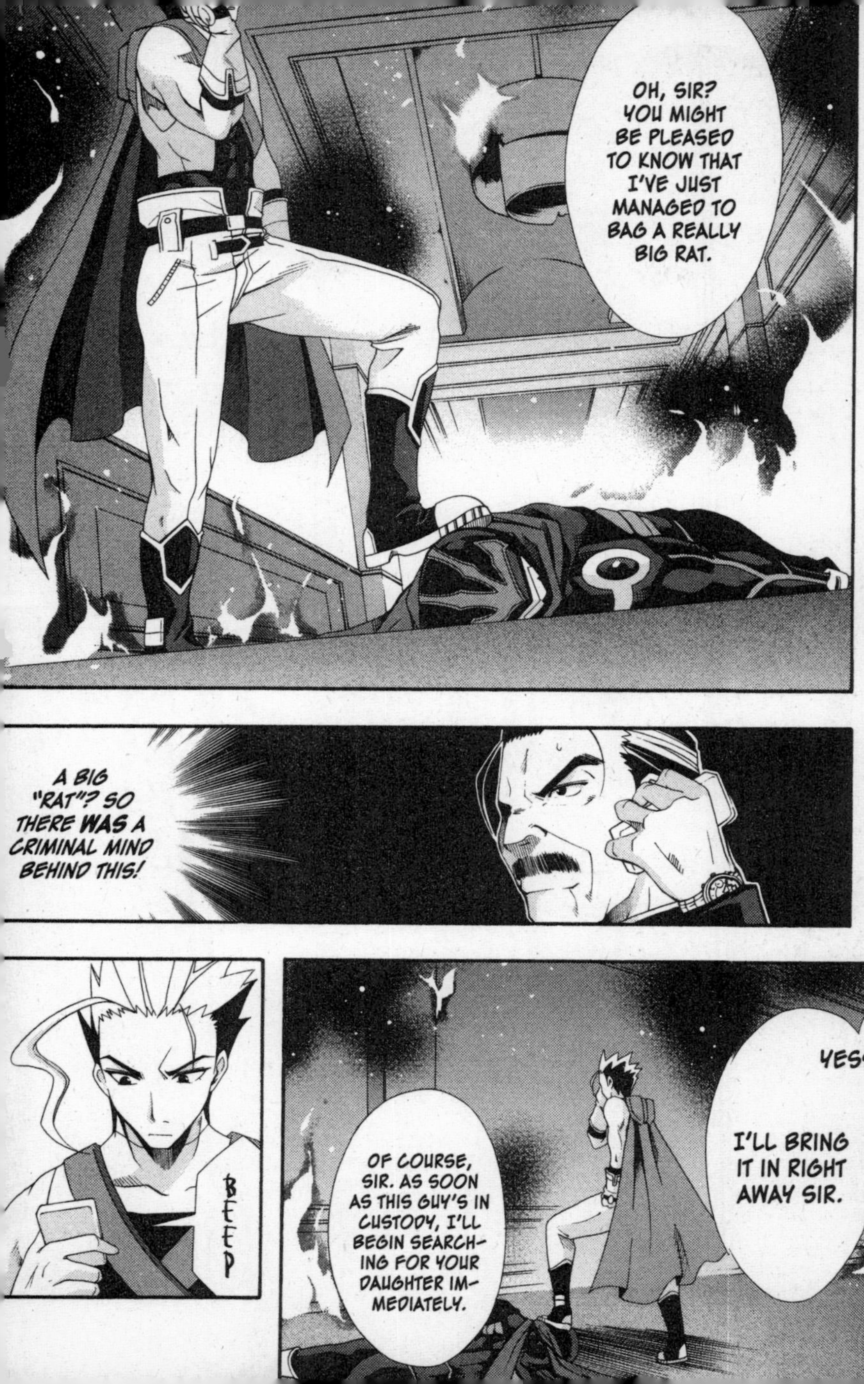
OH, SIR? YOU MIGHT BE PLEASED TO KNOW THAT I'VE JUST MANAGED TO BAG A REALLY BIG RAT.
A BIG "RAT"? SO THERE **WAS** A CRIMINAL MIND BEHIND THIS!
YESSIR.
I'LL BRING IT IN RIGHT AWAY SIR.
OF COURSE, SIR. AS SOON AS THIS GUY'S IN CUSTODY, I'LL BEGIN SEARCHING FOR YOUR DAUGHTER IMMEDIATELY.
BEEP

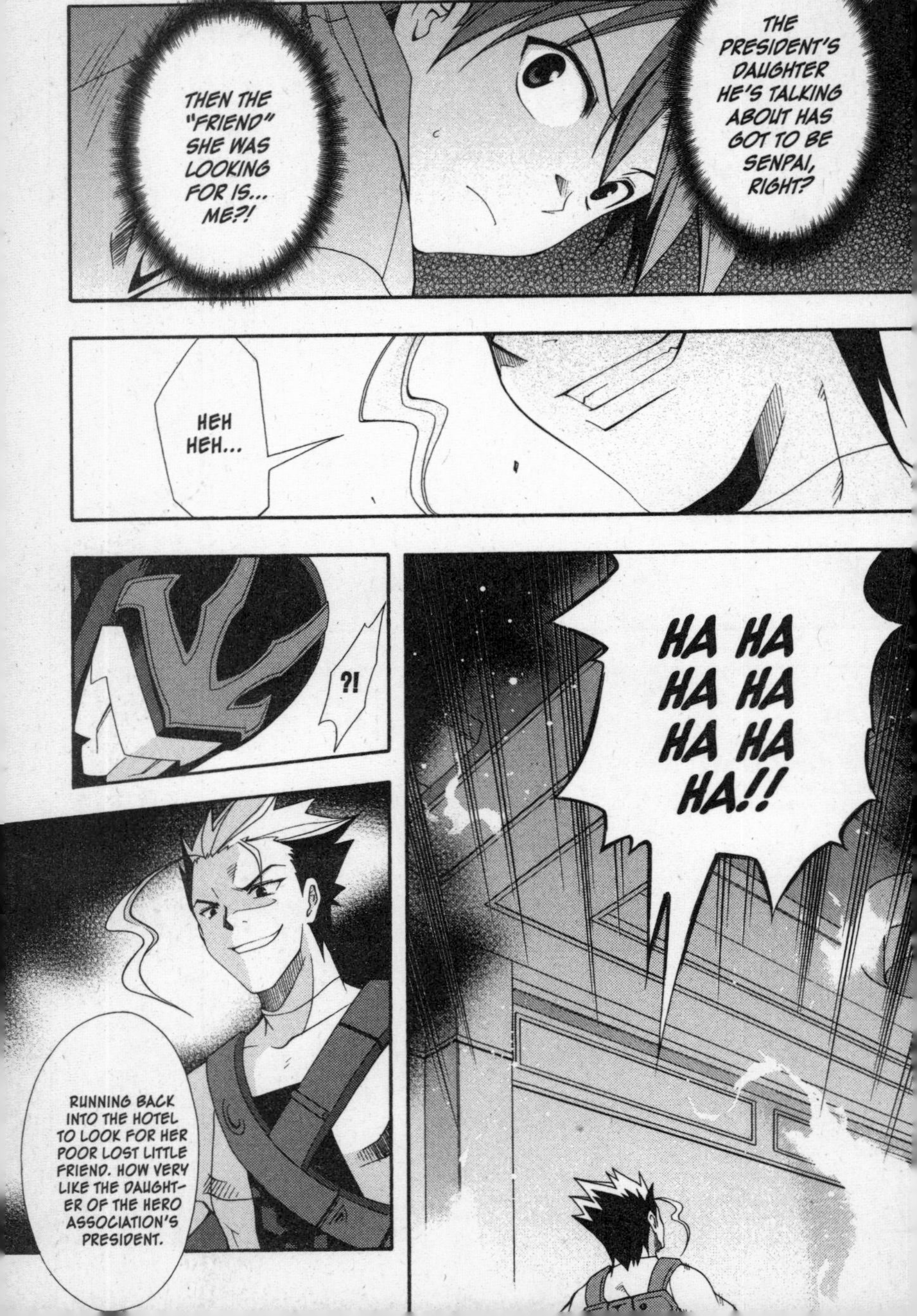
THE PRESIDENT'S DAUGHTER HE'S TALKING ABOUT HAS GOT TO BE SENPAI, RIGHT?
THEN THE "FRIEND" SHE WAS LOOKING FOR IS... ME?!
HEH HEH...
HA HA HA HA HA HA HA!!
?!
RUNNING BACK INTO THE HOTEL TO LOOK FOR HER POOR LOST LITTLE FRIEND. HOW VERY LIKE THE DAUGHTER OF THE HERO ASSOCIATION'S PRESIDENT.

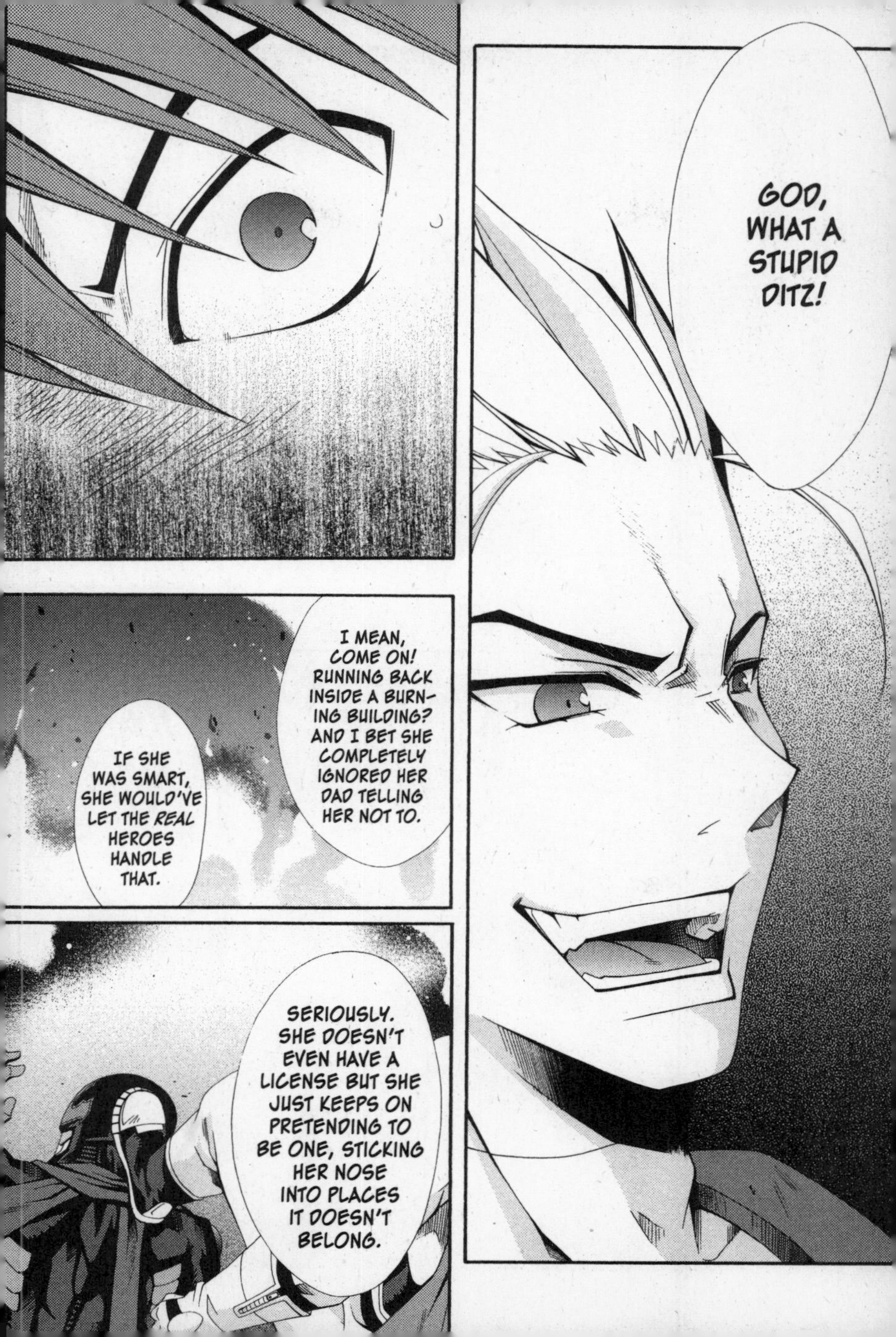
GOD, WHAT A STUPID DITZ!
I MEAN, COME ON! RUNNING BACK INSIDE A BURNING BUILDING? AND I BET SHE COMPLETELY IGNORED HER DAD TELLING HER NOT TO.
IF SHE WAS SMART, SHE WOULD'VE LET THE *REAL* HEROES HANDLE THAT.
SERIOUSLY. SHE DOESN'T EVEN HAVE A LICENSE BUT SHE JUST KEEPS ON PRETENDING TO BE ONE, STICKING HER NOSE INTO PLACES IT DOESN'T BELONG.

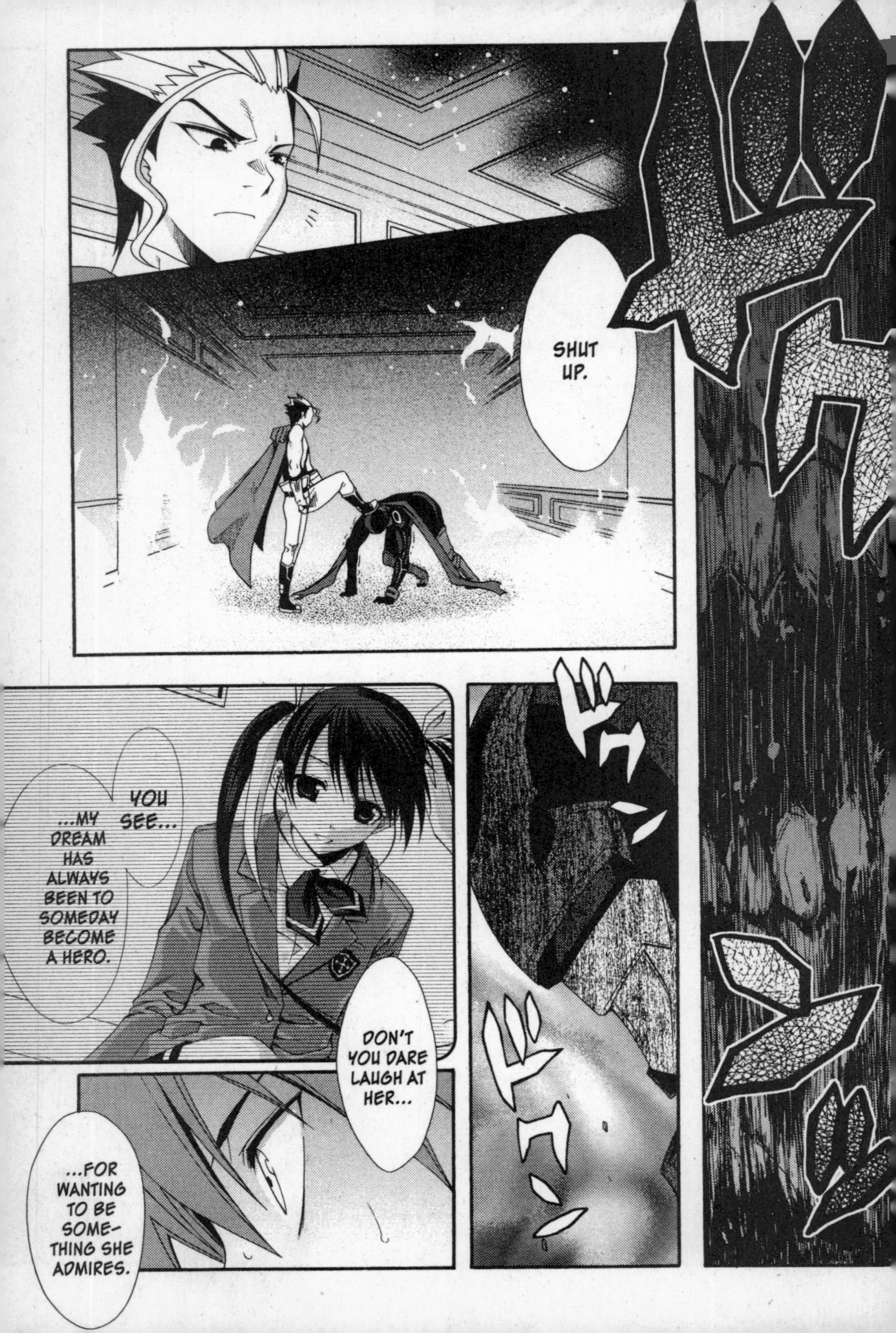
SHUT UP.
YOU SEE...
...MY DREAM HAS ALWAYS BEEN TO SOMEDAY BECOME A HERO.
DON'T YOU DARE LAUGH AT HER...
...FOR WANTING TO BE SOME-THING SHE ADMIRES.

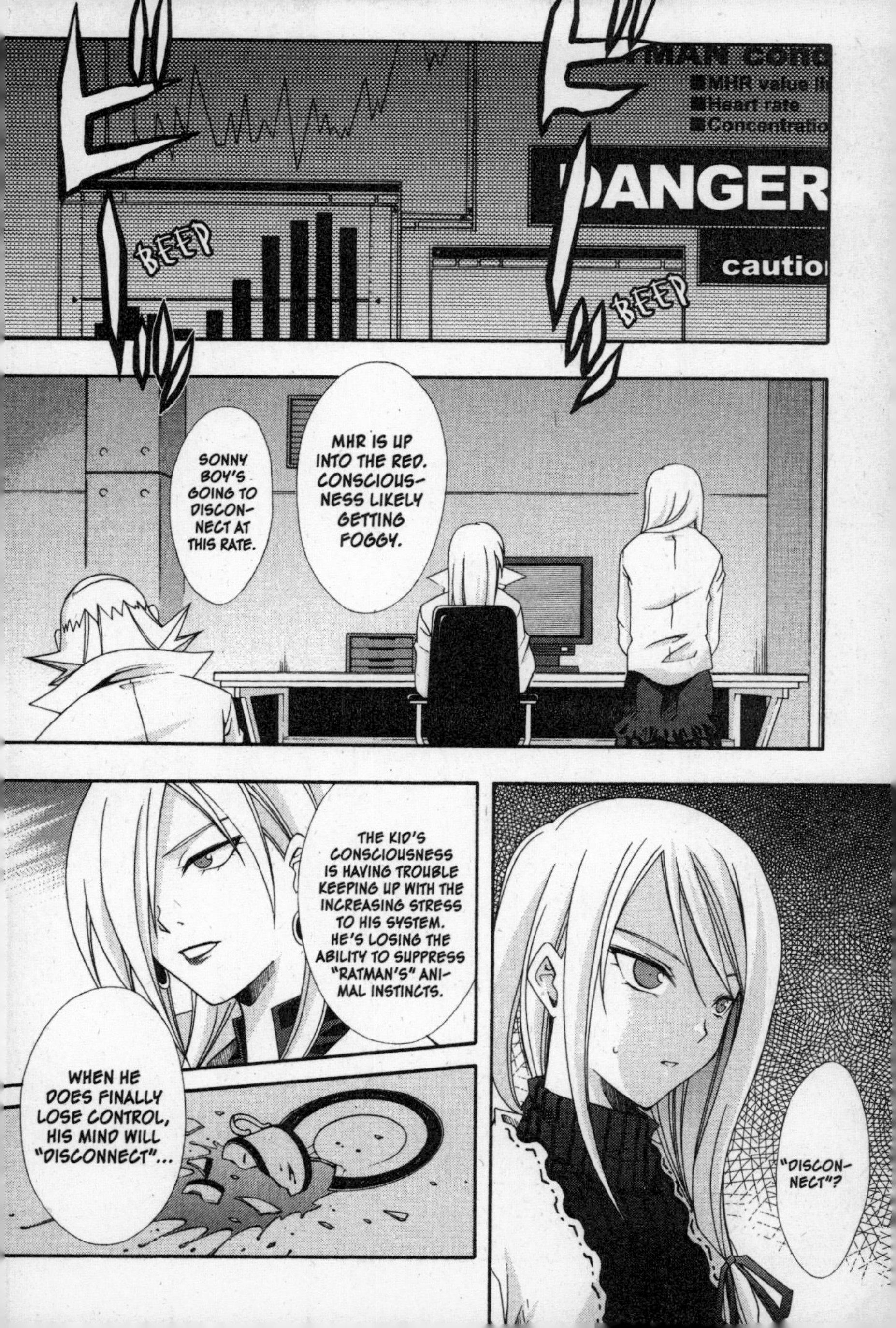
MAN CONC
MHR value li
Heart rate
Concentratio
DANGER
caution
BEEP
BEEP
MHR IS UP INTO THE RED. CONSCIOUS-NESS LIKELY GETTING FOGGY.
SONNY BOY'S GOING TO DISCON-NECT AT THIS RATE.
THE KID'S CONSCIOUSNESS IS HAVING TROUBLE KEEPING UP WITH THE INCREASING STRESS TO HIS SYSTEM. HE'S LOSING THE ABILITY TO SUPPRESS "RATMAN'S" ANI-MAL INSTINCTS.
WHEN HE DOES FINALLY LOSE CONTROL, HIS MIND WILL "DISCONNECT"...
"DISCON-NECT"?

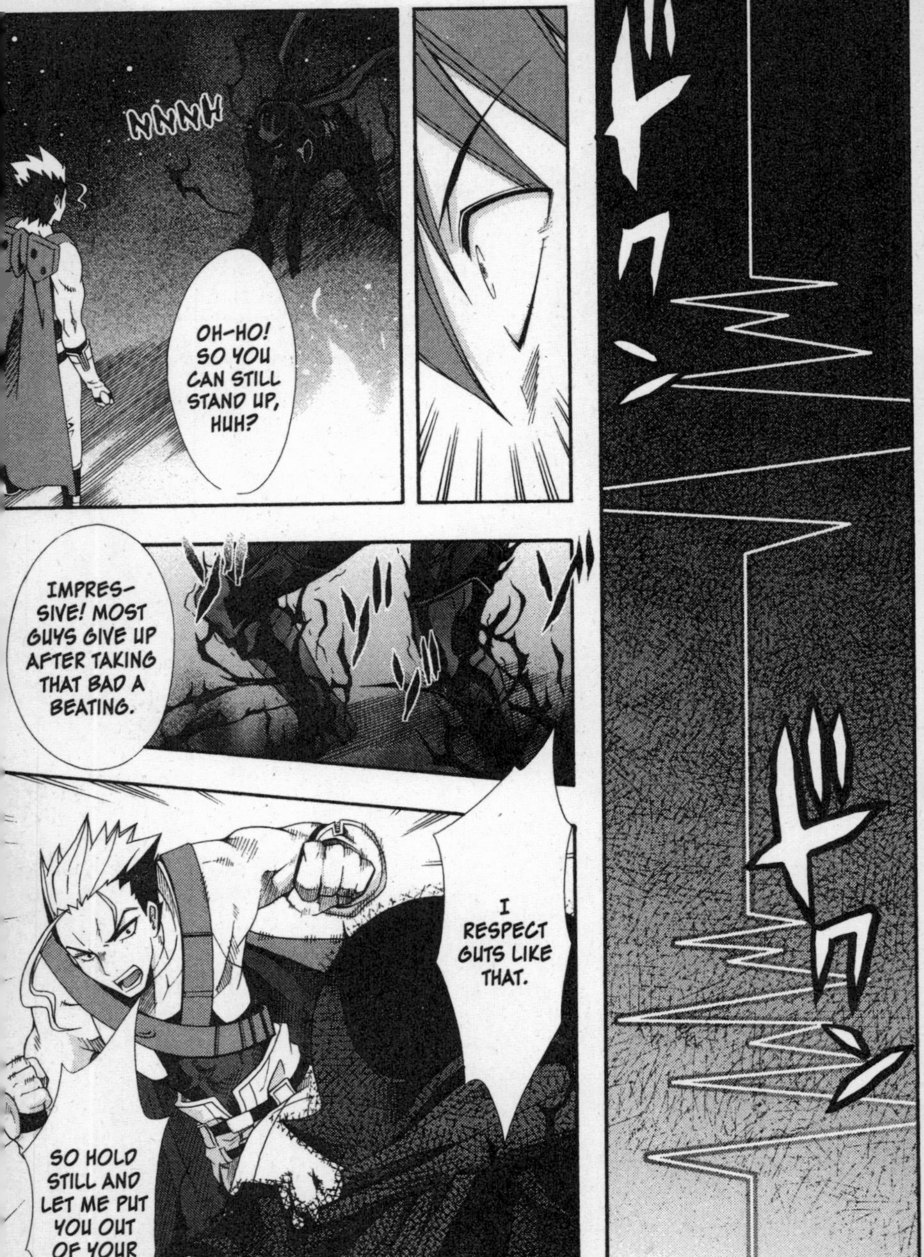
NNNH
OH-HO! SO YOU CAN STILL STAND UP, HUH?
IMPRES-SIVE! MOST GUYS GIVE UP AFTER TAKING THAT BAD A BEATING.
I RESPECT GUTS LIKE THAT.
SO HOLD STILL AND LET ME PUT YOU OUT OF YOUR MISERY!!

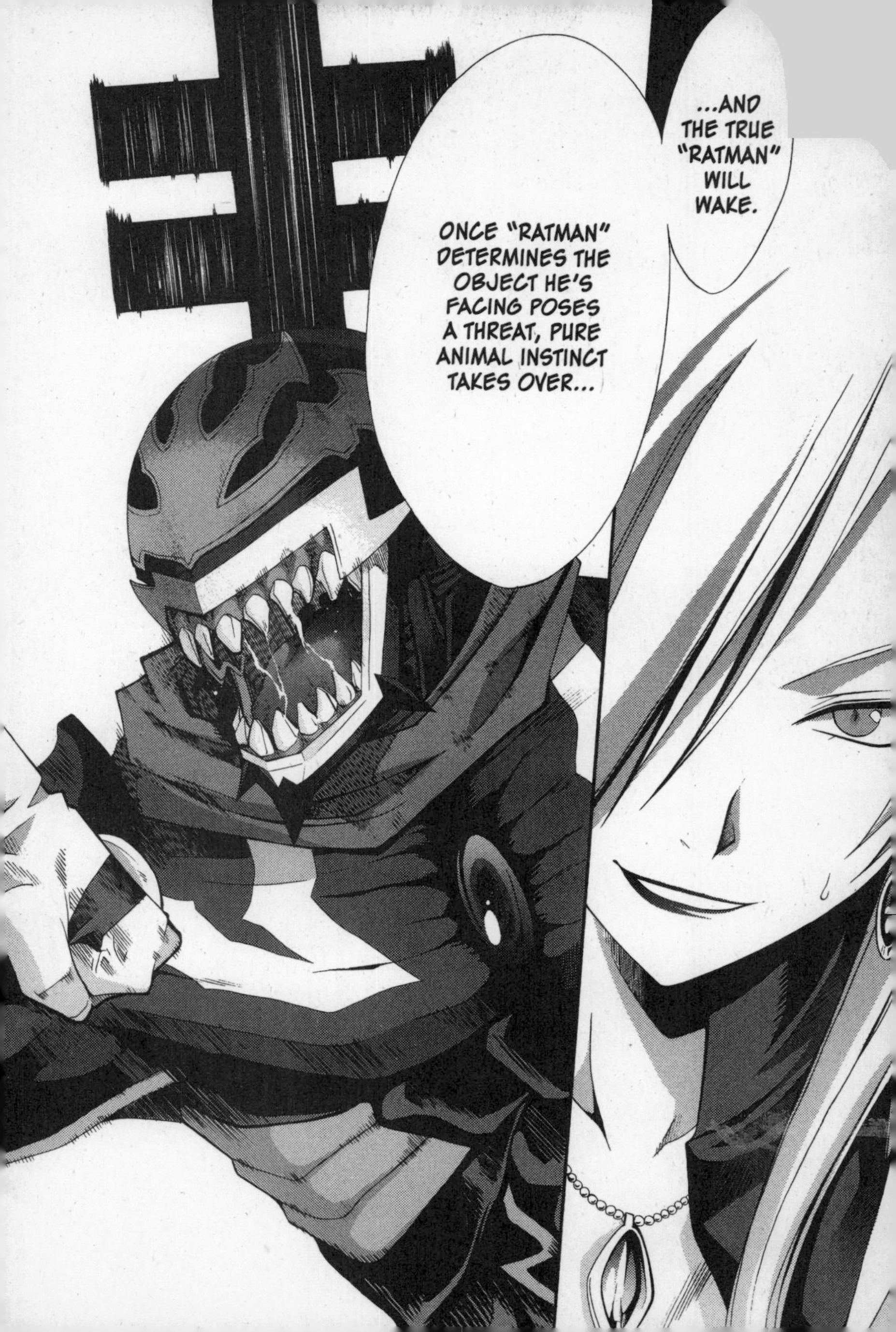
ONCE "RATMAN" DETERMINES THE OBJECT HE'S FACING POSES A THREAT, PURE ANIMAL INSTINCT TAKES OVER...
...AND THE TRUE "RATMAN" WILL WAKE.

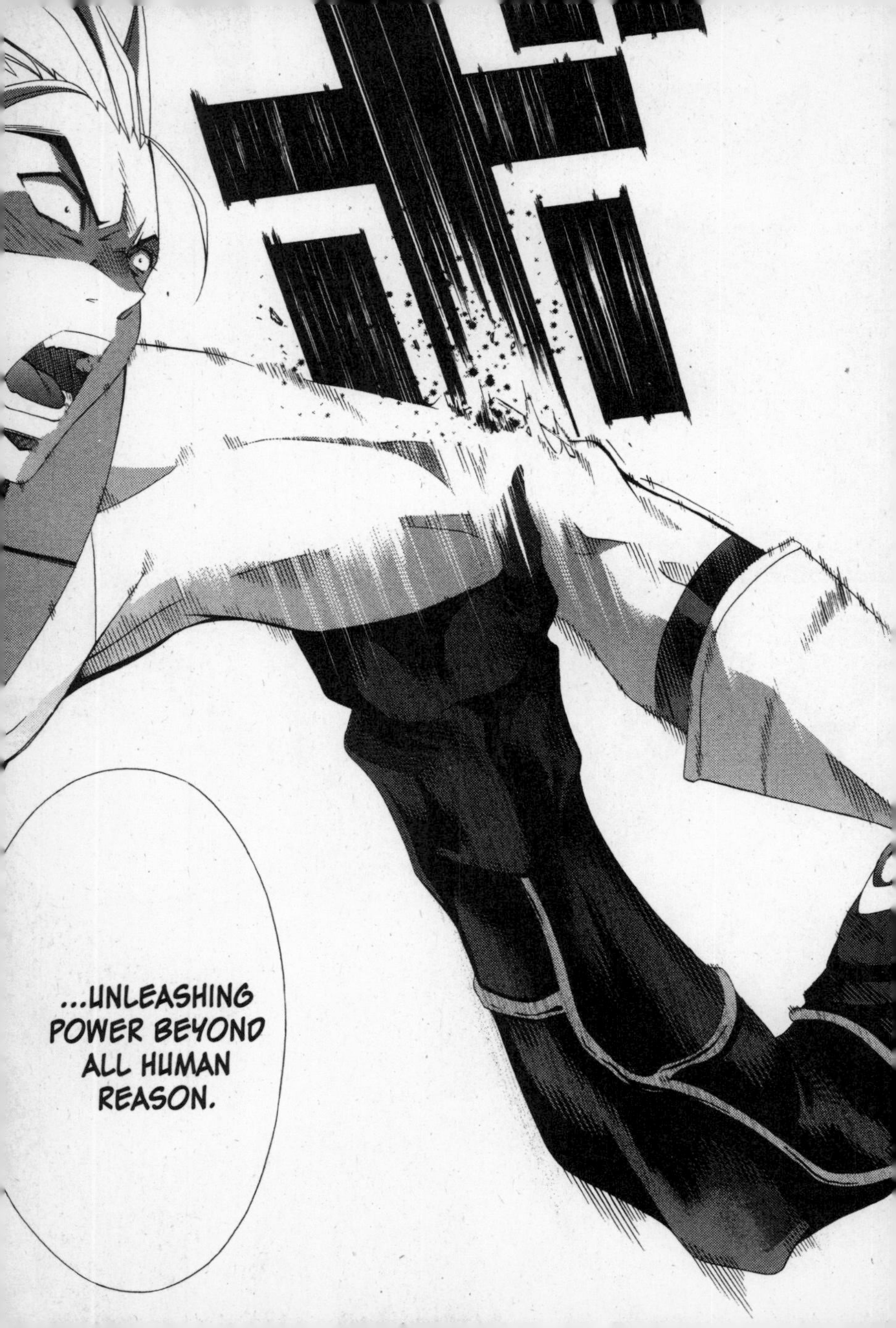
...UNLEASHING POWER BEYOND ALL HUMAN REASON.

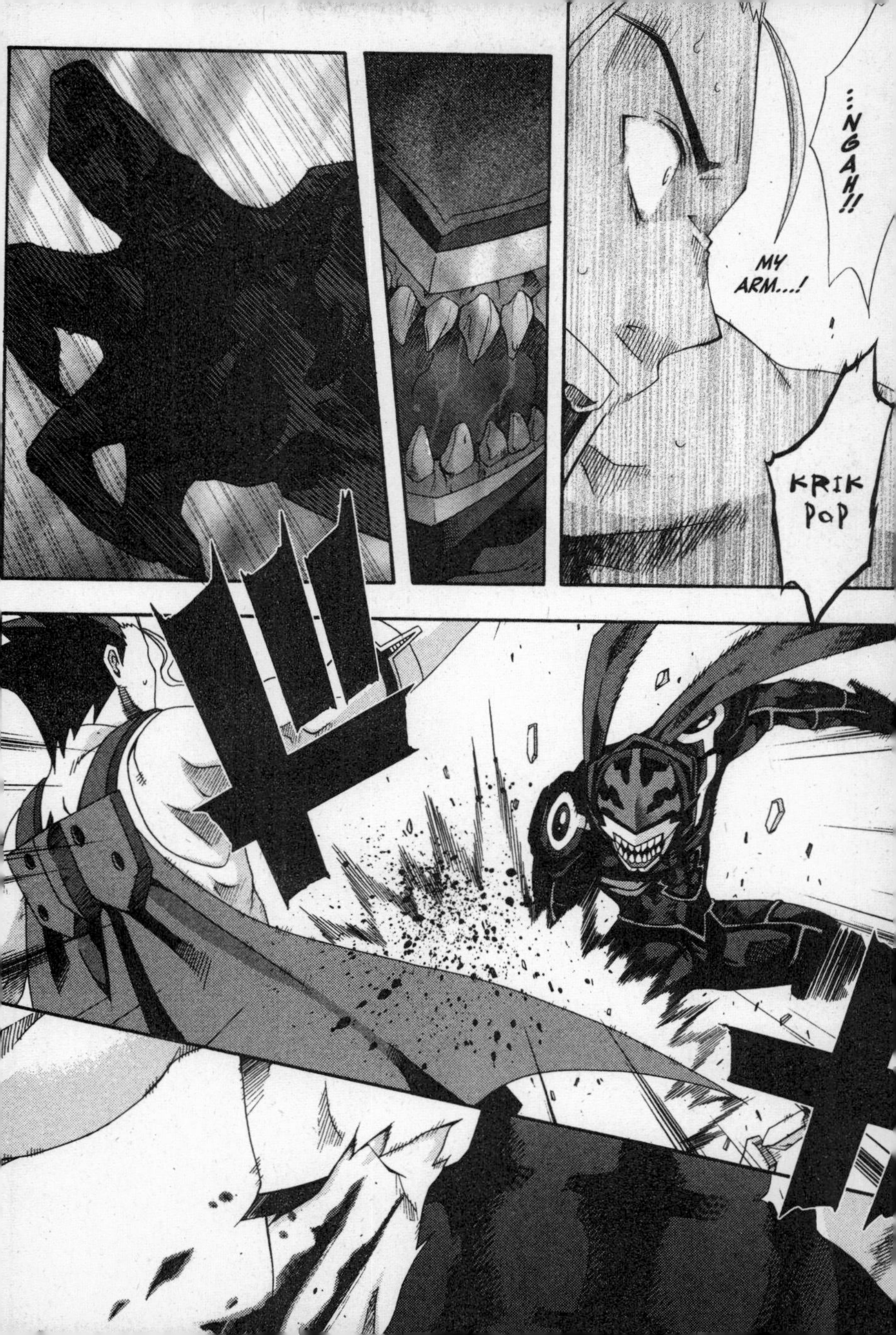
...NGAH!!
MY ARM...!
KRIK POP

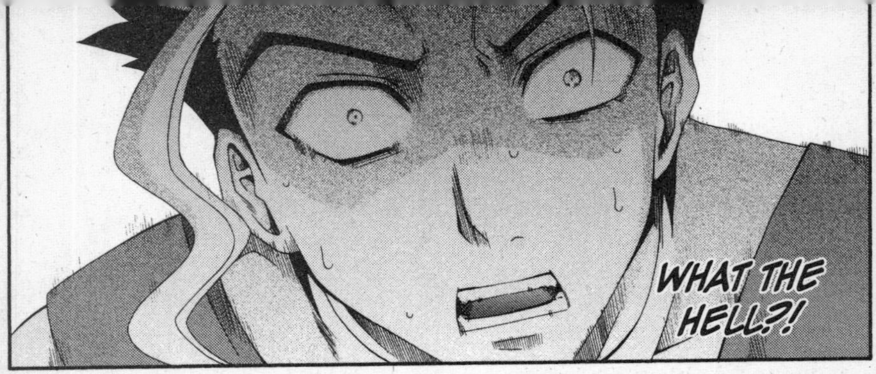
WHAT THE HELL?!
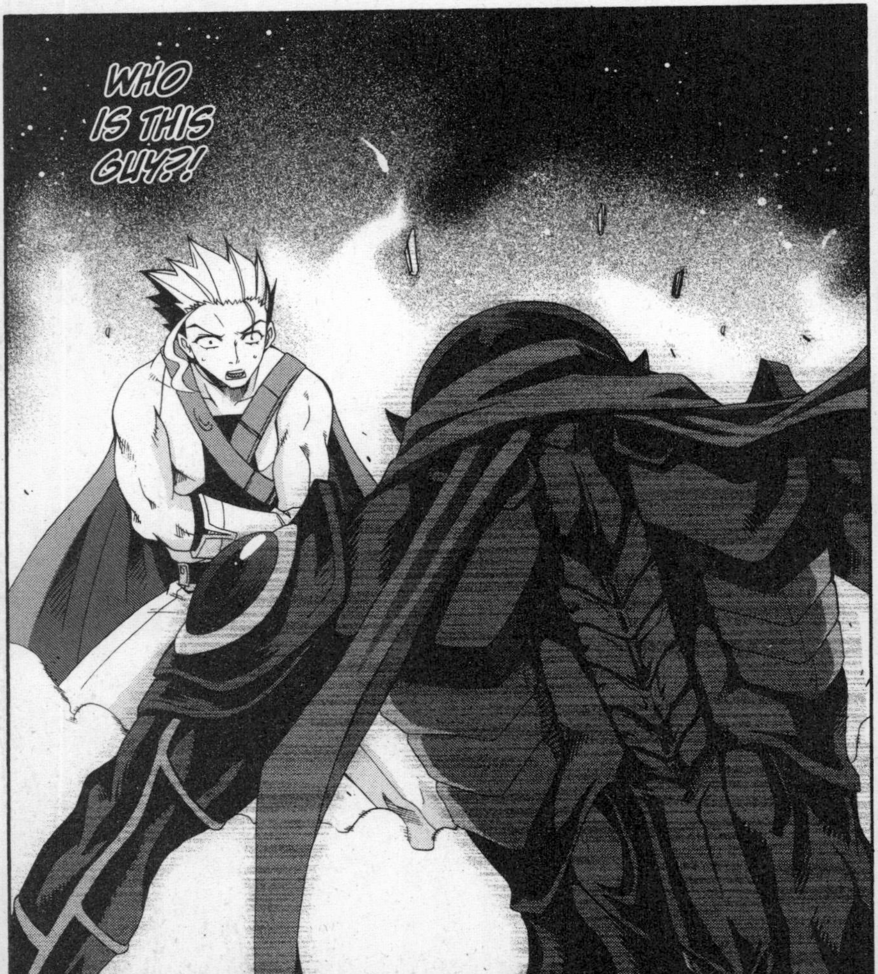
WHO IS THIS GUY?!

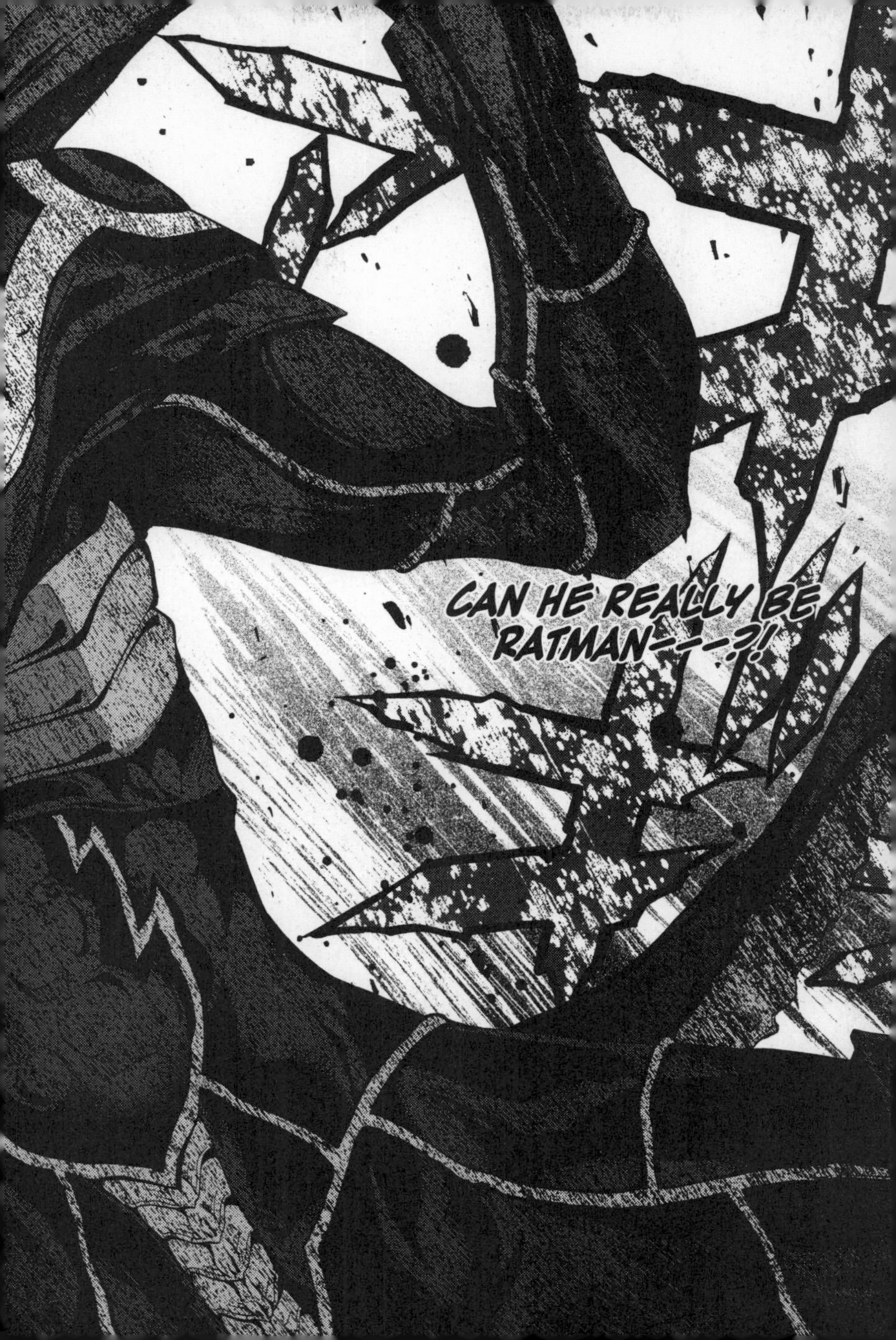
CAN HE REALLY BE RATMAN----?!

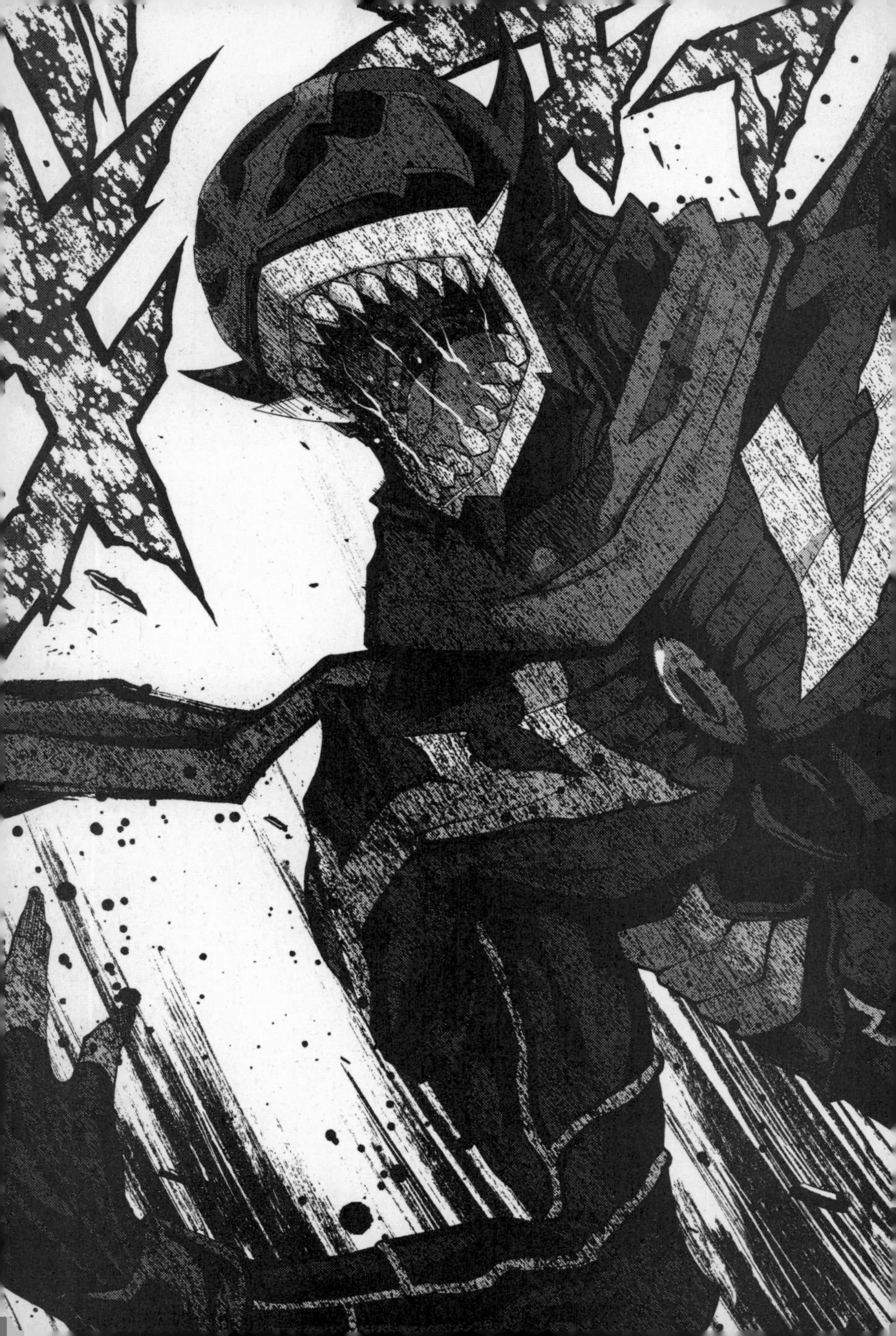

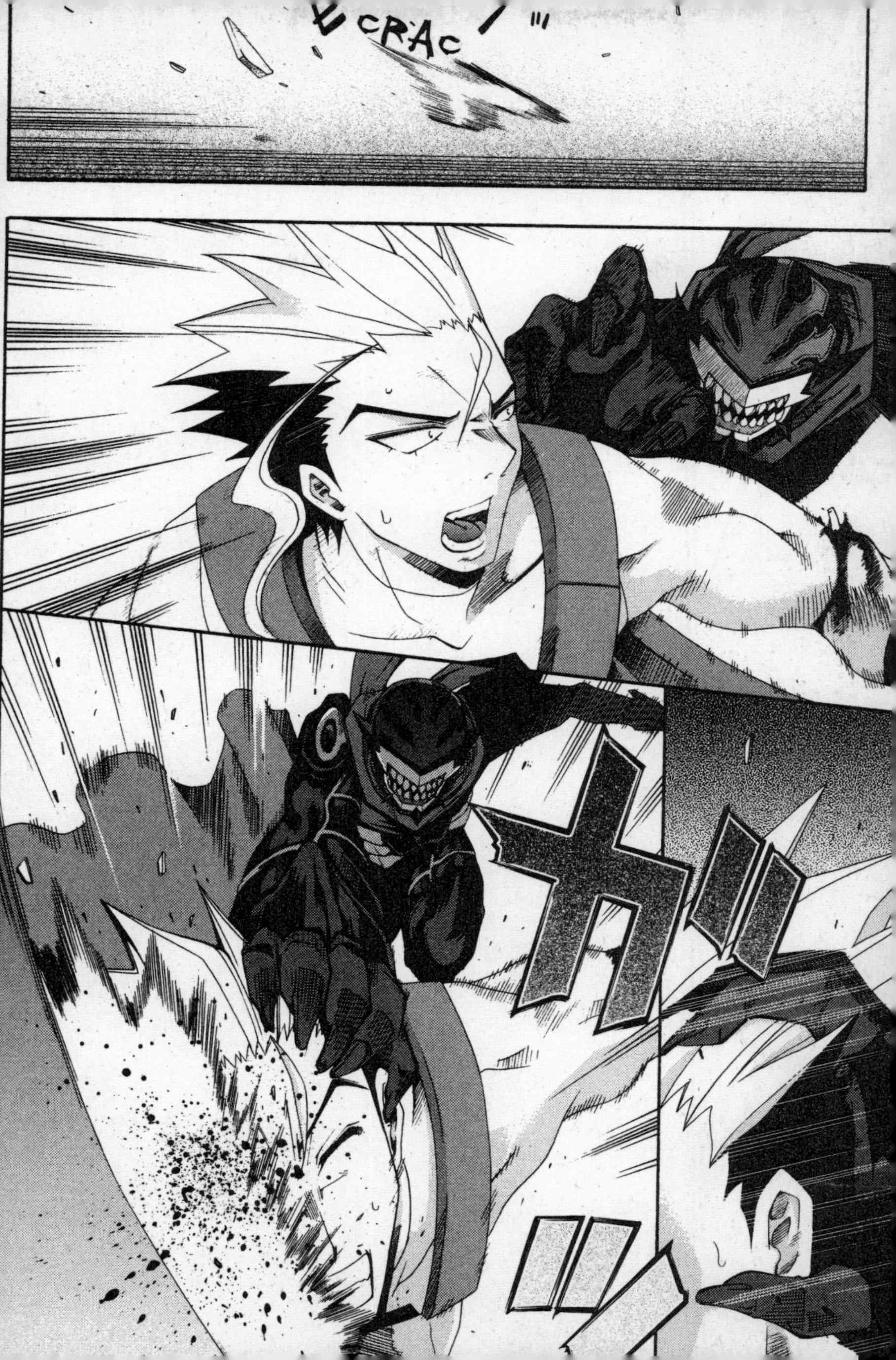
CRAC

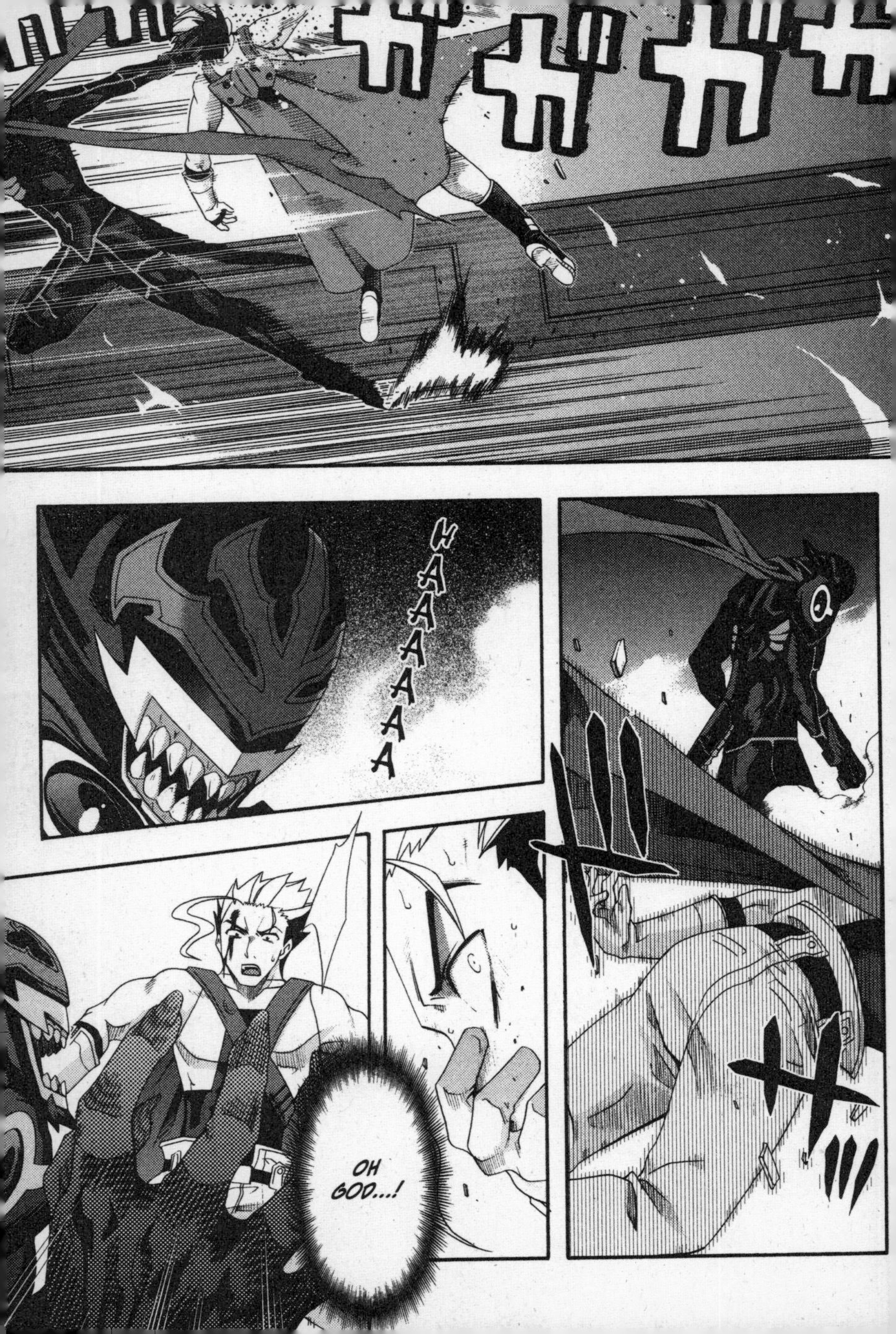
HAAAAAAA
OH GOD...!

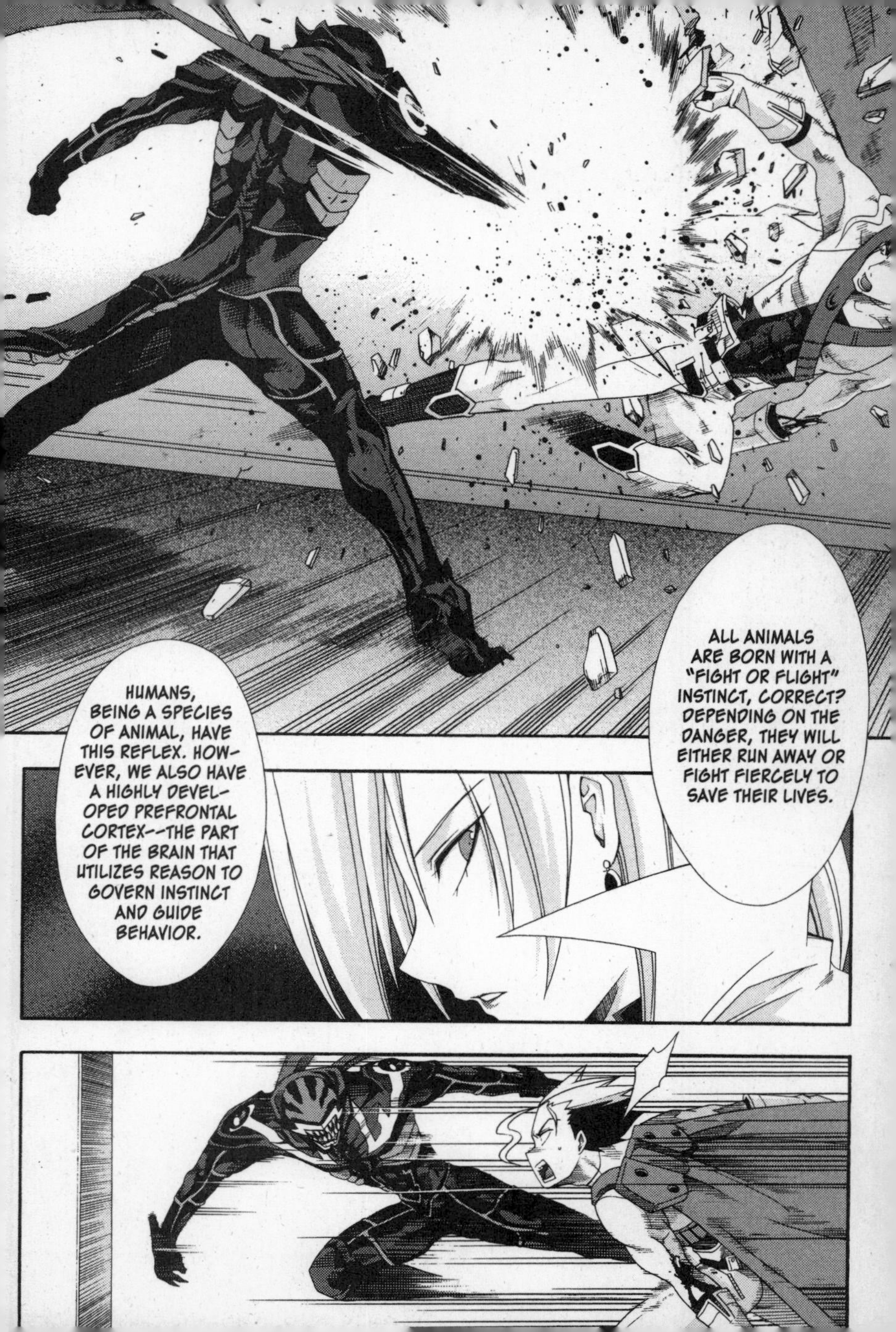
ALL ANIMALS ARE BORN WITH A "FIGHT OR FLIGHT" INSTINCT, CORRECT? DEPENDING ON THE DANGER, THEY WILL EITHER RUN AWAY OR FIGHT FIERCELY TO SAVE THEIR LIVES.
HUMANS, BEING A SPECIES OF ANIMAL, HAVE THIS REFLEX. HOW-EVER, WE ALSO HAVE A HIGHLY DEVEL-OPED PREFRONTAL CORTEX--THE PART OF THE BRAIN THAT UTILIZES REASON TO GOVERN INSTINCT AND GUIDE BEHAVIOR.

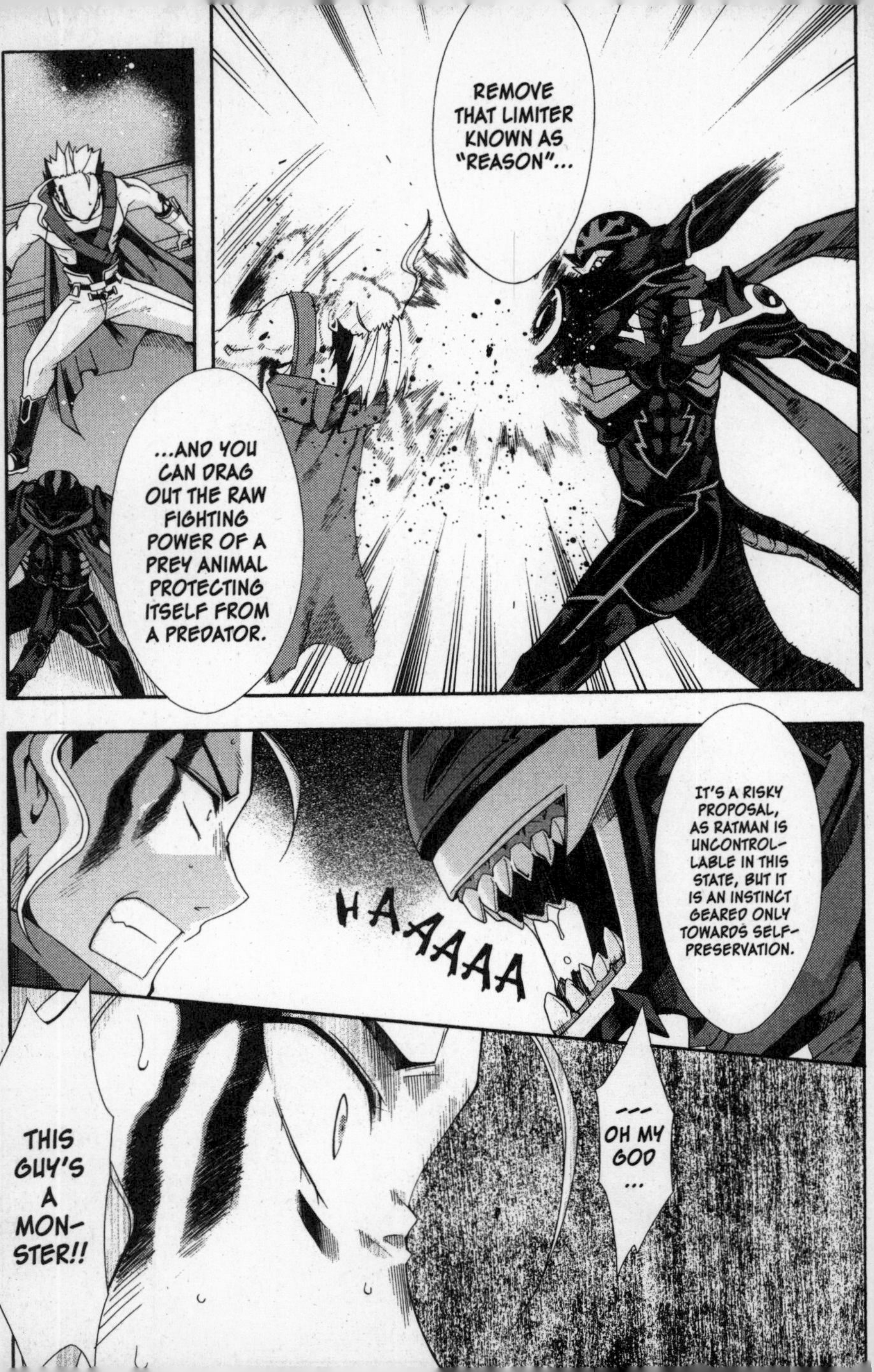
REMOVE THAT LIMITER KNOWN AS "REASON"...
...AND YOU CAN DRAG OUT THE RAW FIGHTING POWER OF A PREY ANIMAL PROTECTING ITSELF FROM A PREDATOR.
IT'S A RISKY PROPOSAL, AS RATMAN IS UNCONTROL-LABLE IN THIS STATE, BUT IT IS AN INSTINCT GEARED ONLY TOWARDS SELF-PRESERVATION.
HAAAAAA
---OH MY GOD...
THIS GUY'S A MON-STER!!

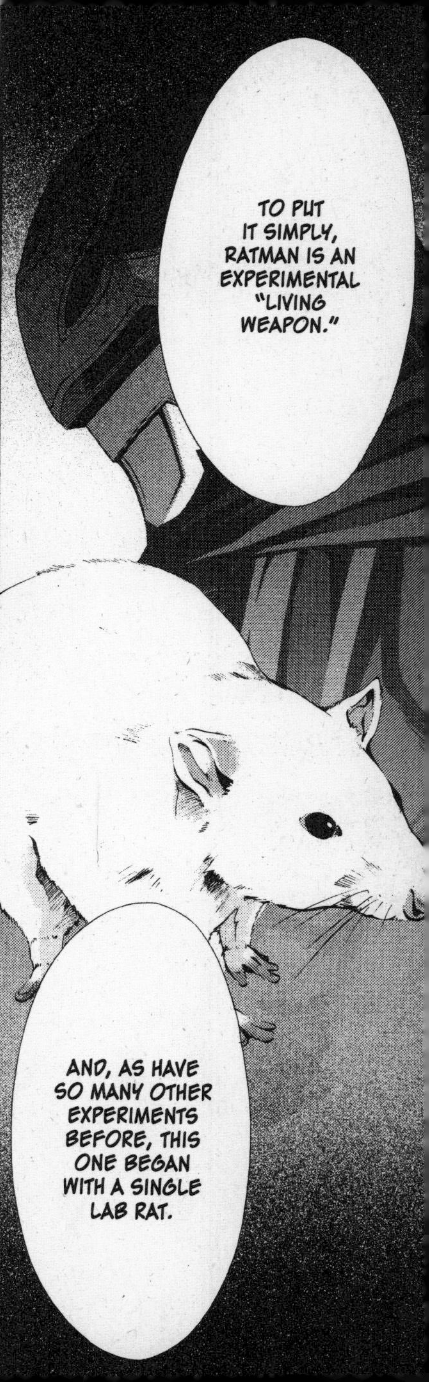
TO PUT IT SIMPLY, RATMAN IS AN EXPERIMENTAL "LIVING WEAPON."
AND, AS HAVE SO MANY OTHER EXPERIMENTS BEFORE, THIS ONE BEGAN WITH A SINGLE LAB RAT.

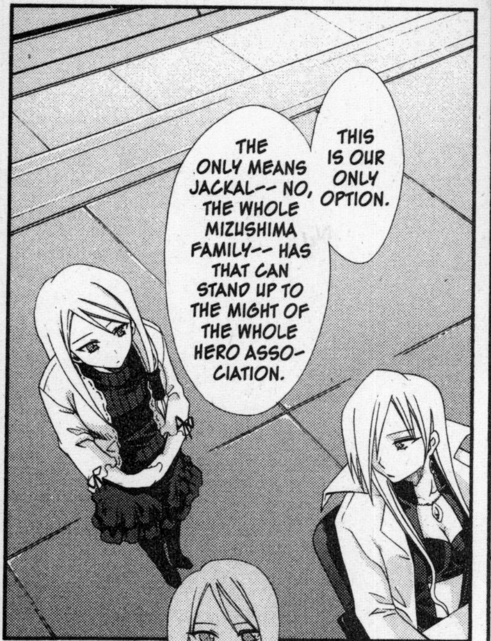
THIS IS OUR ONLY OPTION.
THE ONLY MEANS JACKAL-- NO, THE WHOLE MIZUSHIMA FAMILY-- HAS THAT CAN STAND UP TO THE MIGHT OF THE WHOLE HERO ASSO-CIATION.

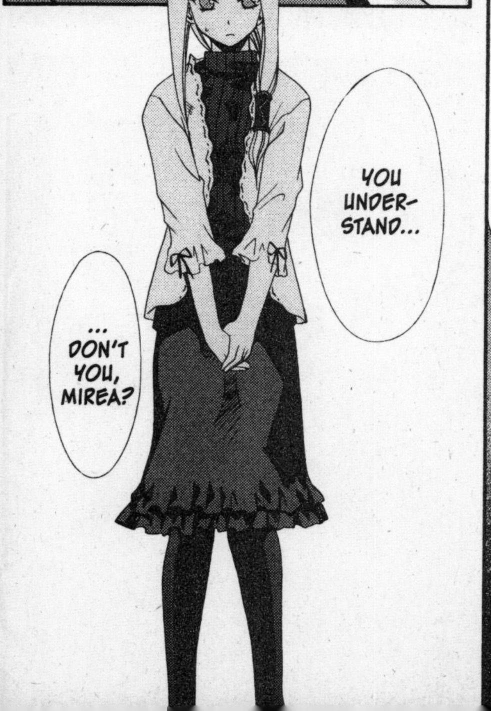
YOU UNDER-STAND...
... DON'T YOU, MIREA?

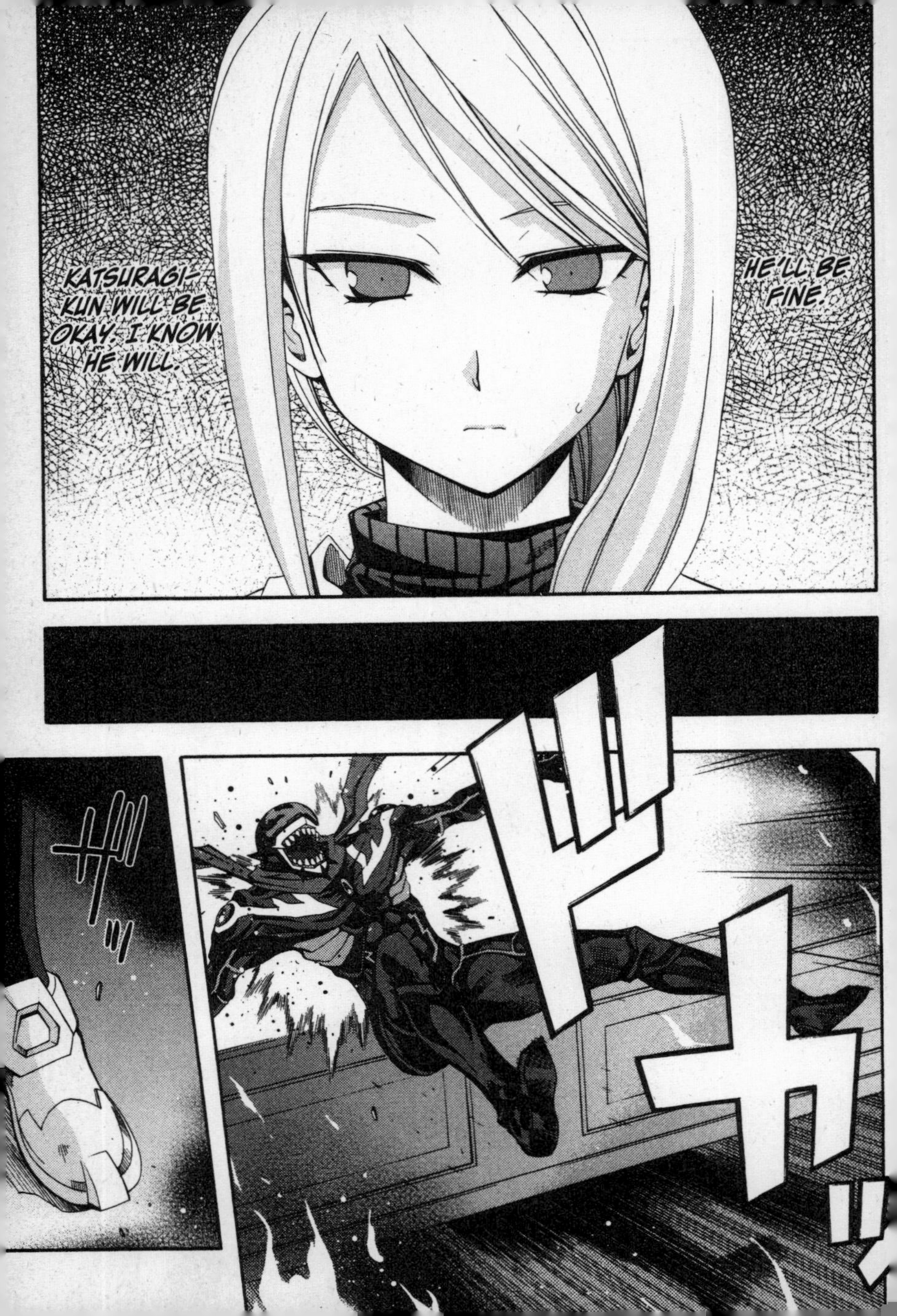
HE'LL BE FINE.
KATSURAGI-KUN WILL BE OKAY. I KNOW HE WILL.

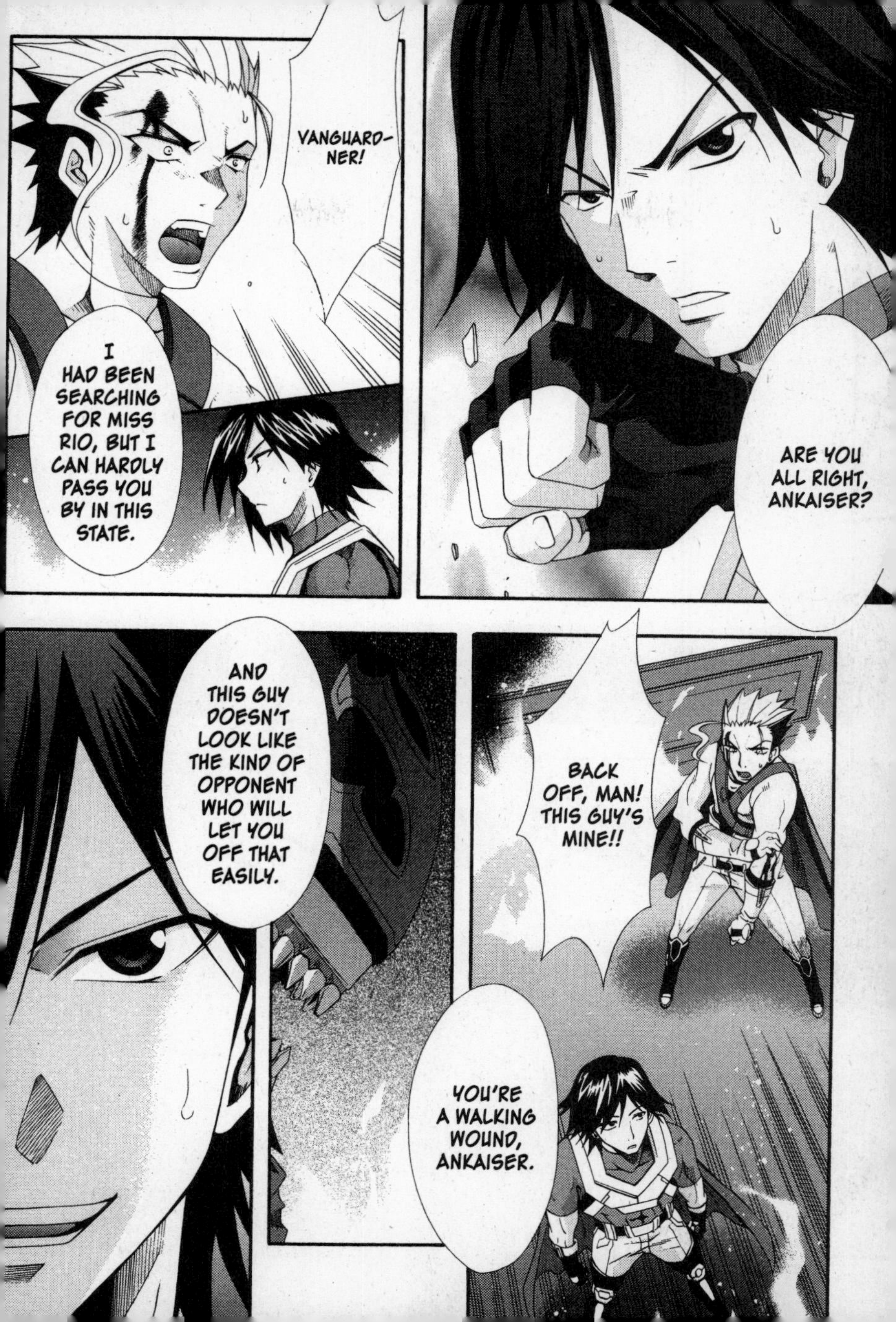
ARE YOU ALL RIGHT, ANKAISER?
VANGUARDNER!
I HAD BEEN SEARCHING FOR MISS RIO, BUT I CAN HARDLY PASS YOU BY IN THIS STATE.
BACK OFF, MAN! THIS GUY'S MINE!!
YOU'RE A WALKING WOUND, ANKAISER.
AND THIS GUY DOESN'T LOOK LIKE THE KIND OF OPPONENT WHO WILL LET YOU OFF THAT EASILY.

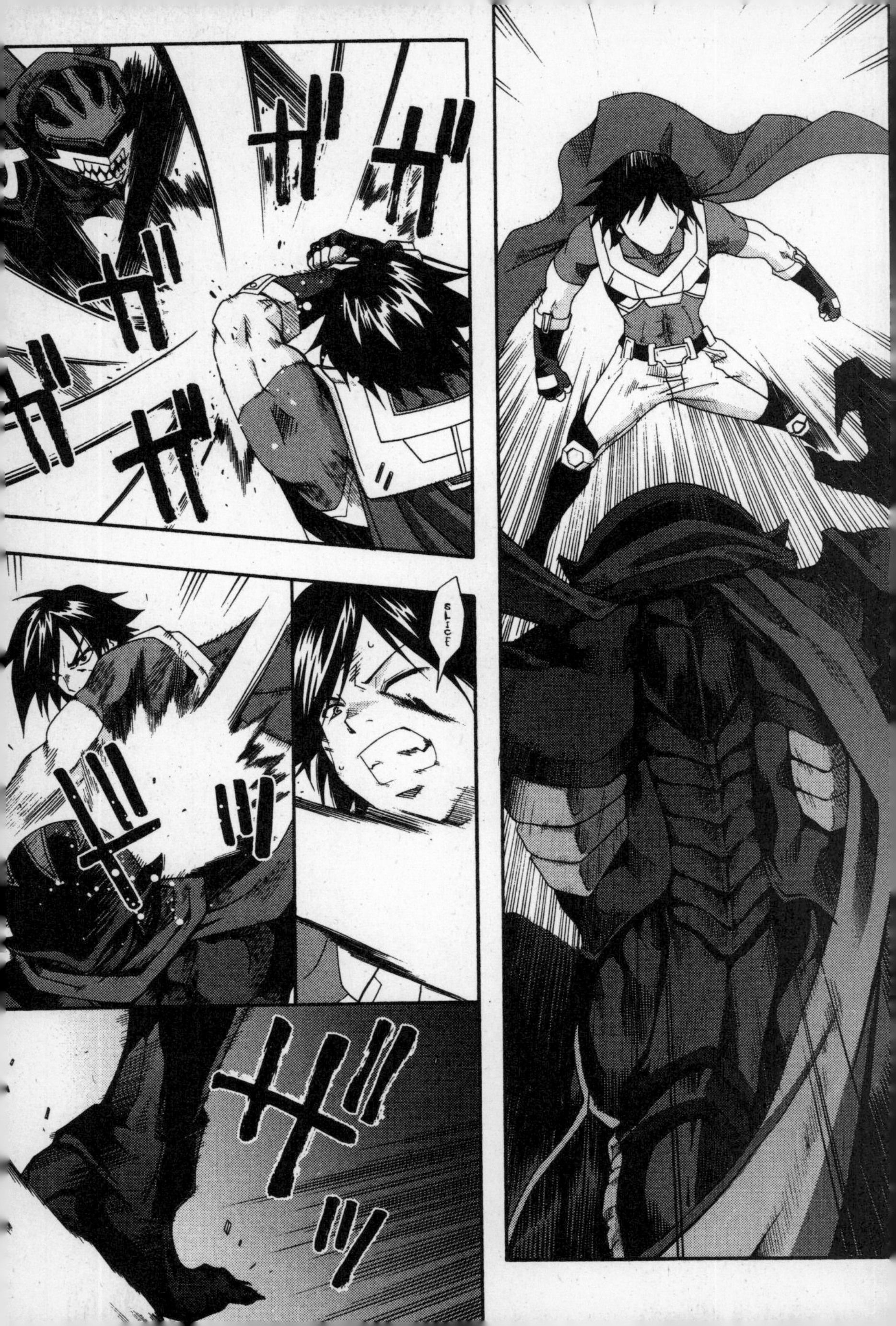
ガガガガガ
SLICE
ザッ

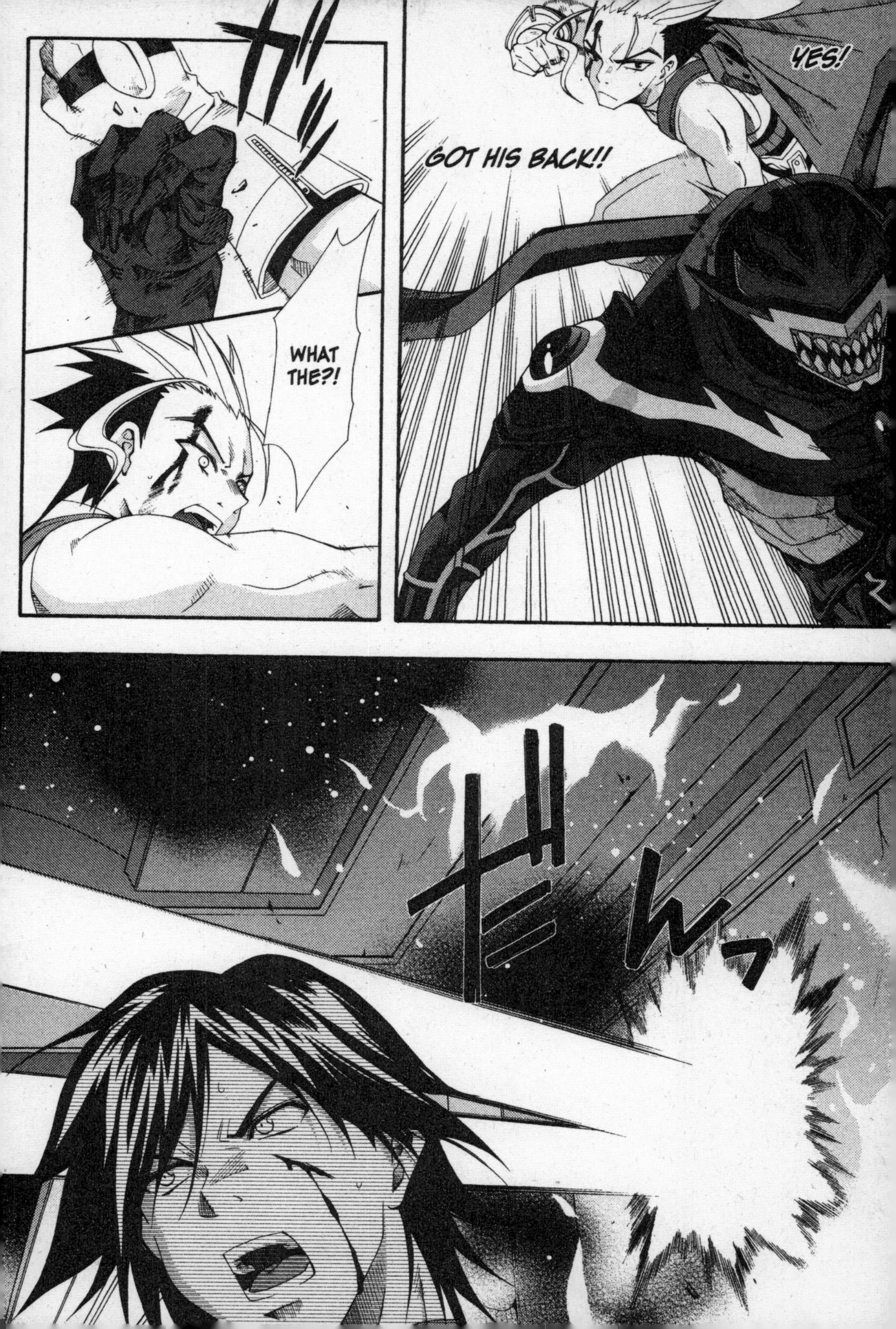
YES!
GOT HIS BACK!!
WHAT THE?!

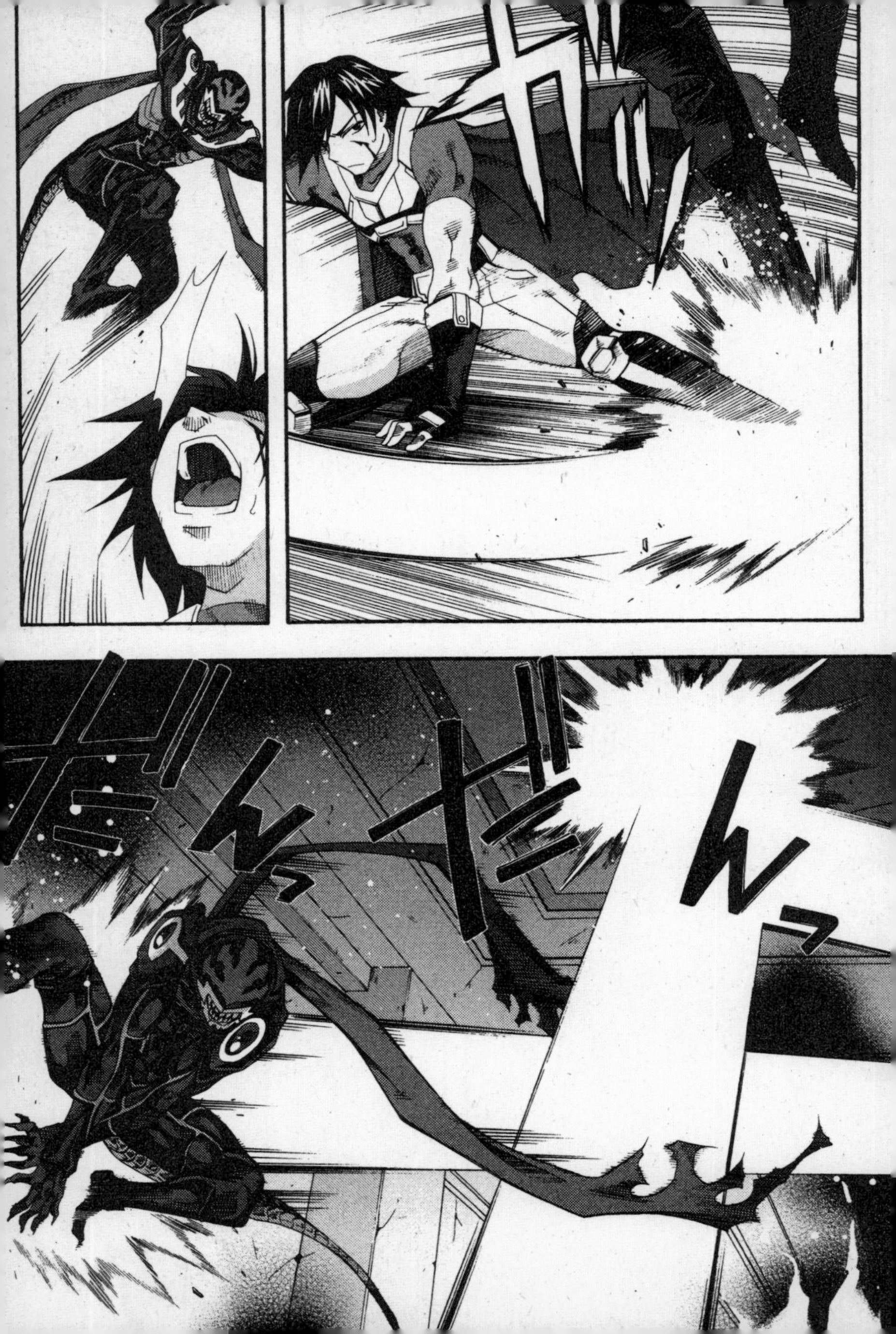

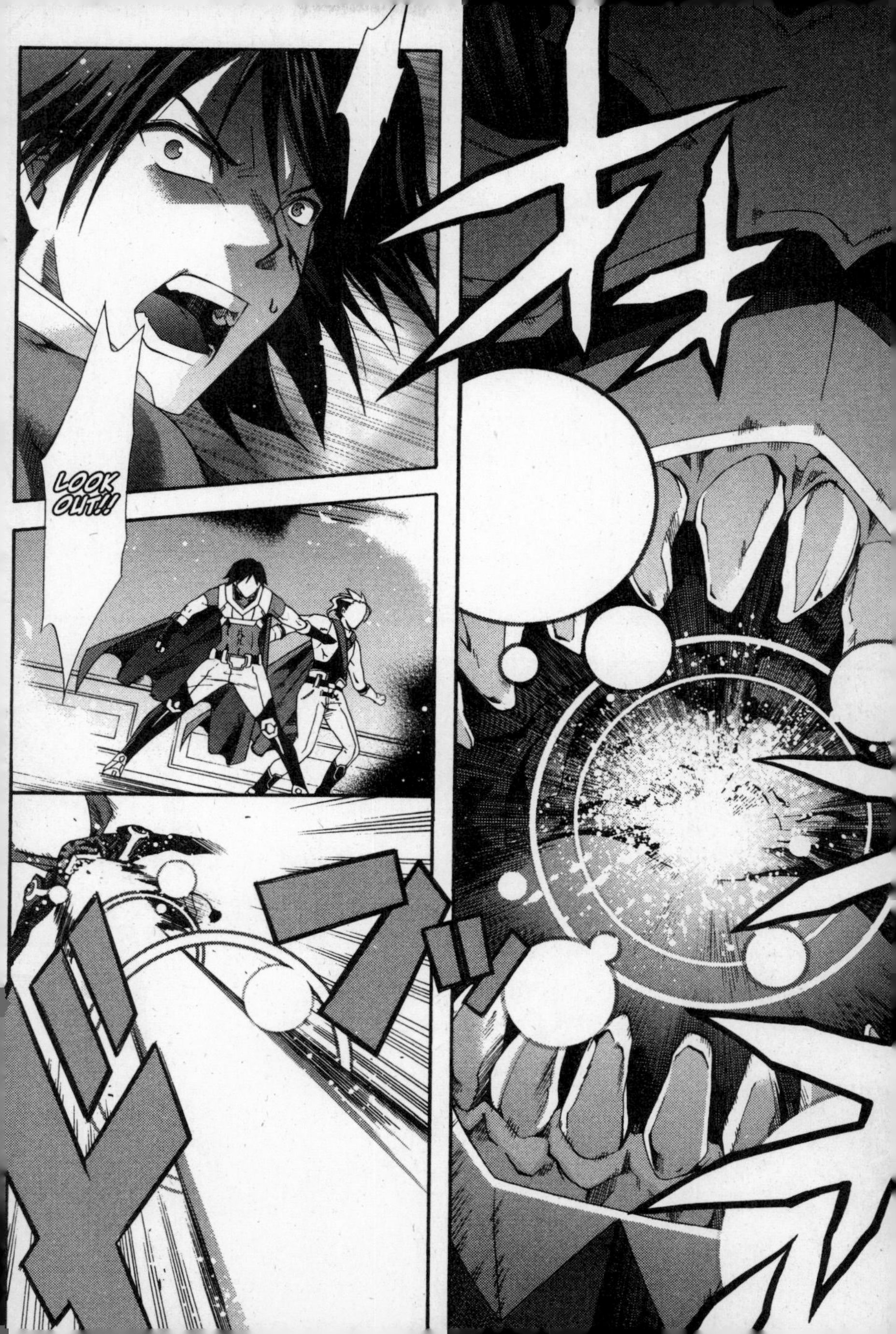
LOOK OUT!!

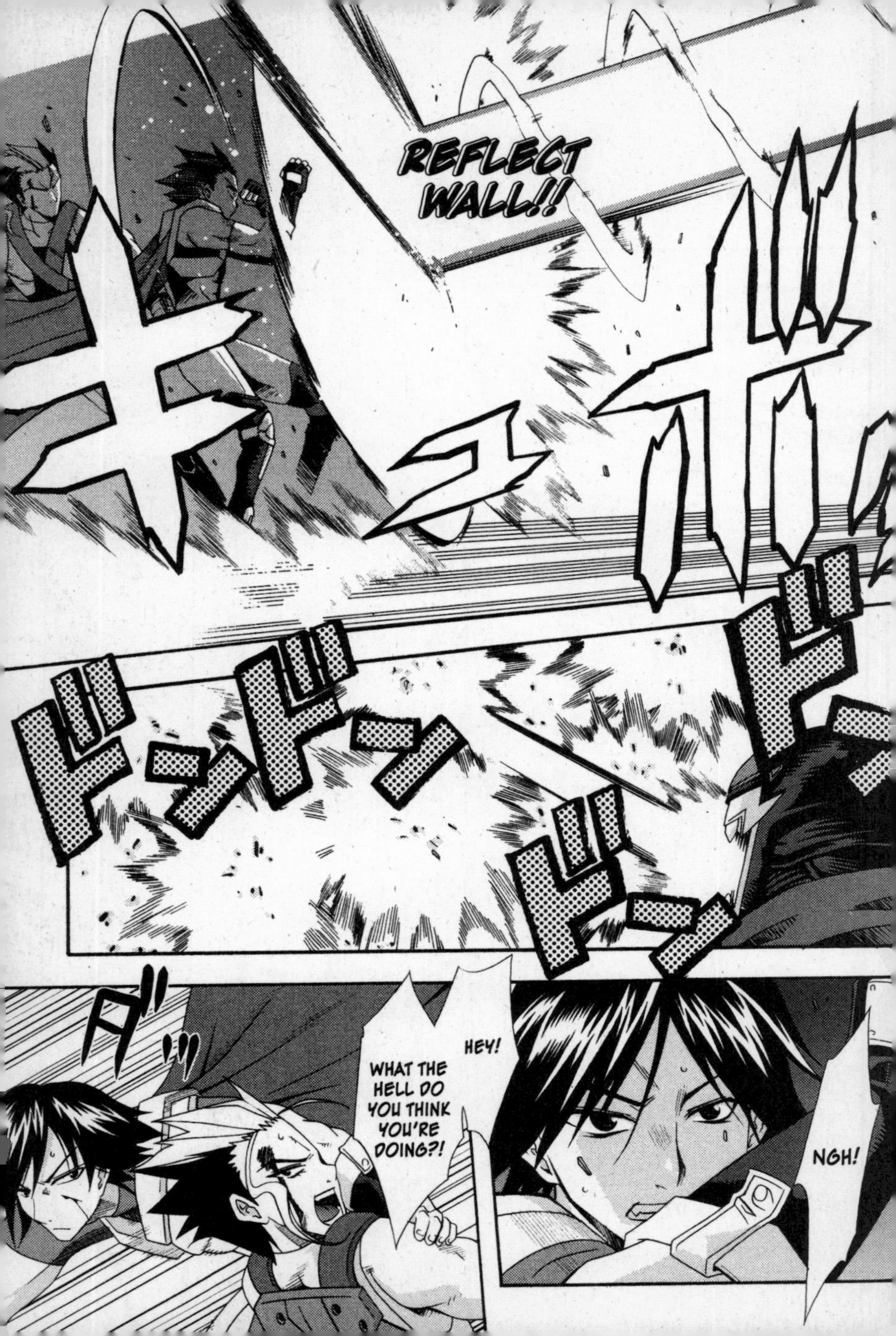
REFLECT WALL!!
ドッドッ
ドッドッ
NGH!
HEY!
WHAT THE HELL DO YOU THINK YOU'RE DOING?!

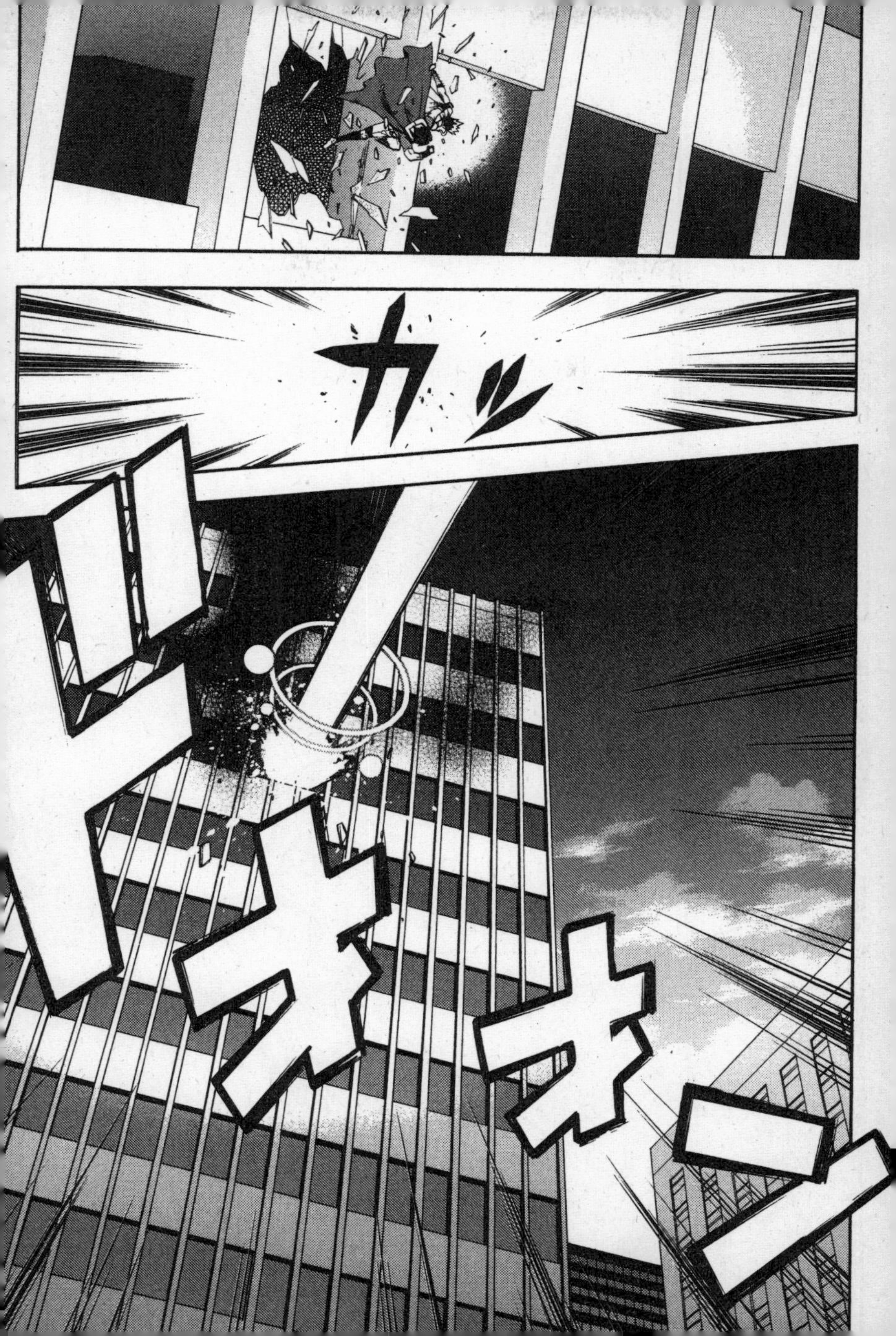
カッ
ドオオン

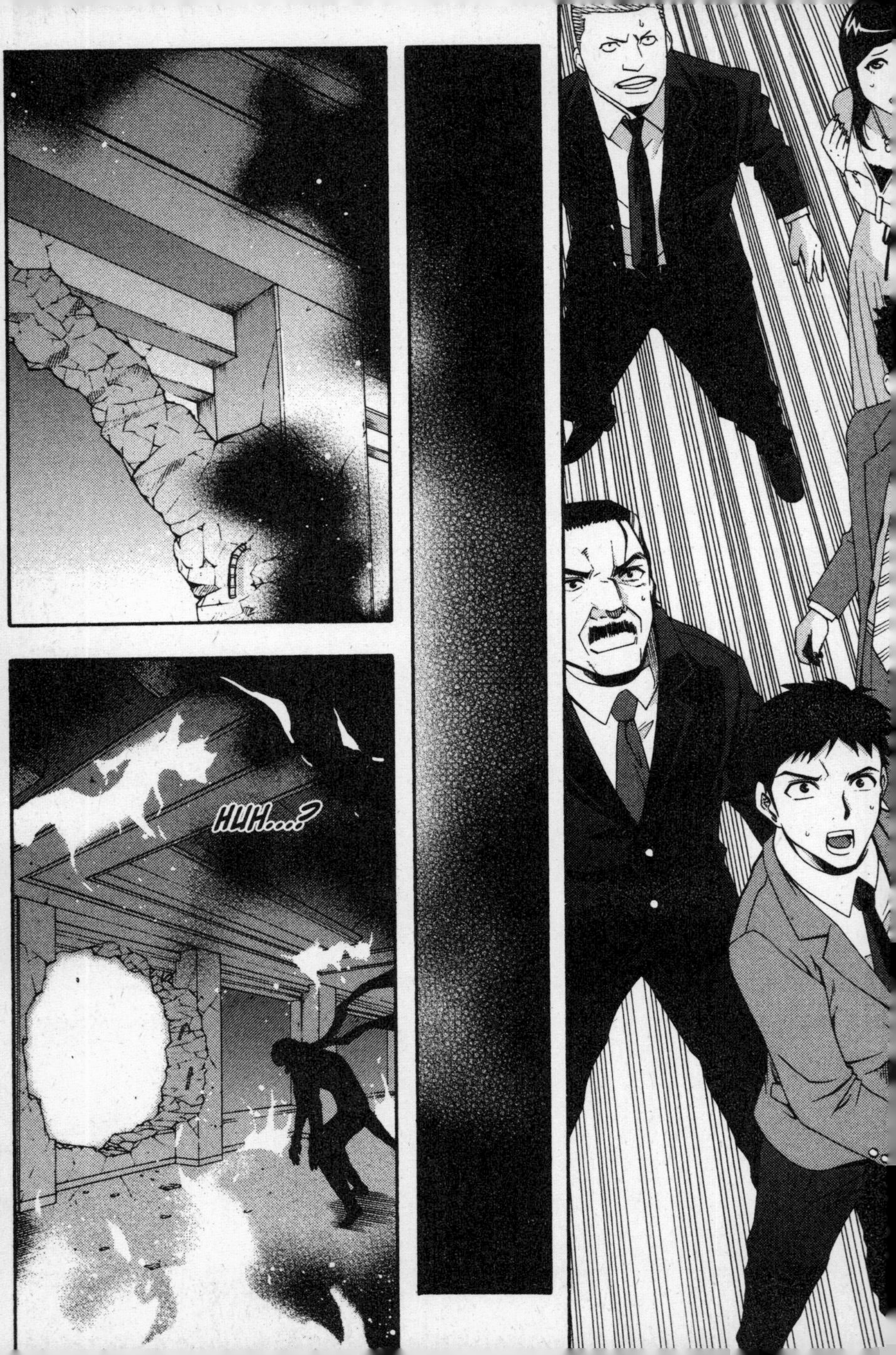
HUH...?

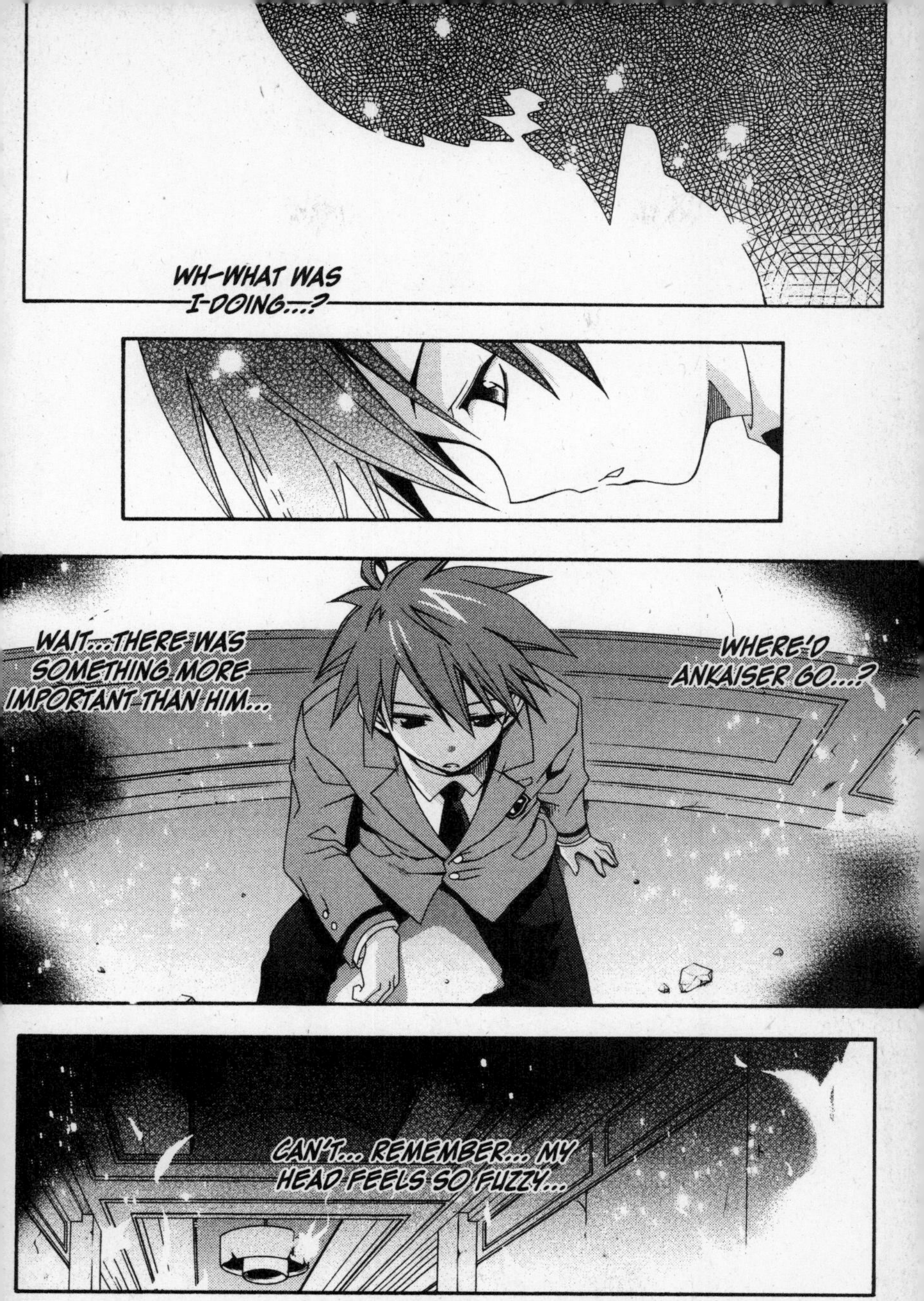
WH-WHAT WAS I-DOING...?
WHERE'D ANKAISER GO...?
WAIT...THERE WAS SOMETHING MORE IMPORTANT THAN HIM...
CAN'T... REMEMBER... MY HEAD FEELS SO FUZZY...

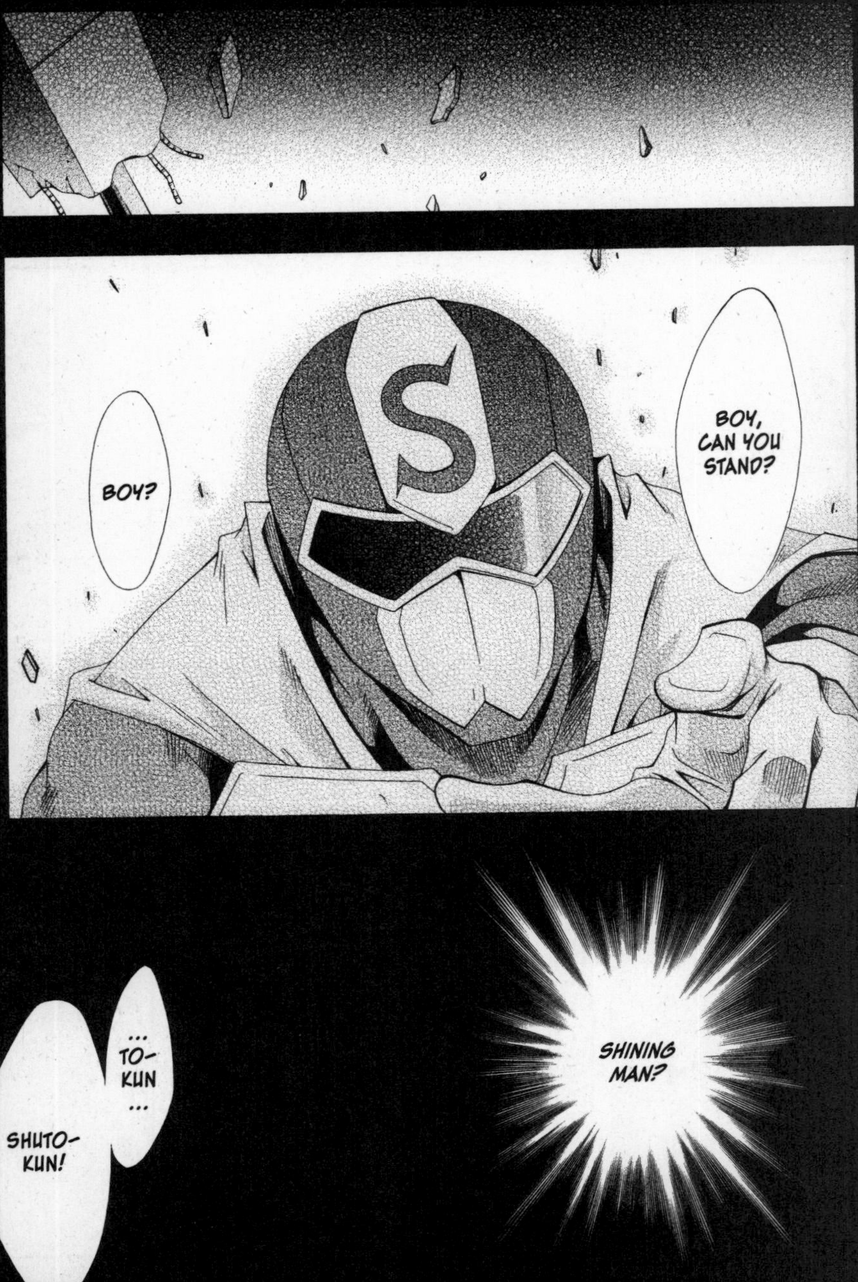
BOY, CAN YOU STAND?
BOY?
SHINING MAN?
...TO-KUN...
SHUTO-KUN!

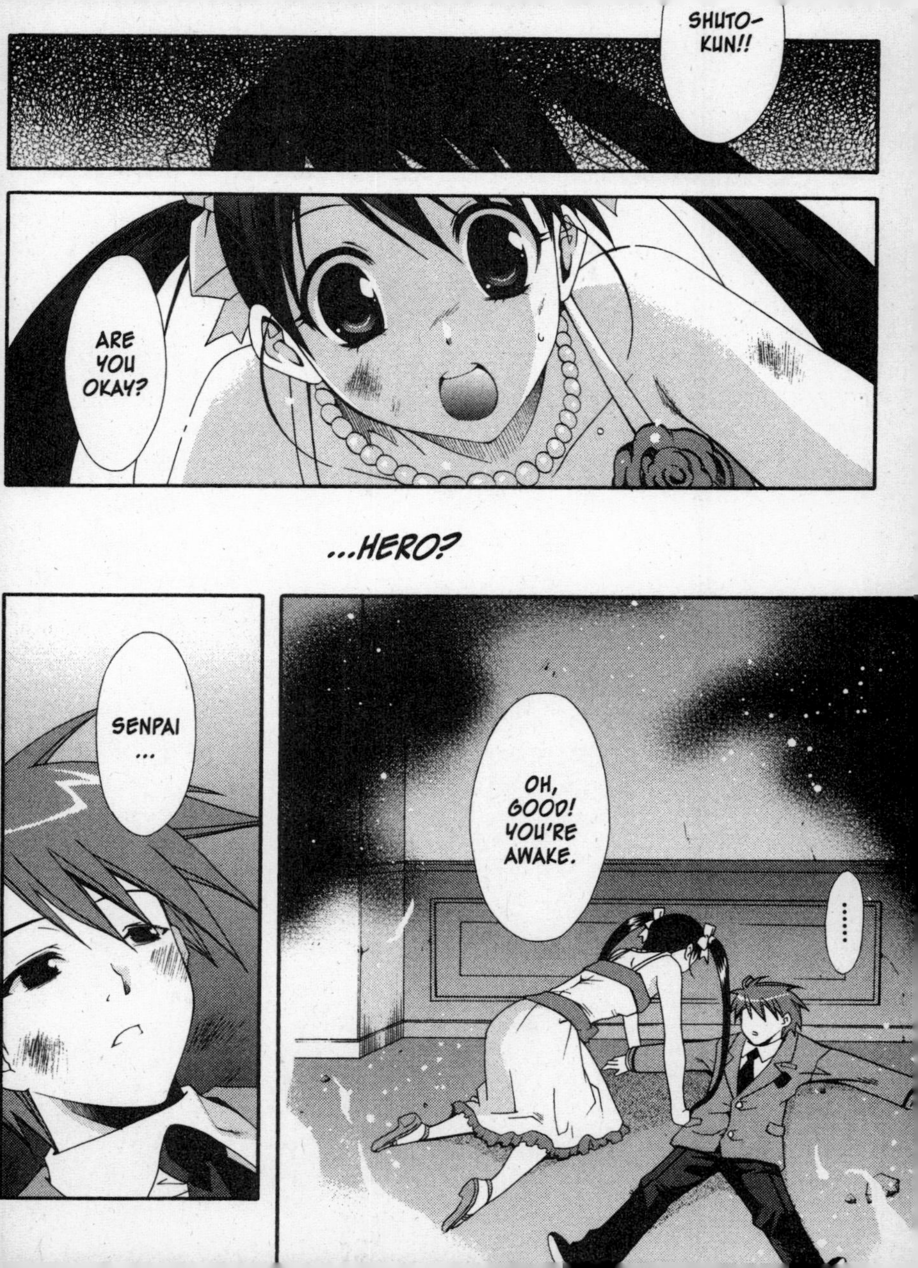
SHUTO-KUN!!
ARE YOU OKAY?
...HERO?
OH, GOOD! YOU'RE AWAKE.
......
SENPAI ...

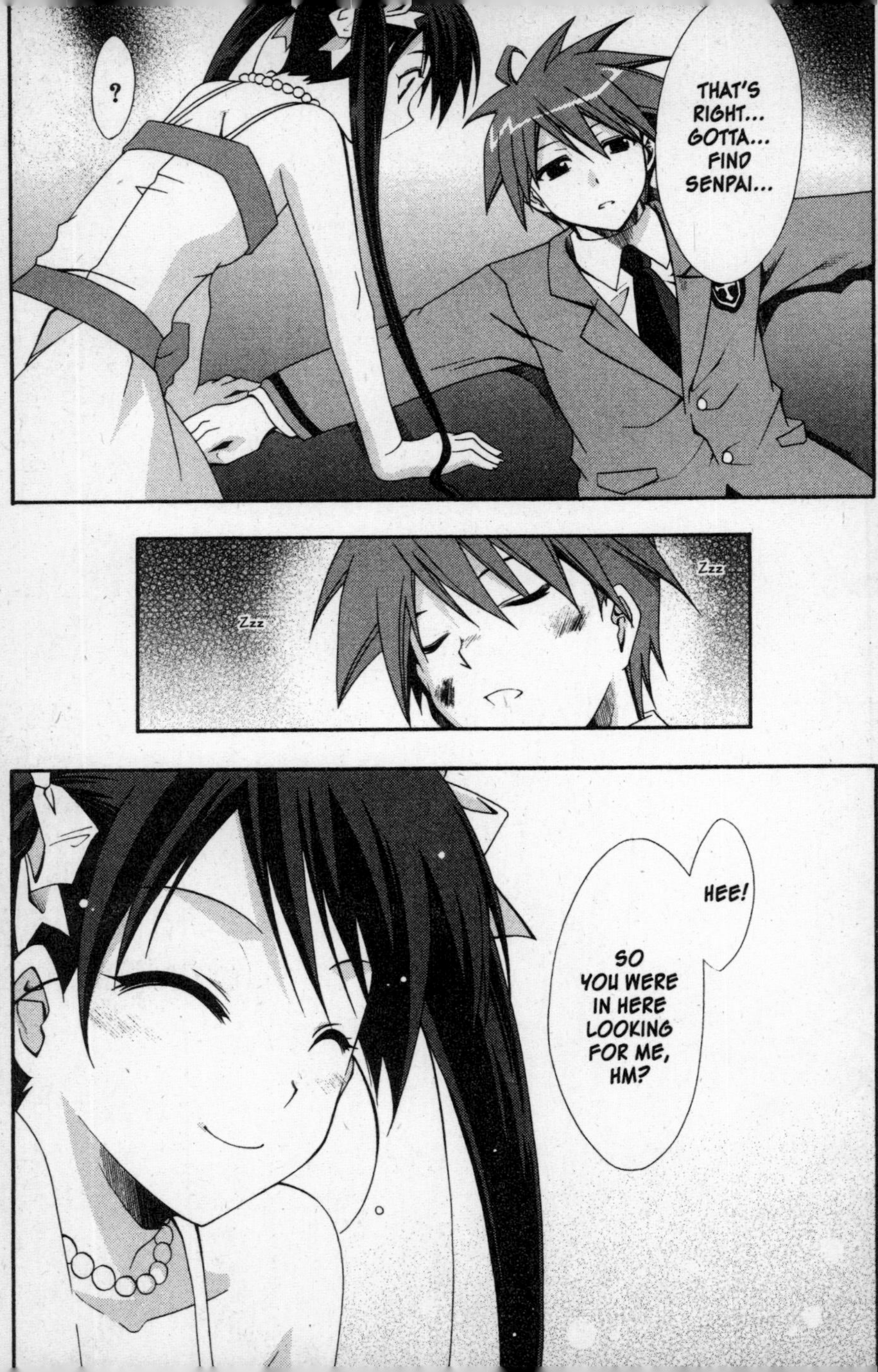
THAT'S RIGHT... GOTTA... FIND SENPAI...
?
Zzz
Zzz
HEE!
SO YOU WERE IN HERE LOOKING FOR ME, HM?

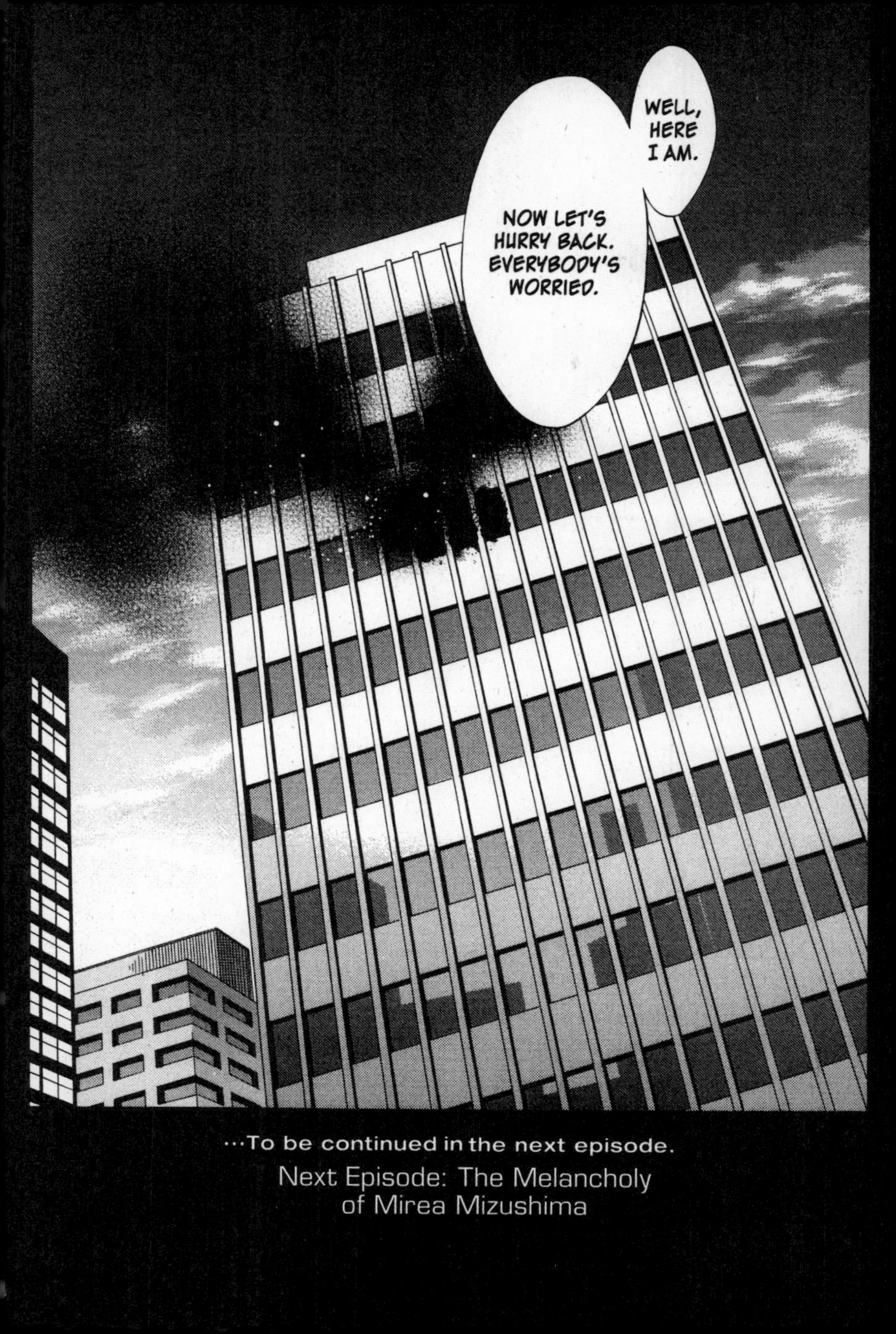
WELL, HERE I AM.
NOW LET'S HURRY BACK. EVERYBODY'S WORRIED.

…To be continued in the next episode.

Next Episode: The Melancholy of Mirea Mizushima

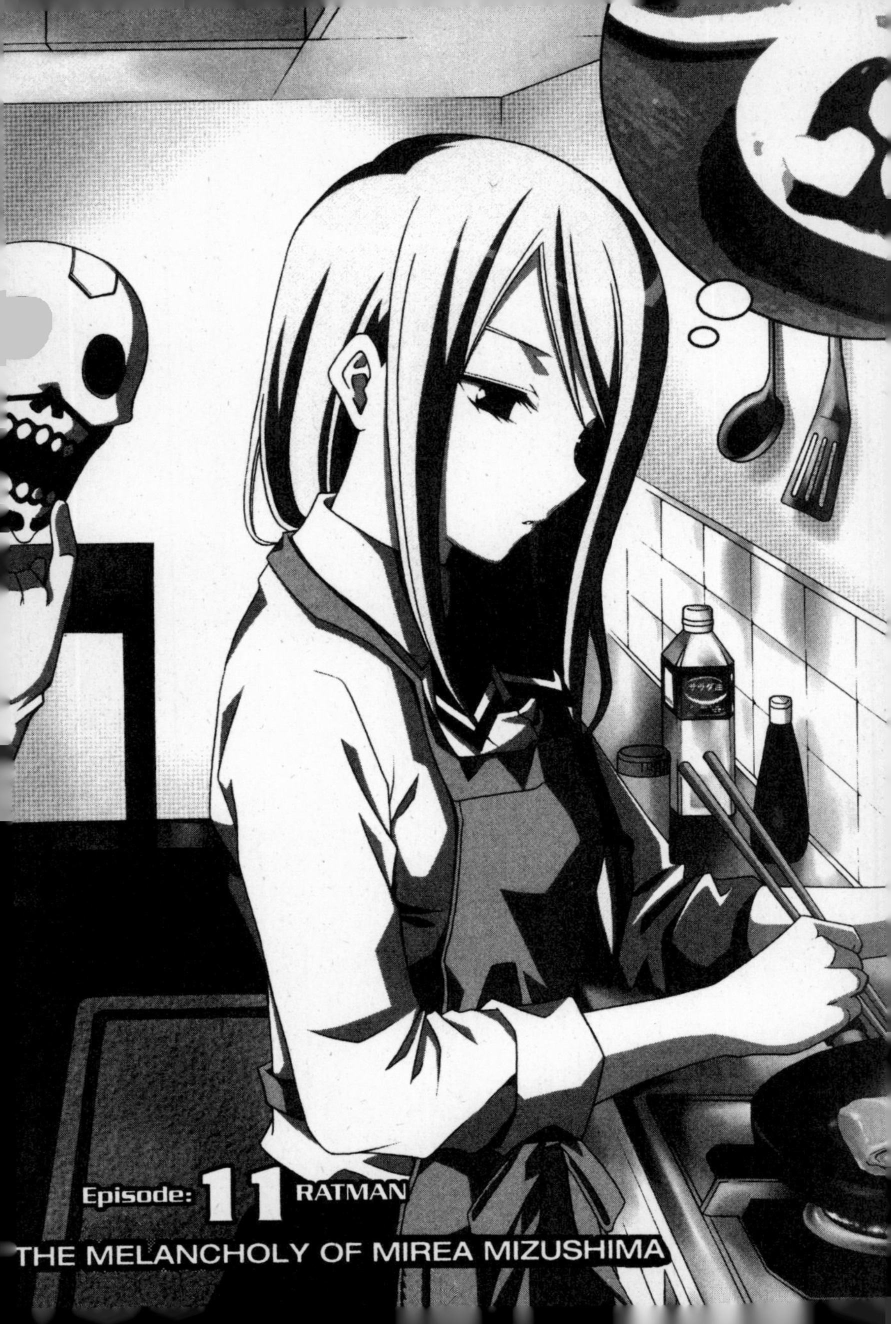
Episode: 11 RATMAN
THE MELANCHOLY OF MIREA MIZUSHIMA

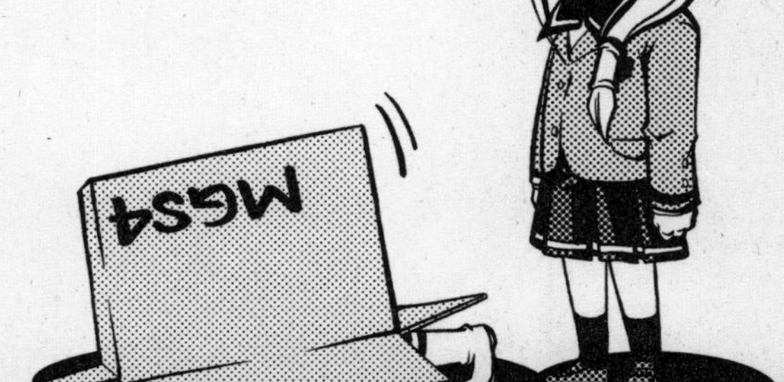
?
MGS4

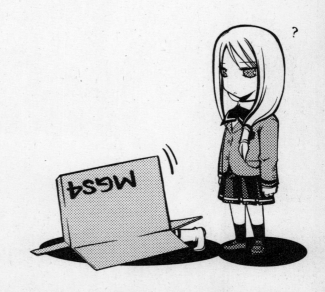

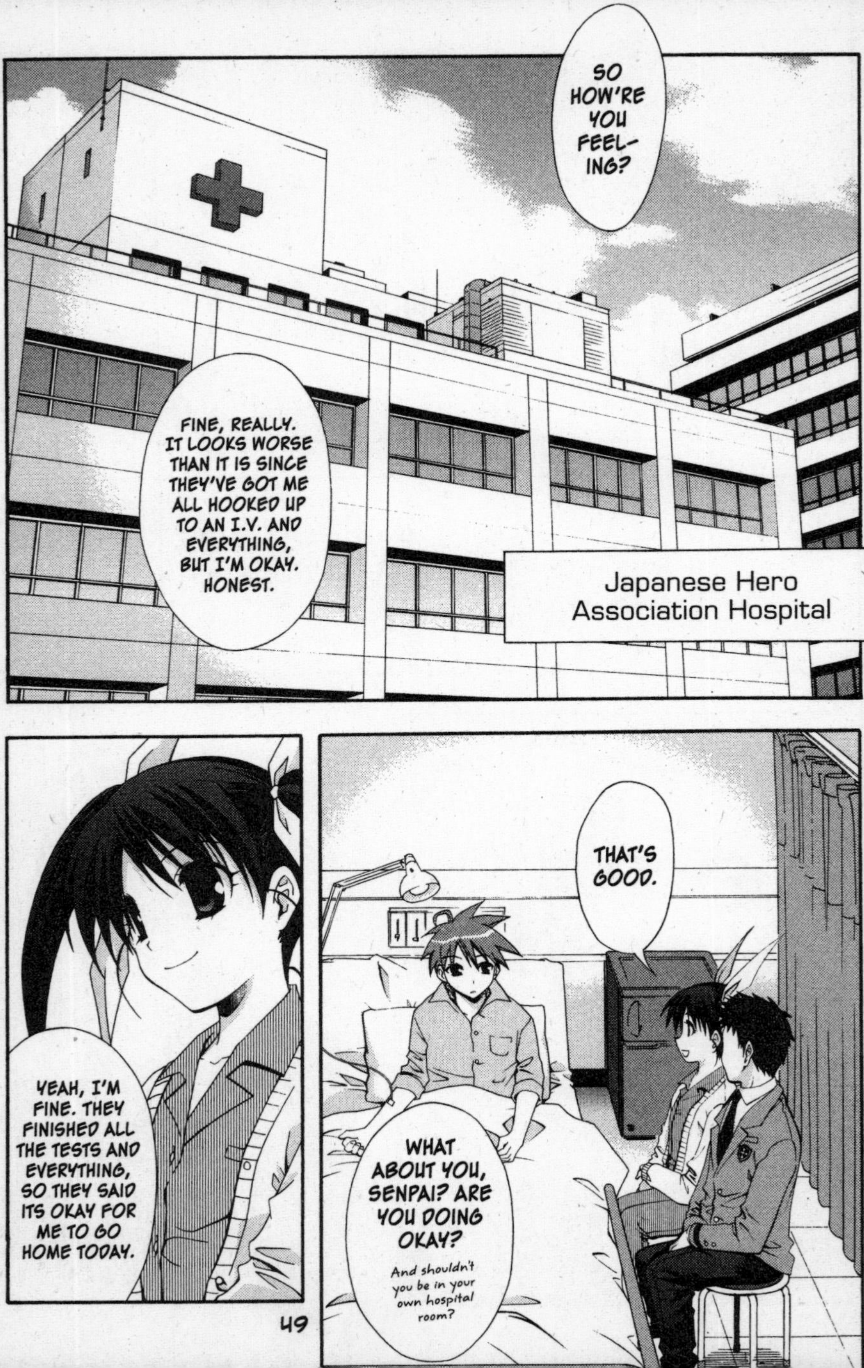
SO HOW'RE YOU FEEL-ING?
Japanese Hero Association Hospital
FINE, REALLY. IT LOOKS WORSE THAN IT IS SINCE THEY'VE GOT ME ALL HOOKED UP TO AN I.V. AND EVERYTHING, BUT I'M OKAY. HONEST.
THAT'S GOOD.
WHAT ABOUT YOU, SENPAI? ARE YOU DOING OKAY?
And shouldn't you be in your own hospital room?
YEAH, I'M FINE. THEY FINISHED ALL THE TESTS AND EVERYTHING, SO THEY SAID ITS OKAY FOR ME TO GO HOME TODAY.

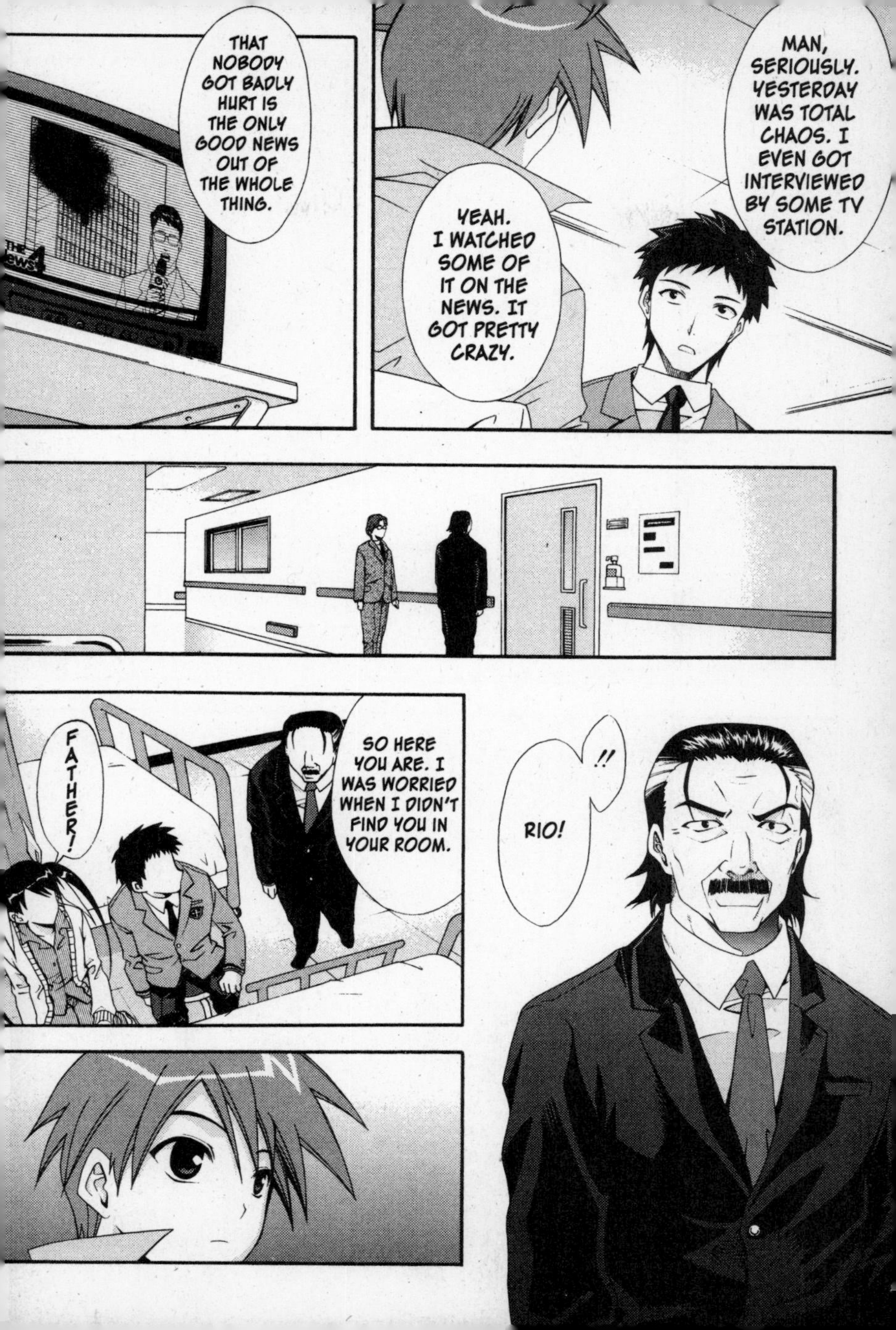
MAN, SERIOUSLY. YESTERDAY WAS TOTAL CHAOS. I EVEN GOT INTERVIEWED BY SOME TV STATION.
YEAH. I WATCHED SOME OF IT ON THE NEWS. IT GOT PRETTY CRAZY.
THAT NOBODY GOT BADLY HURT IS THE ONLY GOOD NEWS OUT OF THE WHOLE THING.
!!
RIO!
SO HERE YOU ARE. I WAS WORRIED WHEN I DIDN'T FIND YOU IN YOUR ROOM.
FATHER!

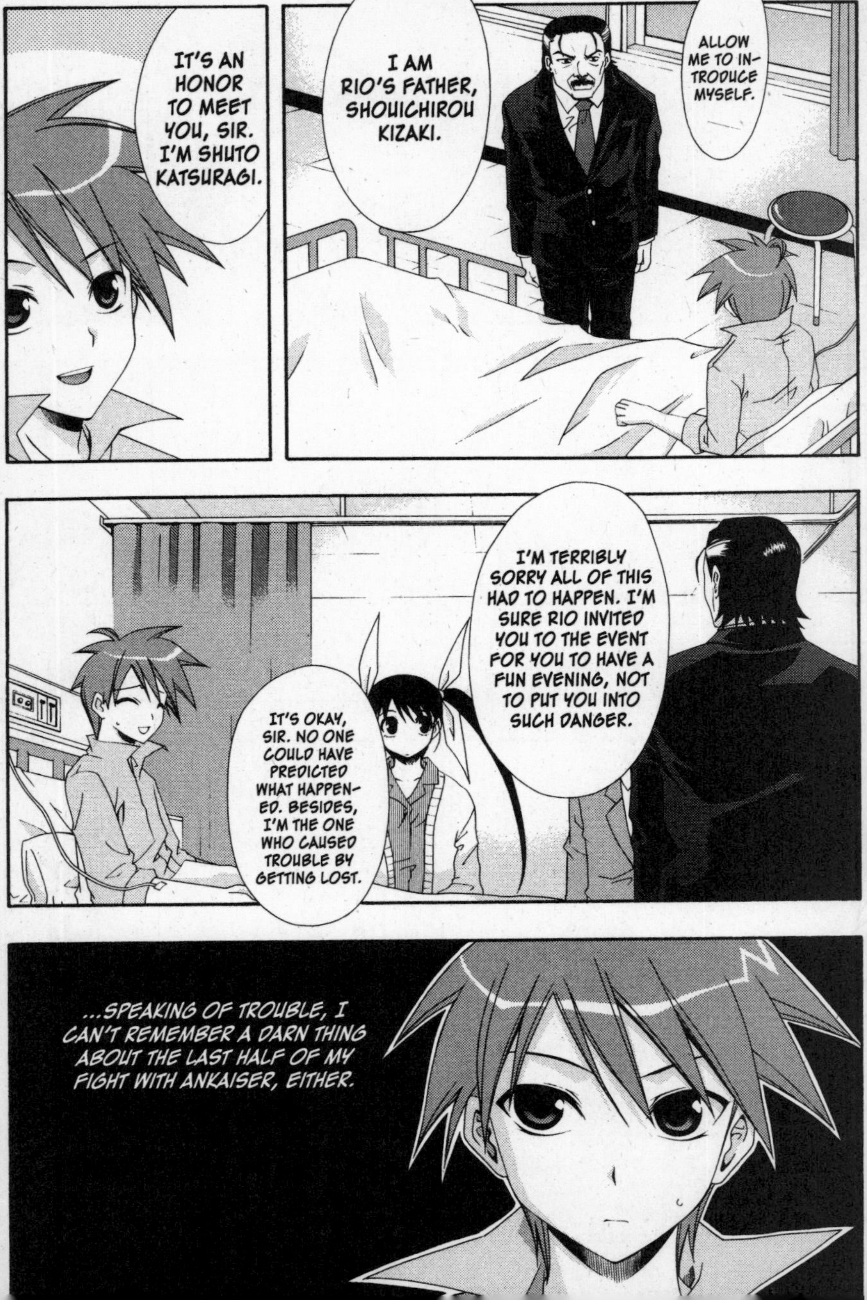
ALLOW ME TO IN-TRODUCE MYSELF.
I AM RIO'S FATHER, SHOUICHIROU KIZAKI.
IT'S AN HONOR TO MEET YOU, SIR. I'M SHUTO KATSURAGI.
I'M TERRIBLY SORRY ALL OF THIS HAD TO HAPPEN. I'M SURE RIO INVITED YOU TO THE EVENT FOR YOU TO HAVE A FUN EVENING, NOT TO PUT YOU INTO SUCH DANGER.
IT'S OKAY, SIR. NO ONE COULD HAVE PREDICTED WHAT HAPPEN-ED. BESIDES, I'M THE ONE WHO CAUSED TROUBLE BY GETTING LOST.
...SPEAKING OF TROUBLE, I CAN'T REMEMBER A DARN THING ABOUT THE LAST HALF OF MY FIGHT WITH ANKAISER, EITHER.

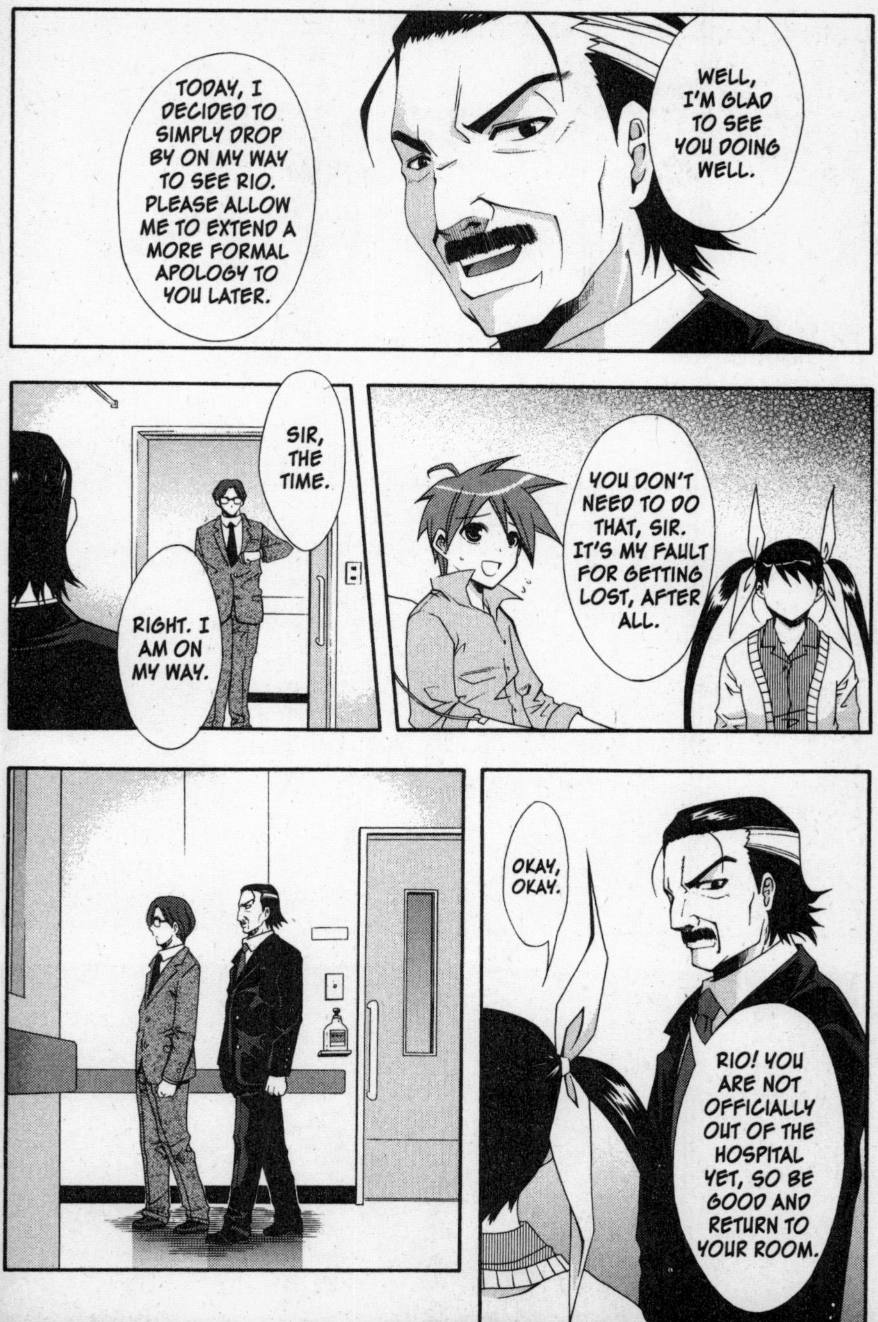
WELL, I'M GLAD TO SEE YOU DOING WELL.
TODAY, I DECIDED TO SIMPLY DROP BY ON MY WAY TO SEE RIO. PLEASE ALLOW ME TO EXTEND A MORE FORMAL APOLOGY TO YOU LATER.
YOU DON'T NEED TO DO THAT, SIR. IT'S MY FAULT FOR GETTING LOST, AFTER ALL.
SIR, THE TIME.
RIGHT. I AM ON MY WAY.
RIO! YOU ARE NOT OFFICIALLY OUT OF THE HOSPITAL YET, SO BE GOOD AND RETURN TO YOUR ROOM.
OKAY, OKAY.

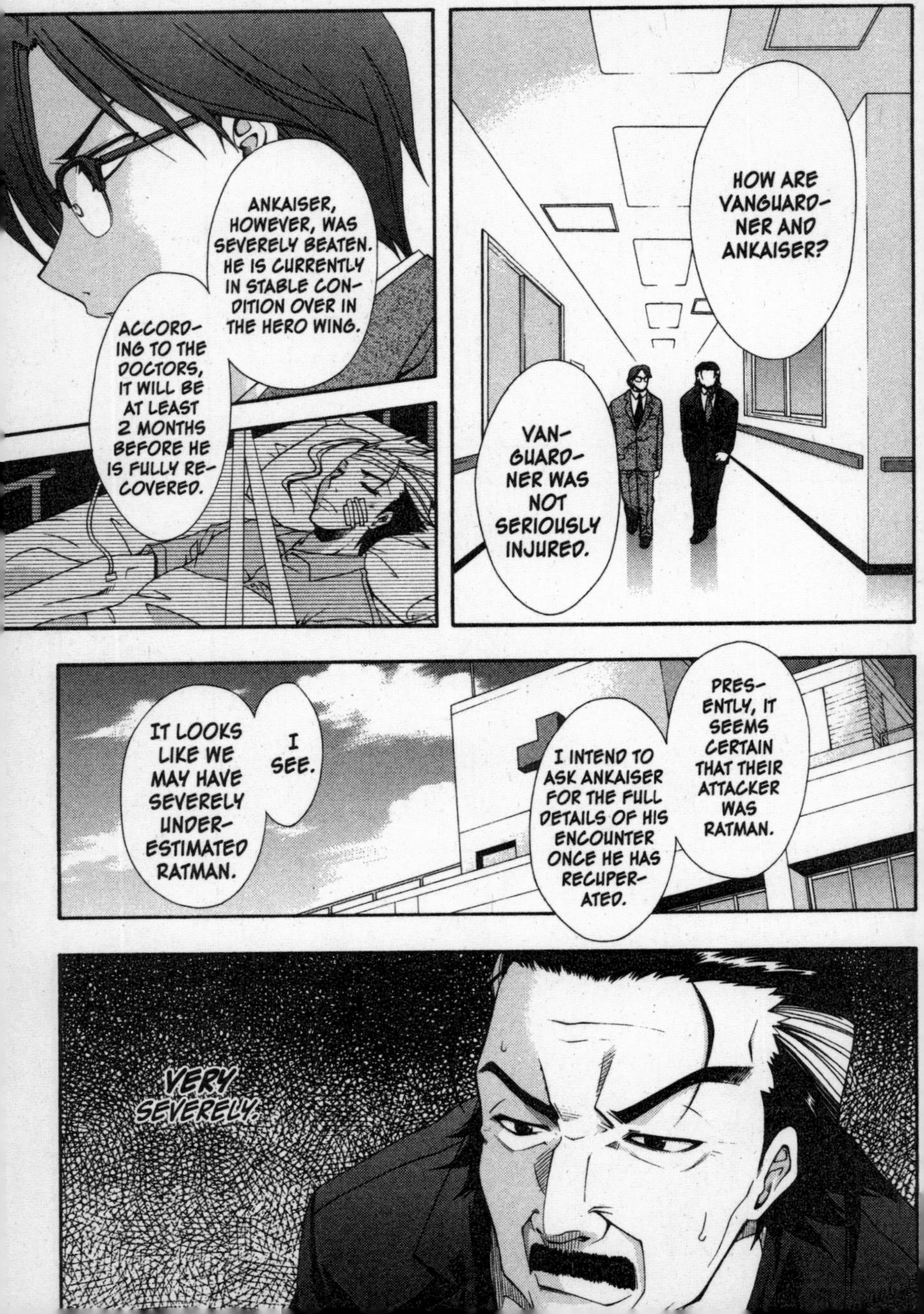
HOW ARE VANGUARDNER AND ANKAISER?
VANGUARDNER WAS NOT SERIOUSLY INJURED.
ANKAISER, HOWEVER, WAS SEVERELY BEATEN. HE IS CURRENTLY IN STABLE CONDITION OVER IN THE HERO WING.
ACCORDING TO THE DOCTORS, IT WILL BE AT LEAST 2 MONTHS BEFORE HE IS FULLY RECOVERED.
PRESENTLY, IT SEEMS CERTAIN THAT THEIR ATTACKER WAS RATMAN.
I INTEND TO ASK ANKAISER FOR THE FULL DETAILS OF HIS ENCOUNTER ONCE HE HAS RECUPERATED.
I SEE.
IT LOOKS LIKE WE MAY HAVE SEVERELY UNDERESTIMATED RATMAN.
VERY SEVERELY.

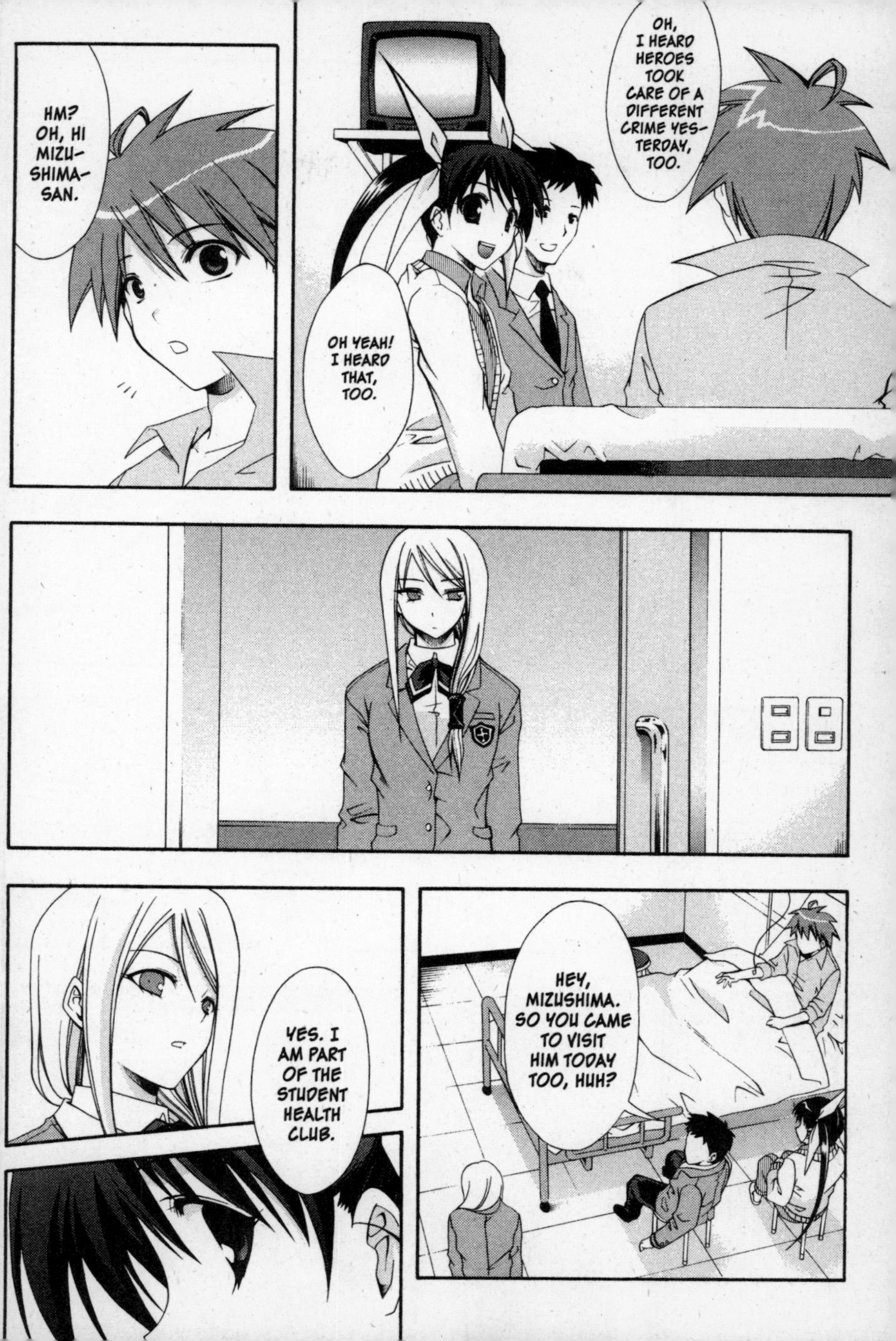
OH, I HEARD HEROES TOOK CARE OF A DIFFERENT CRIME YESTERDAY, TOO.
OH YEAH! I HEARD THAT, TOO.
HM? OH, HI MIZUSHIMA-SAN.
HEY, MIZUSHIMA. SO YOU CAME TO VISIT HIM TODAY TOO, HUH?
YES. I AM PART OF THE STUDENT HEALTH CLUB.

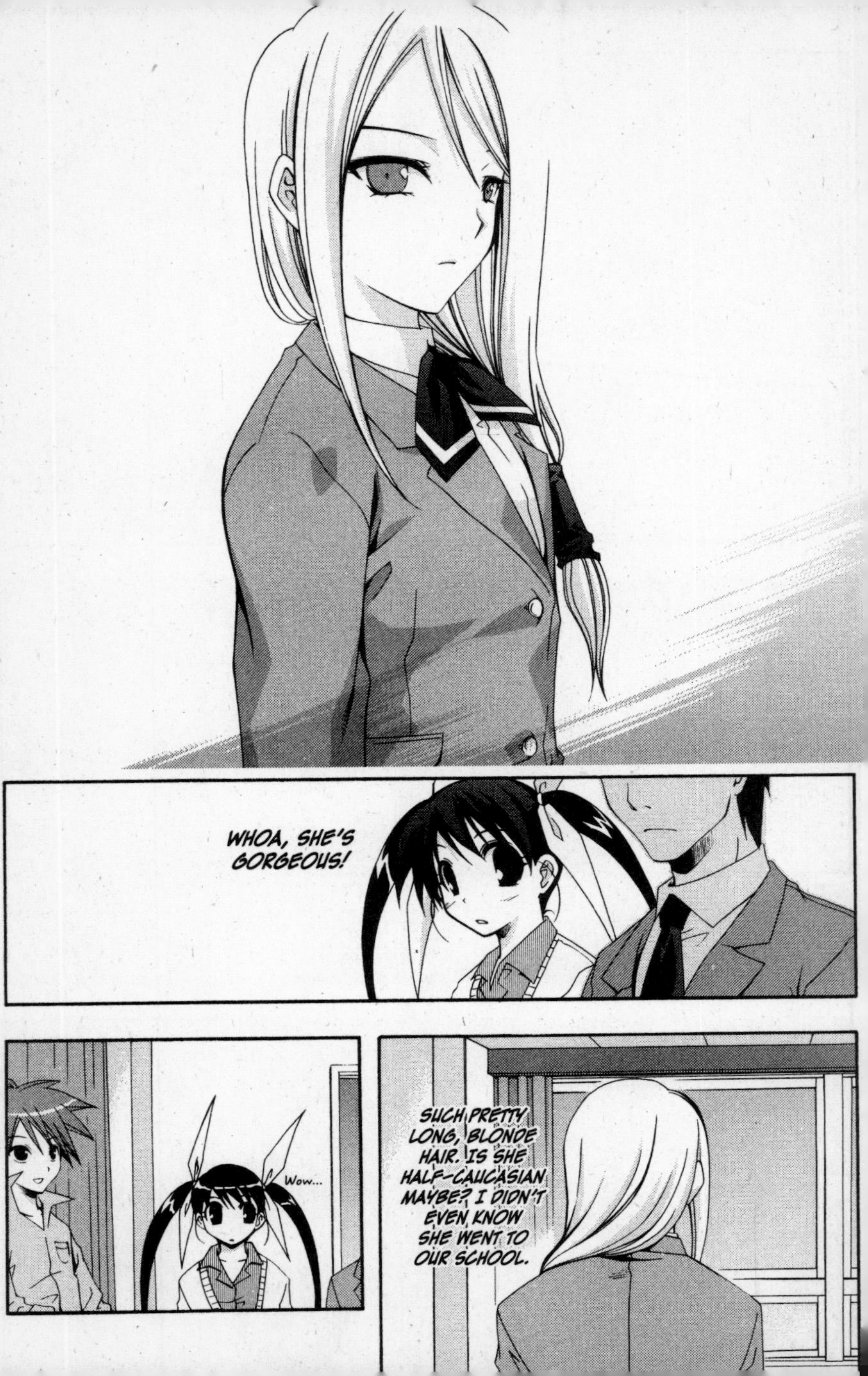
WHOA, SHE'S GORGEOUS!
SUCH PRETTY LONG, BLONDE HAIR. IS SHE HALF-CAUCASIAN MAYBE? I DIDN'T EVEN KNOW SHE WENT TO OUR SCHOOL.
Wow...

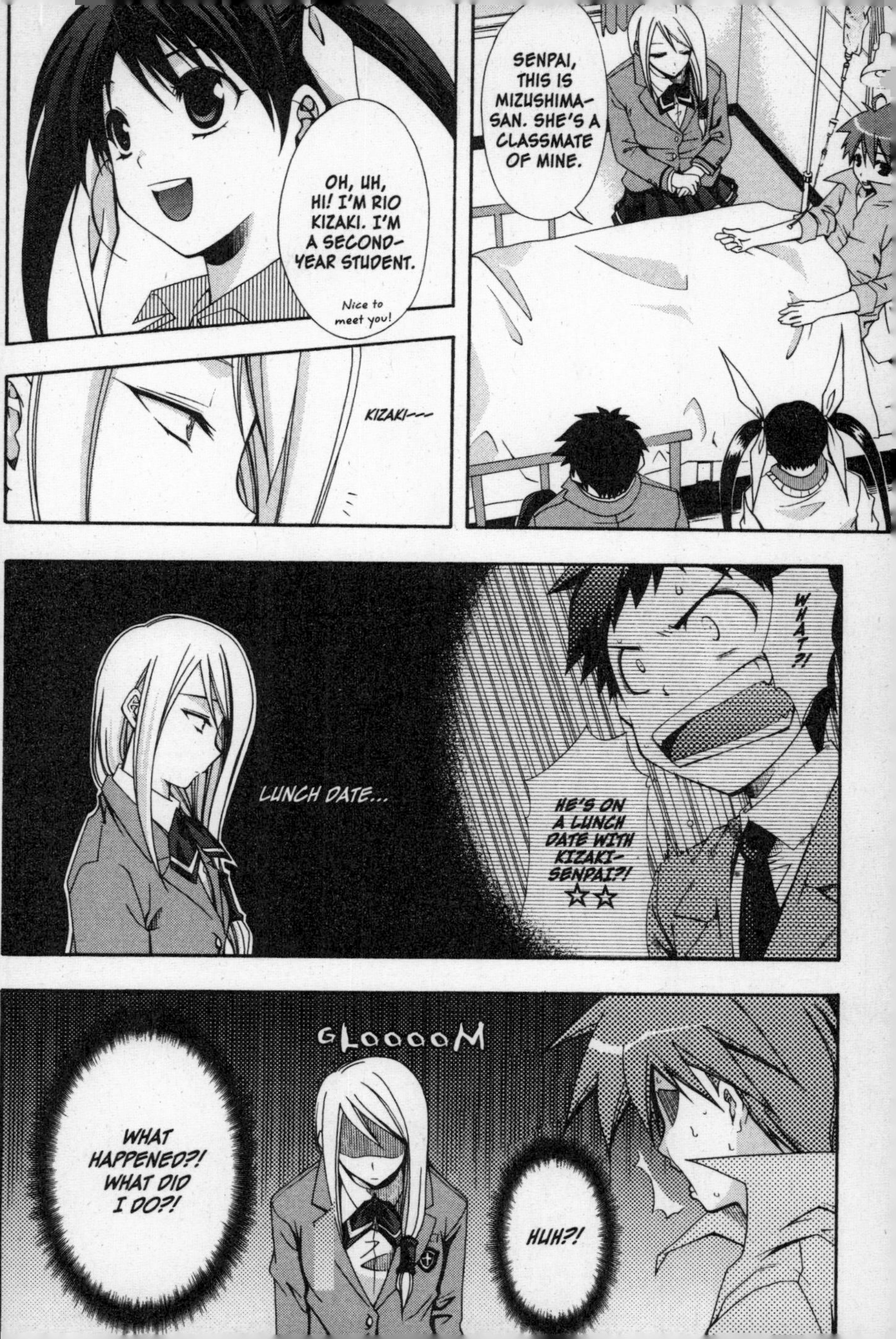
SENPAI, THIS IS MIZUSHIMA-SAN. SHE'S A CLASSMATE OF MINE.
OH, UH, HI! I'M RIO KIZAKI. I'M A SECOND-YEAR STUDENT.
Nice to meet you!
KIZAKI---
WHAT?!
HE'S ON A LUNCH DATE WITH KIZAKI-SENPAI?! ☆☆
LUNCH DATE...
GLOOOOOM
HUH?!
WHAT HAPPENED?! WHAT DID I DO?!

YEAH, ME TOO.

ANYWAYS, I THINK I'D BETTER GET GOING.

YOU TOO.

TAKE CARE!

I AM SUPPOSED TO STILL BE IN BED, AFTER ALL.

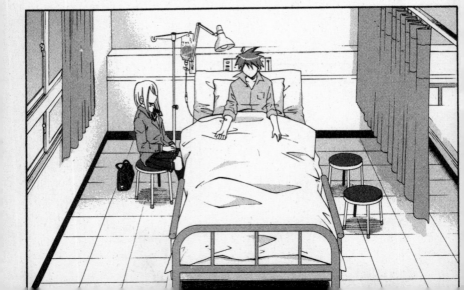

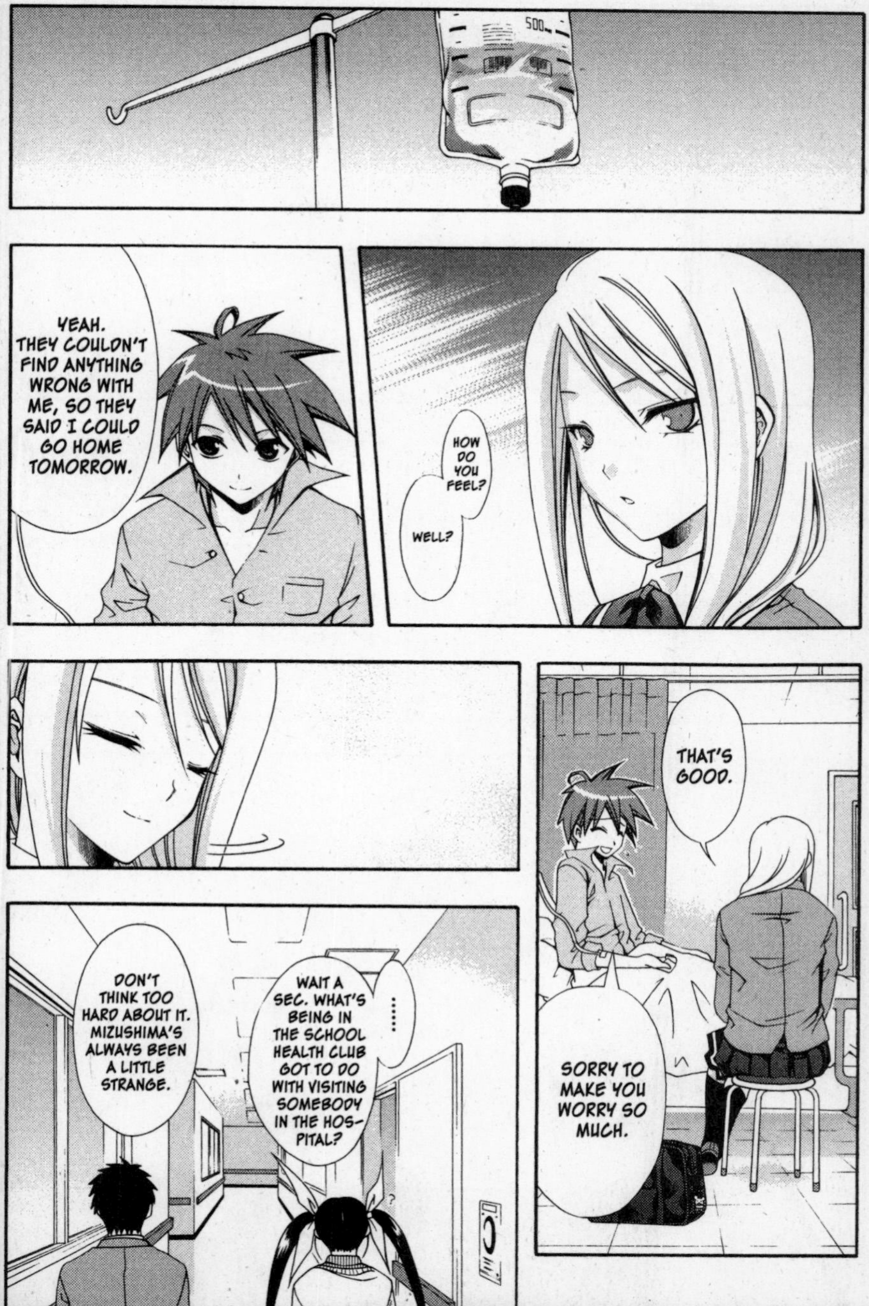
HOW DO YOU FEEL?
WELL?
YEAH. THEY COULDN'T FIND ANYTHING WRONG WITH ME, SO THEY SAID I COULD GO HOME TOMORROW.
THAT'S GOOD.
SORRY TO MAKE YOU WORRY SO MUCH.
......
WAIT A SEC. WHAT'S BEING IN THE SCHOOL HEALTH CLUB GOT TO DO WITH VISITING SOMEBODY IN THE HOS-PITAL?
DON'T THINK TOO HARD ABOUT IT. MIZUSHIMA'S ALWAYS BEEN A LITTLE STRANGE.

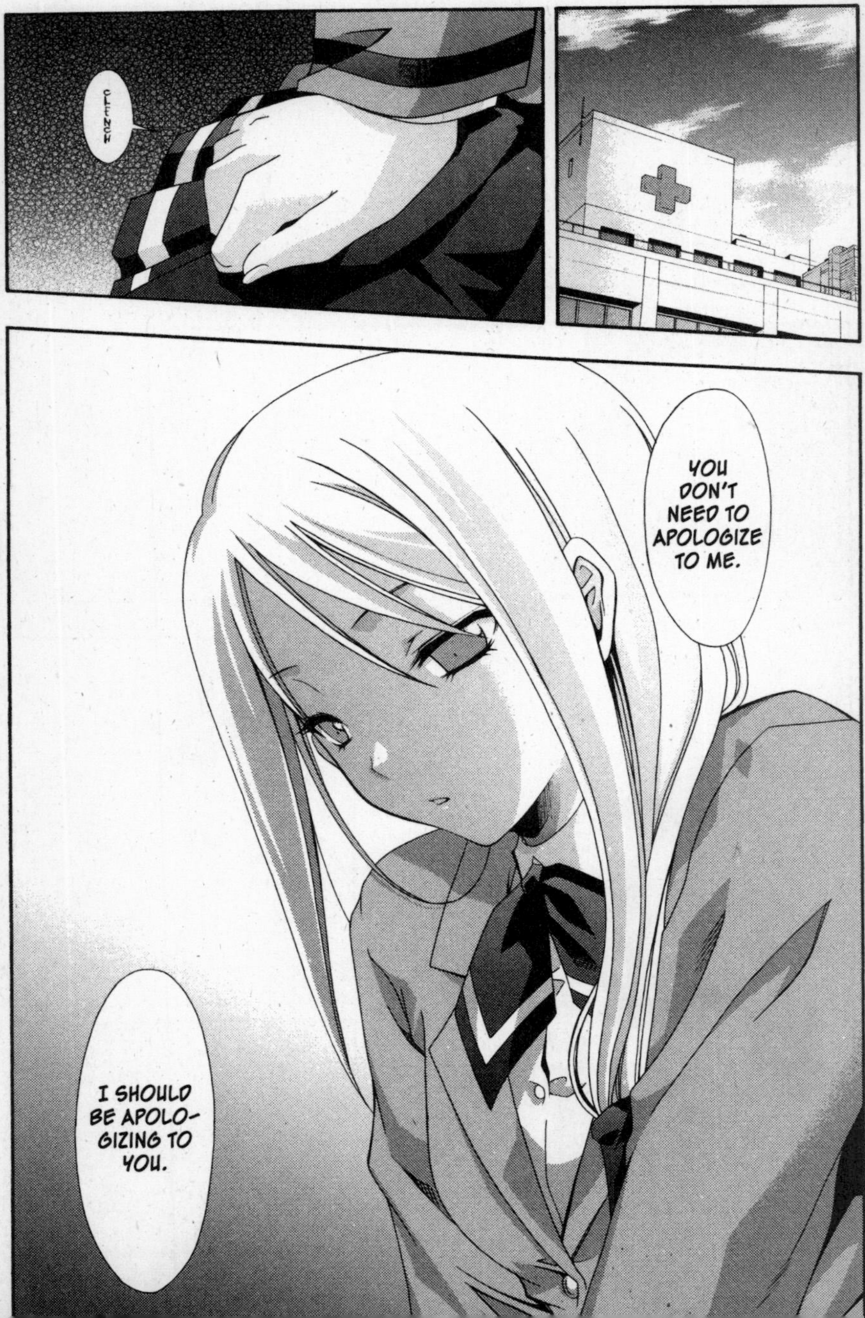
CLENCH
YOU DON'T NEED TO APOLOGIZE TO ME.
I SHOULD BE APOLO-GIZING TO YOU.

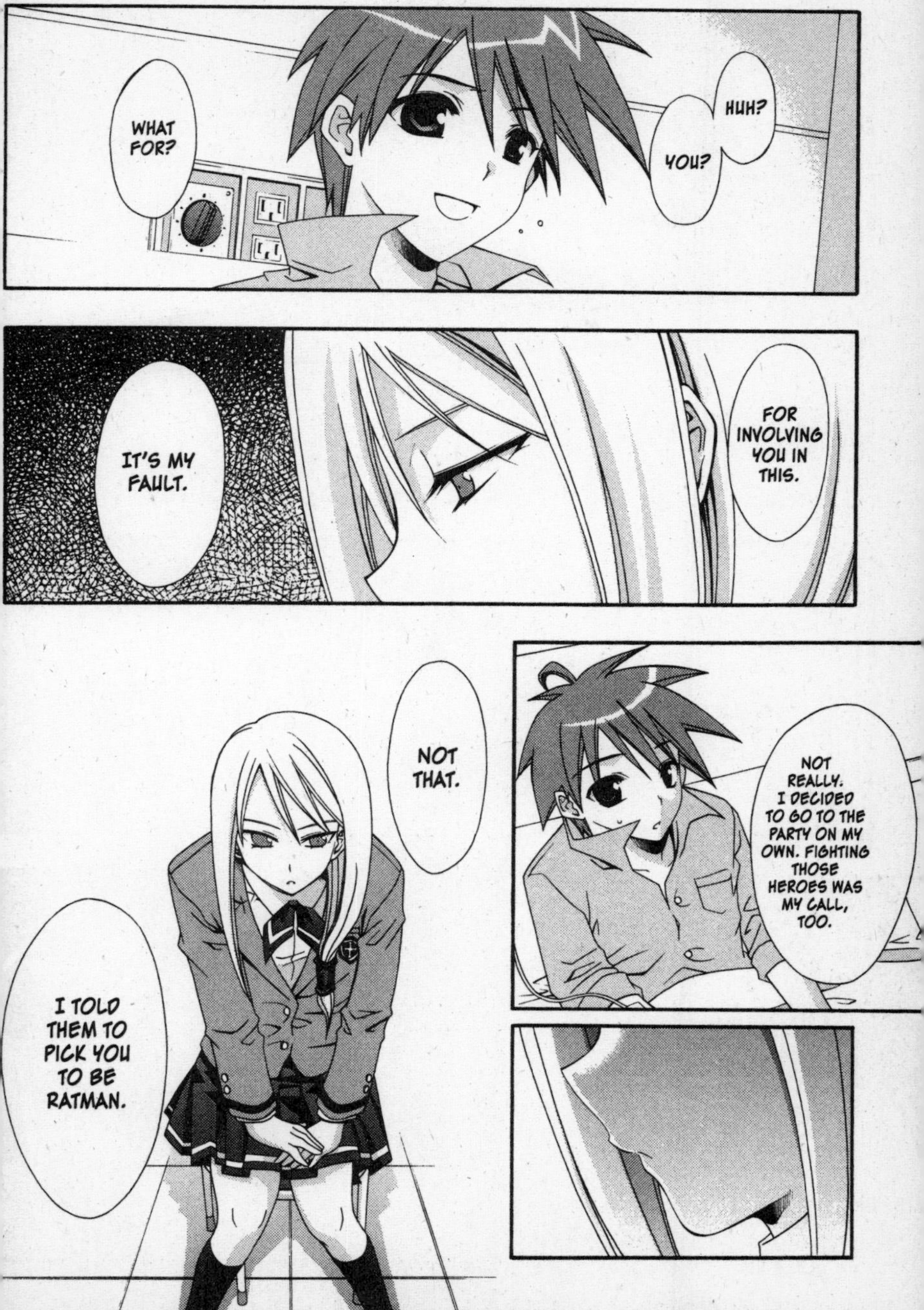
HUH?
YOU?
WHAT FOR?
FOR INVOLVING YOU IN THIS.
IT'S MY FAULT.
NOT REALLY. I DECIDED TO GO TO THE PARTY ON MY OWN. FIGHTING THOSE HEROES WAS MY CALL, TOO.
NOT THAT.
I TOLD THEM TO PICK YOU TO BE RATMAN.

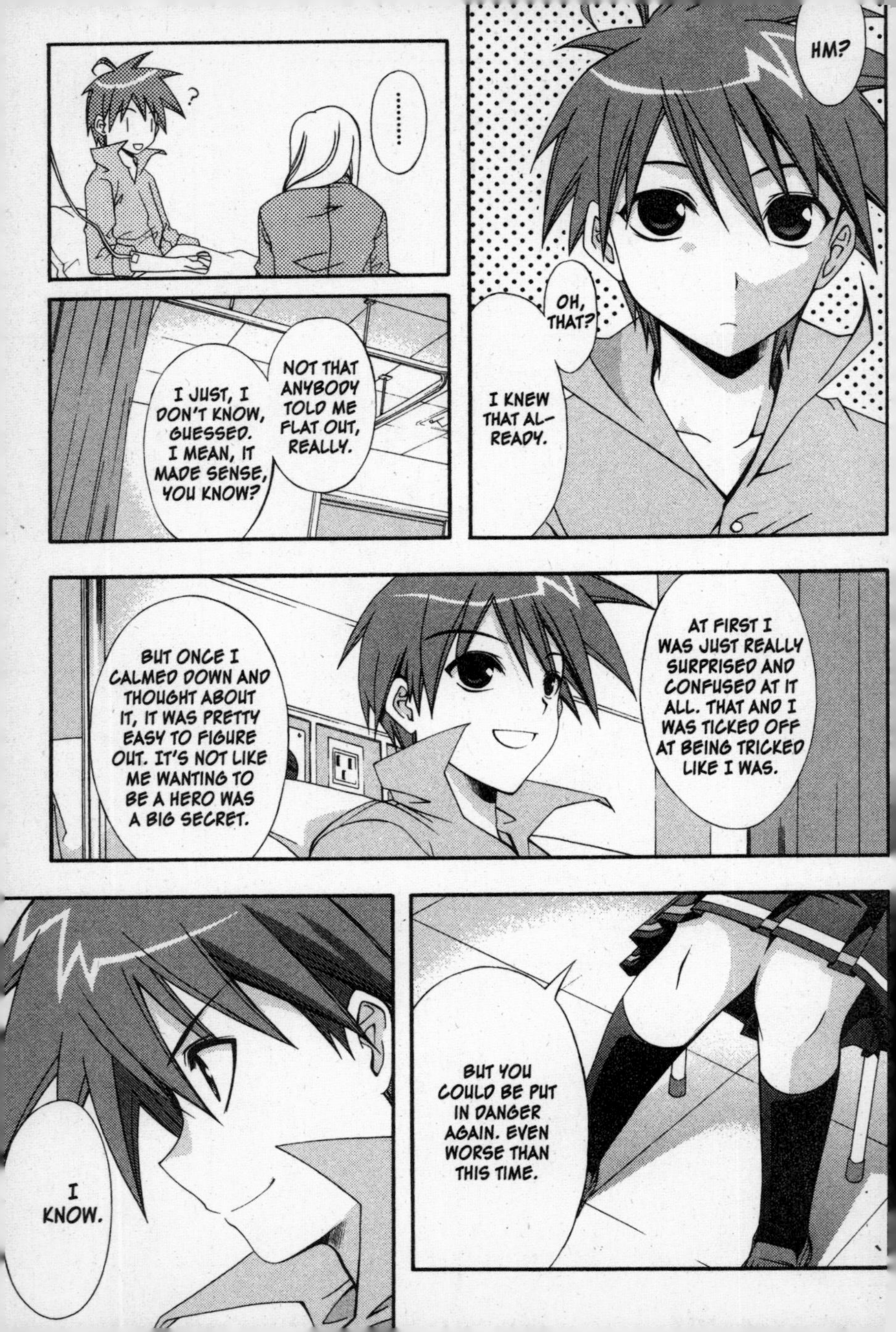
HM?
OH, THAT?
I KNEW THAT AL-READY.
......
NOT THAT ANYBODY TOLD ME FLAT OUT, REALLY.
I JUST, I DON'T KNOW, GUESSED. I MEAN, IT MADE SENSE, YOU KNOW?
AT FIRST I WAS JUST REALLY SURPRISED AND CONFUSED AT IT ALL. THAT AND I WAS TICKED OFF AT BEING TRICKED LIKE I WAS.
BUT ONCE I CALMED DOWN AND THOUGHT ABOUT IT, IT WAS PRETTY EASY TO FIGURE OUT. IT'S NOT LIKE ME WANTING TO BE A HERO WAS A BIG SECRET.
BUT YOU COULD BE PUT IN DANGER AGAIN. EVEN WORSE THAN THIS TIME.
I KNOW.

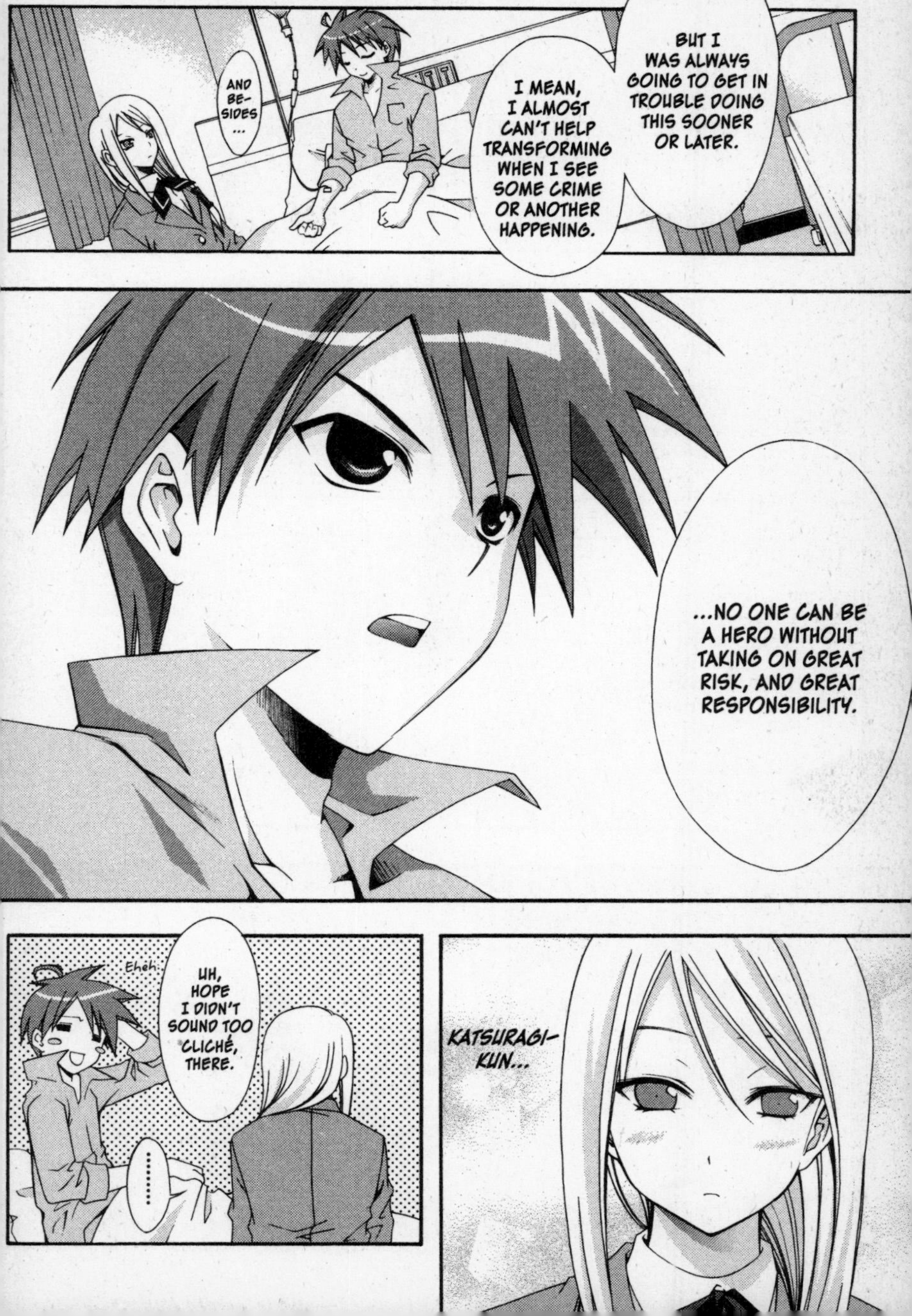
BUT I WAS ALWAYS GOING TO GET IN TROUBLE DOING THIS SOONER OR LATER.
I MEAN, I ALMOST CAN'T HELP TRANSFORMING WHEN I SEE SOME CRIME OR ANOTHER HAPPENING.
AND BE-SIDES ...
...NO ONE CAN BE A HERO WITHOUT TAKING ON GREAT RISK, AND GREAT RESPONSIBILITY.
KATSURAGI-KUN...
UH, HOPE I DIDN'T SOUND TOO CLICHÉ, THERE.
Eheh.
....

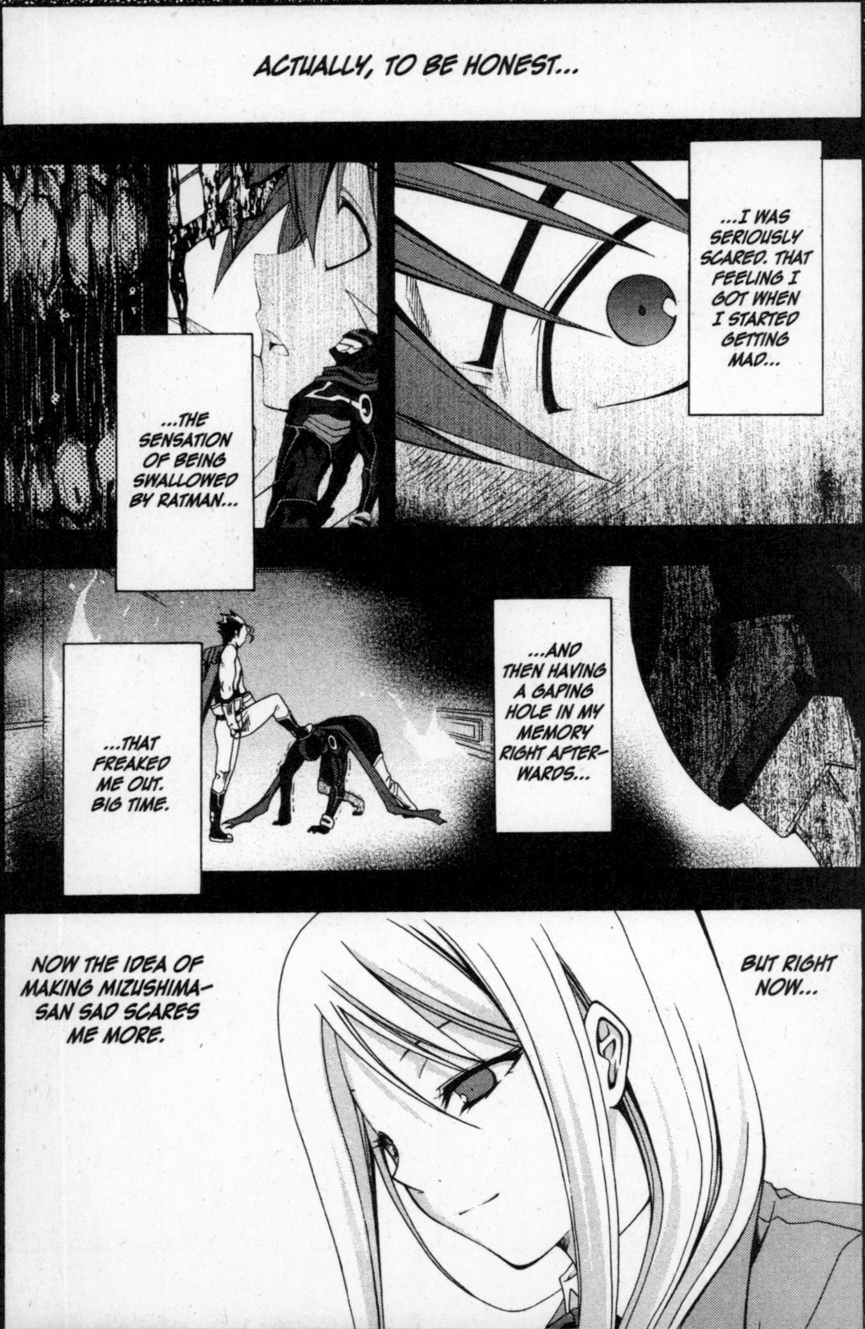
ACTUALLY, TO BE HONEST...
...I WAS SERIOUSLY SCARED. THAT FEELING I GOT WHEN I STARTED GETTING MAD...
...THE SENSATION OF BEING SWALLOWED BY RATMAN...
...AND THEN HAVING A GAPING HOLE IN MY MEMORY RIGHT AFTER-WARDS...
...THAT FREAKED ME OUT. BIG TIME.
BUT RIGHT NOW...
NOW THE IDEA OF MAKING MIZUSHIMA-SAN SAD SCARES ME MORE.

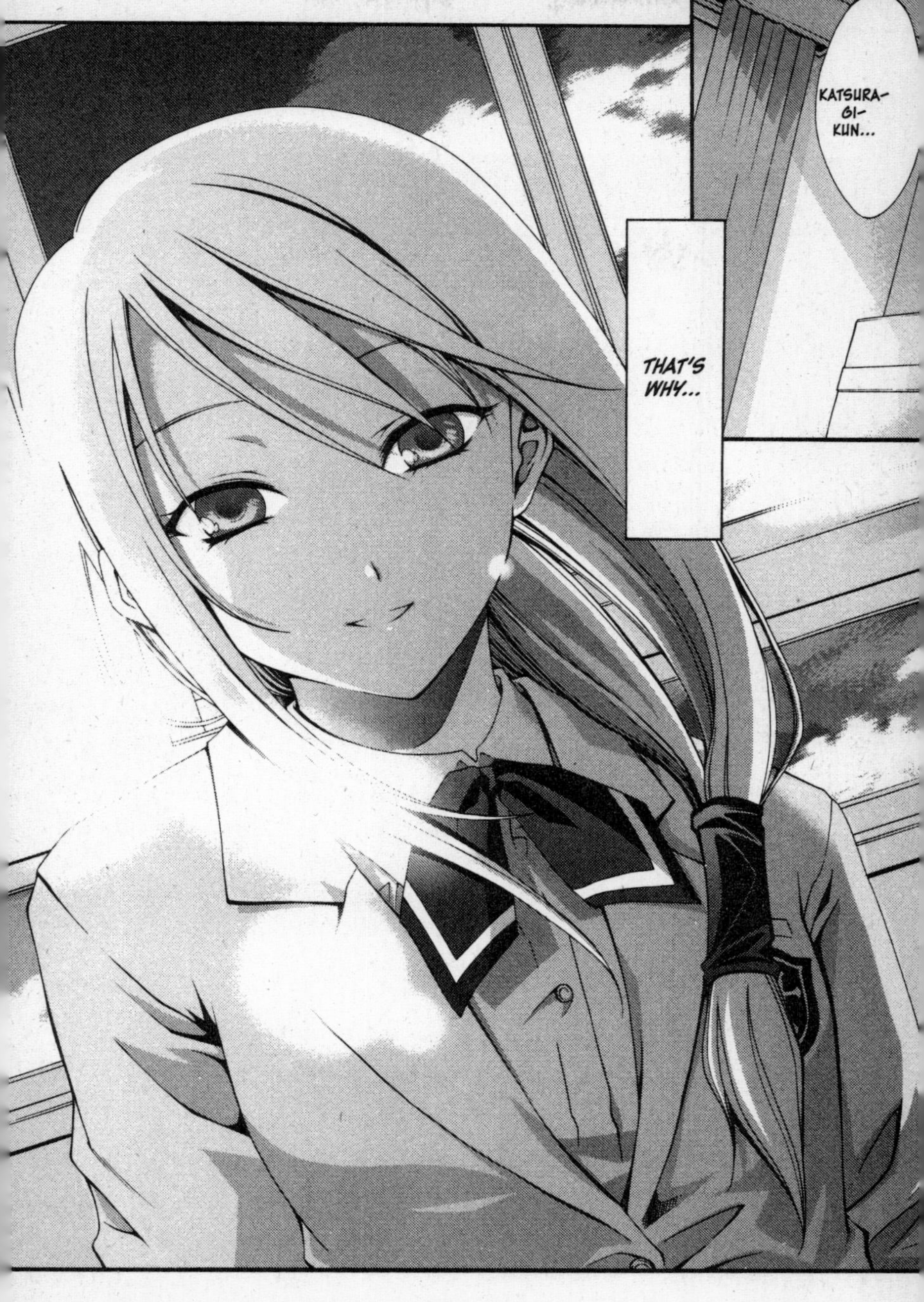
KATSURA-GI-KUN...
THAT'S WHY...

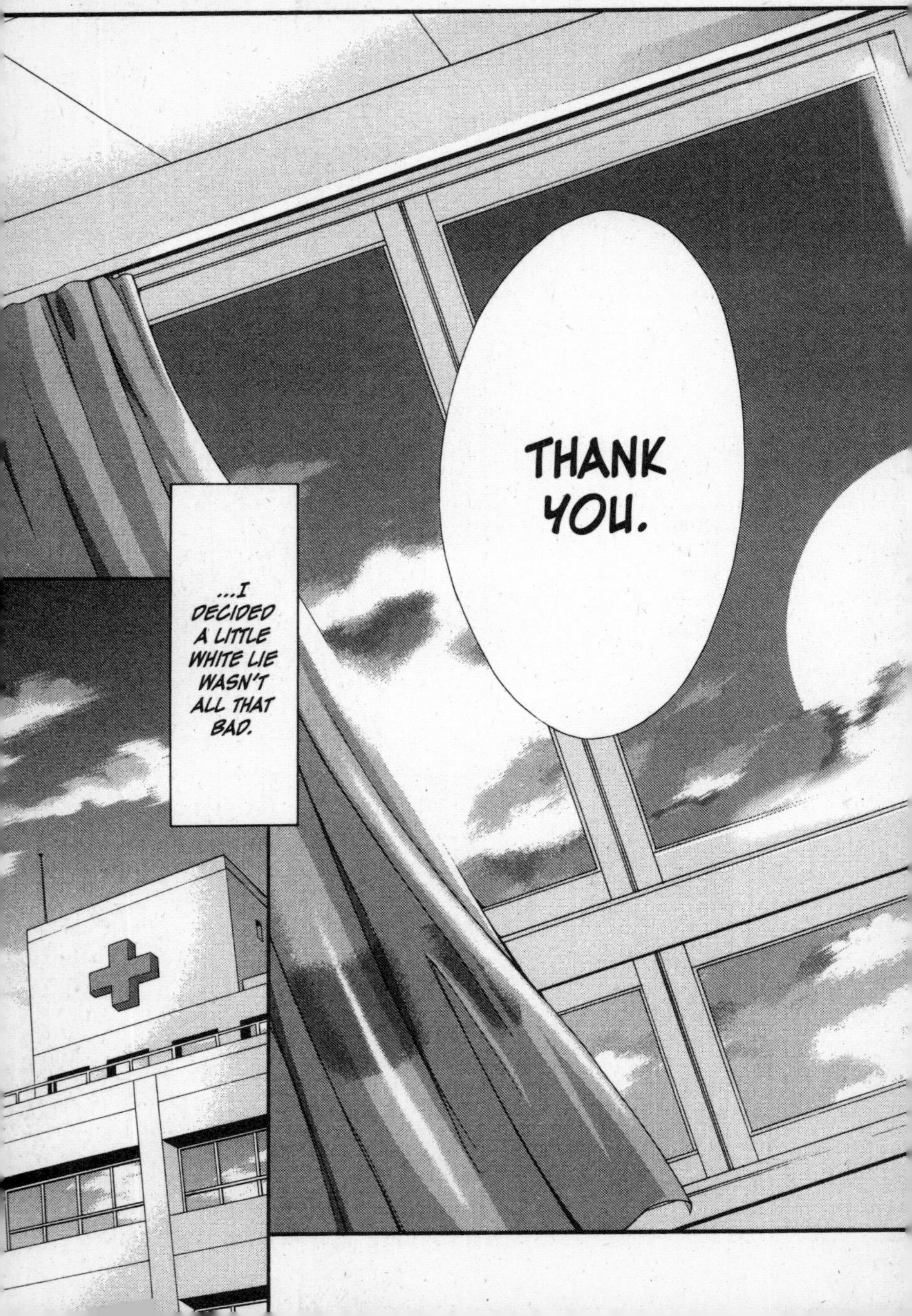
THANK YOU.
...I DECIDED A LITTLE WHITE LIE WASN'T ALL THAT BAD.

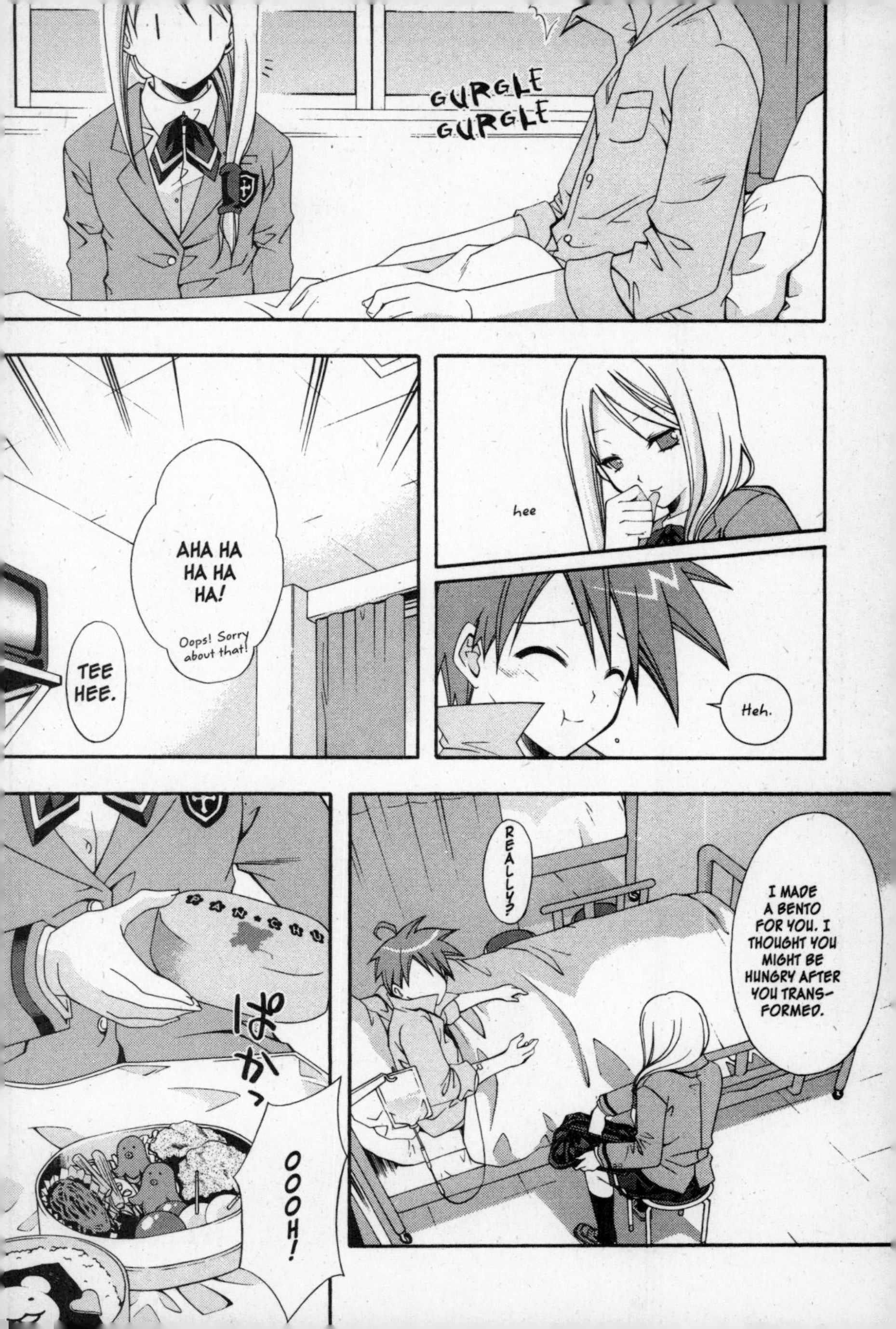
GURGLE
GURGLE
hee
Heh.
AHA HA HA HA HA!
Oops! Sorry about that!
TEE HEE.
I MADE A BENTO FOR YOU. I THOUGHT YOU MIGHT BE HUNGRY AFTER YOU TRANS-FORMED.
REALLY?
PAN-CHU
ぱかっ
OOOH!

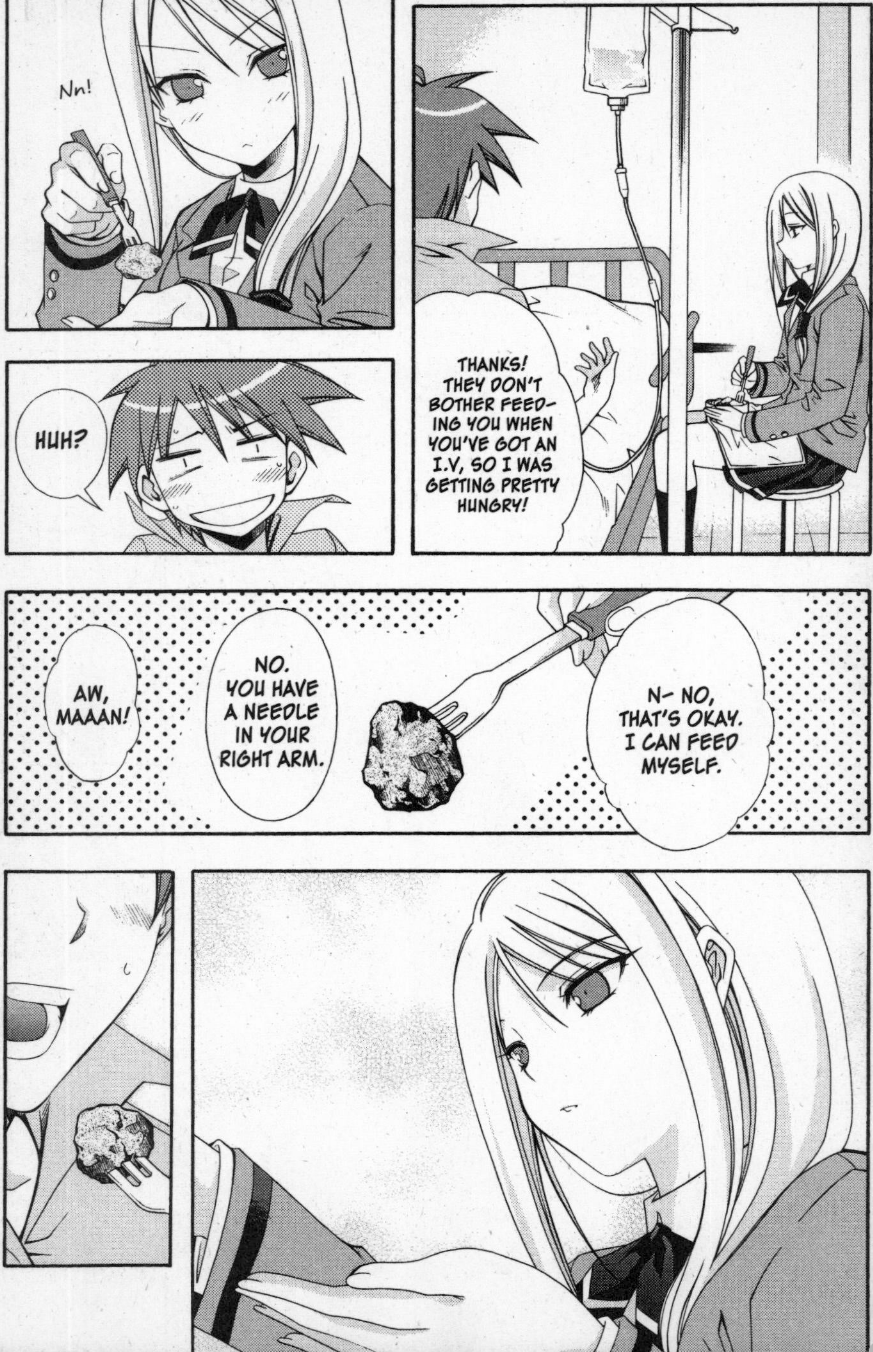
THANKS! THEY DON'T BOTHER FEED-ING YOU WHEN YOU'VE GOT AN I.V, SO I WAS GETTING PRETTY HUNGRY!
Nn!
HUH?
N- NO, THAT'S OKAY. I CAN FEED MYSELF.
NO. YOU HAVE A NEEDLE IN YOUR RIGHT ARM.
AW, MAAAN!

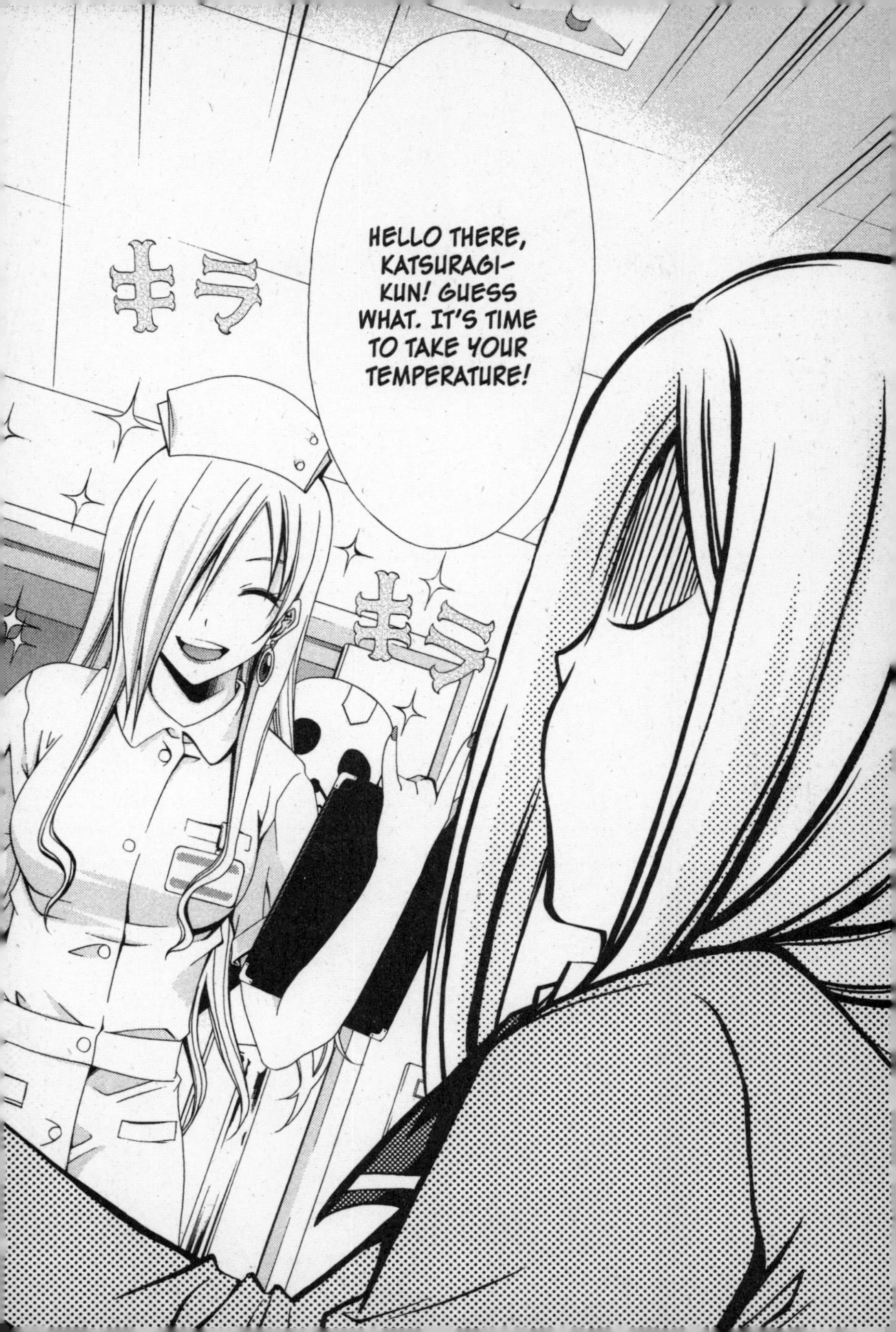
HELLO THERE, KATSURAGI-KUN! GUESS WHAT. IT'S TIME TO TAKE YOUR TEMPERATURE!
キラ
キラ

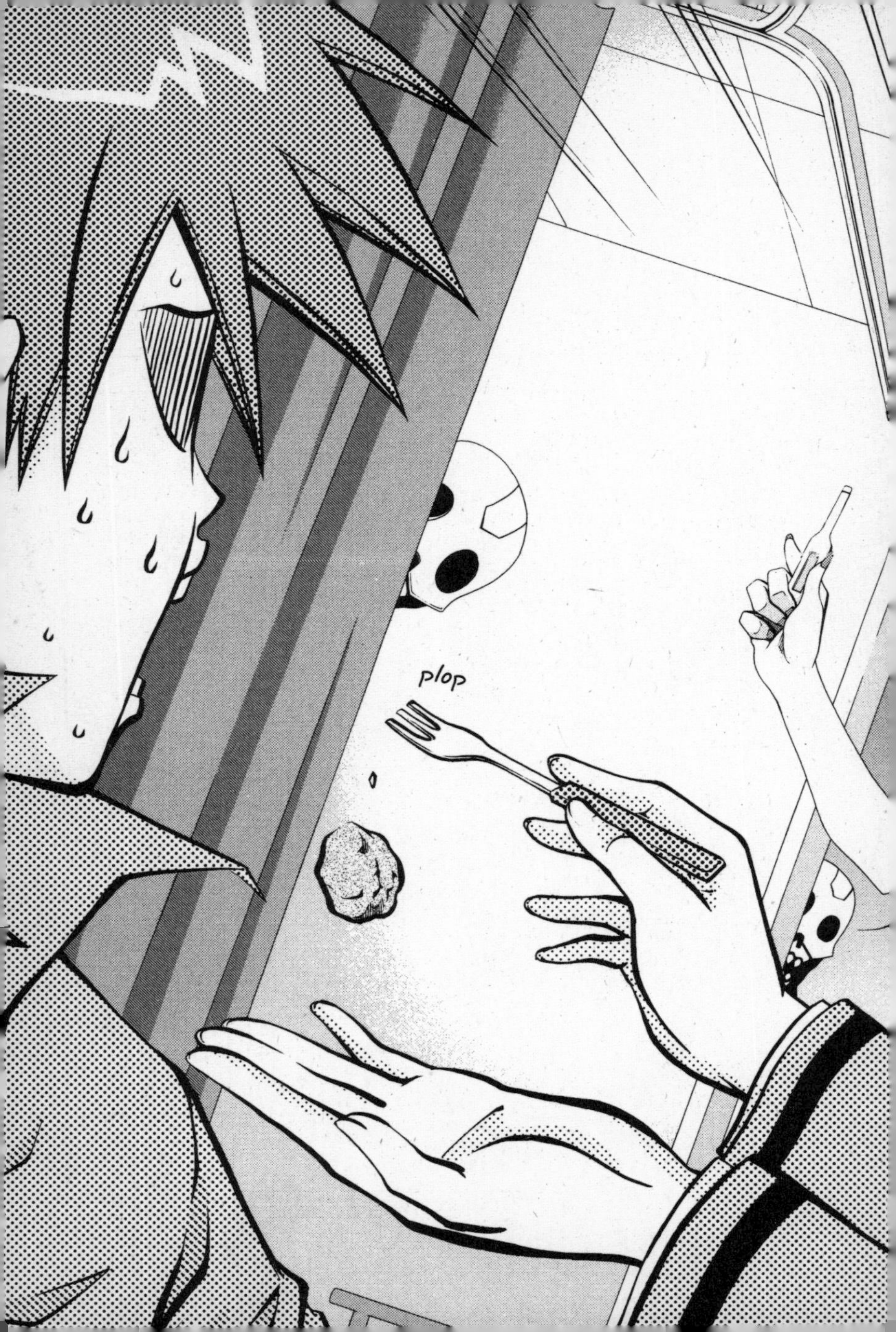
plop

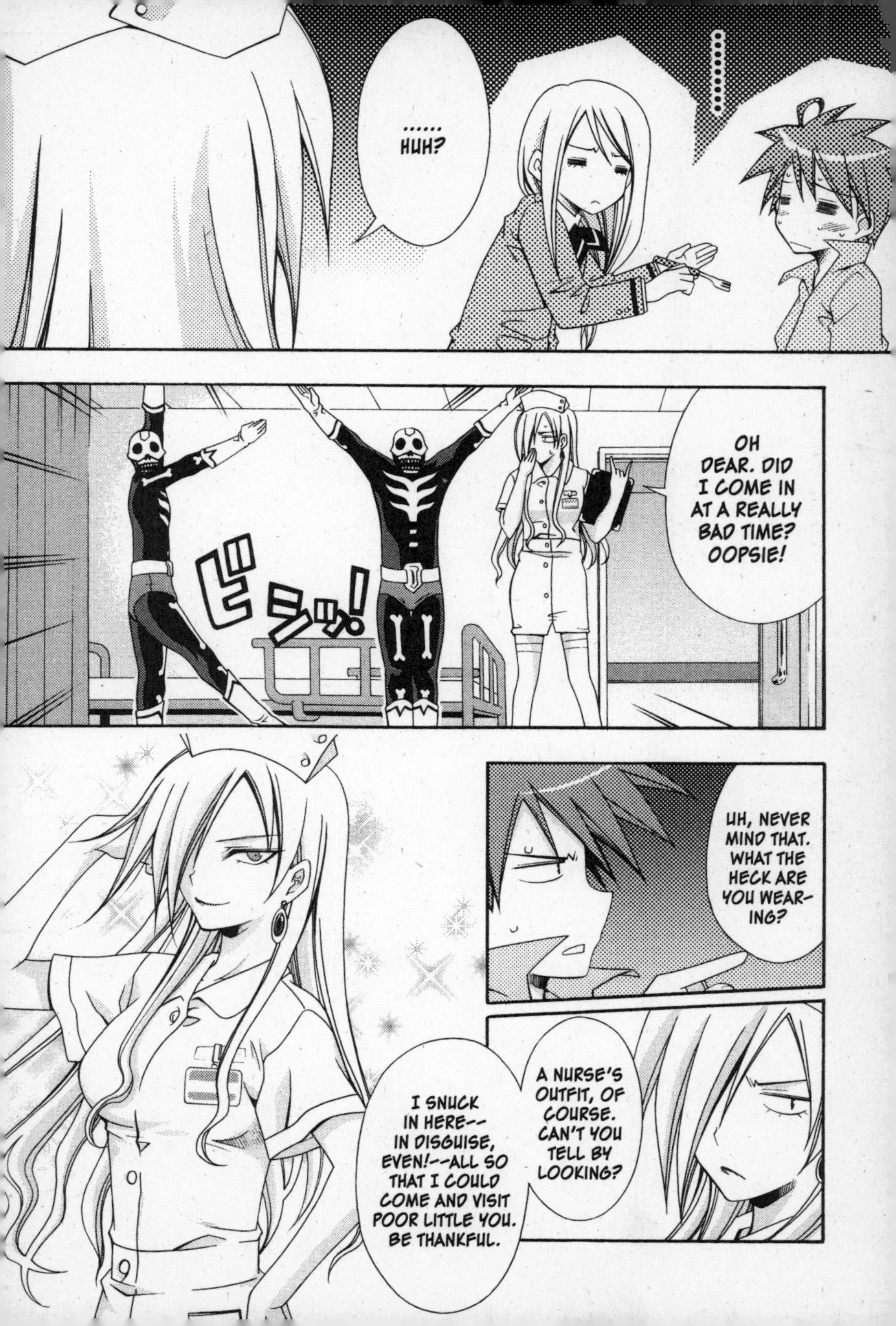
......
......HUH?
OH DEAR. DID I COME IN AT A REALLY BAD TIME? OOPSIE!
ビシッ!
UH, NEVER MIND THAT. WHAT THE HECK ARE YOU WEAR-ING?
A NURSE'S OUTFIT, OF COURSE. CAN'T YOU TELL BY LOOKING?
I SNUCK IN HERE--IN DISGUISE, EVEN!--ALL SO THAT I COULD COME AND VISIT POOR LITTLE YOU. BE THANKFUL.

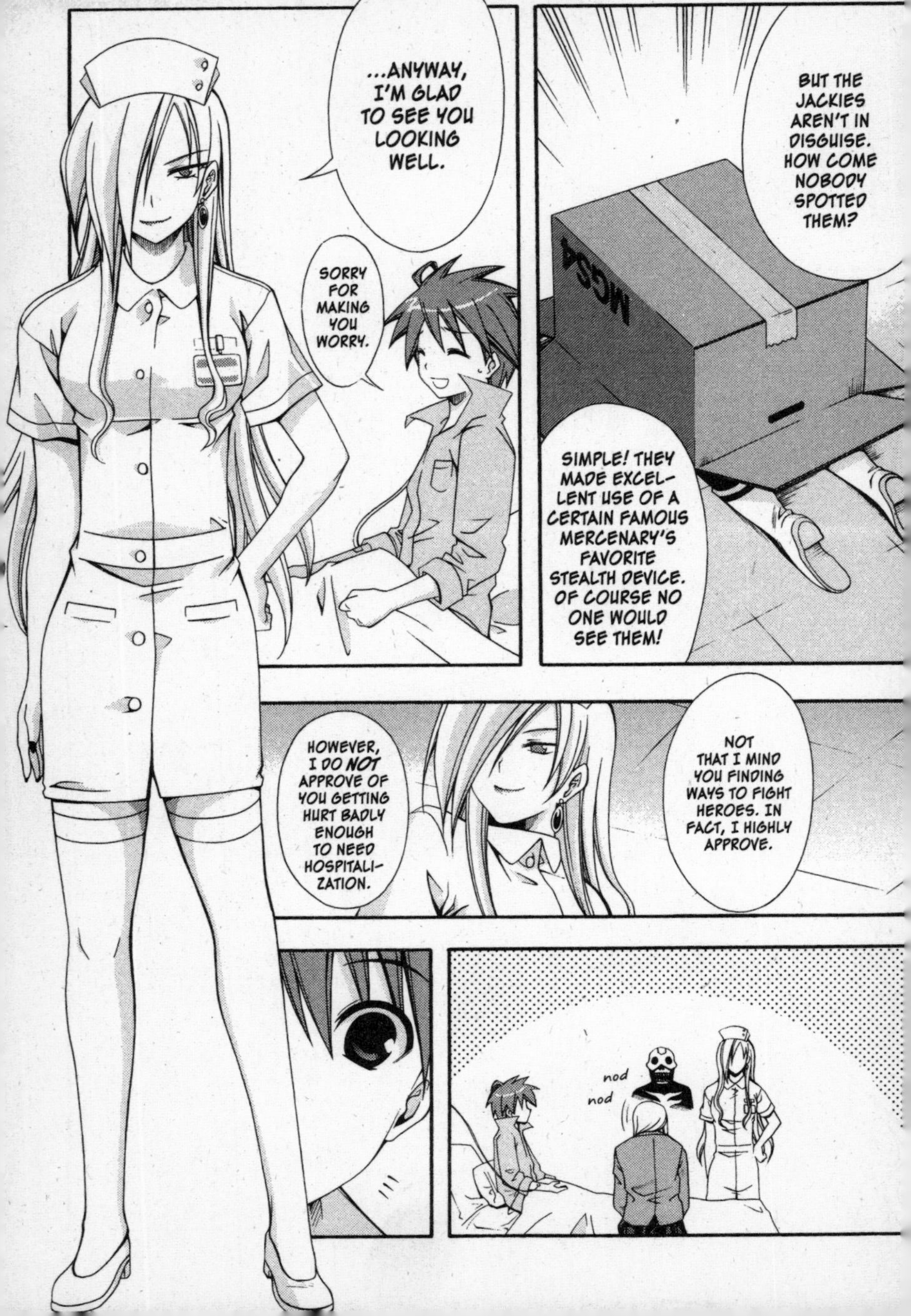
BUT THE JACKIES AREN'T IN DISGUISE. HOW COME NOBODY SPOTTED THEM?
MGS4
SIMPLE! THEY MADE EXCEL-LENT USE OF A CERTAIN FAMOUS MERCENARY'S FAVORITE STEALTH DEVICE. OF COURSE NO ONE WOULD SEE THEM!
...ANYWAY, I'M GLAD TO SEE YOU LOOKING WELL.
SORRY FOR MAKING YOU WORRY.
NOT THAT I MIND YOU FINDING WAYS TO FIGHT HEROES. IN FACT, I HIGHLY APPROVE.
HOWEVER, I DO ***NOT*** APPROVE OF YOU GETTING HURT BADLY ENOUGH TO NEED HOSPITALI-ZATION.
nod
nod

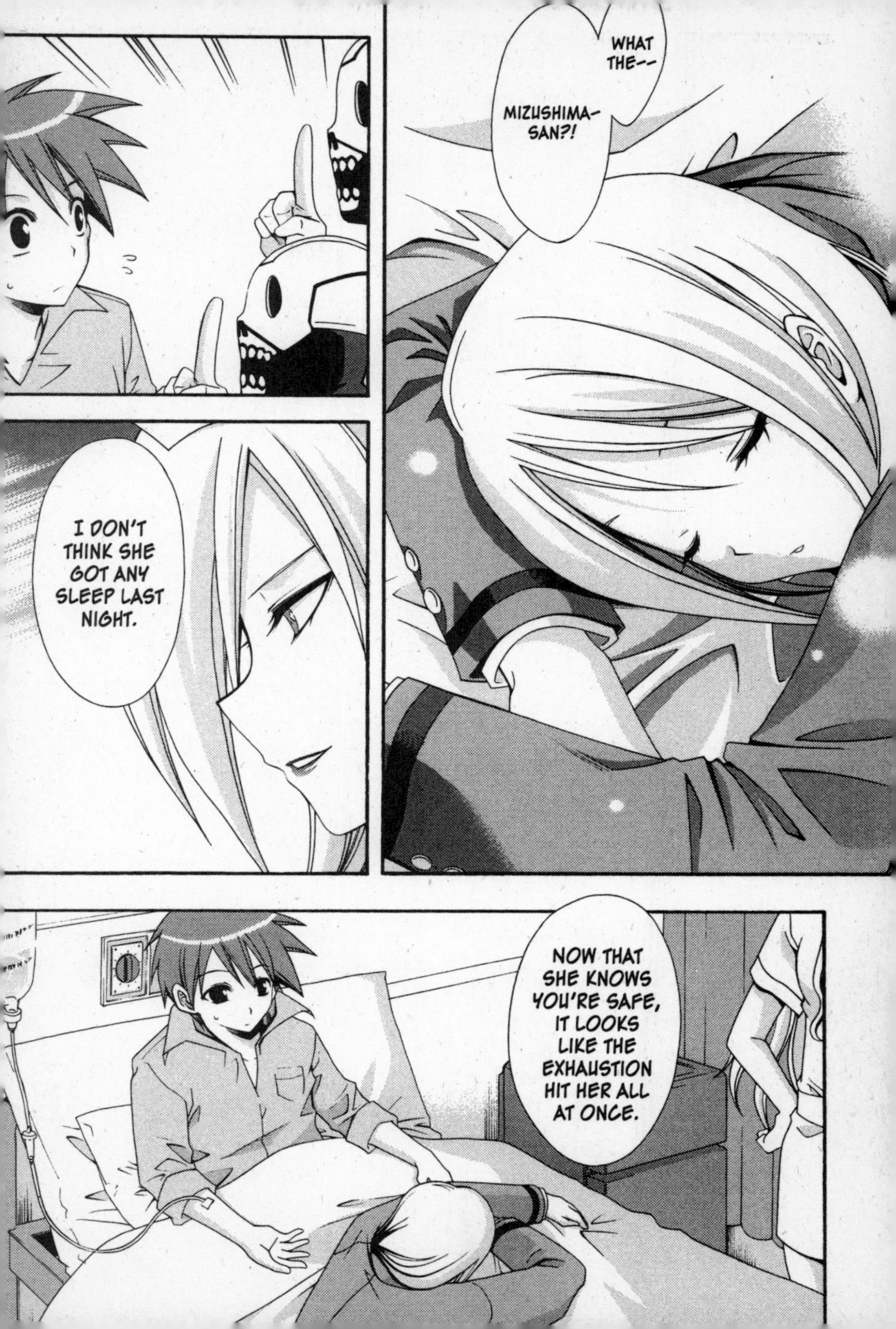
WHAT THE--
MIZUSHIMA-SAN?!
I DON'T THINK SHE GOT ANY SLEEP LAST NIGHT.
NOW THAT SHE KNOWS YOU'RE SAFE, IT LOOKS LIKE THE EXHAUSTION HIT HER ALL AT ONCE.

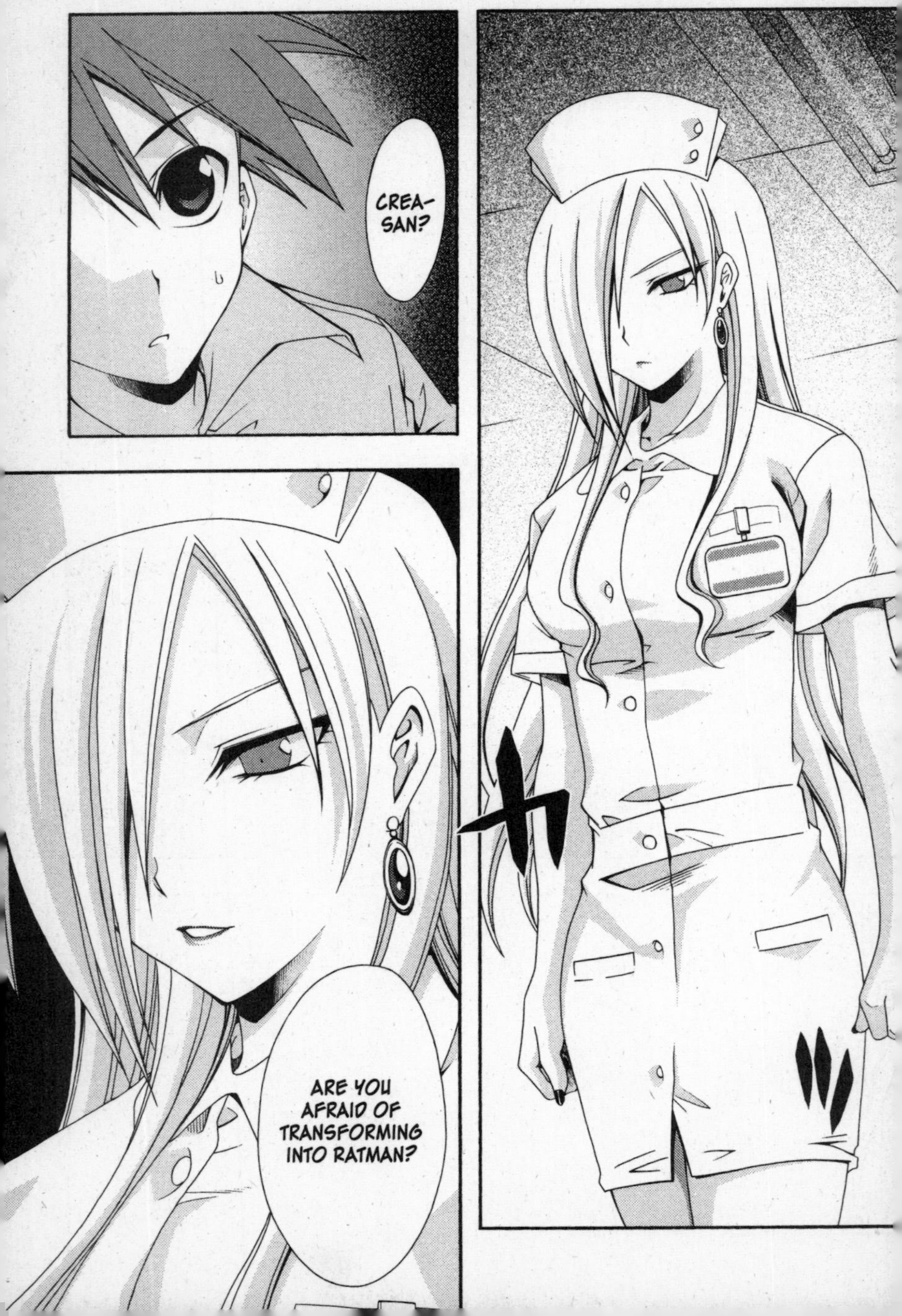
CREA-SAN?
ARE YOU AFRAID OF TRANSFORMING INTO RATMAN?

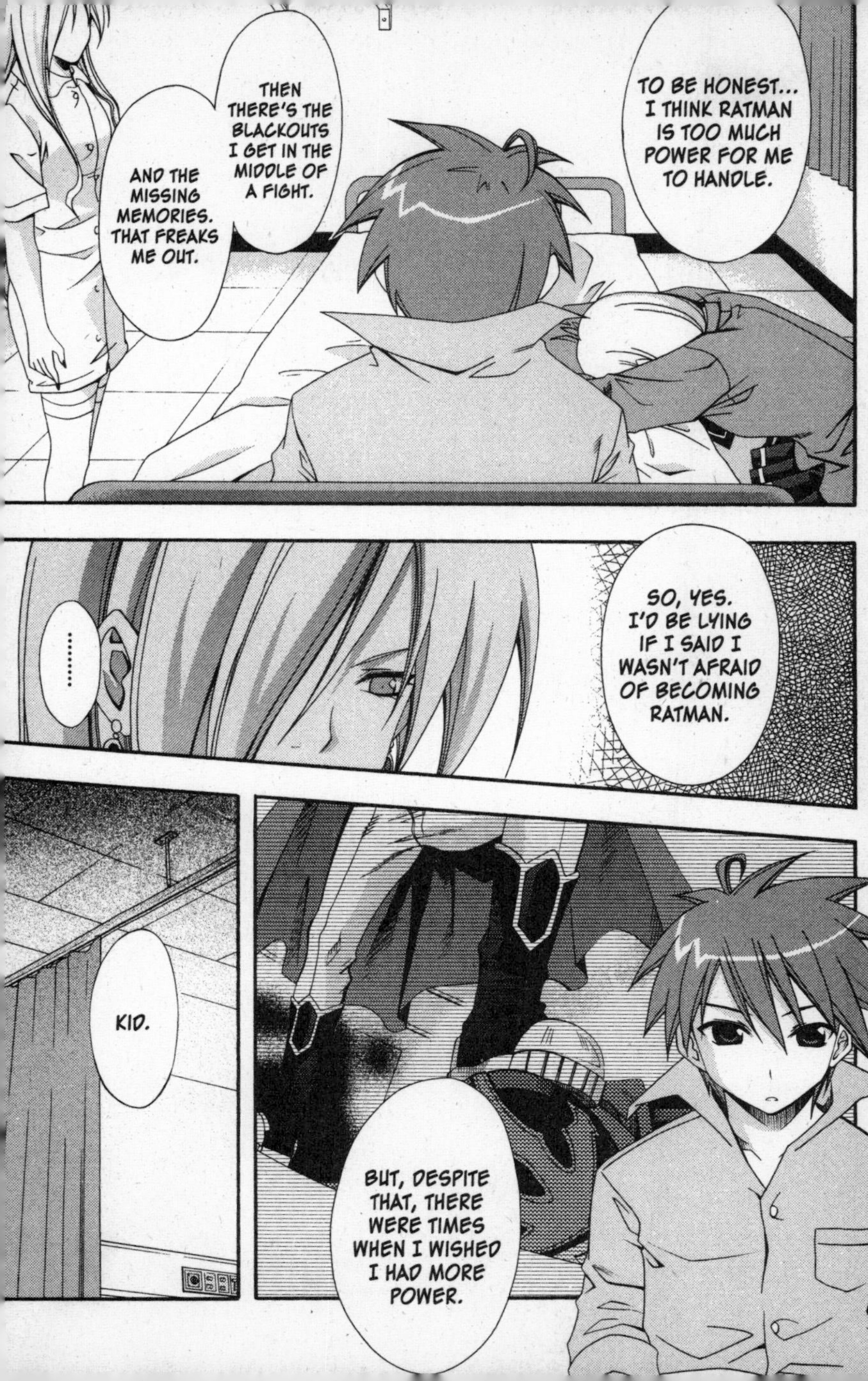
TO BE HONEST... I THINK RATMAN IS TOO MUCH POWER FOR ME TO HANDLE.
THEN THERE'S THE BLACKOUTS I GET IN THE MIDDLE OF A FIGHT.
AND THE MISSING MEMORIES. THAT FREAKS ME OUT.
SO, YES. I'D BE LYING IF I SAID I WASN'T AFRAID OF BECOMING RATMAN.
....
BUT, DESPITE THAT, THERE WERE TIMES WHEN I WISHED I HAD MORE POWER.
KID.

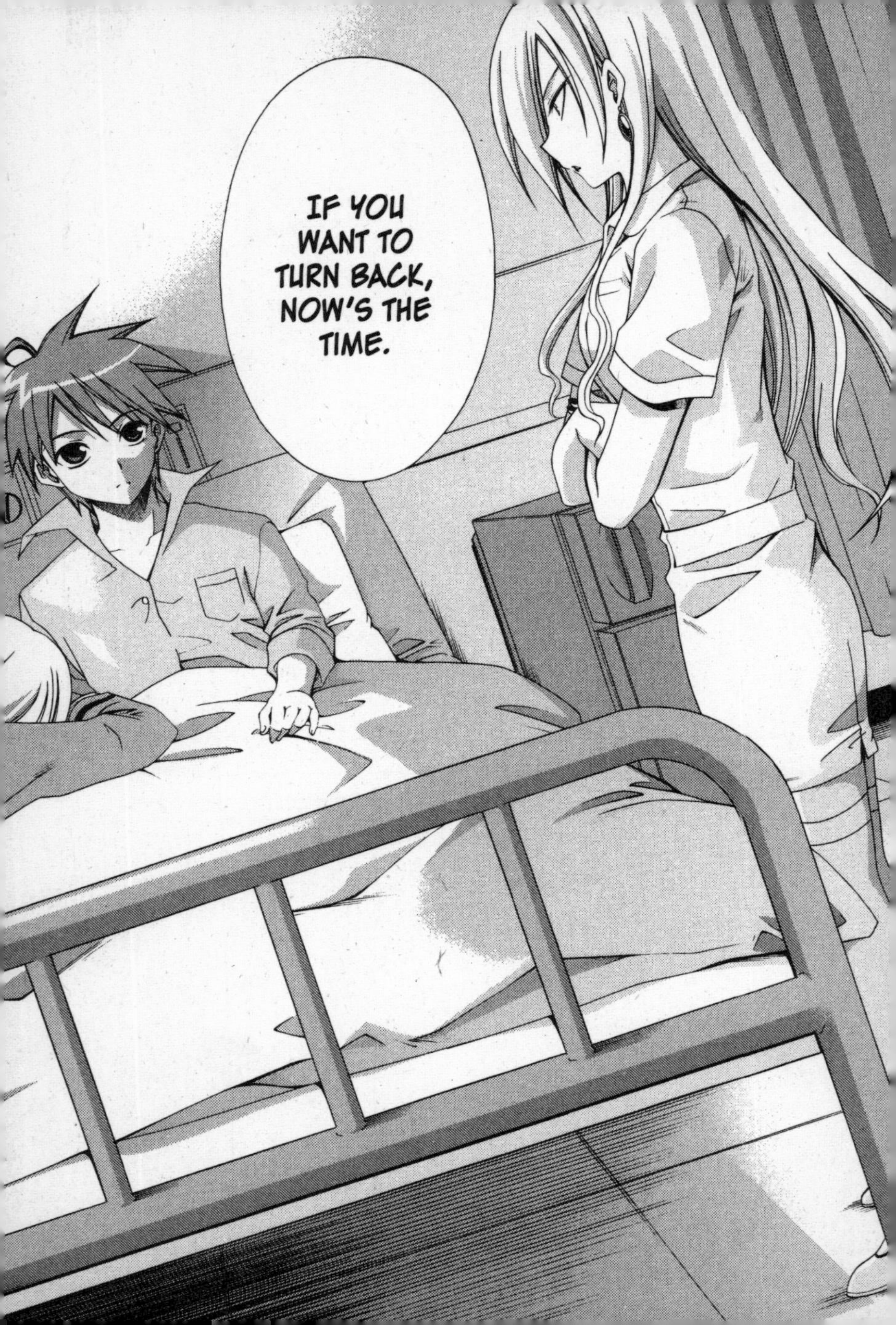
IF YOU WANT TO TURN BACK, NOW'S THE TIME.

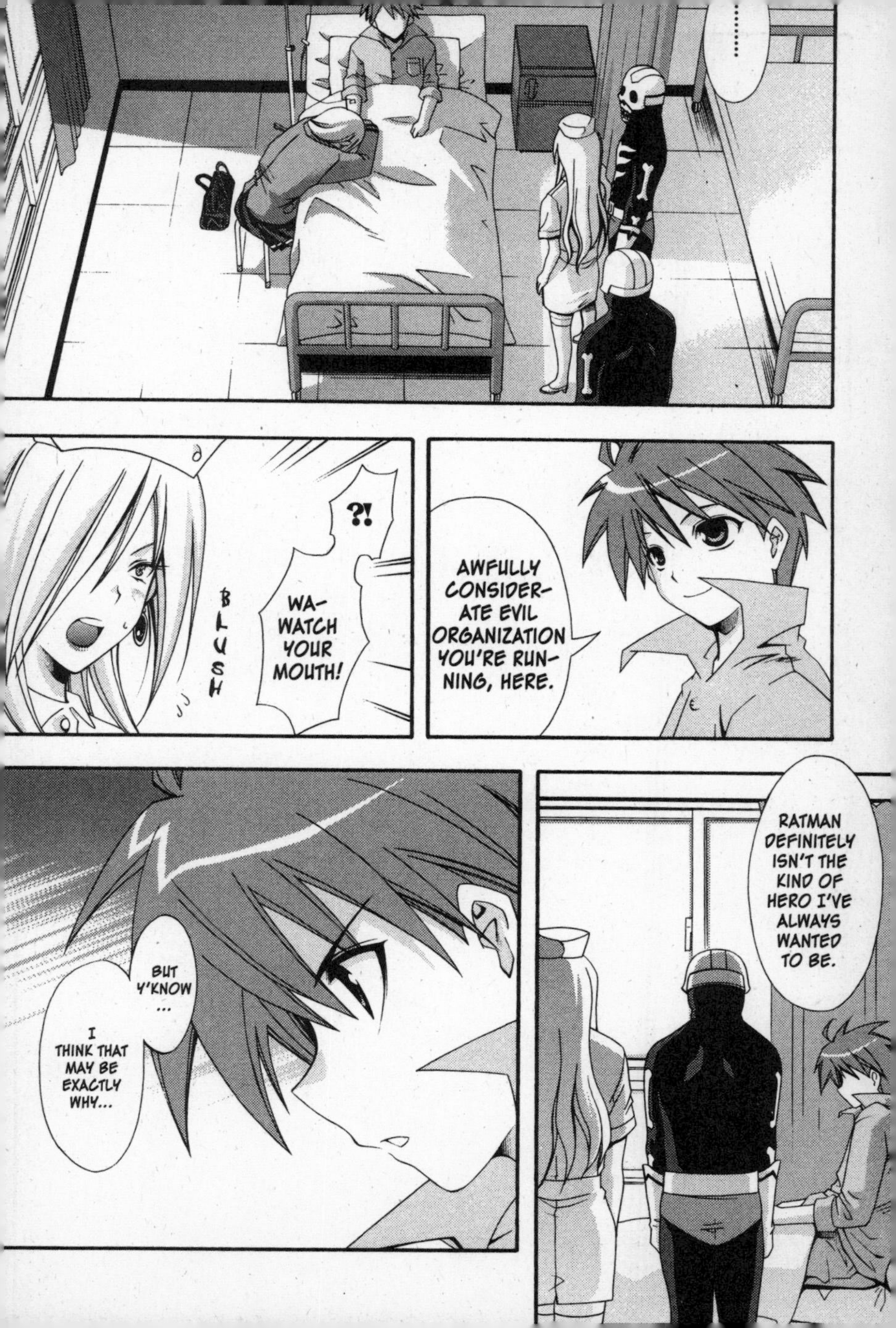
......
AWFULLY CONSIDERATE EVIL ORGANIZATION YOU'RE RUNNING, HERE.
?!
WA-WATCH YOUR MOUTH!
BLUSH
RATMAN DEFINITELY ISN'T THE KIND OF HERO I'VE ALWAYS WANTED TO BE.
BUT Y'KNOW ...
I THINK THAT MAY BE EXACTLY WHY...

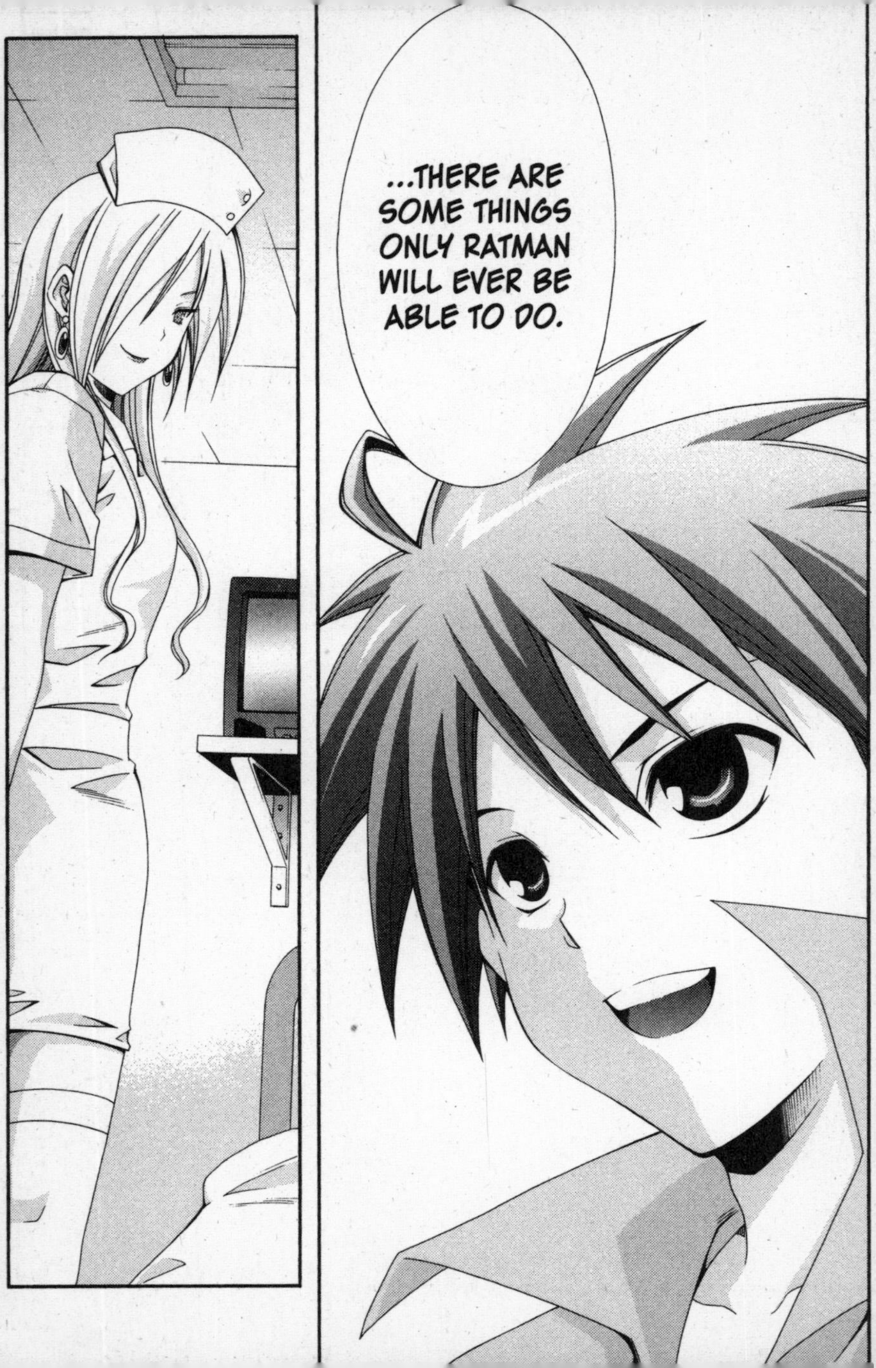
...THERE ARE SOME THINGS ONLY RATMAN WILL EVER BE ABLE TO DO.

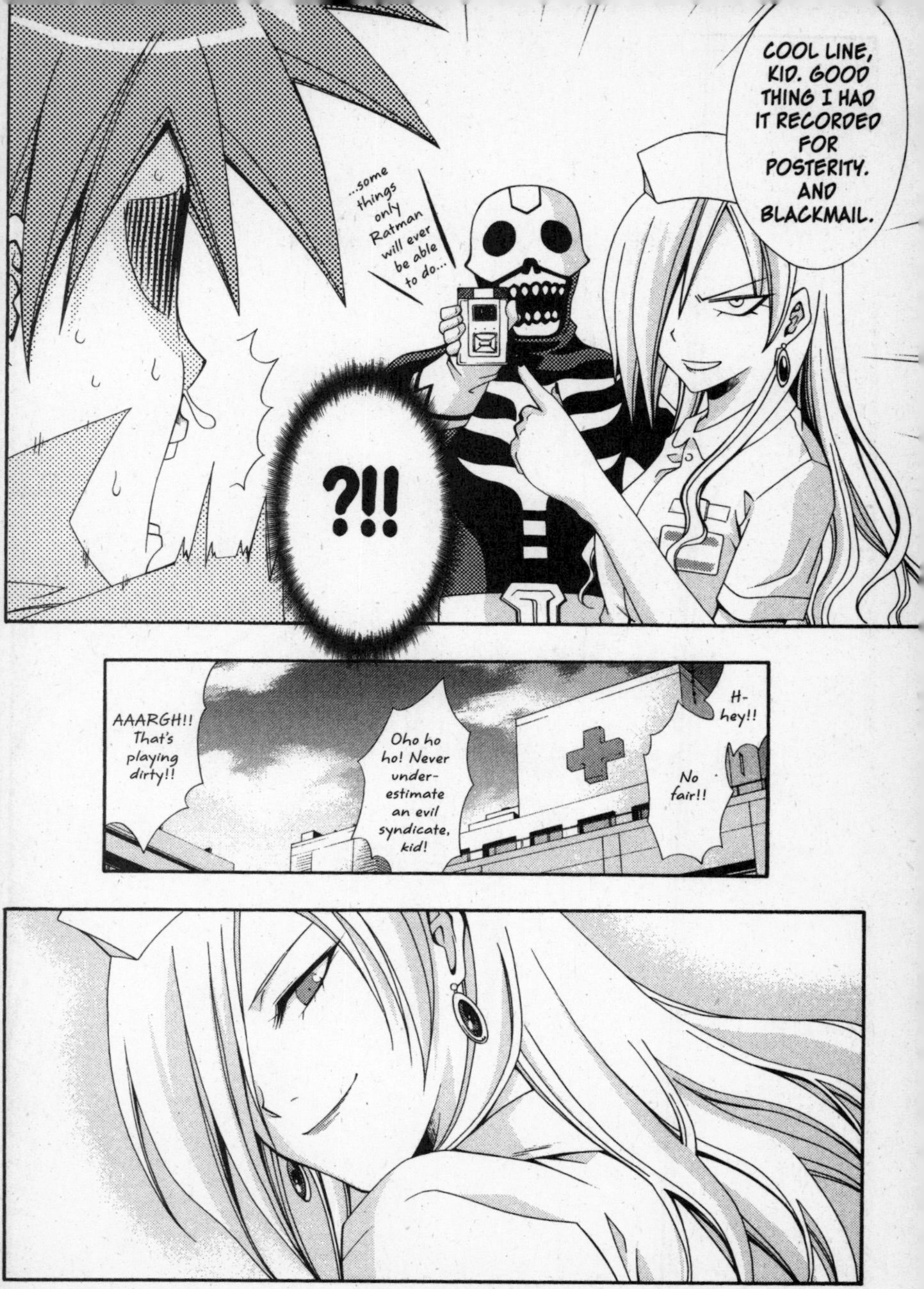
COOL LINE, KID. GOOD THING I HAD IT RECORDED FOR POSTERITY. AND BLACKMAIL.
...some things only Ratman will ever be able to do...
?!!
H-hey!!
No fair!!
Oho ho ho! Never under-estimate an evil syndicate, kid!
AAARGH!! That's playing dirty!!

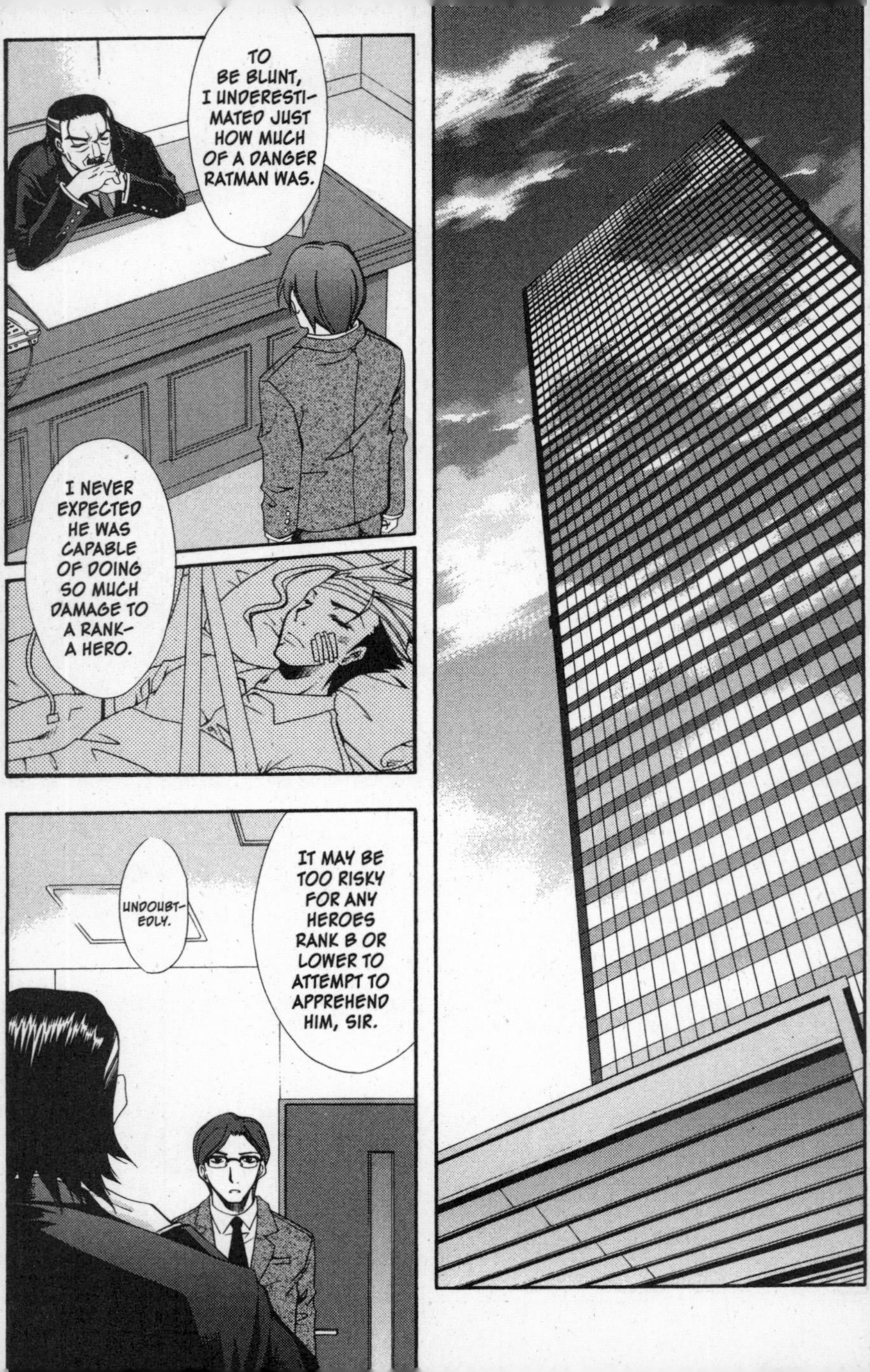
TO BE BLUNT, I UNDERESTIMATED JUST HOW MUCH OF A DANGER RATMAN WAS.
I NEVER EXPECTED HE WAS CAPABLE OF DOING SO MUCH DAMAGE TO A RANK-A HERO.
IT MAY BE TOO RISKY FOR ANY HEROES RANK B OR LOWER TO ATTEMPT TO APPREHEND HIM, SIR.
UNDOUBTEDLY.

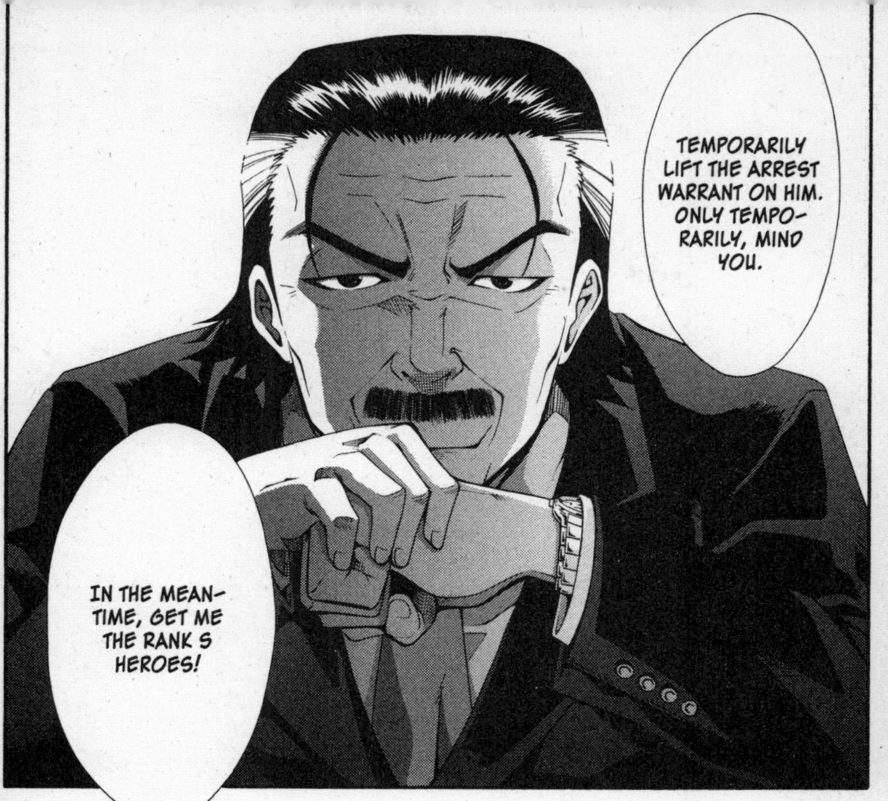
TEMPORARILY LIFT THE ARREST WARRANT ON HIM. ONLY TEMPO-RARILY, MIND YOU.
IN THE MEAN-TIME, GET ME THE RANK S HEROES!

...To be continued in the next episode.

Next Episode: Akihabara Defense Corps

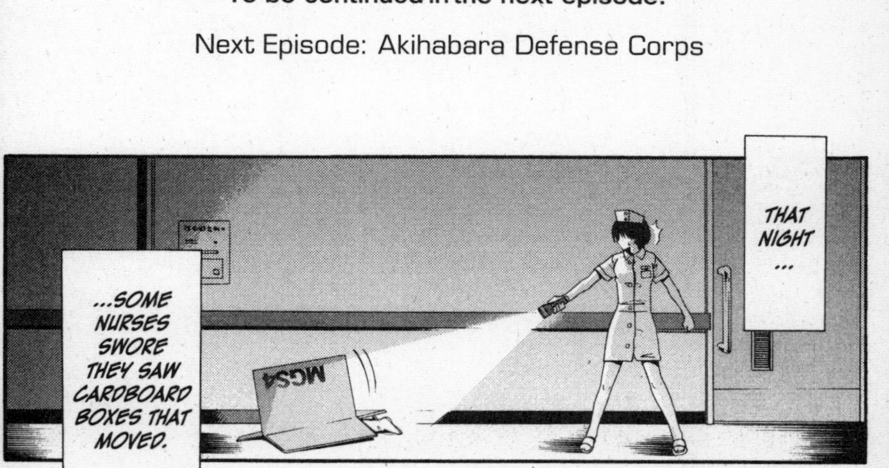
THAT NIGHT ...
...SOME NURSES SWORE THEY SAW CARDBOARD BOXES THAT MOVED.

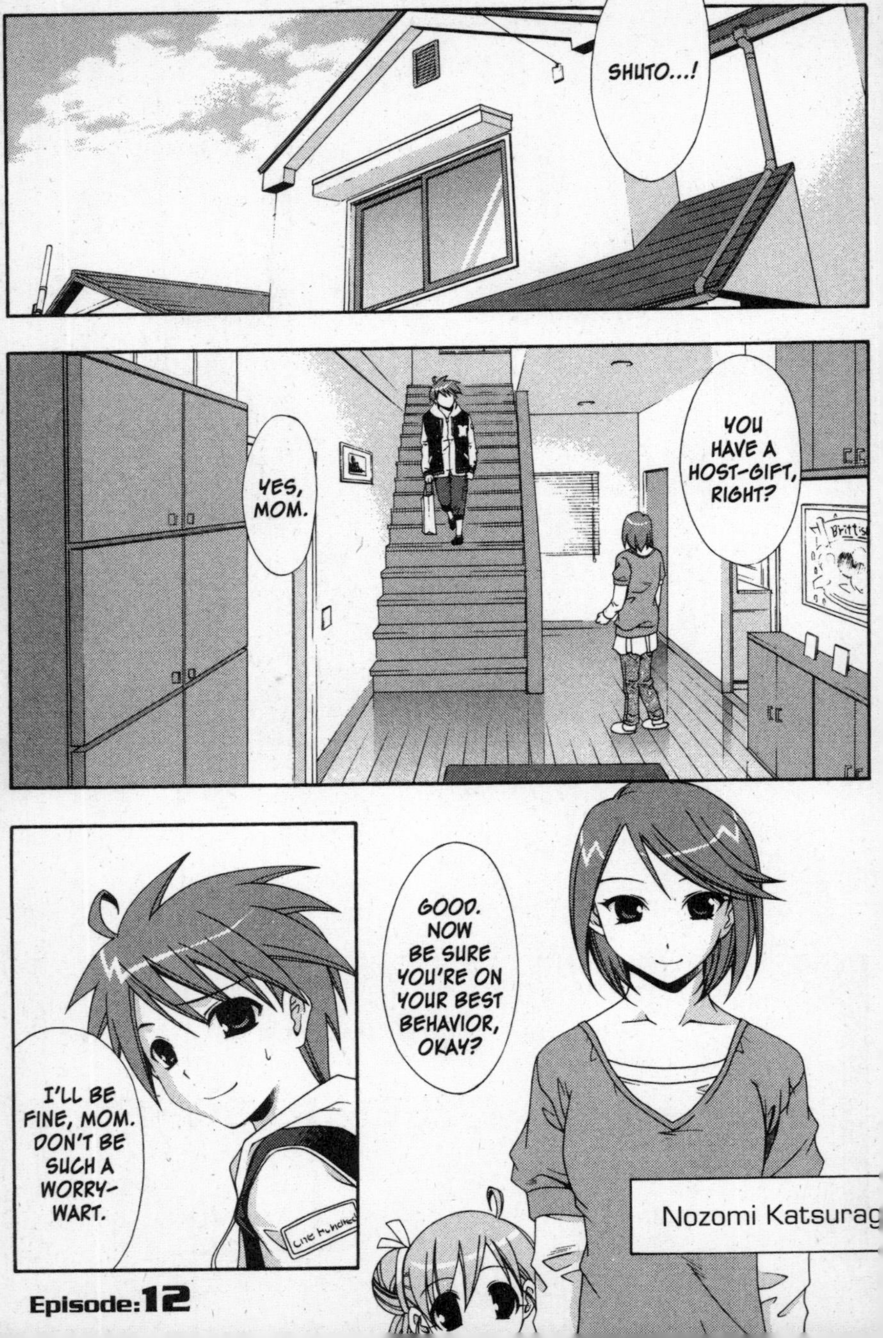
SHUTO...!
YOU HAVE A HOST-GIFT, RIGHT?
YES, MOM.
GOOD. NOW BE SURE YOU'RE ON YOUR BEST BEHAVIOR, OKAY?
Nozomi Katsurag
I'LL BE FINE, MOM. DON'T BE SUCH A WORRY-WART.

Episode:12

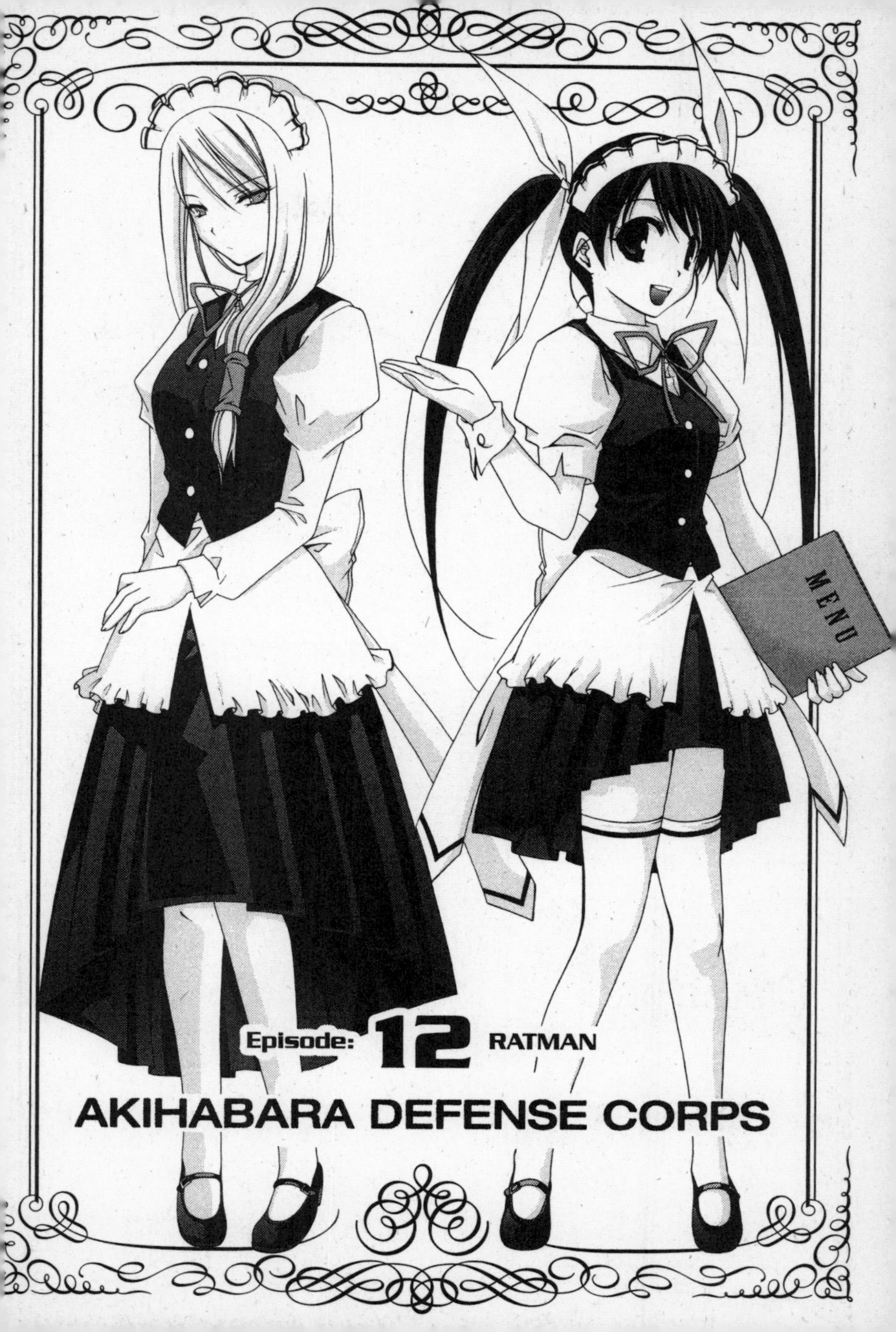
MENU
Episode: 12 RATMAN
AKIHABARA DEFENSE CORPS

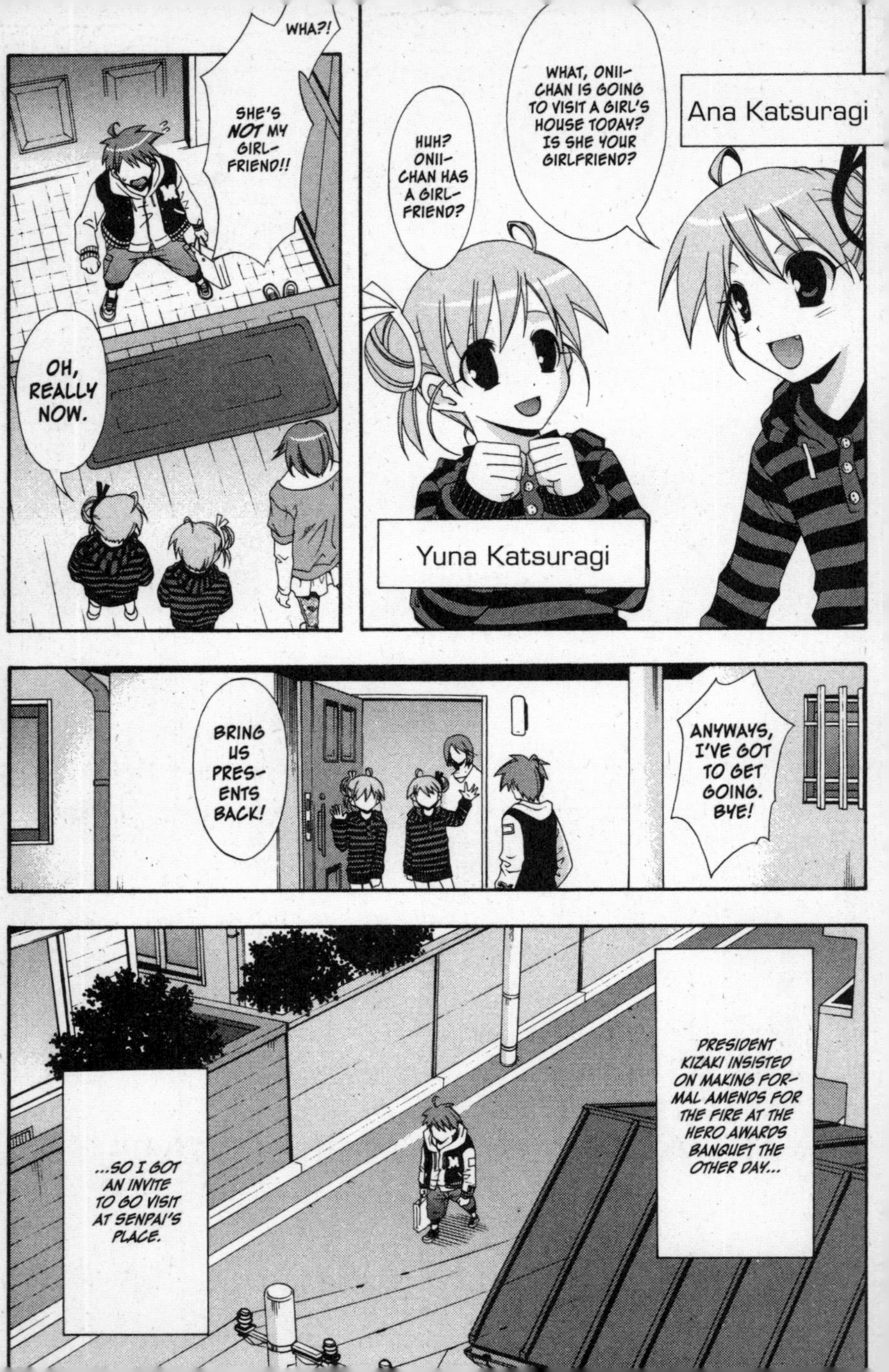
Ana Katsuragi
WHAT, ONII-CHAN IS GOING TO VISIT A GIRL'S HOUSE TODAY? IS SHE YOUR GIRLFRIEND?
HUH? ONII-CHAN HAS A GIRL-FRIEND?
Yuna Katsuragi
WHA?!
SHE'S *NOT* MY GIRL-FRIEND!!
OH, REALLY NOW.
ANYWAYS, I'VE GOT TO GET GOING. BYE!
BRING US PRES-ENTS BACK!
PRESIDENT KIZAKI INSISTED ON MAKING FOR-MAL AMENDS FOR THE FIRE AT THE HERO AWARDS BANQUET THE OTHER DAY...
...SO I GOT AN INVITE TO GO VISIT AT SENPAI'S PLACE.

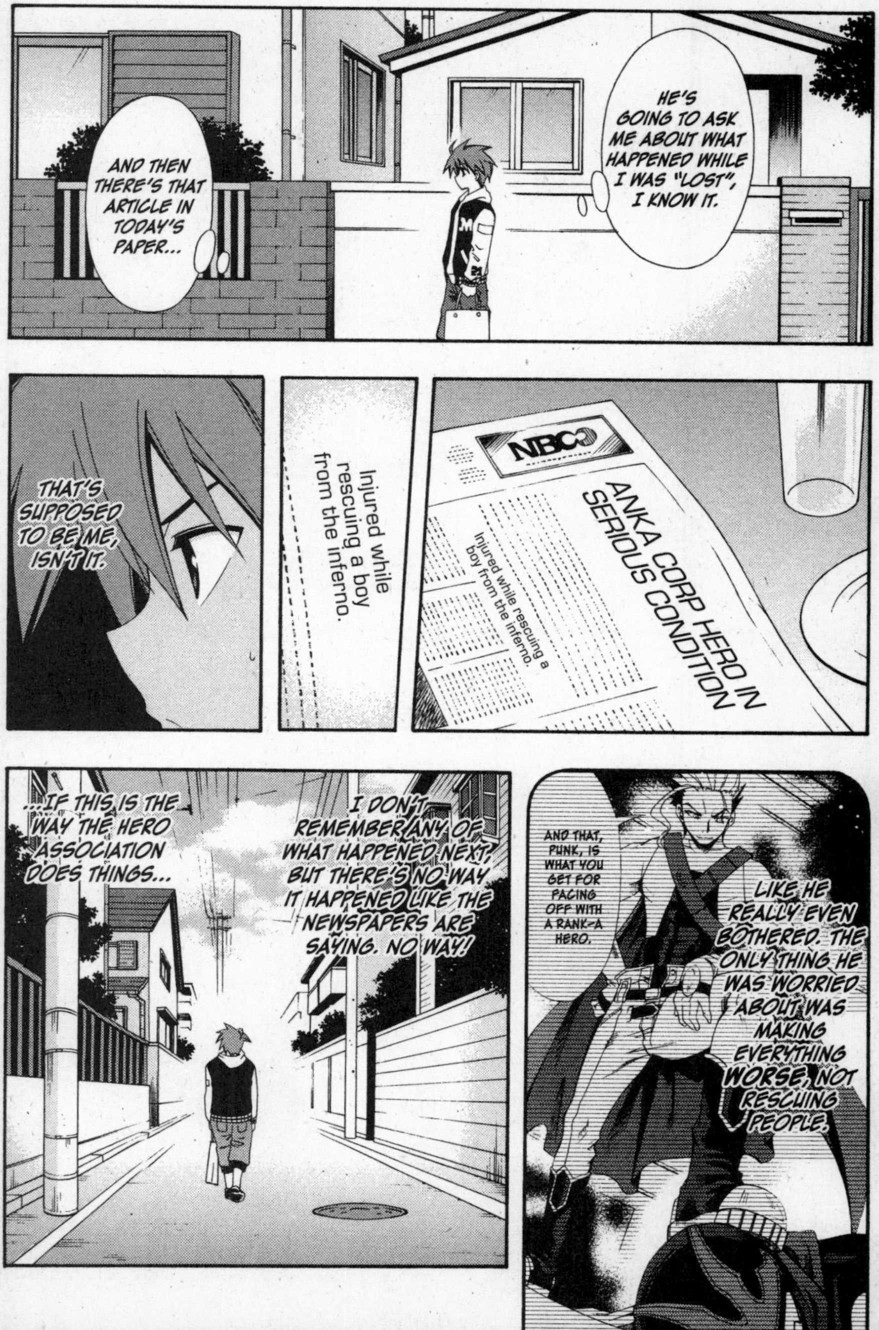
HE'S GOING TO ASK ME ABOUT WHAT HAPPENED WHILE I WAS "LOST", I KNOW IT.
AND THEN THERE'S THAT ARTICLE IN TODAY'S PAPER...
NBC
ANKA CORP HERO IN SERIOUS CONDITION
Injured while rescuing a boy from the inferno.
Injured while rescuing a boy from the inferno.
THAT'S SUPPOSED TO BE ME, ISN'T IT.
AND THAT, PUNK, IS WHAT YOU GET FOR FACING OFF WITH A RANK-A HERO.
LIKE HE REALLY EVEN BOTHERED. THE ONLY THING HE WAS WORRIED ABOUT WAS MAKING EVERYTHING WORSE, NOT RESCUING PEOPLE.
I DON'T REMEMBER ANY OF WHAT HAPPENED NEXT, BUT THERE'S NO WAY IT HAPPENED LIKE THE NEWSPAPERS ARE SAYING. NO WAY!
...IF THIS IS THE WAY THE HERO ASSOCIATION DOES THINGS...

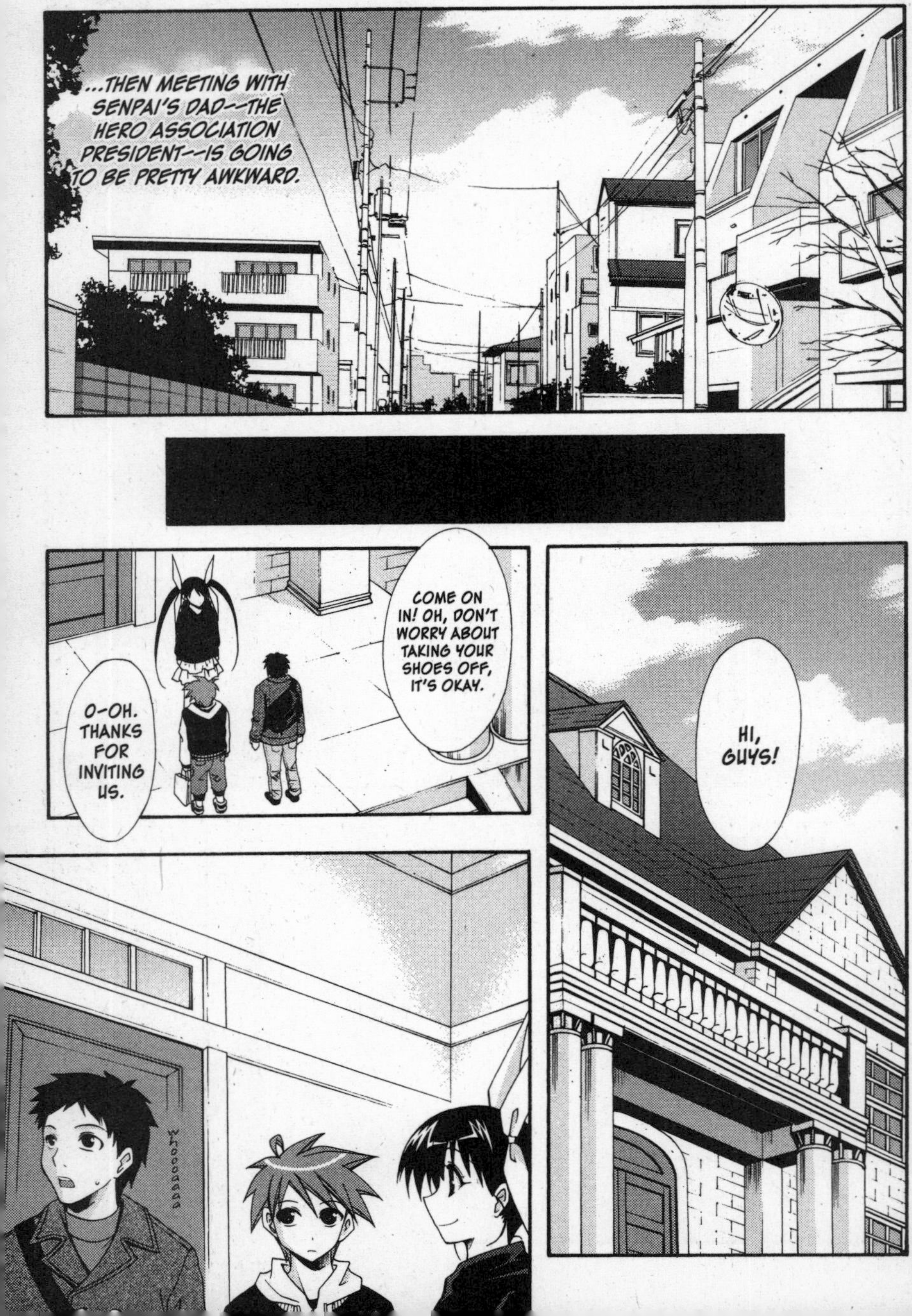
...THEN MEETING WITH SENPAI'S DAD--THE HERO ASSOCIATION PRESIDENT--IS GOING TO BE PRETTY AWKWARD.
HI, GUYS!
COME ON IN! OH, DON'T WORRY ABOUT TAKING YOUR SHOES OFF, IT'S OKAY.
O-OH. THANKS FOR INVITING US.

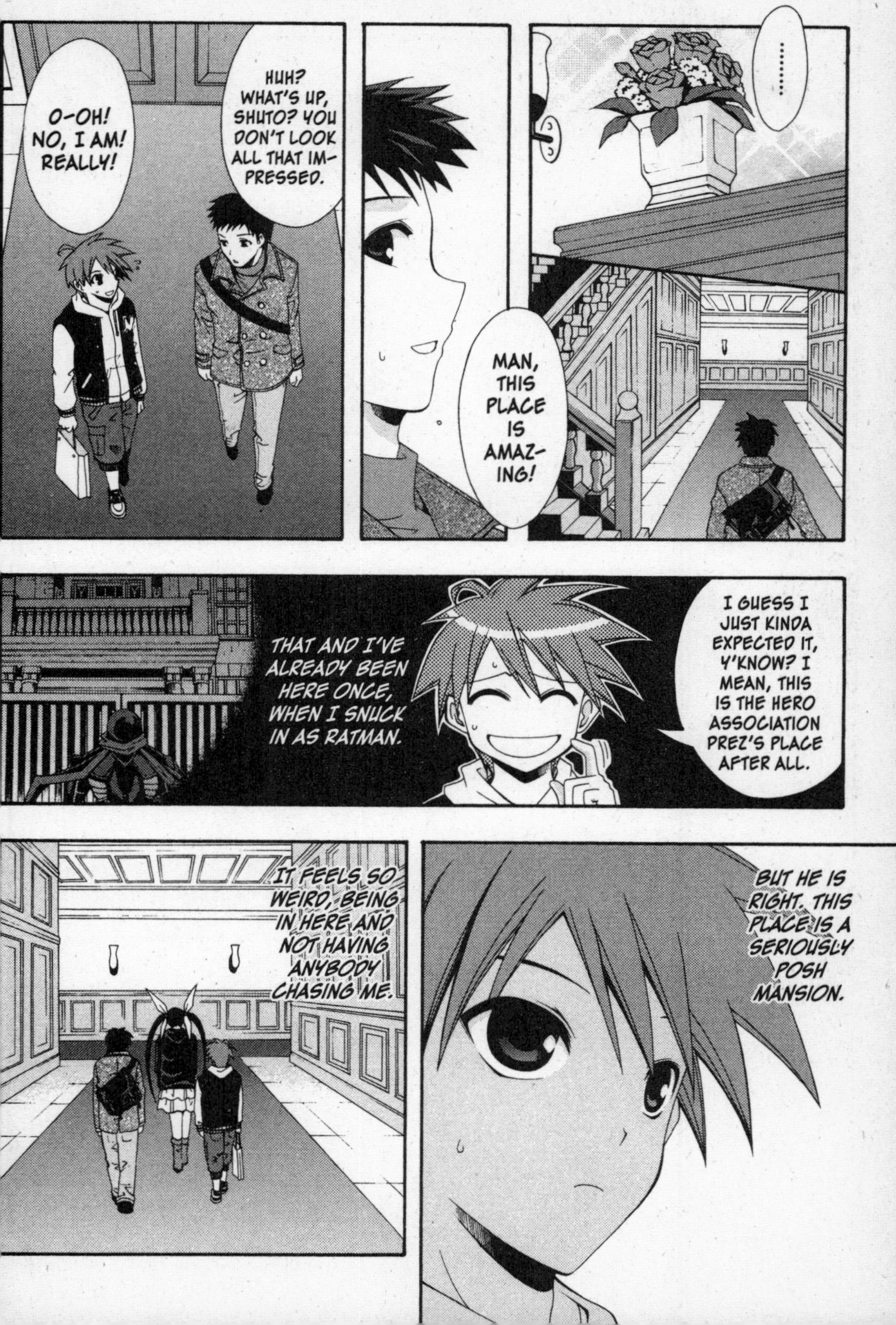
......
MAN, THIS PLACE IS AMAZ-ING!
HUH? WHAT'S UP, SHUTO? YOU DON'T LOOK ALL THAT IM-PRESSED.
O-OH! NO, I AM! REALLY!
I GUESS I JUST KINDA EXPECTED IT, Y'KNOW? I MEAN, THIS IS THE HERO ASSOCIATION PREZ'S PLACE AFTER ALL.
THAT AND I'VE ALREADY BEEN HERE ONCE, WHEN I SNUCK IN AS RATMAN.
BUT HE IS RIGHT. THIS PLACE IS A SERIOUSLY POSH MANSION.
IT FEELS SO WEIRD, BEING IN HERE AND NOT HAVING ANYBODY CHASING ME.

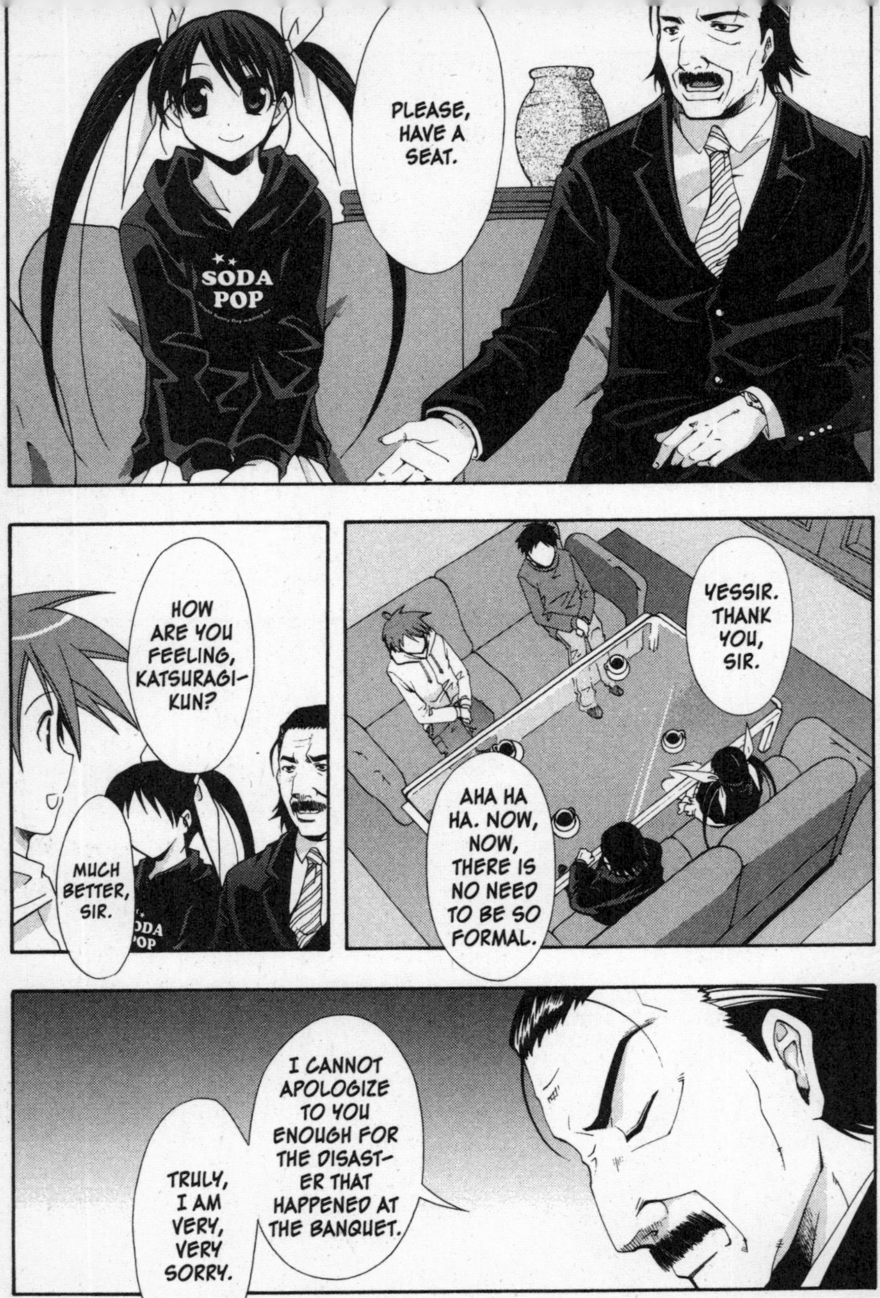
PLEASE, HAVE A SEAT.
SODA POP
YESSIR. THANK YOU, SIR.
AHA HA HA. NOW, NOW, THERE IS NO NEED TO BE SO FORMAL.
HOW ARE YOU FEELING, KATSURAGI-KUN?
MUCH BETTER, SIR.
I CANNOT APOLOGIZE TO YOU ENOUGH FOR THE DISASTER THAT HAPPENED AT THE BANQUET.
TRULY, I AM VERY, VERY SORRY.

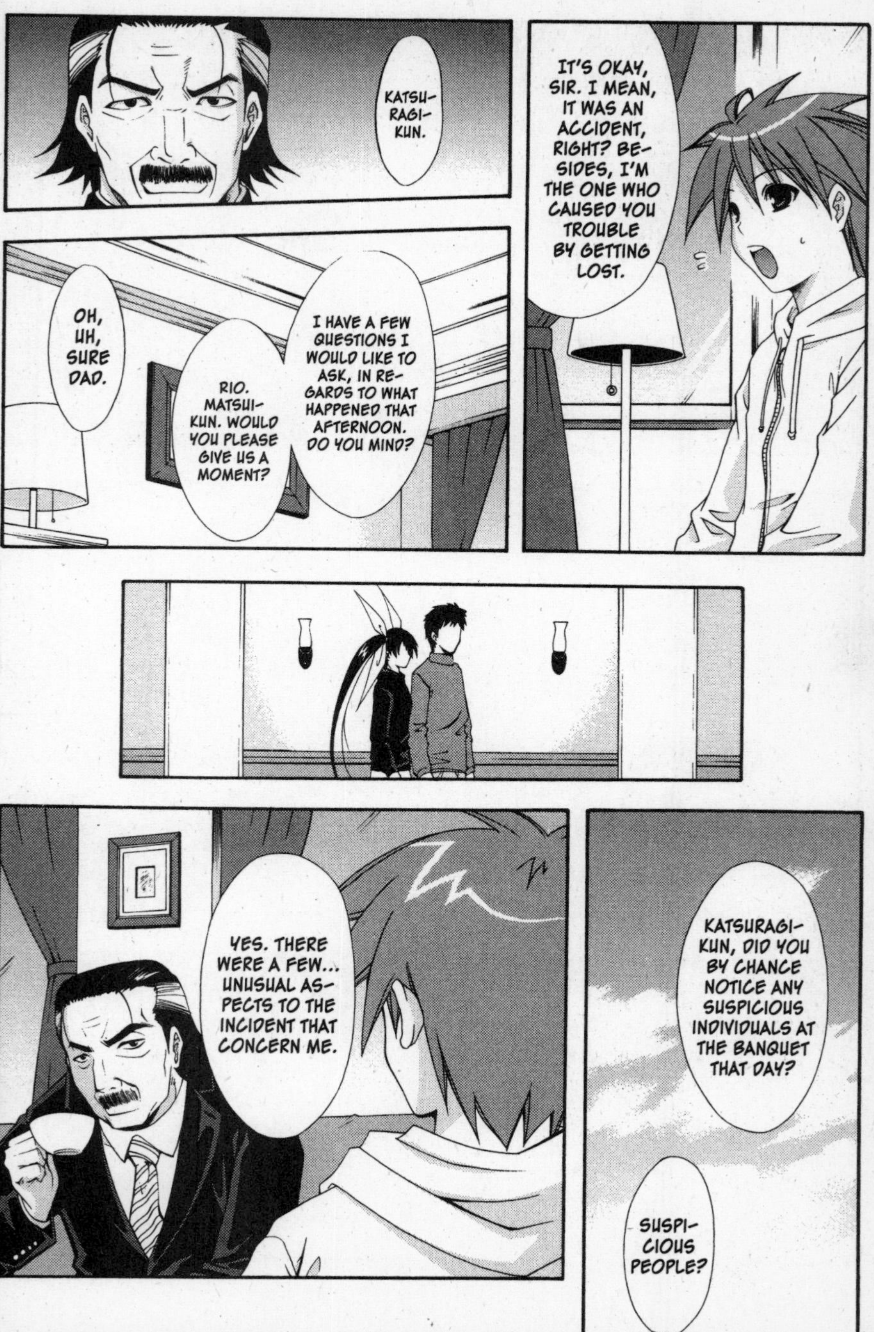
IT'S OKAY, SIR. I MEAN, IT WAS AN ACCIDENT, RIGHT? BESIDES, I'M THE ONE WHO CAUSED YOU TROUBLE BY GETTING LOST.
KATSURAGI-KUN.
I HAVE A FEW QUESTIONS I WOULD LIKE TO ASK, IN REGARDS TO WHAT HAPPENED THAT AFTERNOON. DO YOU MIND?
RIO. MATSUI-KUN. WOULD YOU PLEASE GIVE US A MOMENT?
OH, UH, SURE DAD.
KATSURAGI-KUN, DID YOU BY CHANCE NOTICE ANY SUSPICIOUS INDIVIDUALS AT THE BANQUET THAT DAY?
SUSPICIOUS PEOPLE?
YES. THERE WERE A FEW... UNUSUAL ASPECTS TO THE INCIDENT THAT CONCERN ME.

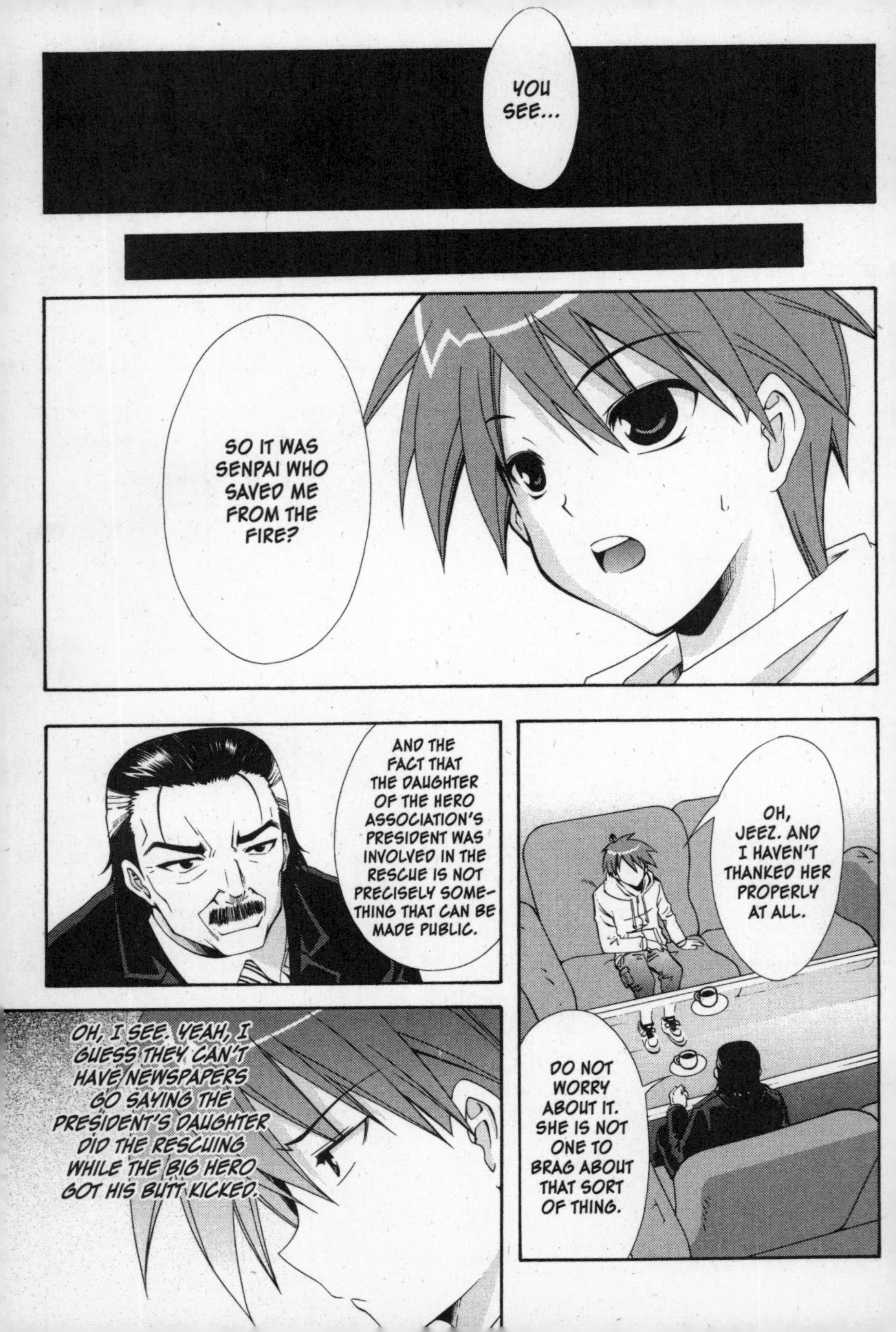
YOU SEE...
SO IT WAS SENPAI WHO SAVED ME FROM THE FIRE?
OH, JEEZ. AND I HAVEN'T THANKED HER PROPERLY AT ALL.
DO NOT WORRY ABOUT IT. SHE IS NOT ONE TO BRAG ABOUT THAT SORT OF THING.
AND THE FACT THAT THE DAUGHTER OF THE HERO ASSOCIATION'S PRESIDENT WAS INVOLVED IN THE RESCUE IS NOT PRECISELY SOME-THING THAT CAN BE MADE PUBLIC.
OH, I SEE. YEAH, I GUESS THEY CAN'T HAVE NEWSPAPERS GO SAYING THE PRESIDENT'S DAUGHTER DID THE RESCUING WHILE THE BIG HERO GOT HIS BUTT KICKED.

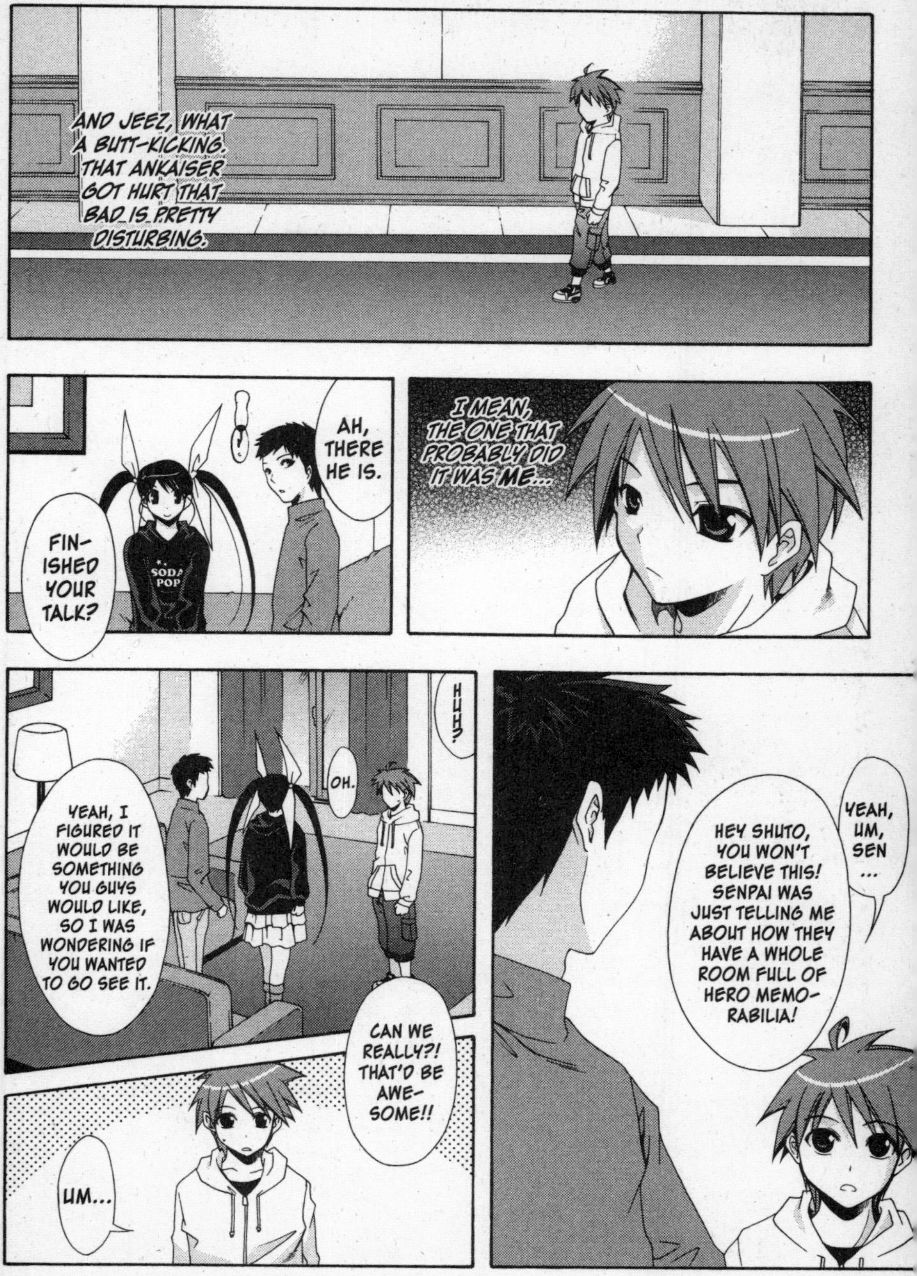
AND JEEZ, WHAT A BUTT-KICKING. THAT ANKAISER GOT HURT THAT BAD IS PRETTY DISTURBING.
AH, THERE HE IS.
FIN-ISHED YOUR TALK?
I MEAN, THE ONE THAT PROBABLY DID IT WAS ME...
HUH?
OH.
YEAH, I FIGURED IT WOULD BE SOMETHING YOU GUYS WOULD LIKE, SO I WAS WONDERING IF YOU WANTED TO GO SEE IT.
CAN WE REALLY?! THAT'D BE AWE-SOME!!
UM...
HEY SHUTO, YOU WON'T BELIEVE THIS! SENPAI WAS JUST TELLING ME ABOUT HOW THEY HAVE A WHOLE ROOM FULL OF HERO MEMO-RABILIA!
YEAH, UM, SEN...

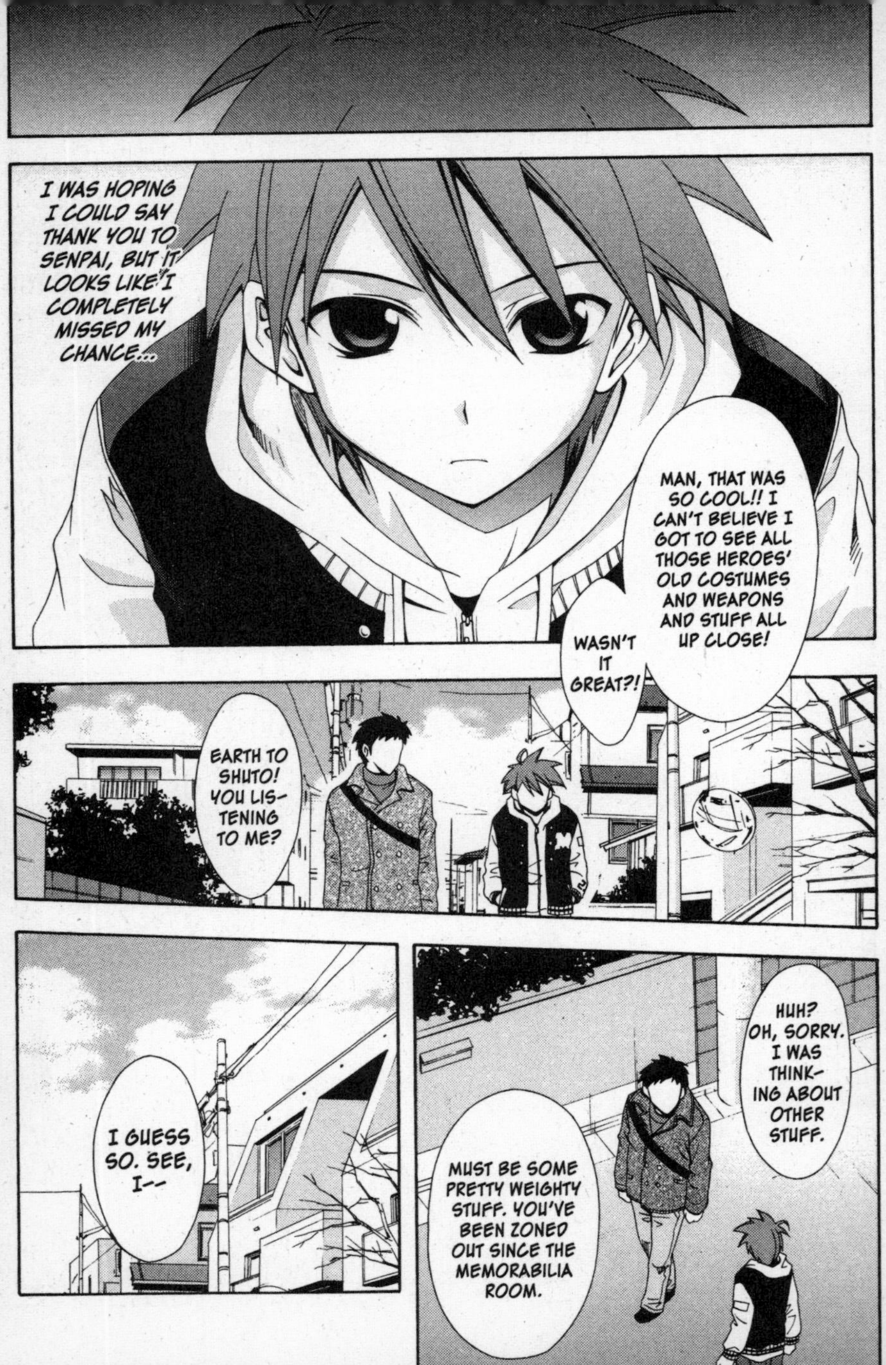
I WAS HOPING I COULD SAY THANK YOU TO SENPAI, BUT IT LOOKS LIKE I COMPLETELY MISSED MY CHANCE...
MAN, THAT WAS SO COOL!! I CAN'T BELIEVE I GOT TO SEE ALL THOSE HEROES' OLD COSTUMES AND WEAPONS AND STUFF ALL UP CLOSE!
WASN'T IT GREAT?!
EARTH TO SHUTO! YOU LIS-TENING TO ME?
HUH? OH, SORRY. I WAS THINK-ING ABOUT OTHER STUFF.
MUST BE SOME PRETTY WEIGHTY STUFF. YOU'VE BEEN ZONED OUT SINCE THE MEMORABILIA ROOM.
I GUESS SO. SEE, I--

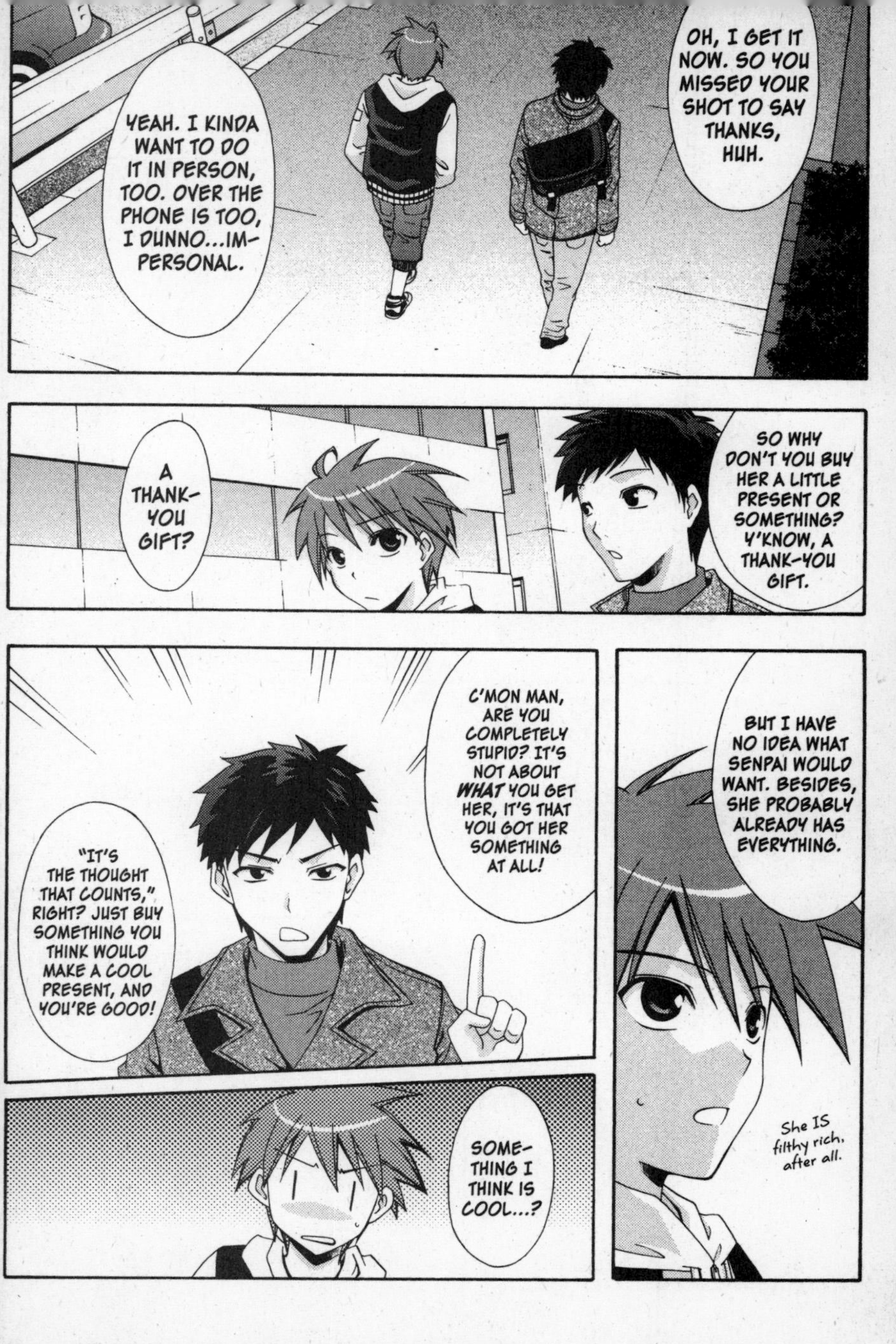
OH, I GET IT NOW. SO YOU MISSED YOUR SHOT TO SAY THANKS, HUH.
YEAH. I KINDA WANT TO DO IT IN PERSON, TOO. OVER THE PHONE IS TOO, I DUNNO...IM-PERSONAL.
SO WHY DON'T YOU BUY HER A LITTLE PRESENT OR SOMETHING? Y'KNOW, A THANK-YOU GIFT.
A THANK-YOU GIFT?
BUT I HAVE NO IDEA WHAT SENPAI WOULD WANT. BESIDES, SHE PROBABLY ALREADY HAS EVERYTHING.
She IS filthy rich, after all.
C'MON MAN, ARE YOU COMPLETELY STUPID? IT'S NOT ABOUT WHAT YOU GET HER, IT'S THAT YOU GOT HER SOMETHING AT ALL!
"IT'S THE THOUGHT THAT COUNTS," RIGHT? JUST BUY SOMETHING YOU THINK WOULD MAKE A COOL PRESENT, AND YOU'RE GOOD!
SOME-THING I THINK IS COOL...?

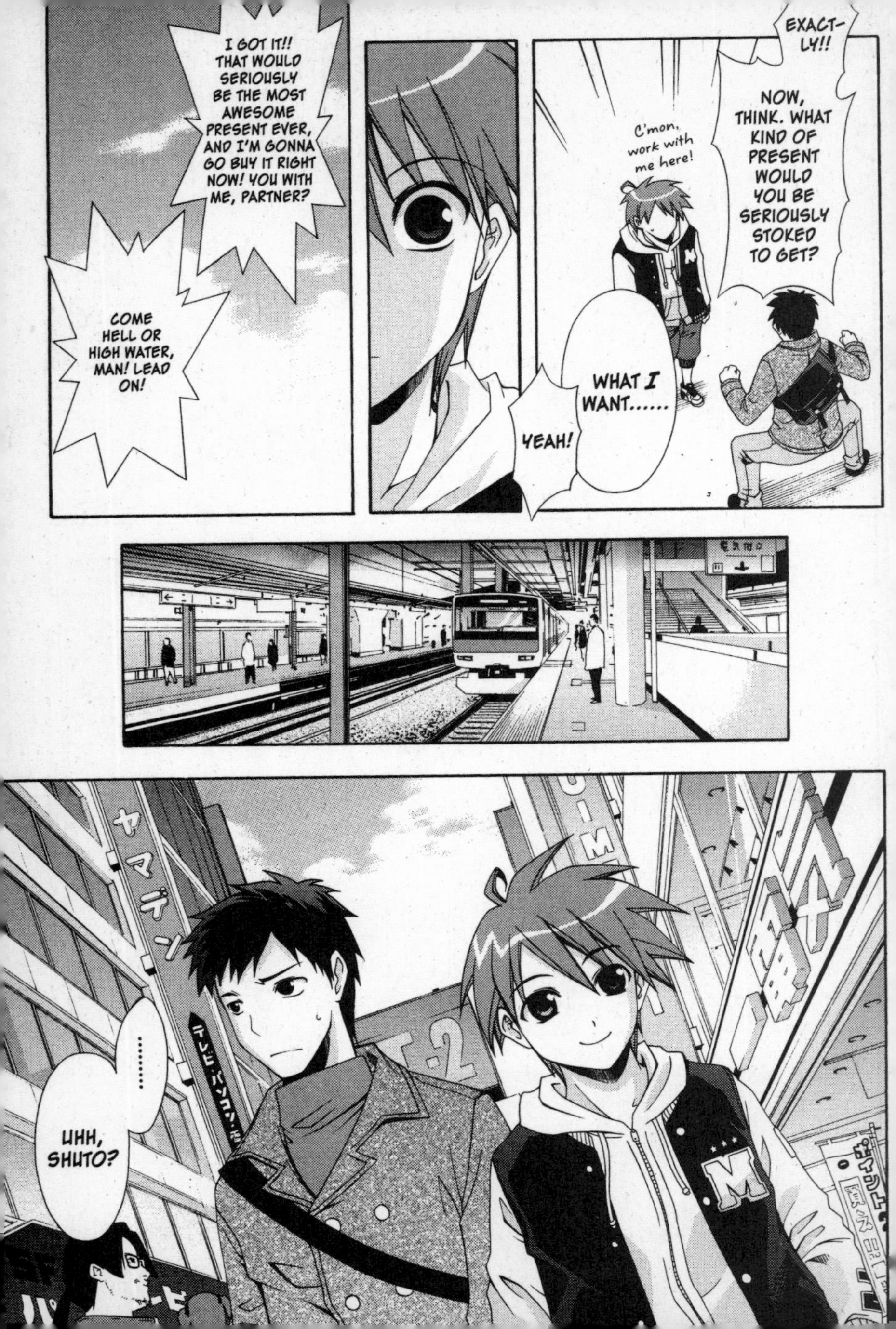
EXACT-LY!!
NOW, THINK. WHAT KIND OF PRESENT WOULD YOU BE SERIOUSLY STOKED TO GET?
C'mon, work with me here!
WHAT I WANT......
YEAH!
I GOT IT!! THAT WOULD SERIOUSLY BE THE MOST AWESOME PRESENT EVER, AND I'M GONNA GO BUY IT RIGHT NOW! YOU WITH ME, PARTNER?
COME HELL OR HIGH WATER, MAN! LEAD ON!
......
UHH, SHUTO?

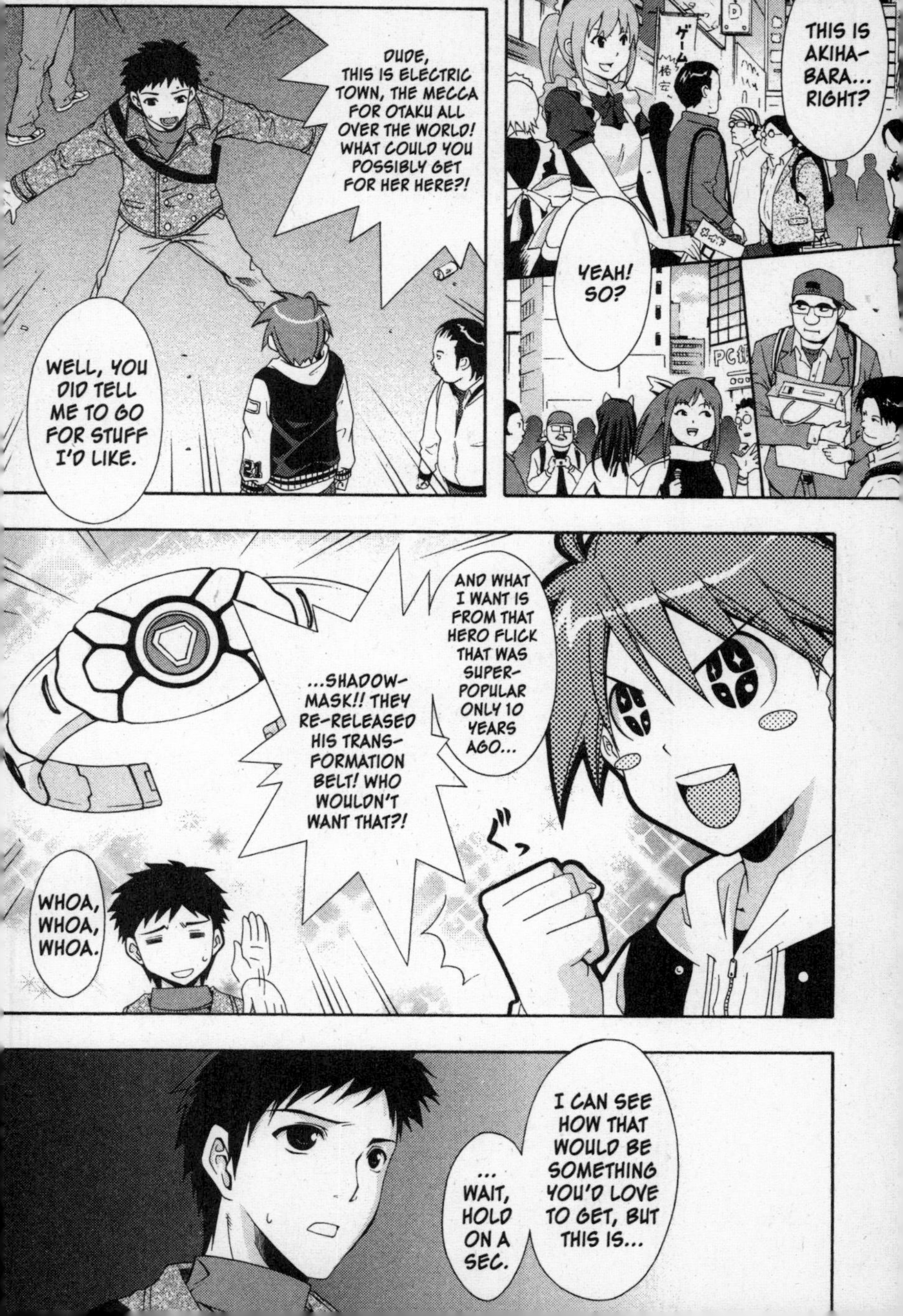
THIS IS AKIHABARA... RIGHT?
YEAH! SO?
DUDE, THIS IS ELECTRIC TOWN, THE MECCA FOR OTAKU ALL OVER THE WORLD! WHAT COULD YOU POSSIBLY GET FOR HER HERE?!
WELL, YOU DID TELL ME TO GO FOR STUFF I'D LIKE.
AND WHAT I WANT IS FROM THAT HERO FLICK THAT WAS SUPER-POPULAR ONLY 10 YEARS AGO...
...SHADOW-MASK!! THEY RE-RELEASED HIS TRANSFORMATION BELT! WHO WOULDN'T WANT THAT?!
ぐっ
WHOA, WHOA, WHOA.
I CAN SEE HOW THAT WOULD BE SOMETHING YOU'D LOVE TO GET, BUT THIS IS...
... WAIT, HOLD ON A SEC.

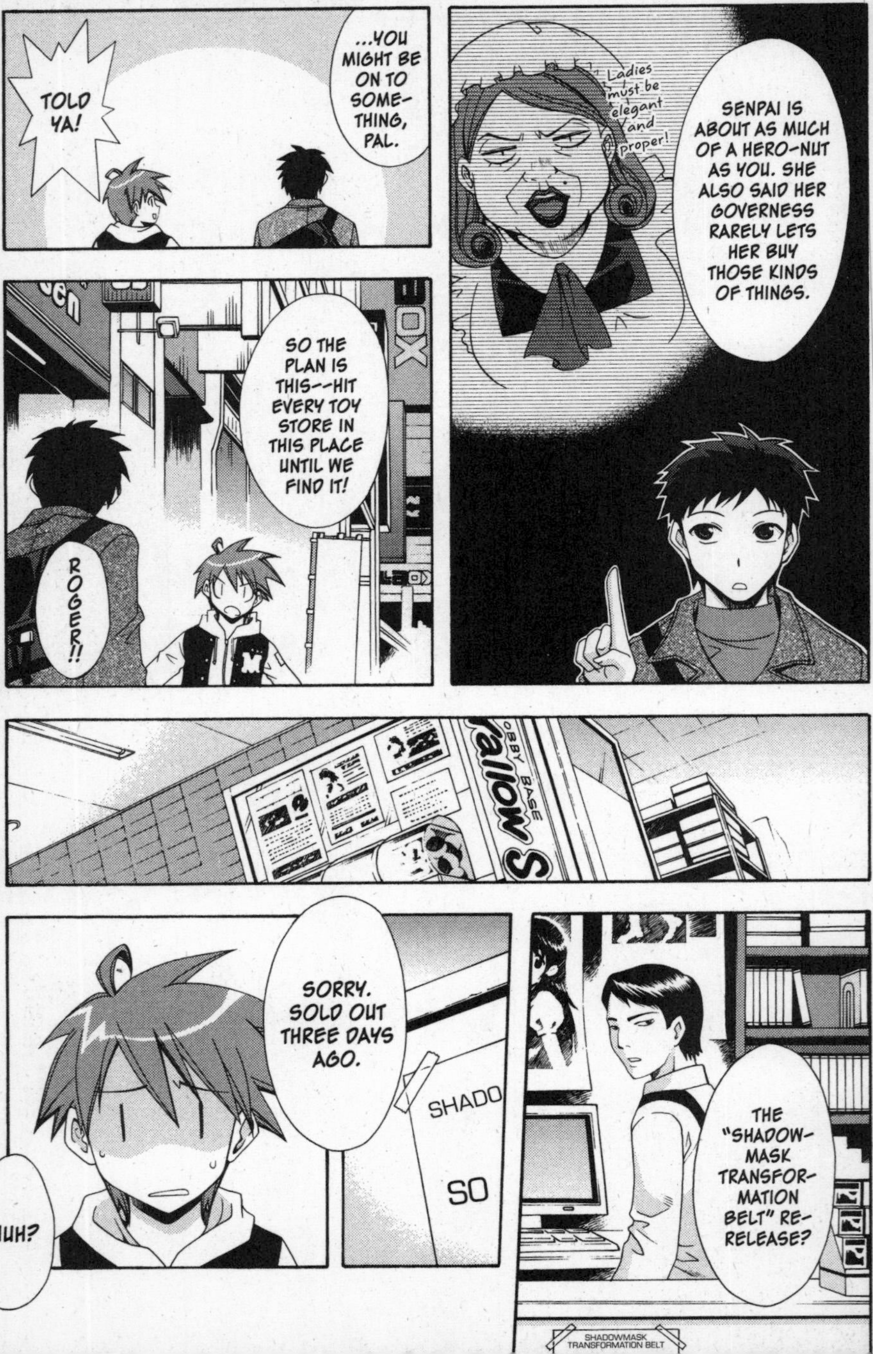
SENPAI IS ABOUT AS MUCH OF A HERO-NUT AS YOU. SHE ALSO SAID HER GOVERNESS RARELY LETS HER BUY THOSE KINDS OF THINGS.
Ladies must be elegant and proper!
...YOU MIGHT BE ON TO SOME-THING, PAL.
TOLD YA!
SO THE PLAN IS THIS--HIT EVERY TOY STORE IN THIS PLACE UNTIL WE FIND IT!
ROGER!!
THE "SHADOW-MASK TRANSFOR-MATION BELT" RE-RELEASE?
SHADOWMASK TRANSFORMATION BELT
SORRY. SOLD OUT THREE DAYS AGO.
SHADO
SO
HUH?

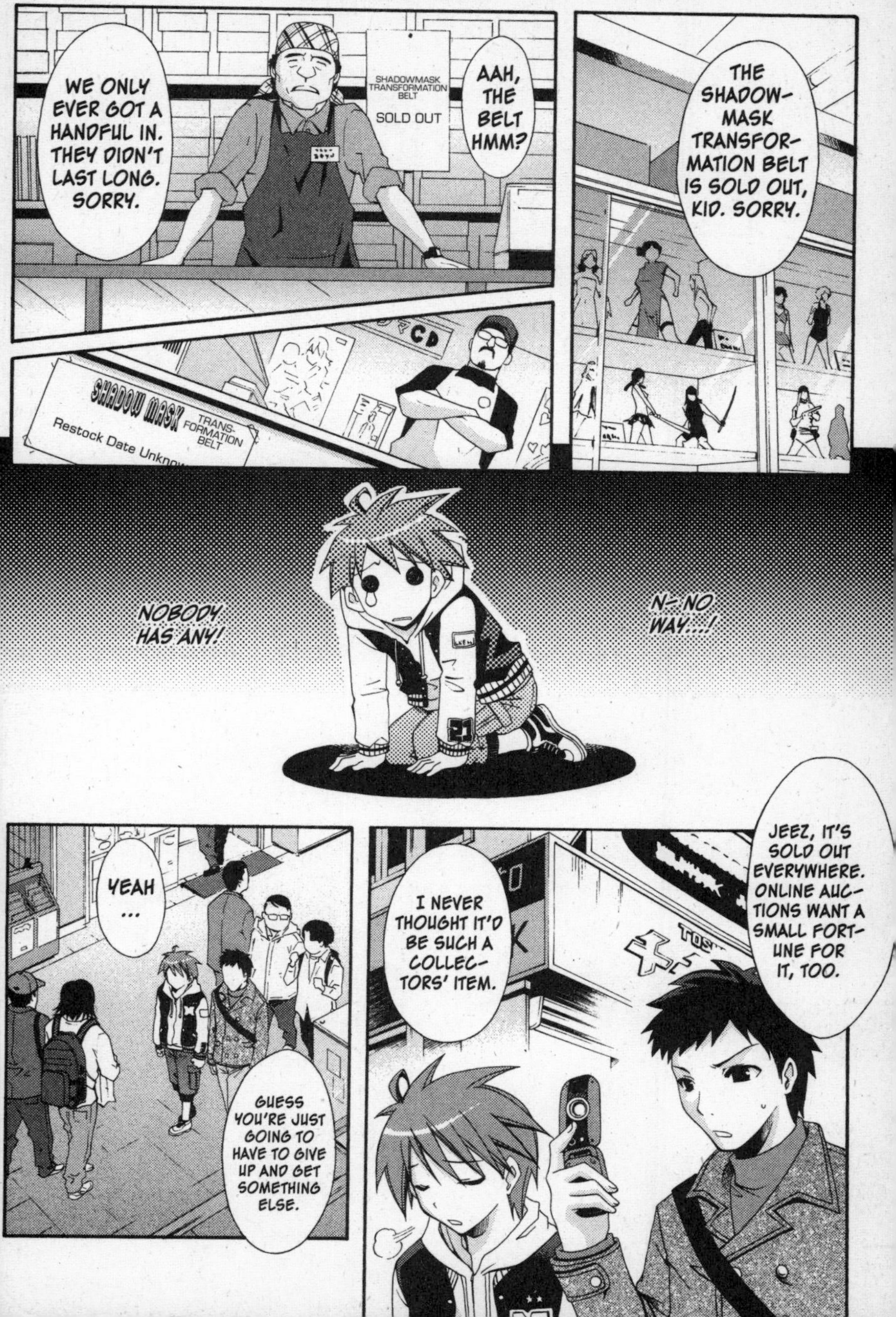
THE SHADOW-MASK TRANSFORMATION BELT IS SOLD OUT, KID. SORRY.
AAH, THE BELT HMM?
SHADOWMASK TRANSFORMATION BELT
SOLD OUT
WE ONLY EVER GOT A HANDFUL IN. THEY DIDN'T LAST LONG. SORRY.
CD
SHADOW MASK TRANS-FORMATION BELT
Restock Date Unknow
N-NO WAY...!
NOBODY HAS ANY!
JEEZ, IT'S SOLD OUT EVERYWHERE. ONLINE AUC-TIONS WANT A SMALL FORT-UNE FOR IT, TOO.
I NEVER THOUGHT IT'D BE SUCH A COLLEC-TORS' ITEM.
GUESS YOU'RE JUST GOING TO HAVE TO GIVE UP AND GET SOMETHING ELSE.
YEAH ...

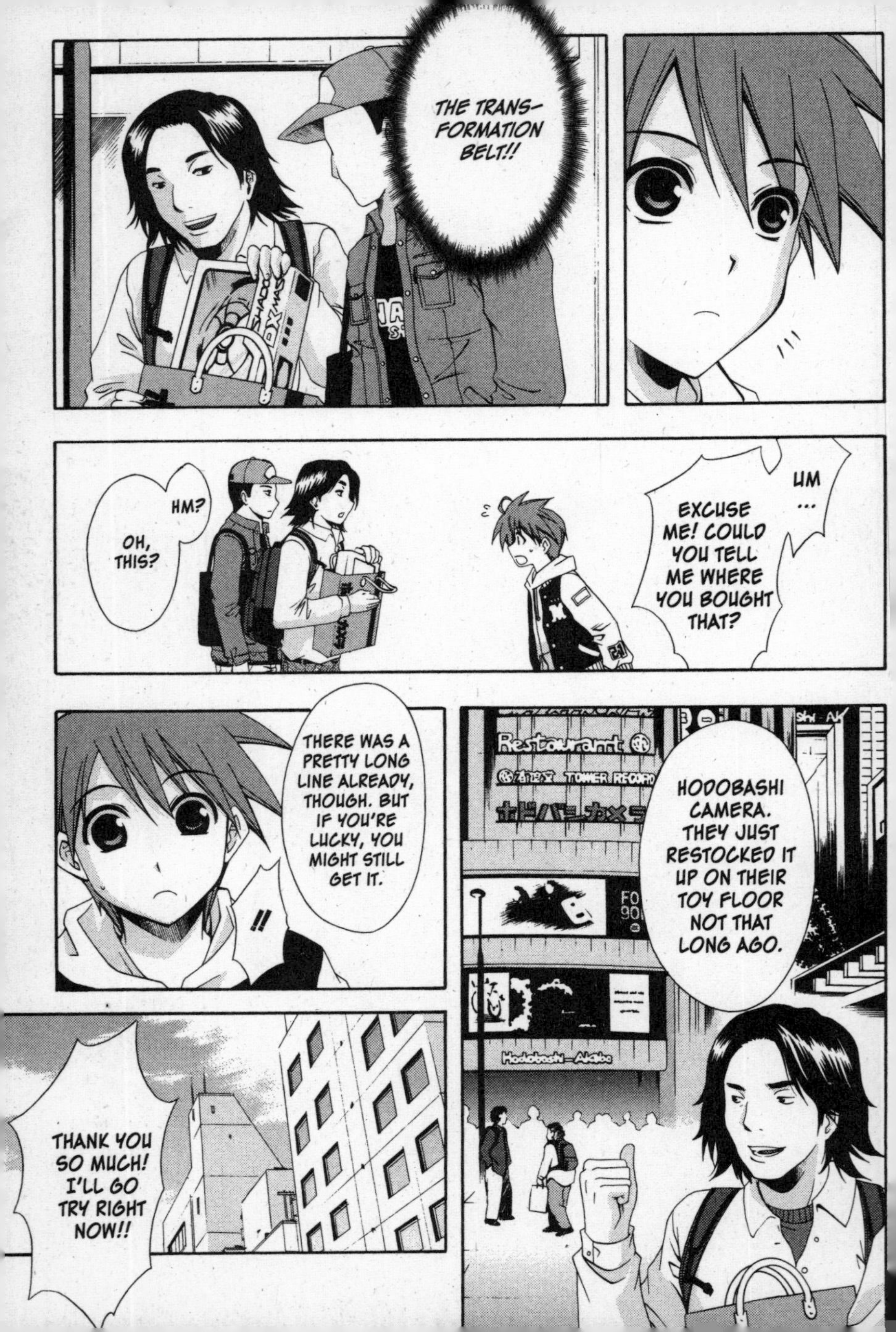
THE TRANS-FORMATION BELT!!
UM ...
EXCUSE ME! COULD YOU TELL ME WHERE YOU BOUGHT THAT?
HM?
OH, THIS?
Restaurant
TOWER RECORD
Hodobashi-Akiba
HODOBASHI CAMERA. THEY JUST RESTOCKED IT UP ON THEIR TOY FLOOR NOT THAT LONG AGO.
THERE WAS A PRETTY LONG LINE ALREADY, THOUGH. BUT IF YOU'RE LUCKY, YOU MIGHT STILL GET IT.
!!
THANK YOU SO MUCH! I'LL GO TRY RIGHT NOW!!

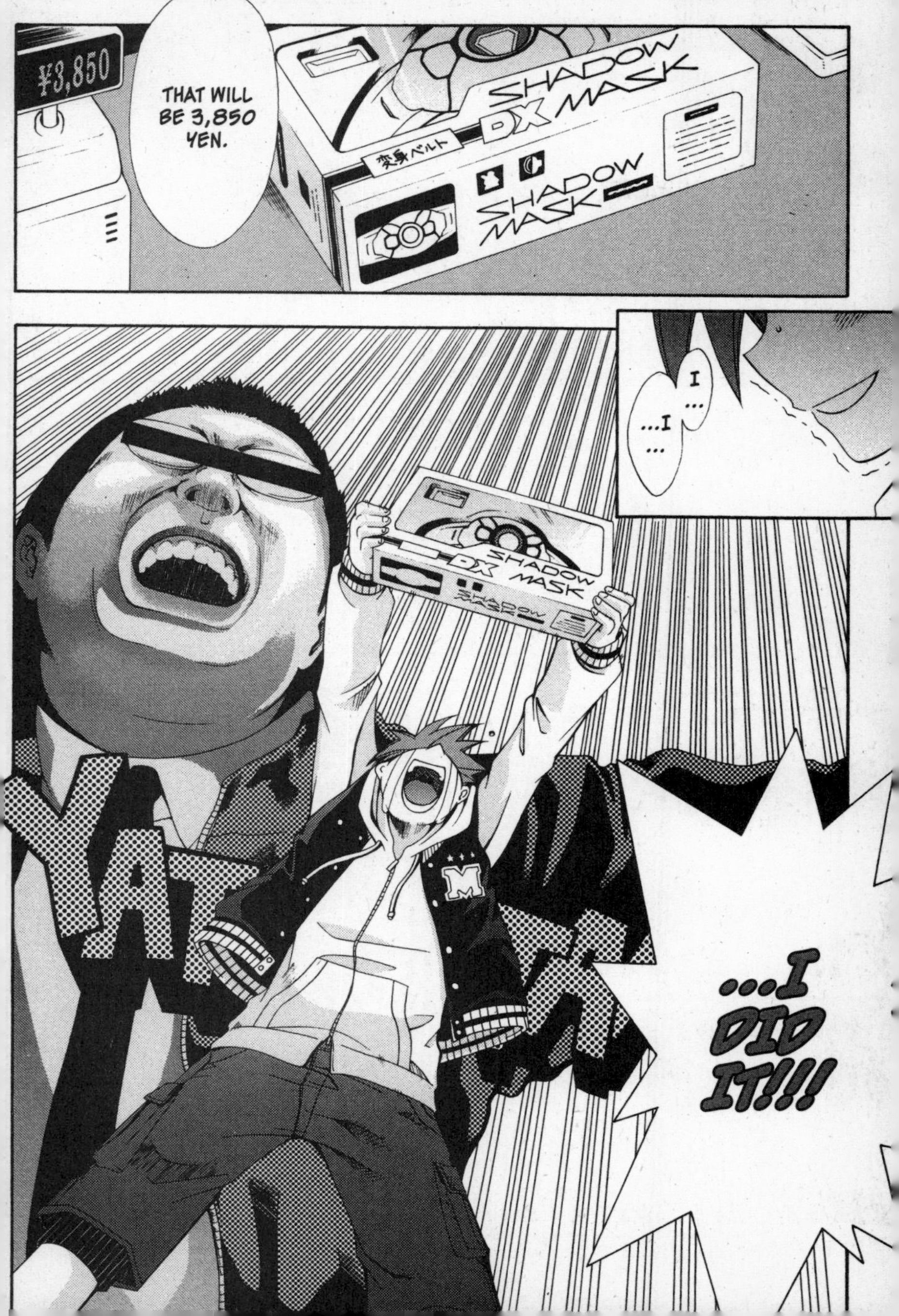
SHADOW DX MASK
変身ベルト
SHADOW MASK
THAT WILL BE 3,850 YEN.
¥3,850
I ...
...I ...
SHADOW DX MASK
...I DID IT!!!
YAT

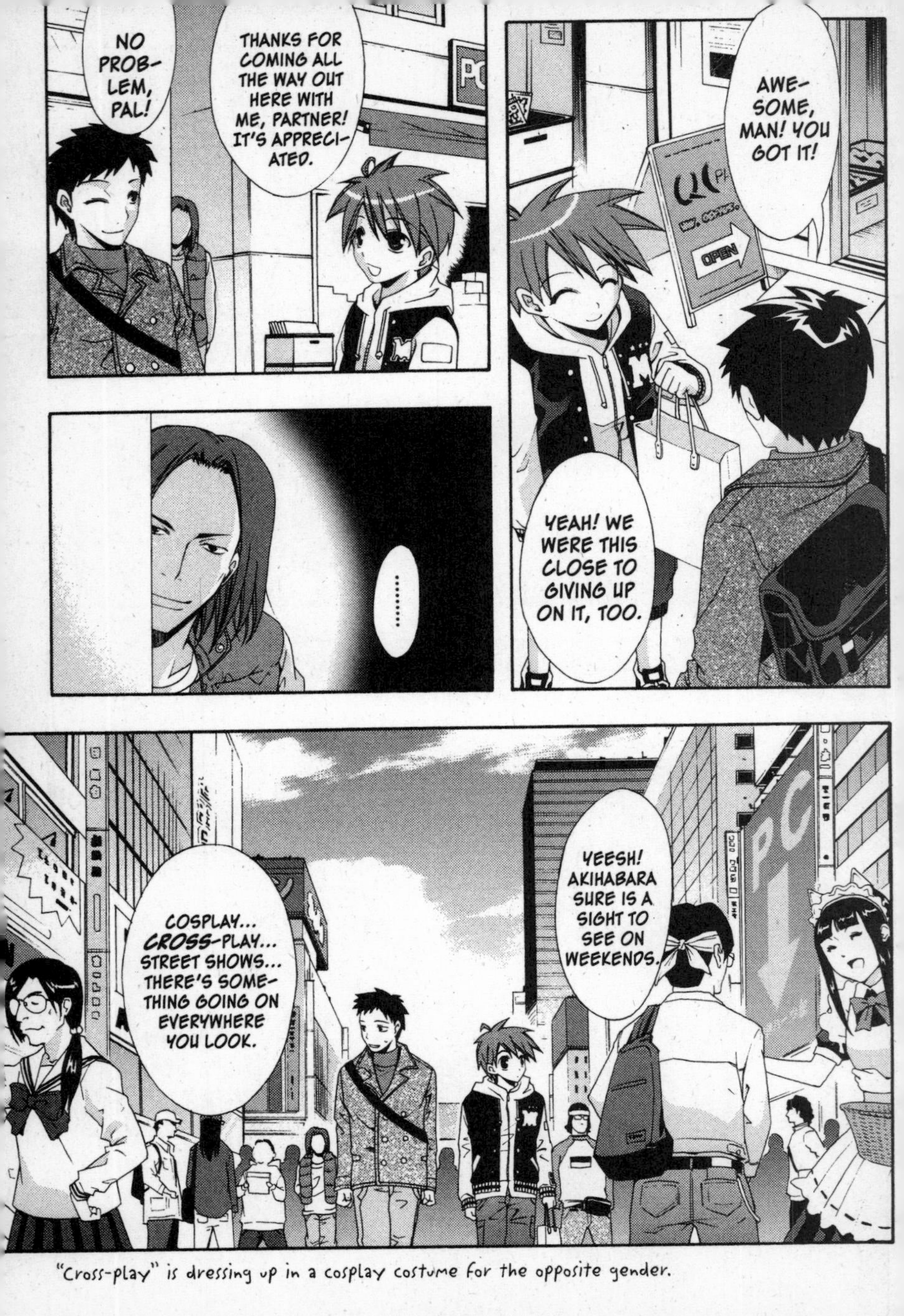
AWE-SOME, MAN! YOU GOT IT!
YEAH! WE WERE THIS CLOSE TO GIVING UP ON IT, TOO.
THANKS FOR COMING ALL THE WAY OUT HERE WITH ME, PARTNER! IT'S APPRECI-ATED.
NO PROB-LEM, PAL!
....
YEESH! AKIHABARA SURE IS A SIGHT TO SEE ON WEEKENDS.
COSPLAY... CROSS-PLAY... STREET SHOWS... THERE'S SOME-THING GOING ON EVERYWHERE YOU LOOK.

"Cross-play" is dressing up in a cosplay costume for the opposite gender.

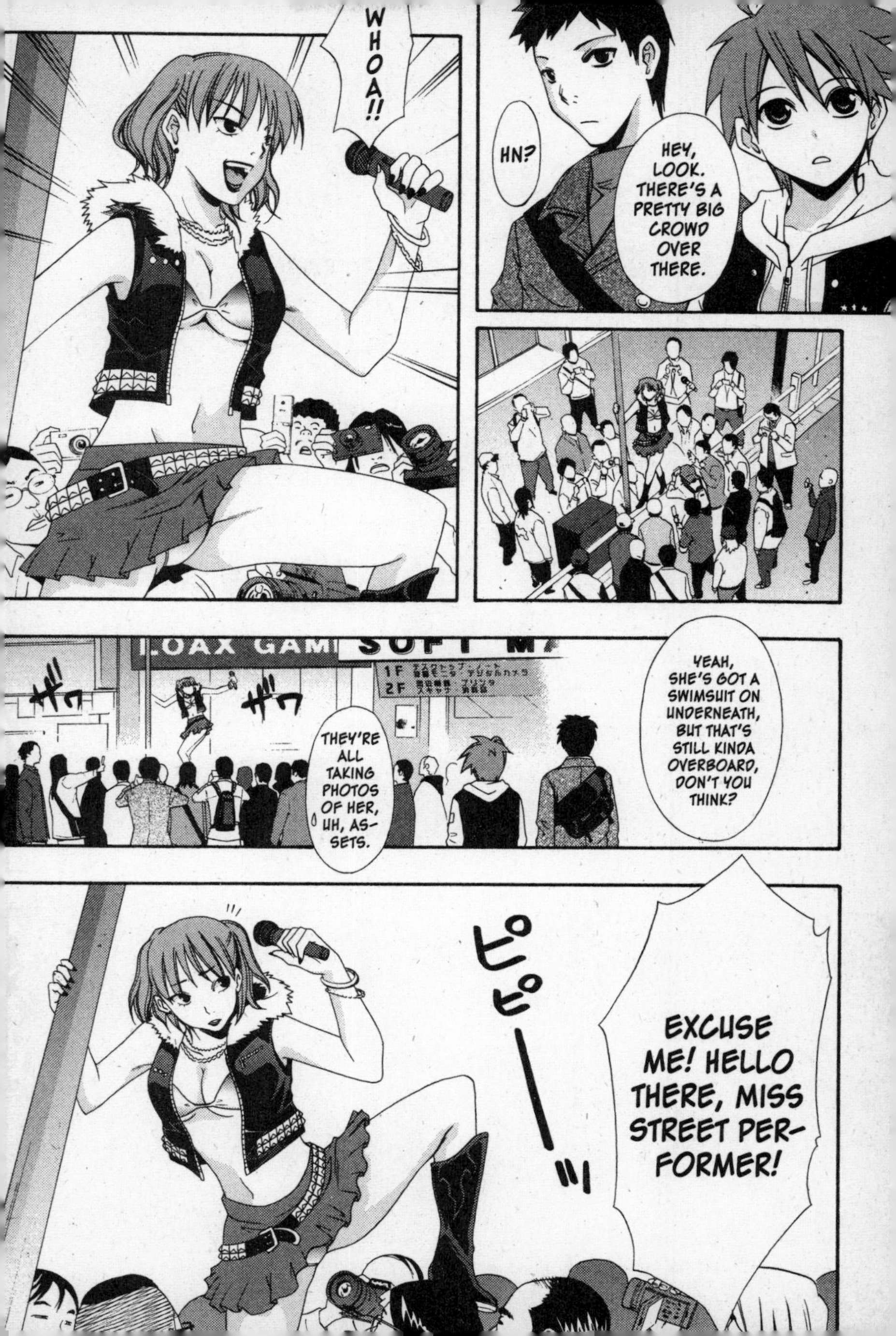
HEY, LOOK. THERE'S A PRETTY BIG CROWD OVER THERE.
HN?
WHOA!!
YEAH, SHE'S GOT A SWIMSUIT ON UNDERNEATH, BUT THAT'S STILL KINDA OVERBOARD, DON'T YOU THINK?
THEY'RE ALL TAKING PHOTOS OF HER, UH, AS-SETS.
LOAX GAM
SOFT M
ザワ
ザワ
ピピーーッ
EXCUSE ME! HELLO THERE, MISS STREET PER-FORMER!

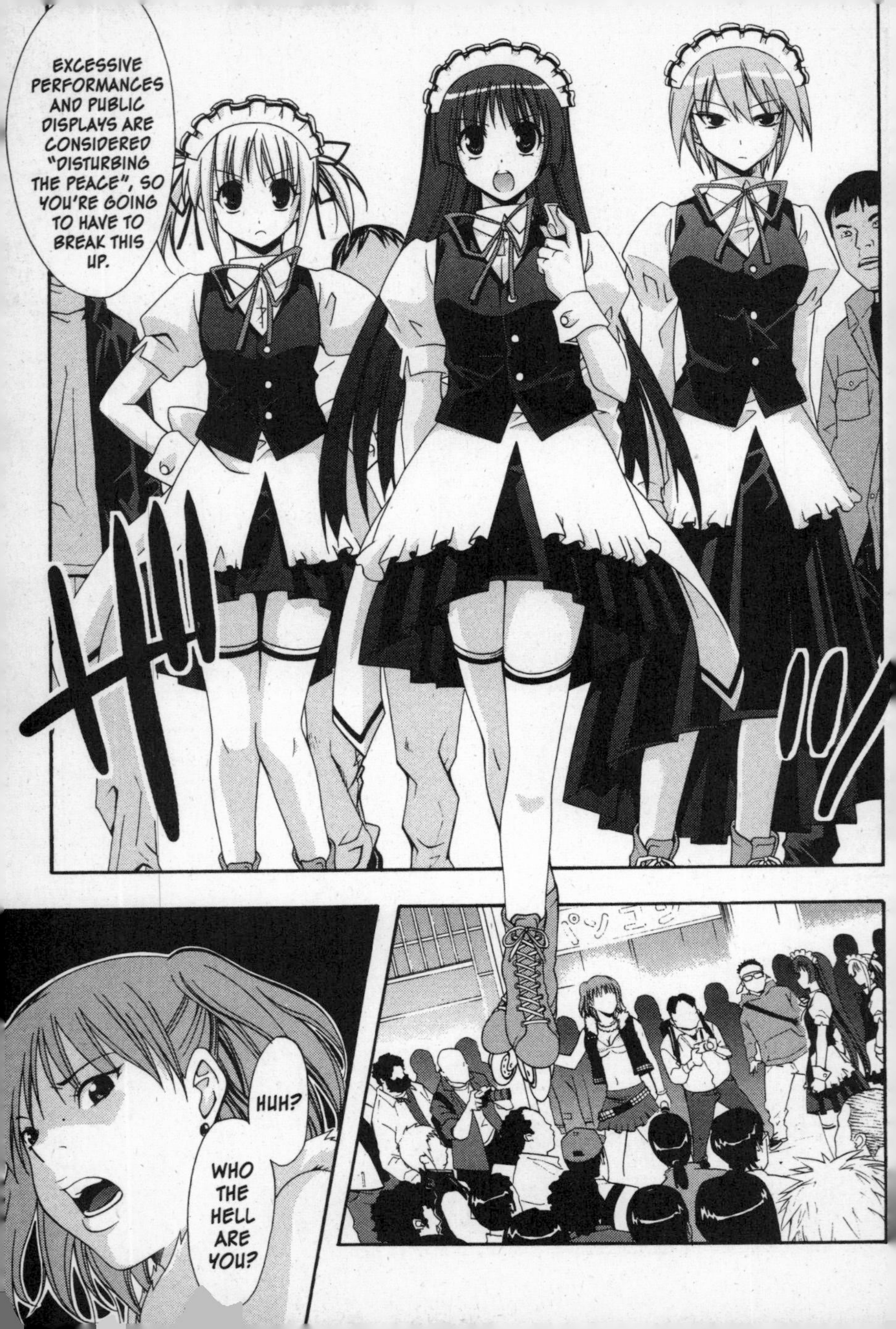
EXCESSIVE PERFORMANCES AND PUBLIC DISPLAYS ARE CONSIDERED "DISTURBING THE PEACE", SO YOU'RE GOING TO HAVE TO BREAK THIS UP.
HUH?
WHO THE HELL ARE YOU?

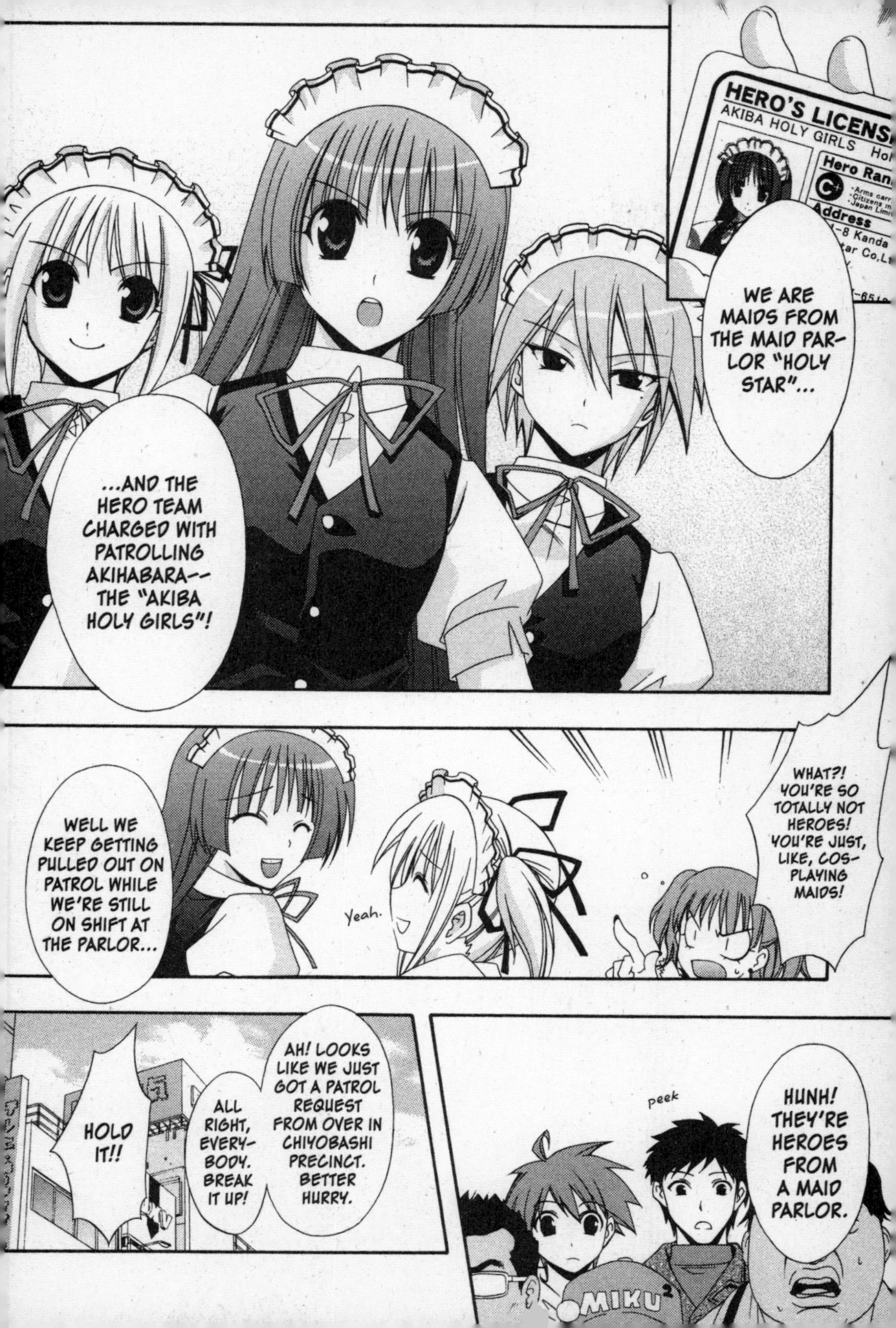
HERO'S LICENS
AKIBA HOLY GIRLS
WE ARE MAIDS FROM THE MAID PARLOR "HOLY STAR"...
...AND THE HERO TEAM CHARGED WITH PATROLLING AKIHABARA-- THE "AKIBA HOLY GIRLS"!
WHAT?! YOU'RE SO TOTALLY NOT HEROES! YOU'RE JUST, LIKE, COSPLAYING MAIDS!
WELL WE KEEP GETTING PULLED OUT ON PATROL WHILE WE'RE STILL ON SHIFT AT THE PARLOR...
Yeah.
peek
HUNH! THEY'RE HEROES FROM A MAID PARLOR.
MIKU
AH! LOOKS LIKE WE JUST GOT A PATROL REQUEST FROM OVER IN CHIYOBASHI PRECINCT. BETTER HURRY.
ALL RIGHT, EVERYBODY. BREAK IT UP!
HOLD IT!!

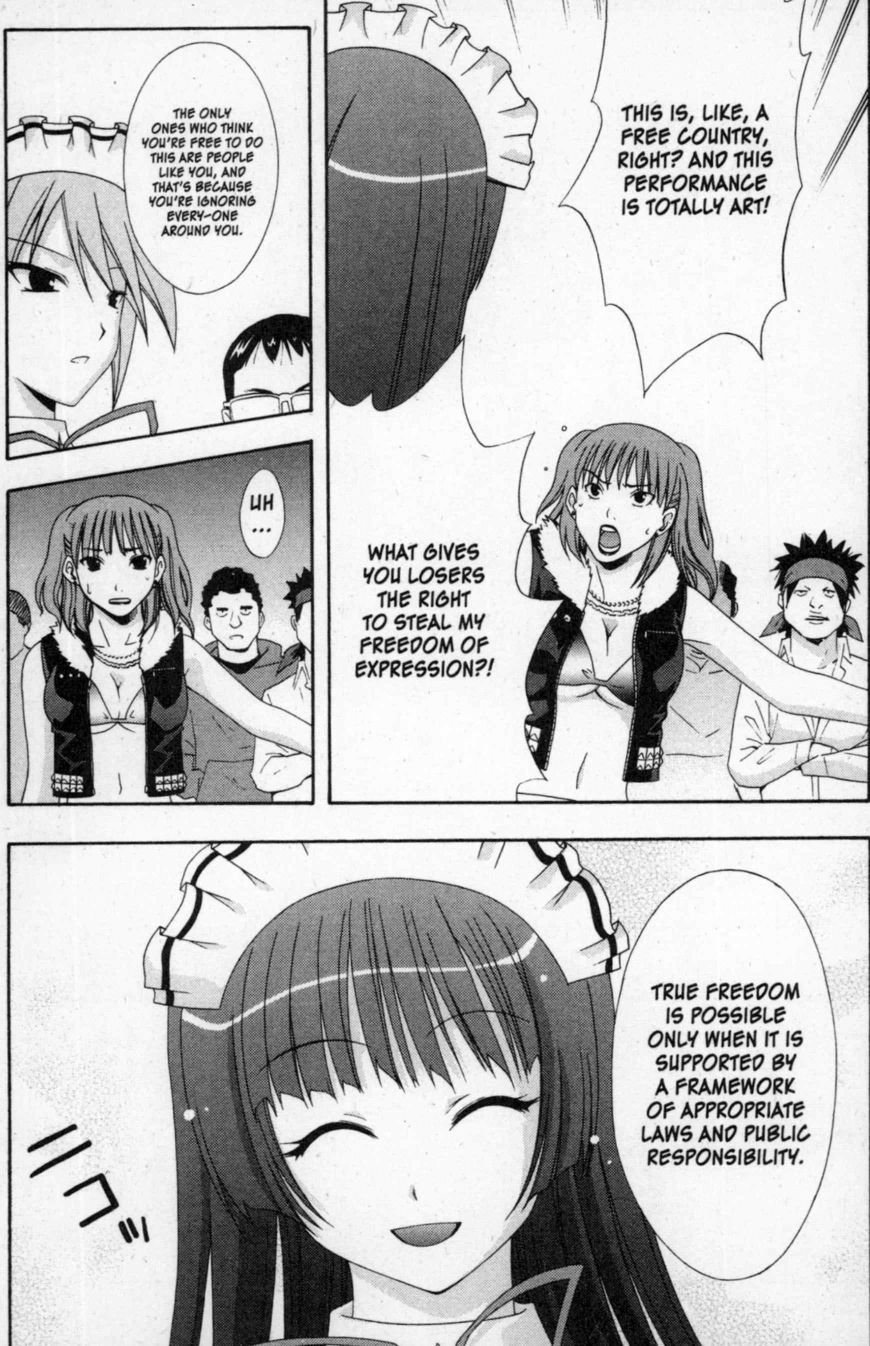
THIS IS, LIKE, A FREE COUNTRY, RIGHT? AND THIS PERFORMANCE IS TOTALLY ART!
WHAT GIVES YOU LOSERS THE RIGHT TO STEAL MY FREEDOM OF EXPRESSION?!
THE ONLY ONES WHO THINK YOU'RE FREE TO DO THIS ARE PEOPLE LIKE YOU, AND THAT'S BECAUSE YOU'RE IGNORING EVERY-ONE AROUND YOU.
UH ...
TRUE FREEDOM IS POSSIBLE ONLY WHEN IT IS SUPPORTED BY A FRAMEWORK OF APPROPRIATE LAWS AND PUBLIC RESPONSIBILITY.
ニコッ

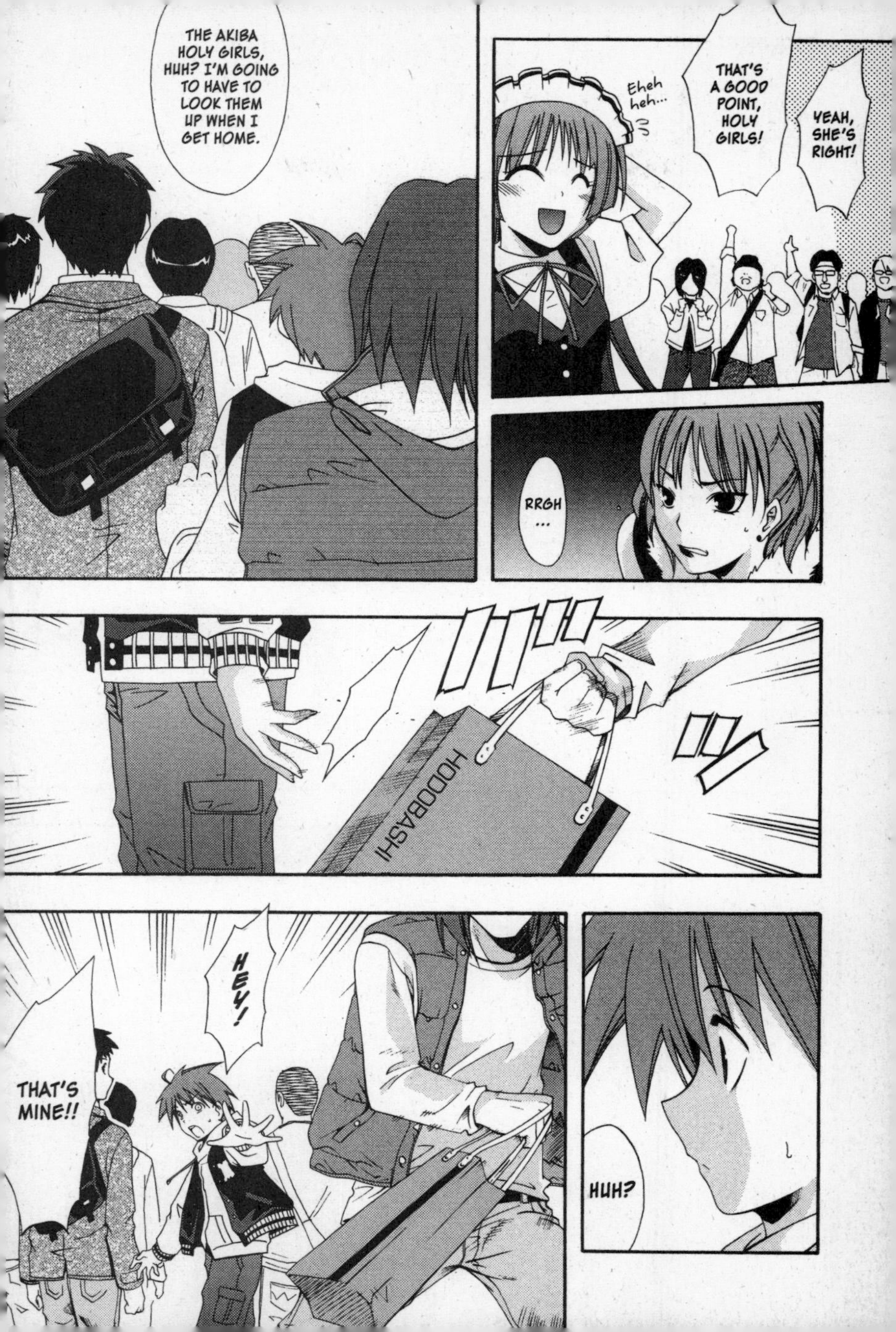

THAT'S A GOOD POINT, HOLY GIRLS!
YEAH, SHE'S RIGHT!
Eheh heh...
RRGH ...
THE AKIBA HOLY GIRLS, HUH? I'M GOING TO HAVE TO LOOK THEM UP WHEN I GET HOME.
HODOBASHI
HUH?
HEY!
THAT'S MINE!!

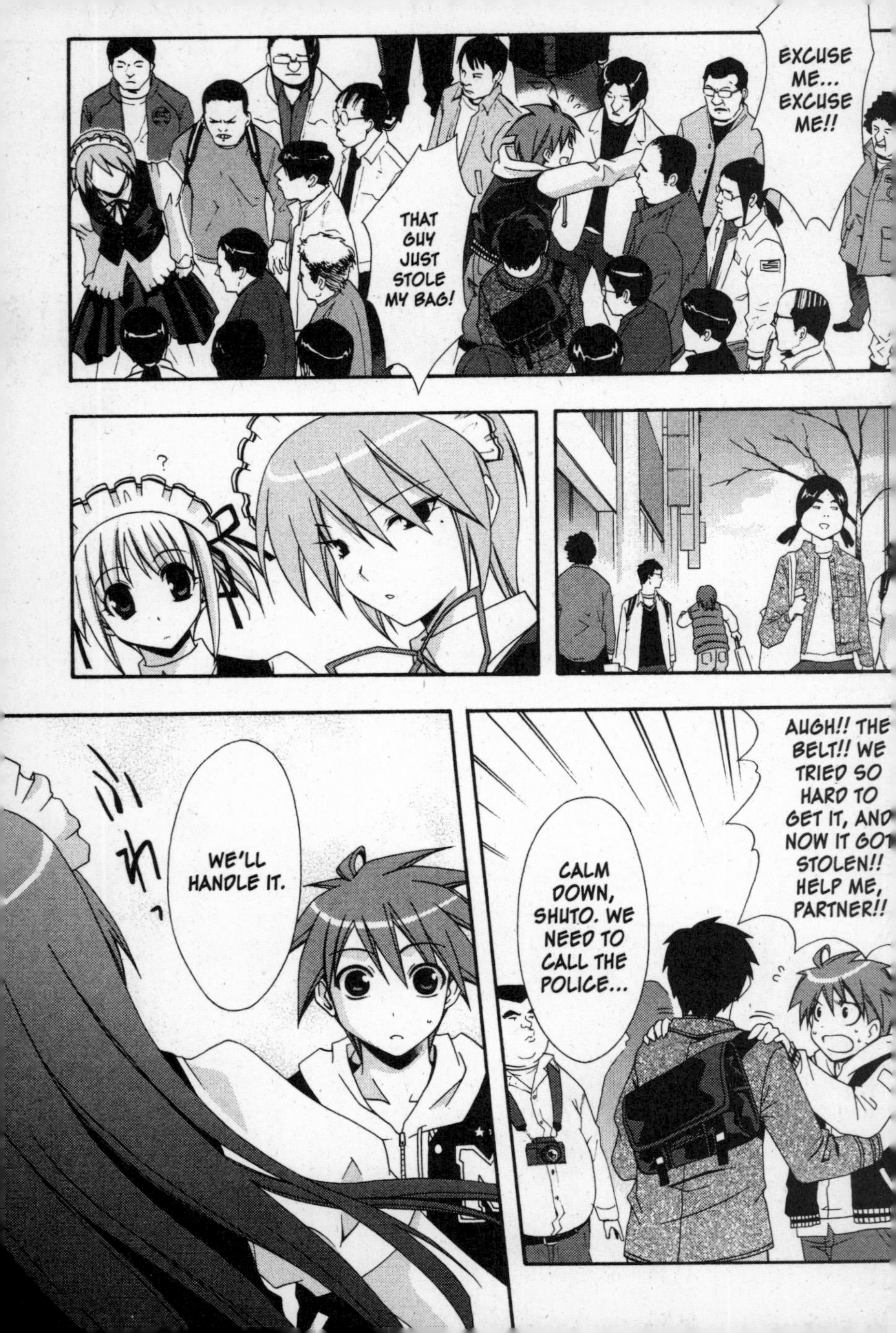
EXCUSE ME... EXCUSE ME!!
THAT GUY JUST STOLE MY BAG!
?
AUGH!! THE BELT!! WE TRIED SO HARD TO GET IT, AND NOW IT GOT STOLEN!! HELP ME, PARTNER!!
CALM DOWN, SHUTO. WE NEED TO CALL THE POLICE...
WE'LL HANDLE IT.

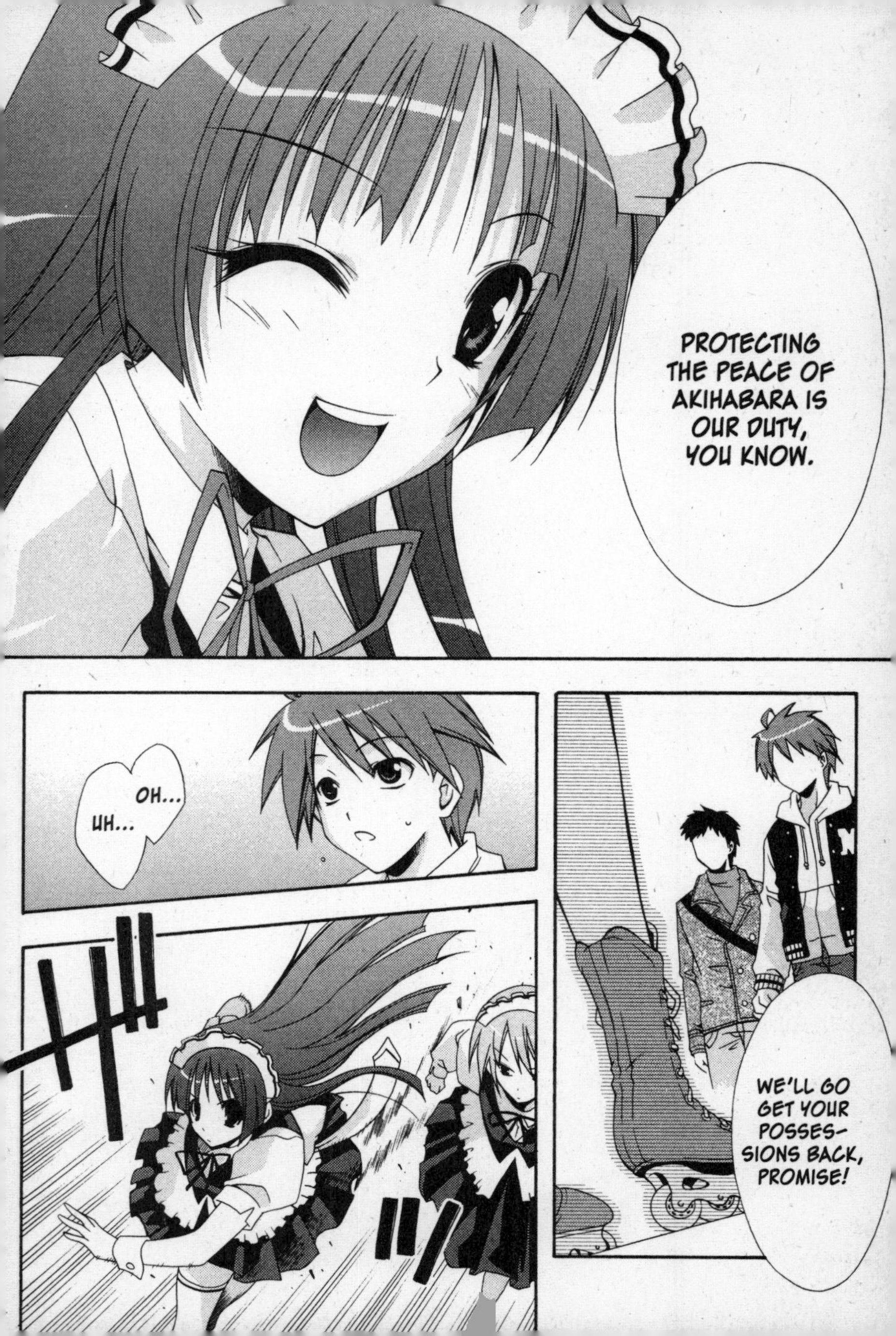
PROTECTING THE PEACE OF AKIHABARA IS OUR DUTY, YOU KNOW.
WE'LL GO GET YOUR POSSES-SIONS BACK, PROMISE!
OH... UH...

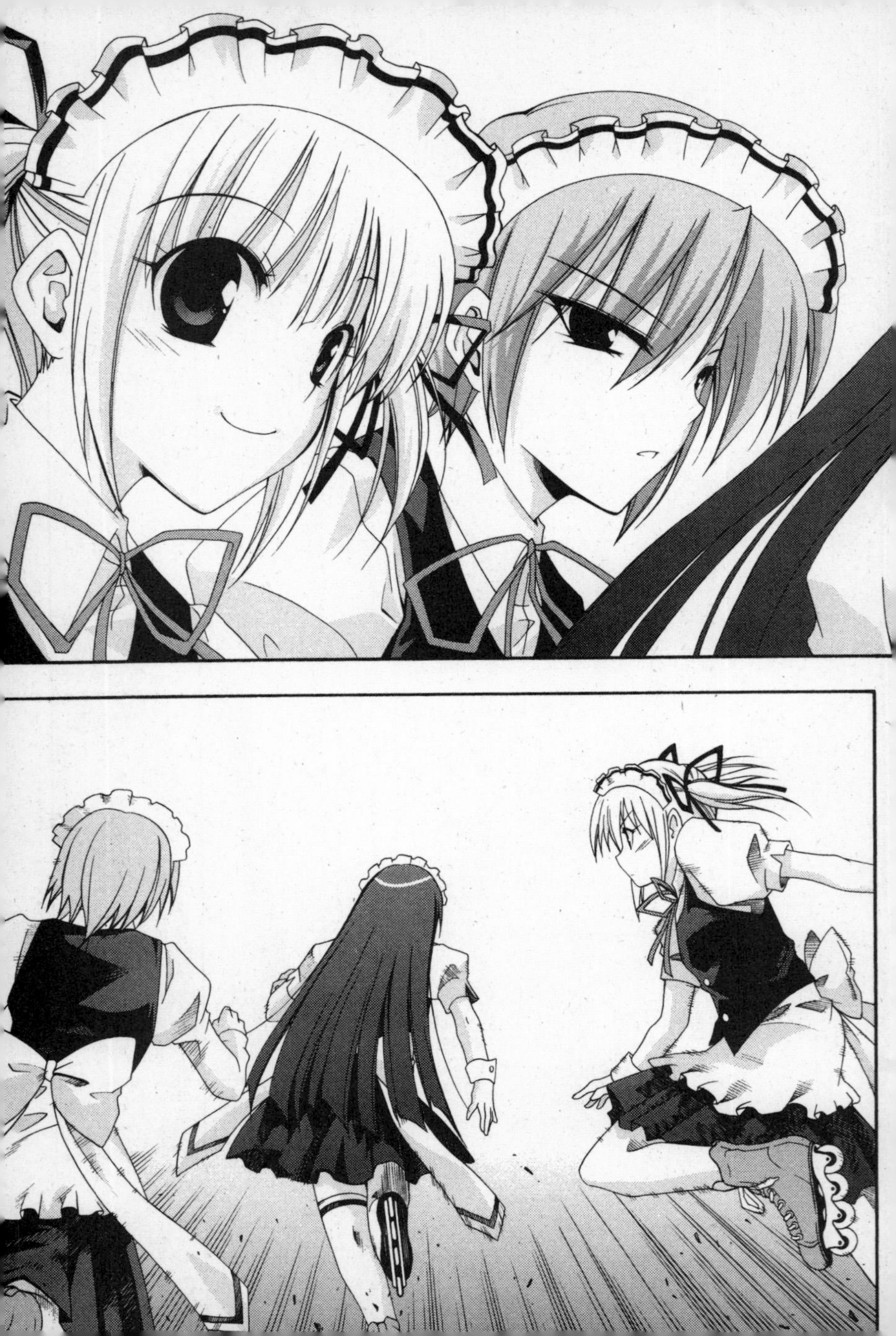

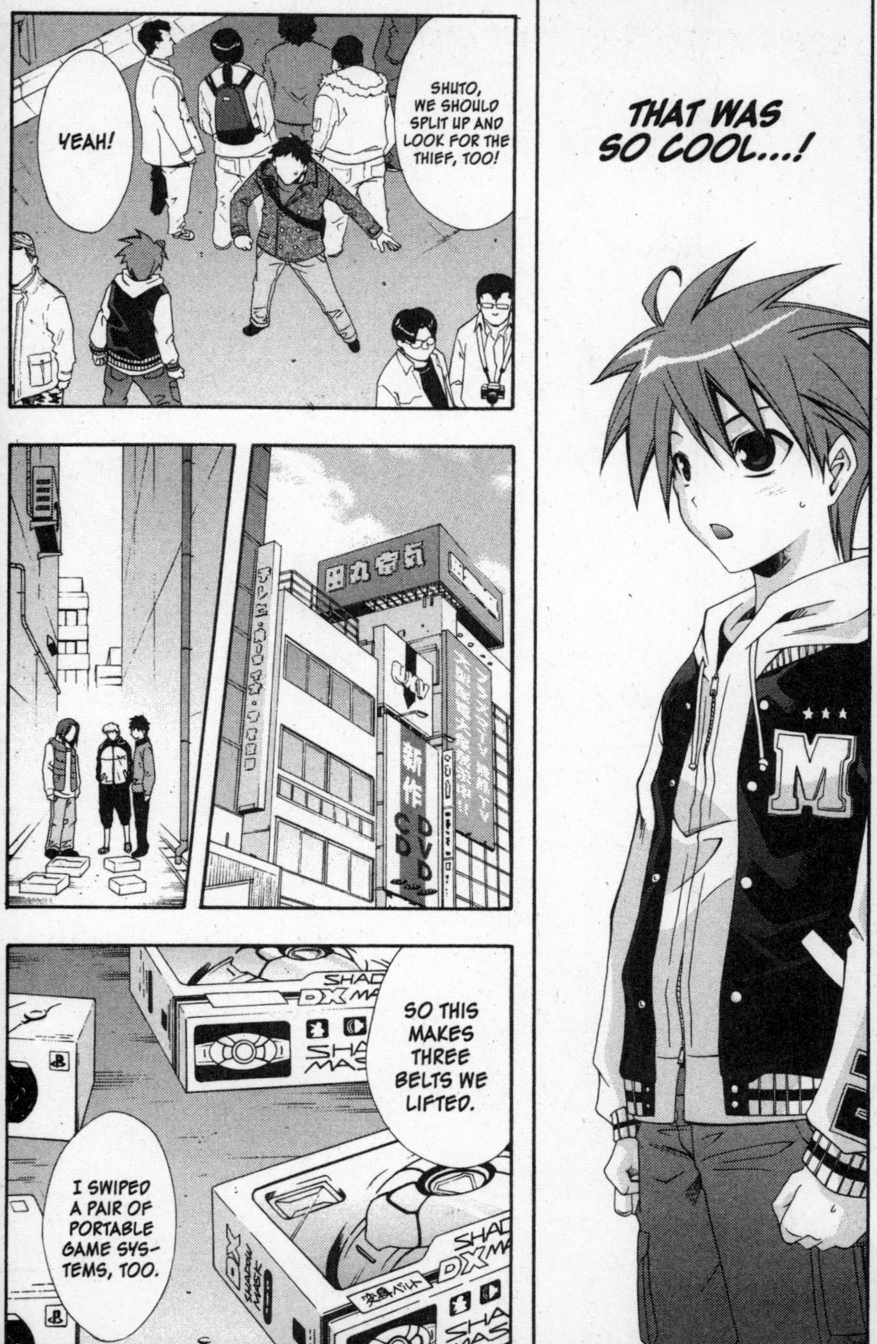
THAT WAS SO COOL...!
SHUTO, WE SHOULD SPLIT UP AND LOOK FOR THE THIEF, TOO!
YEAH!
SO THIS MAKES THREE BELTS WE LIFTED.
I SWIPED A PAIR OF PORTABLE GAME SYS-TEMS, TOO.

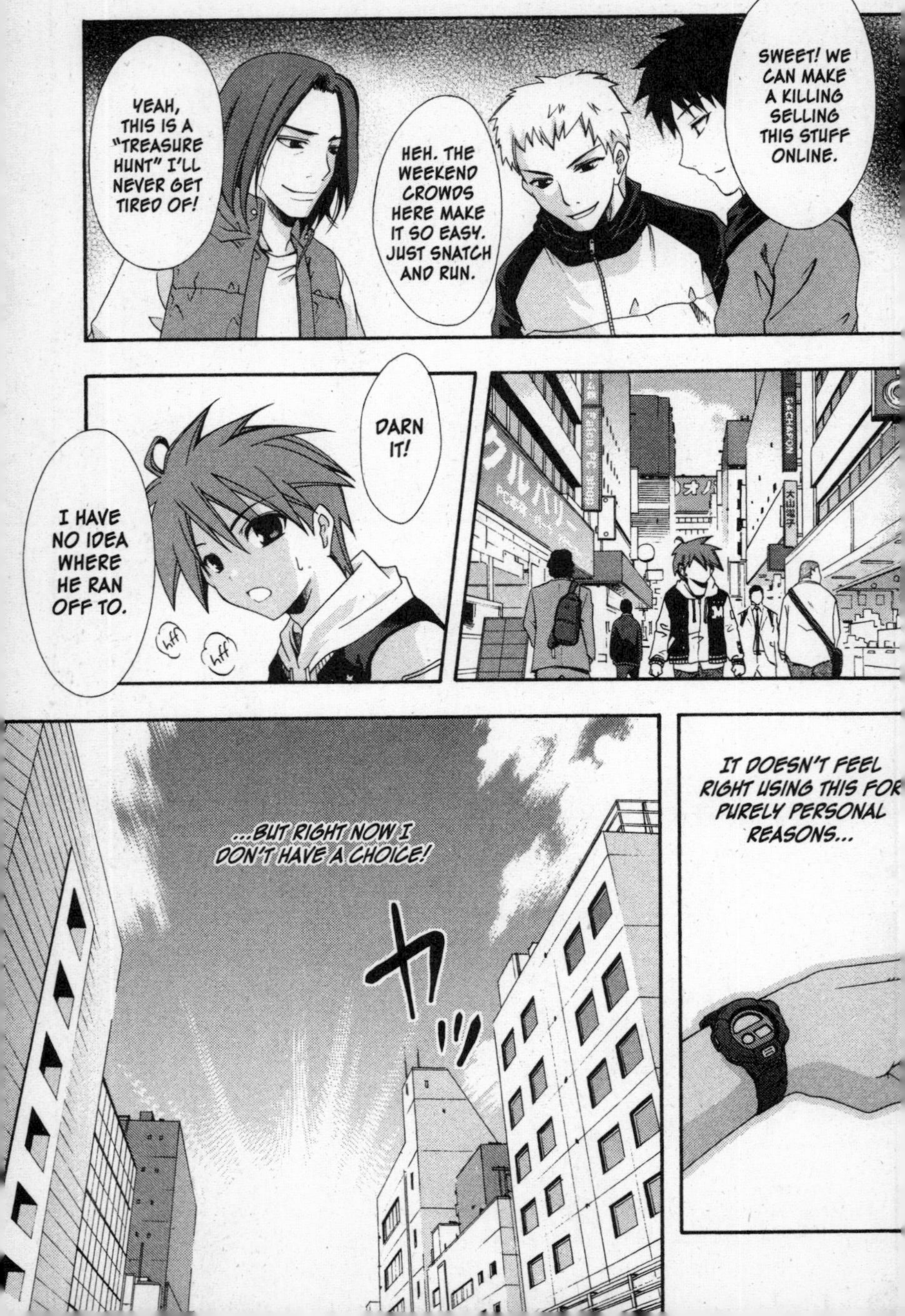
SWEET! WE CAN MAKE A KILLING SELLING THIS STUFF ONLINE.
HEH. THE WEEKEND CROWDS HERE MAKE IT SO EASY. JUST SNATCH AND RUN.
YEAH, THIS IS A "TREASURE HUNT" I'LL NEVER GET TIRED OF!
GACHAPON
DARN IT!
I HAVE NO IDEA WHERE HE RAN OFF TO.
hff
hff
IT DOESN'T FEEL RIGHT USING THIS FOR PURELY PERSONAL REASONS...
...BUT RIGHT NOW I DON'T HAVE A CHOICE!

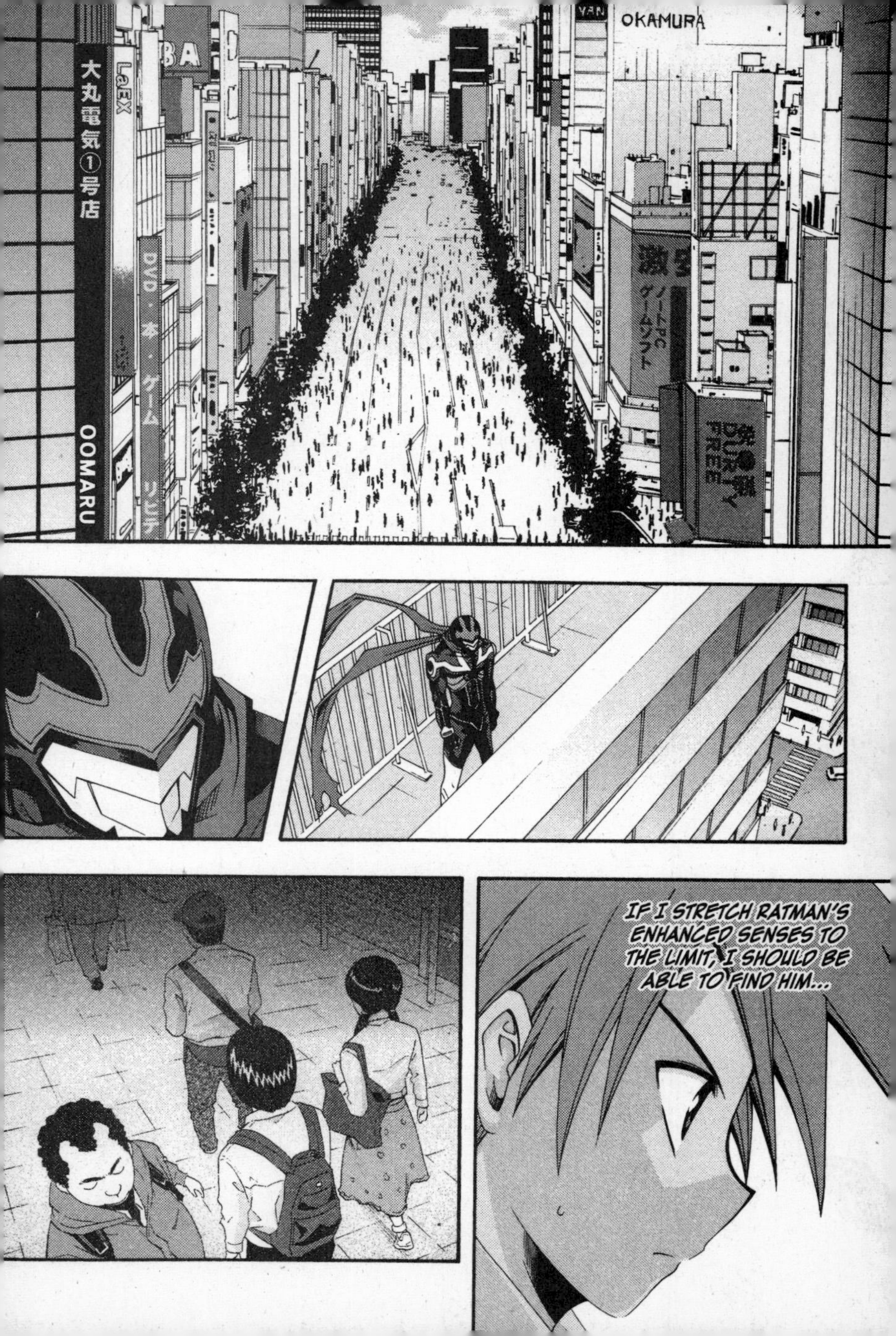
OKAMURA
大丸電気①号店
OOMARU
DVD・本・ゲーム
激多
DUTY FREE
IF I STRETCH RATMAN'S ENHANCED SENSES TO THE LIMIT, I SHOULD BE ABLE TO FIND HIM...

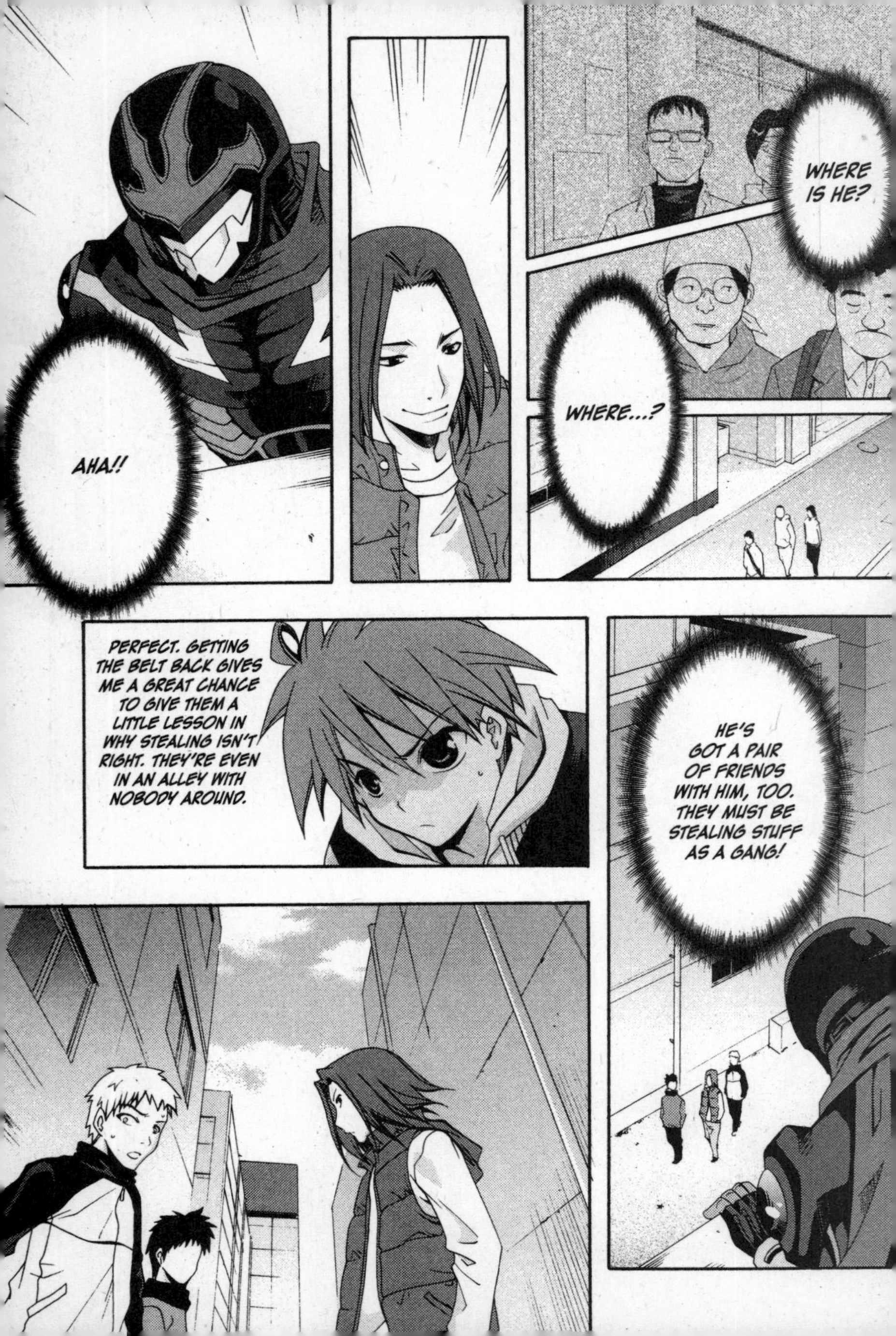
WHERE IS HE?
WHERE...?
AHA!!
HE'S GOT A PAIR OF FRIENDS WITH HIM, TOO. THEY MUST BE STEALING STUFF AS A GANG!
PERFECT. GETTING THE BELT BACK GIVES ME A GREAT CHANCE TO GIVE THEM A LITTLE LESSON IN WHY STEALING ISN'T RIGHT. THEY'RE EVEN IN AN ALLEY WITH NOBODY AROUND.

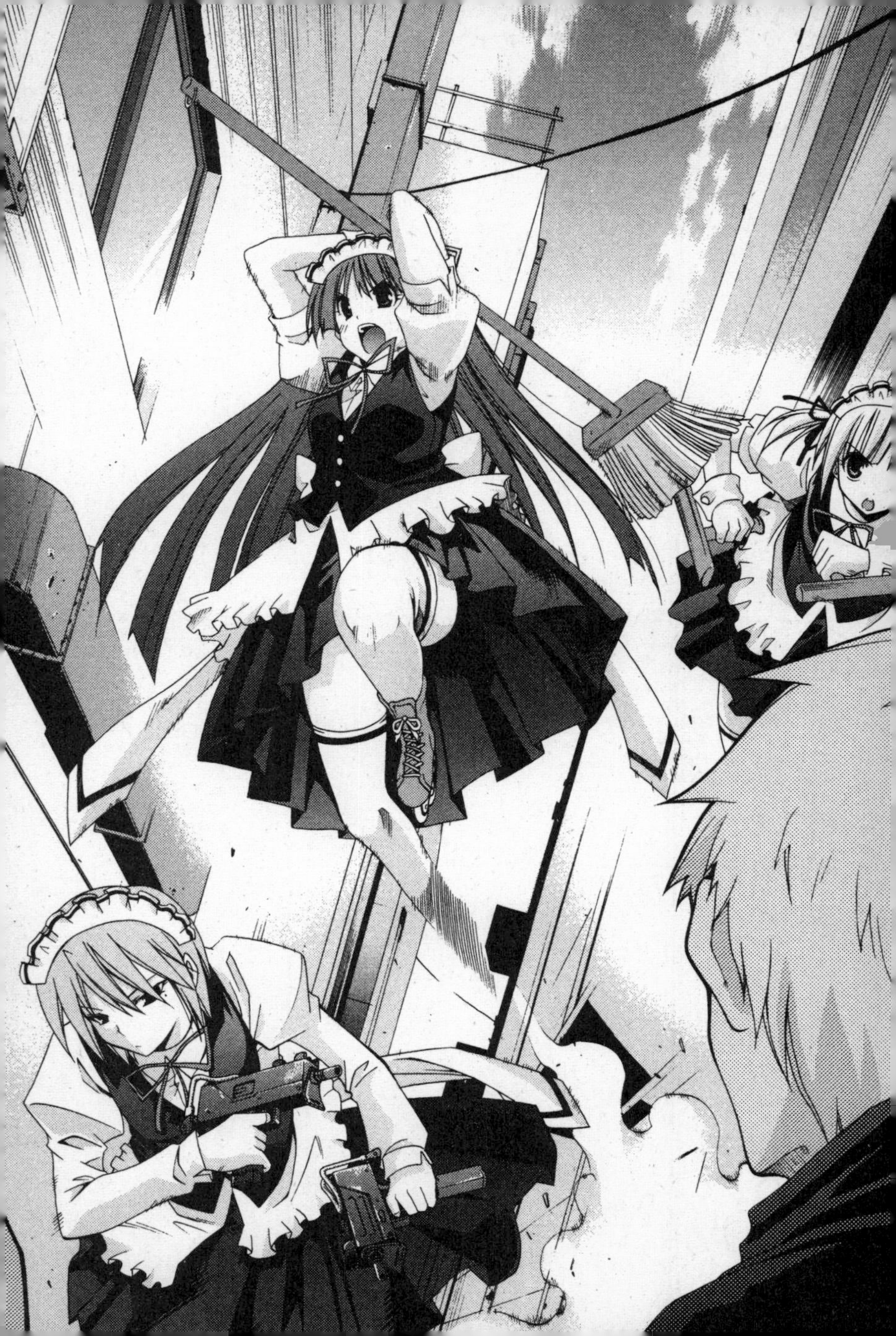

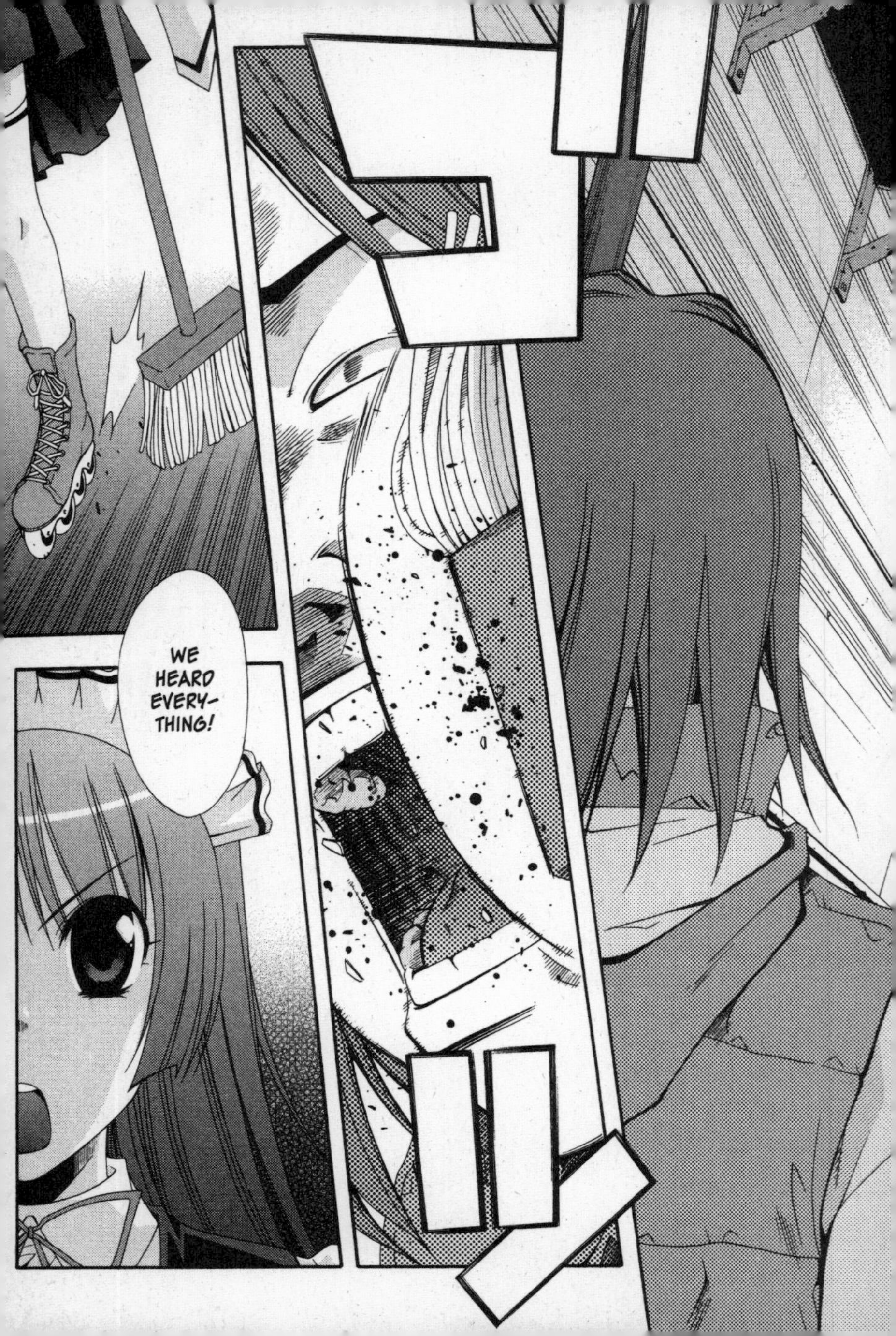
WE HEARD EVERY-THING!

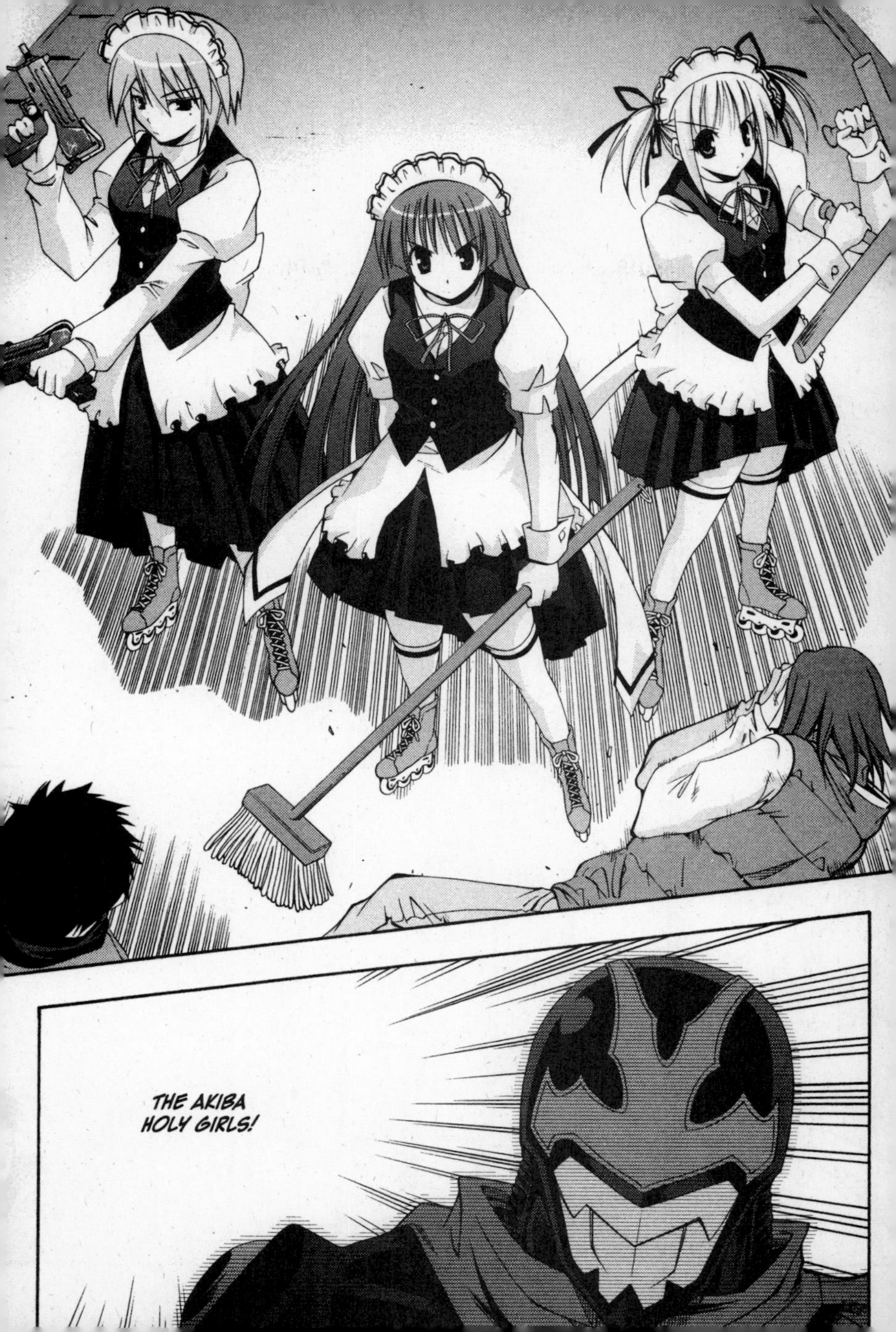
THE AKIBA
HOLY GIRLS!

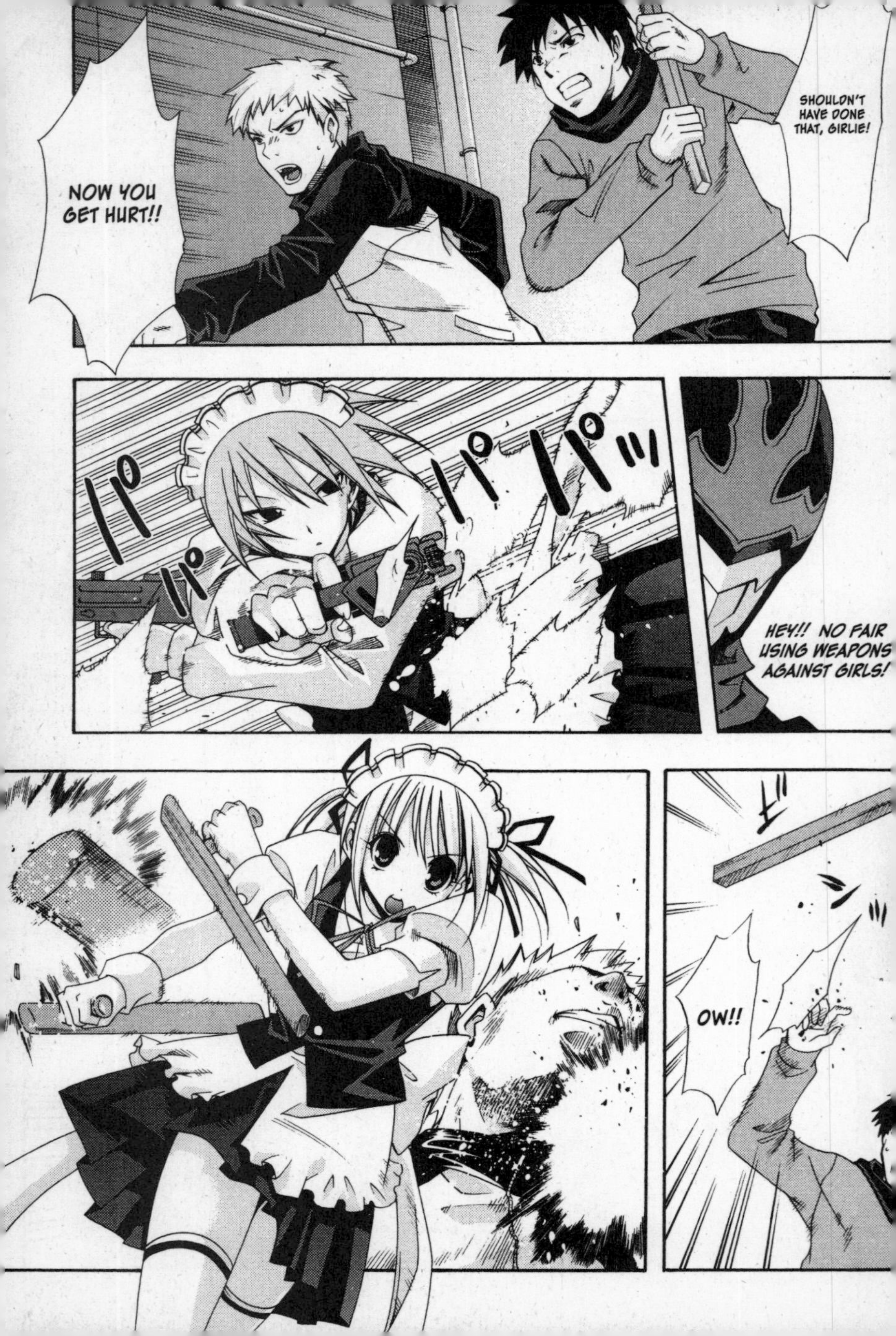
SHOULDN'T HAVE DONE THAT, GIRLIE!
NOW YOU GET HURT!!
HEY!! NO FAIR USING WEAPONS AGAINST GIRLS!
パパッ
パ
パ
パ
ビ
OW!!

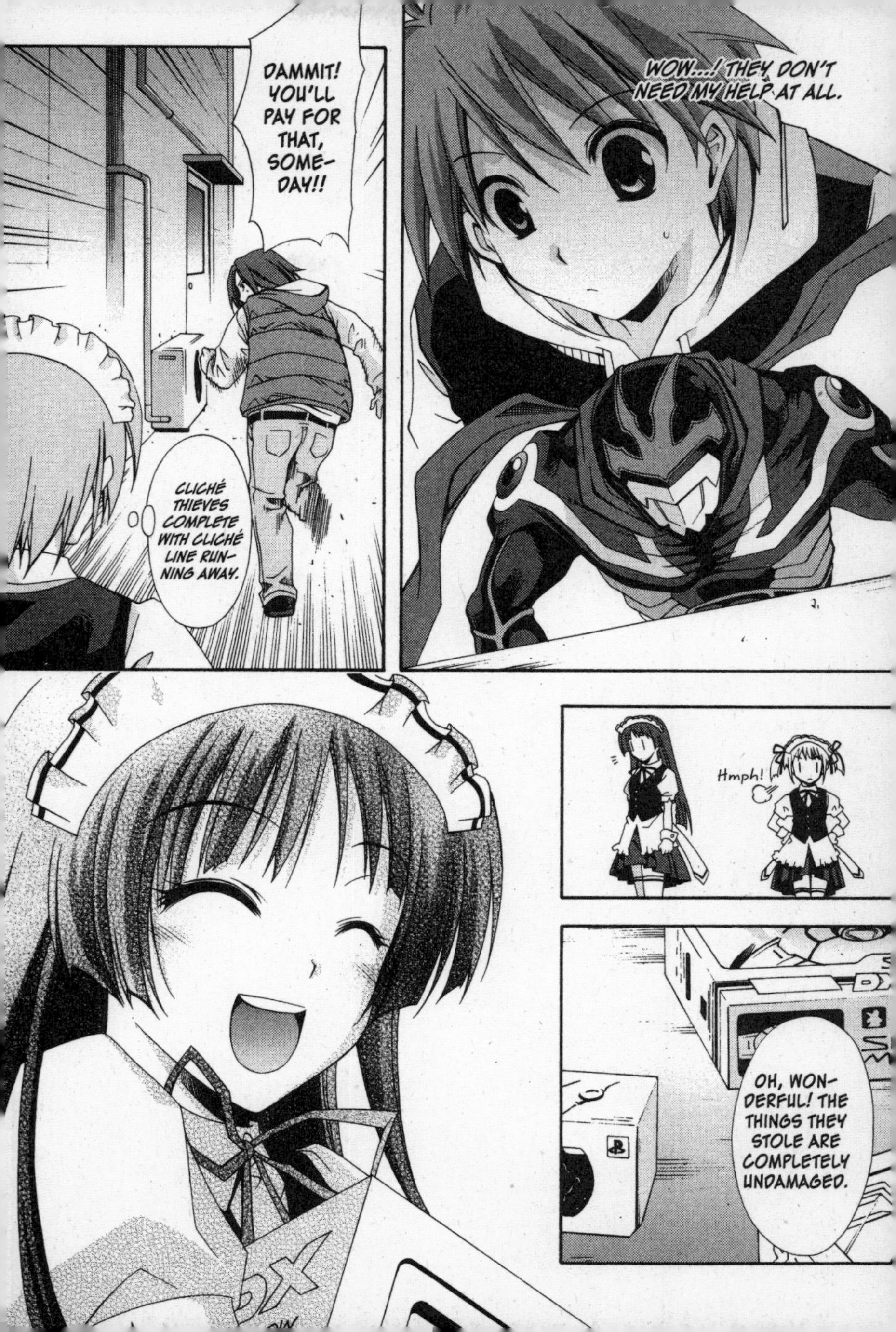
WOW...! THEY DON'T NEED MY HELP AT ALL.
DAMMIT! YOU'LL PAY FOR THAT, SOME-DAY!!
CLICHÉ THIEVES COMPLETE WITH CLICHÉ LINE RUN-NING AWAY.
Hmph!
OH, WON-DERFUL! THE THINGS THEY STOLE ARE COMPLETELY UNDAMAGED.

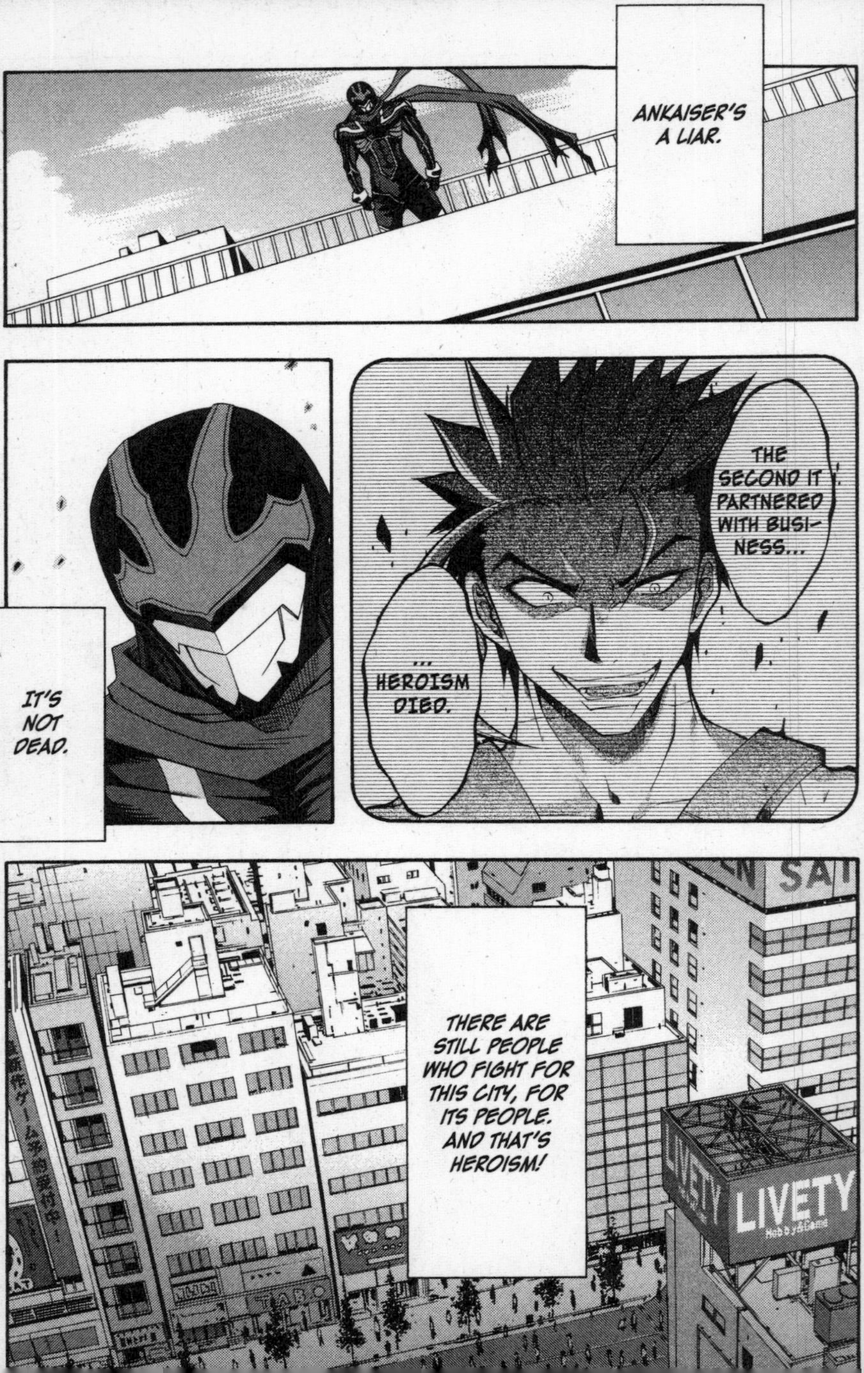
ANKAISER'S A LIAR.
THE SECOND IT PARTNERED WITH BUSI- NESS...
... HEROISM DIED.
IT'S NOT DEAD.
THERE ARE STILL PEOPLE WHO FIGHT FOR THIS CITY, FOR ITS PEOPLE. AND THAT'S HEROISM!
LIVETY
LIVETY

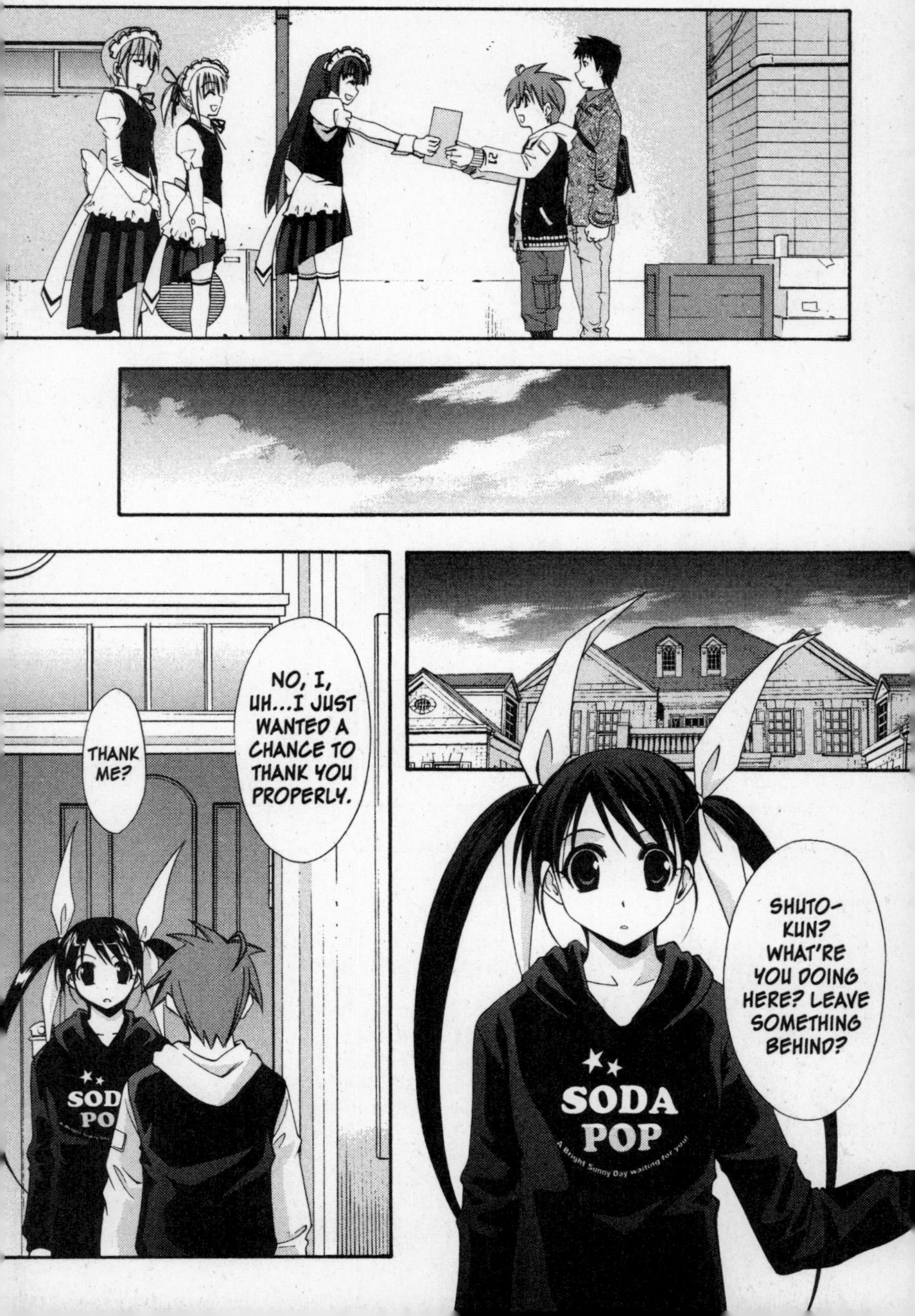
SHUTO-KUN? WHAT'RE YOU DOING HERE? LEAVE SOMETHING BEHIND?
SODA POP
A Bright Sunny Day waiting for you!
NO, I, UH...I JUST WANTED A CHANCE TO THANK YOU PROPERLY.
THANK ME?

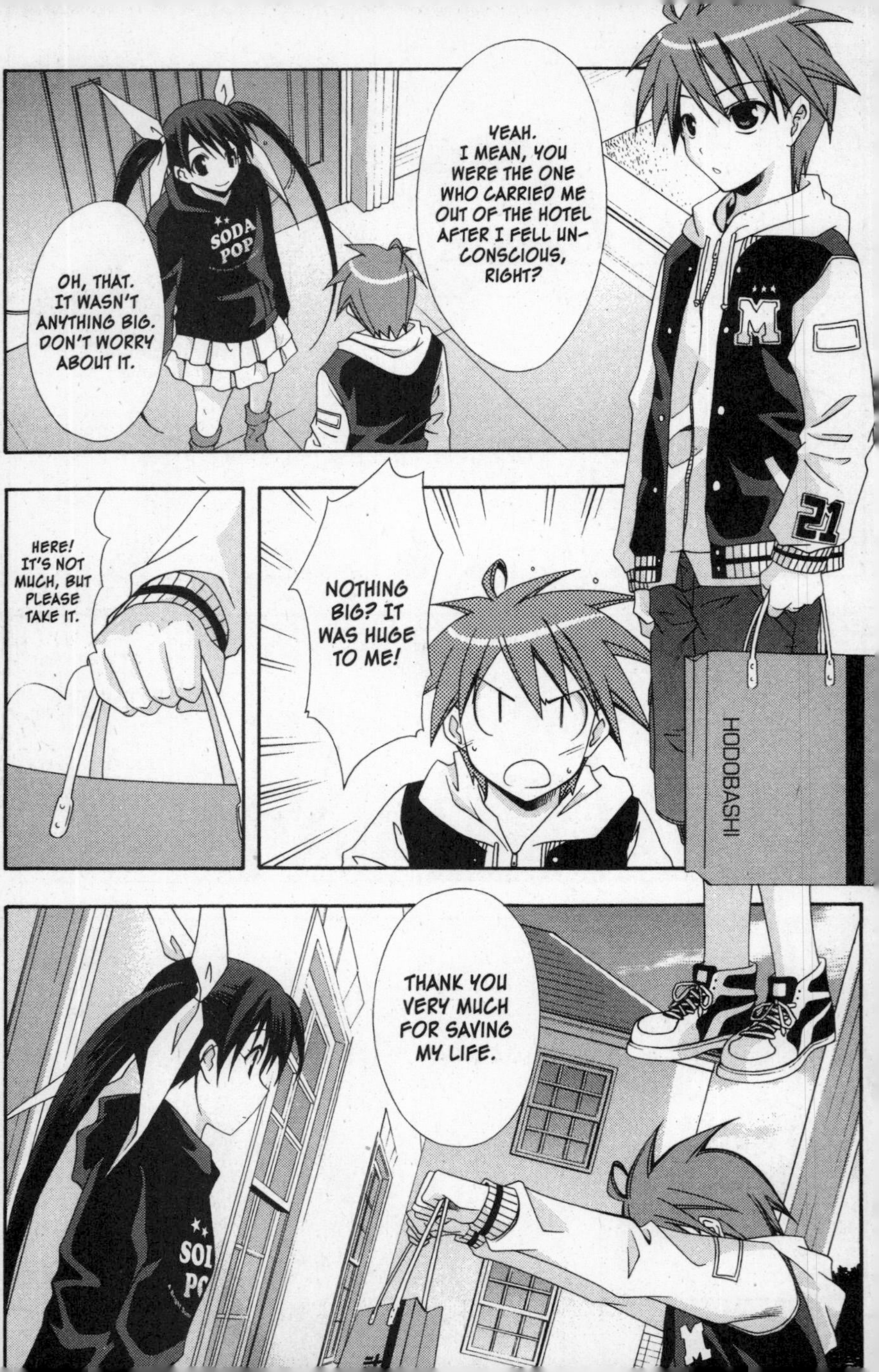
YEAH. I MEAN, YOU WERE THE ONE WHO CARRIED ME OUT OF THE HOTEL AFTER I FELL UN-CONSCIOUS, RIGHT?
OH, THAT. IT WASN'T ANYTHING BIG. DON'T WORRY ABOUT IT.
SODA POP
HODOBASHI
NOTHING BIG? IT WAS HUGE TO ME!
HERE! IT'S NOT MUCH, BUT PLEASE TAKE IT.
THANK YOU VERY MUCH FOR SAVING MY LIFE.

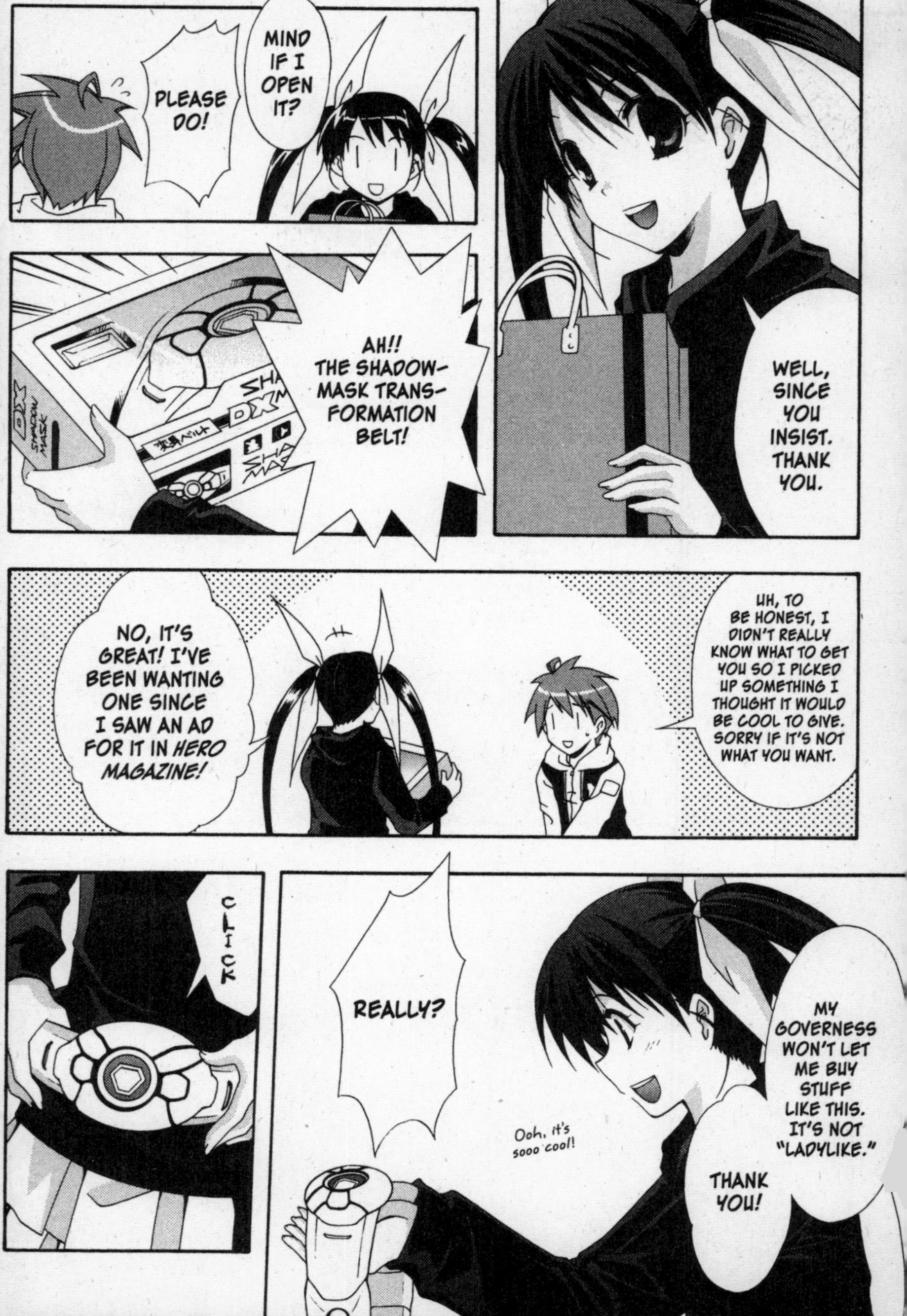
WELL, SINCE YOU INSIST. THANK YOU.
MIND IF I OPEN IT?
PLEASE DO!
AH!! THE SHADOW-MASK TRANS-FORMATION BELT!
UH, TO BE HONEST, I DIDN'T REALLY KNOW WHAT TO GET YOU SO I PICKED UP SOMETHING I THOUGHT IT WOULD BE COOL TO GIVE. SORRY IF IT'S NOT WHAT YOU WANT.
NO, IT'S GREAT! I'VE BEEN WANTING ONE SINCE I SAW AN AD FOR IT IN *HERO MAGAZINE*!
MY GOVERNESS WON'T LET ME BUY STUFF LIKE THIS. IT'S NOT "LADYLIKE."
THANK YOU!
Ooh, it's sooo cool!
REALLY?
CLICK

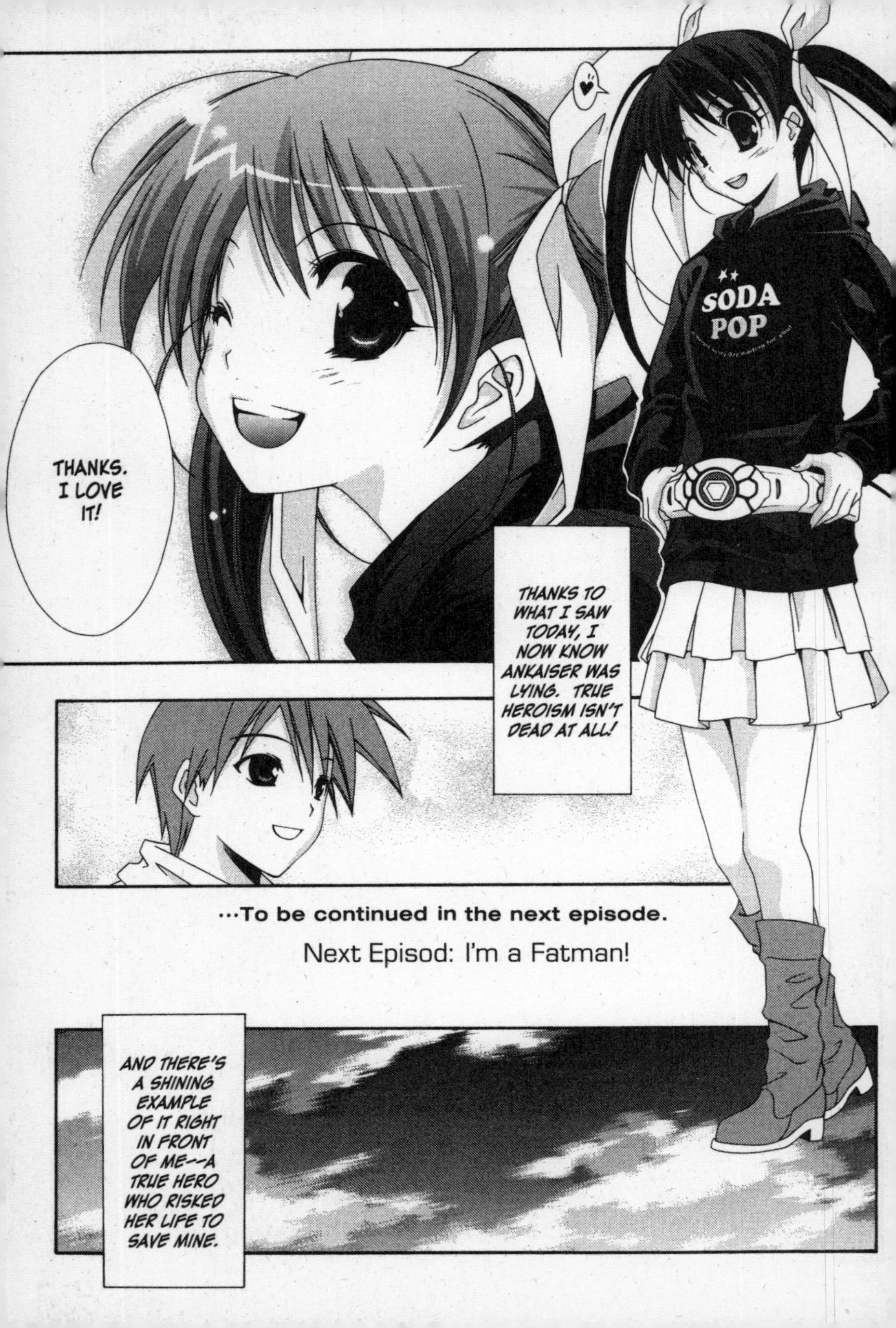
THANKS. I LOVE IT!
SODA POP
THANKS TO WHAT I SAW TODAY, I NOW KNOW ANKAISER WAS LYING. TRUE HEROISM ISN'T DEAD AT ALL!
...To be continued in the next episode.
Next Episod: I'm a Fatman!
AND THERE'S A SHINING EXAMPLE OF IT RIGHT IN FRONT OF ME--A TRUE HERO WHO RISKED HER LIFE TO SAVE MINE.

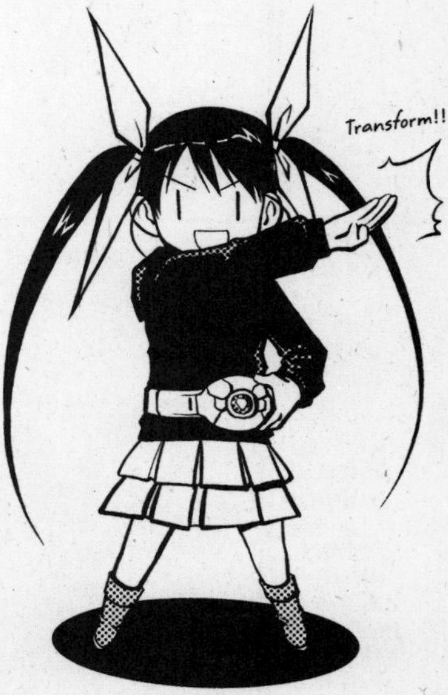
Transform!!

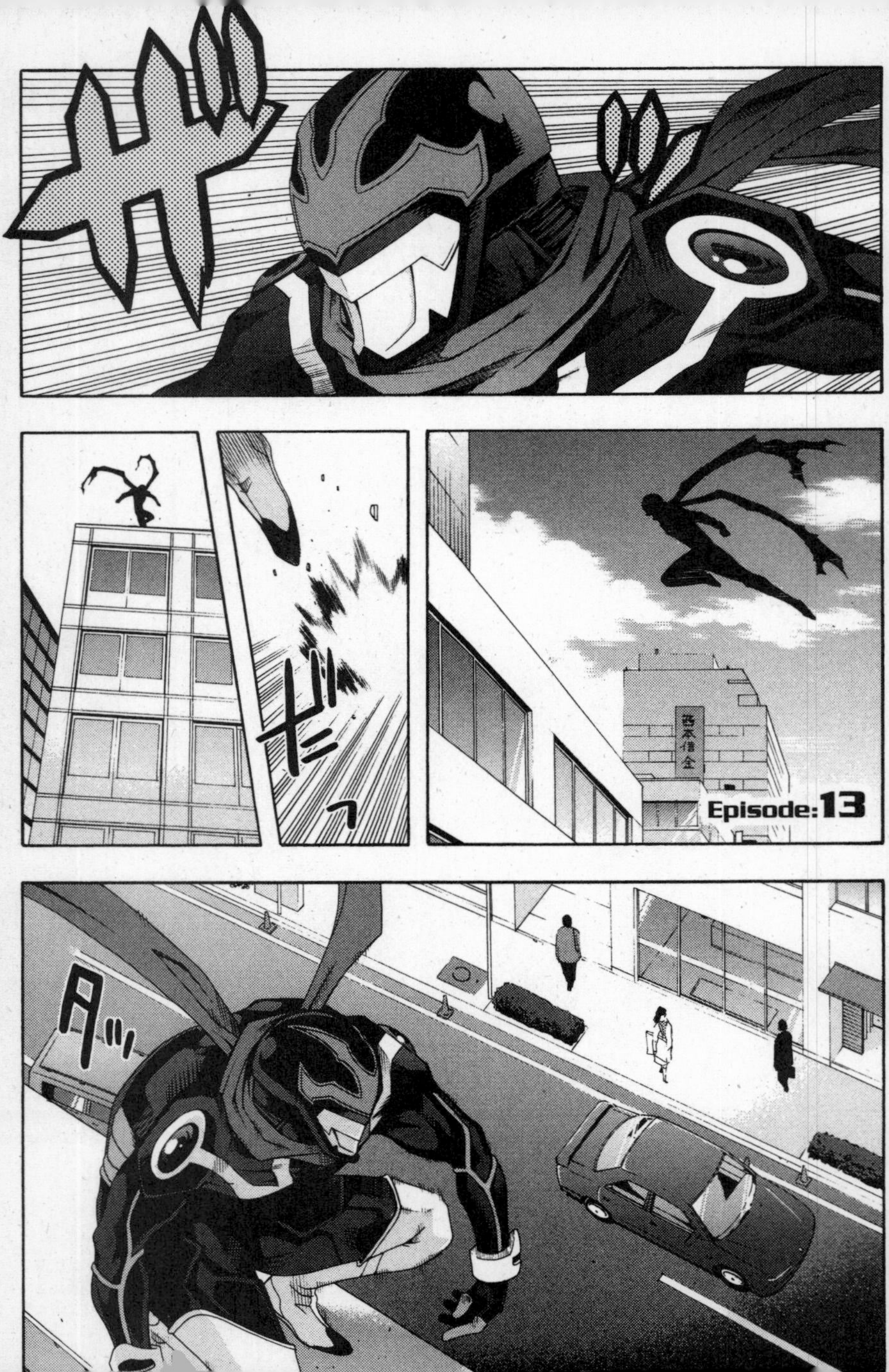
Episode:13

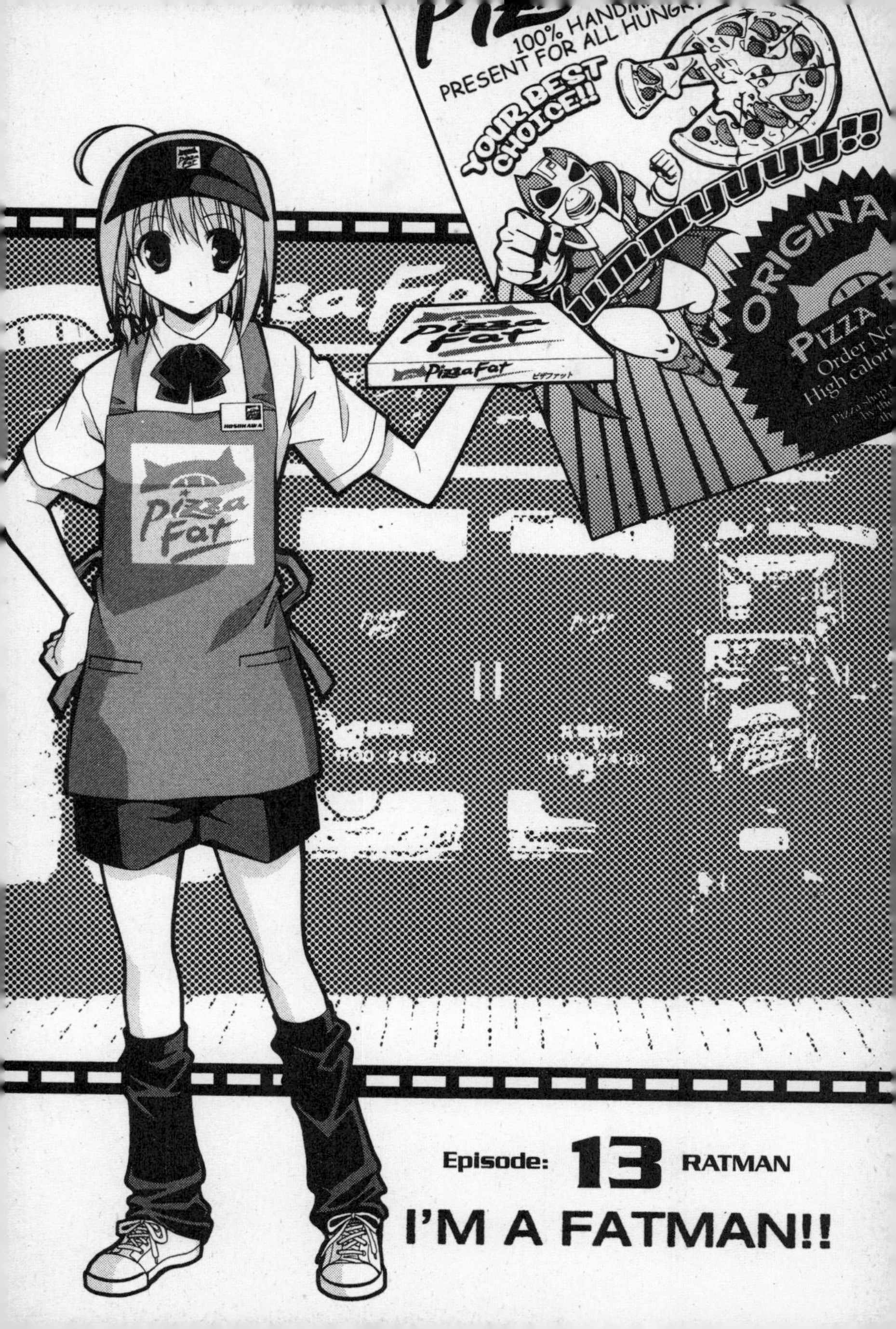
YOUR BEST CHOICE!!
Pizza Fat
Pizza Fat
ピザファット
Pizza Fat

Episode: 13 RATMAN

I'M A FATMAN!!

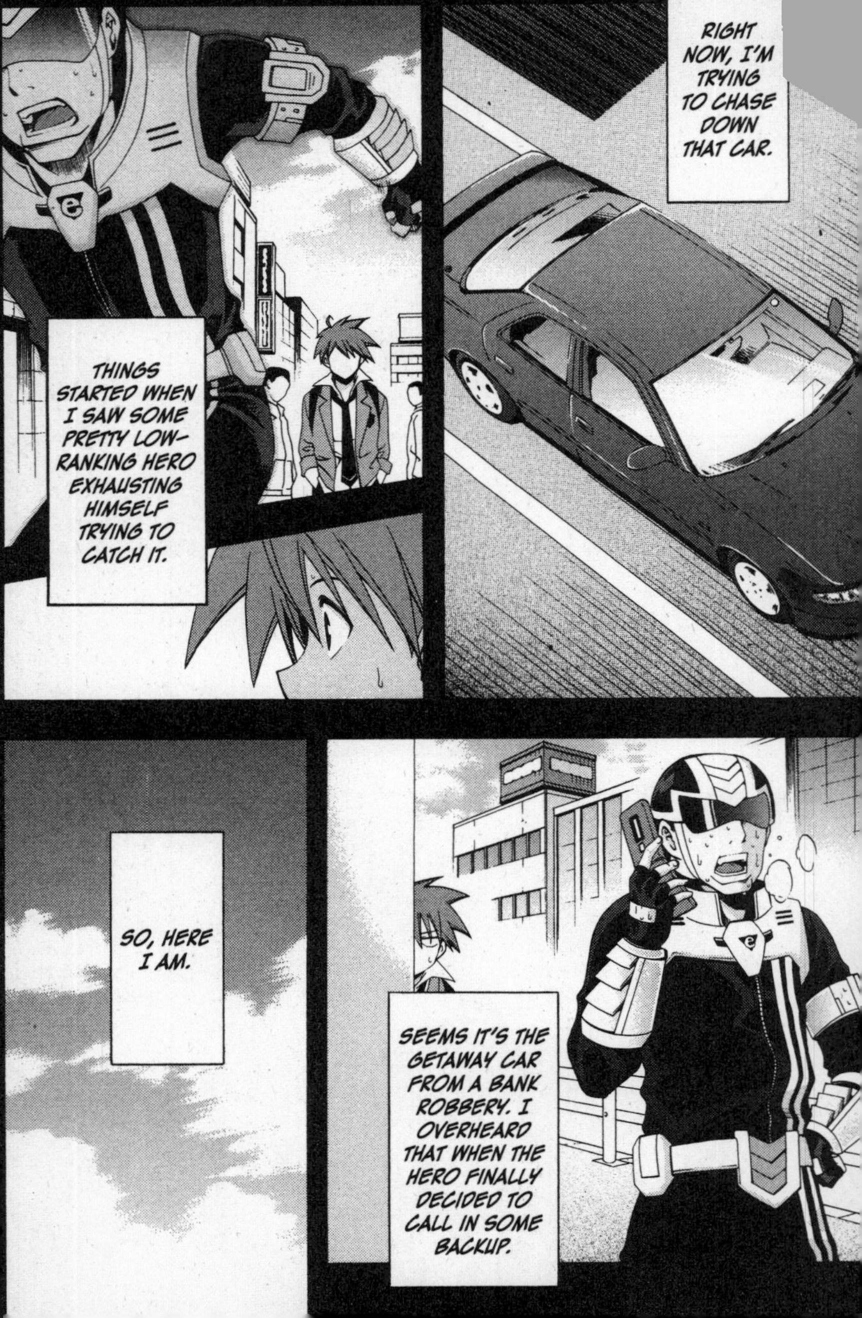
RIGHT NOW, I'M TRYING TO CHASE DOWN THAT CAR.
THINGS STARTED WHEN I SAW SOME PRETTY LOW-RANKING HERO EXHAUSTING HIMSELF TRYING TO CATCH IT.
SEEMS IT'S THE GETAWAY CAR FROM A BANK ROBBERY. I OVERHEARD THAT WHEN THE HERO FINALLY DECIDED TO CALL IN SOME BACKUP.
SO, HERE I AM.

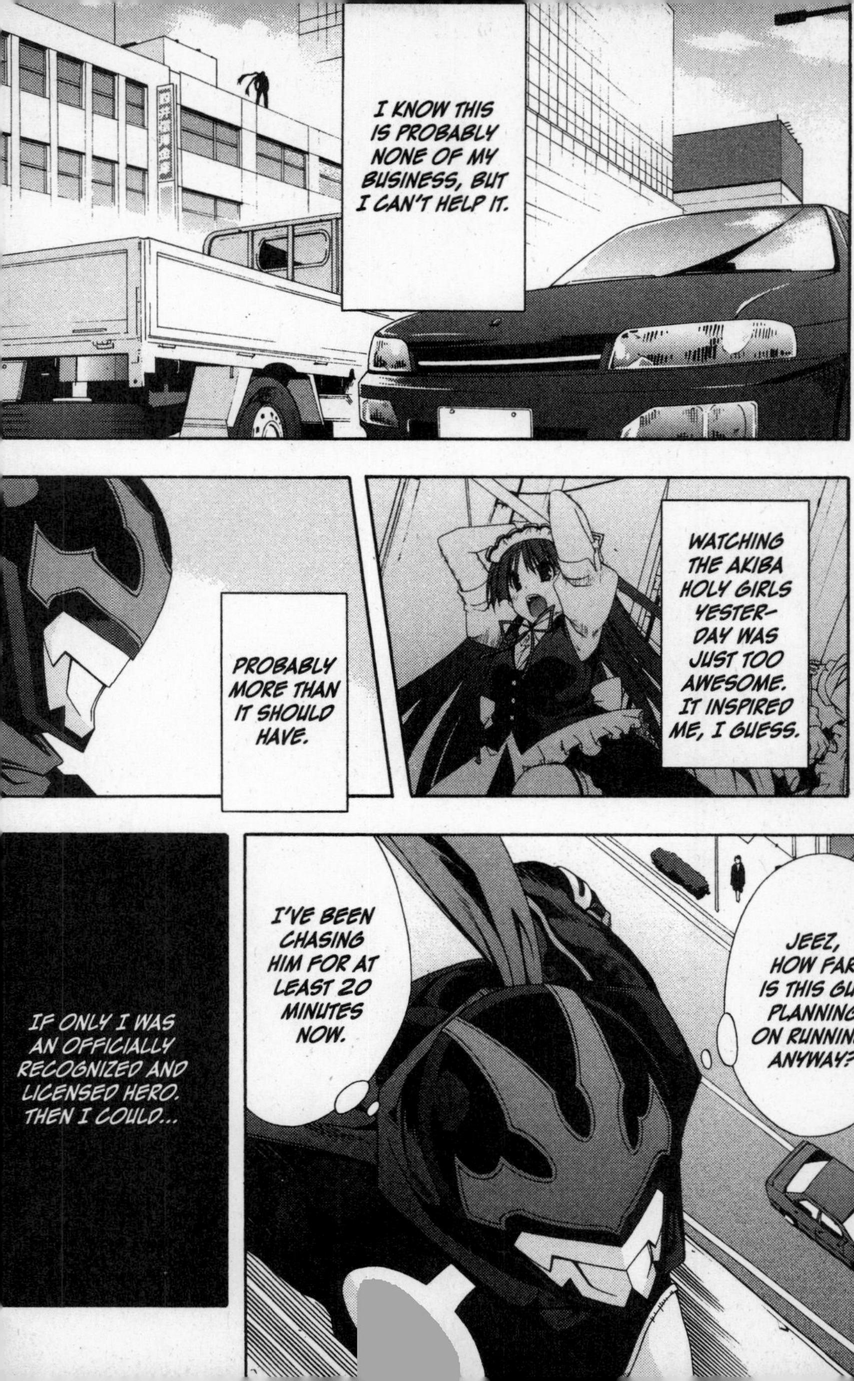
I KNOW THIS IS PROBABLY NONE OF MY BUSINESS, BUT I CAN'T HELP IT.
WATCHING THE AKIBA HOLY GIRLS YESTER-DAY WAS JUST TOO AWESOME. IT INSPIRED ME, I GUESS.
PROBABLY MORE THAN IT SHOULD HAVE.
JEEZ, HOW FAR IS THIS GUY PLANNING ON RUNNING, ANYWAY?
I'VE BEEN CHASING HIM FOR AT LEAST 20 MINUTES NOW.
IF ONLY I WAS AN OFFICIALLY RECOGNIZED AND LICENSED HERO. THEN I COULD...

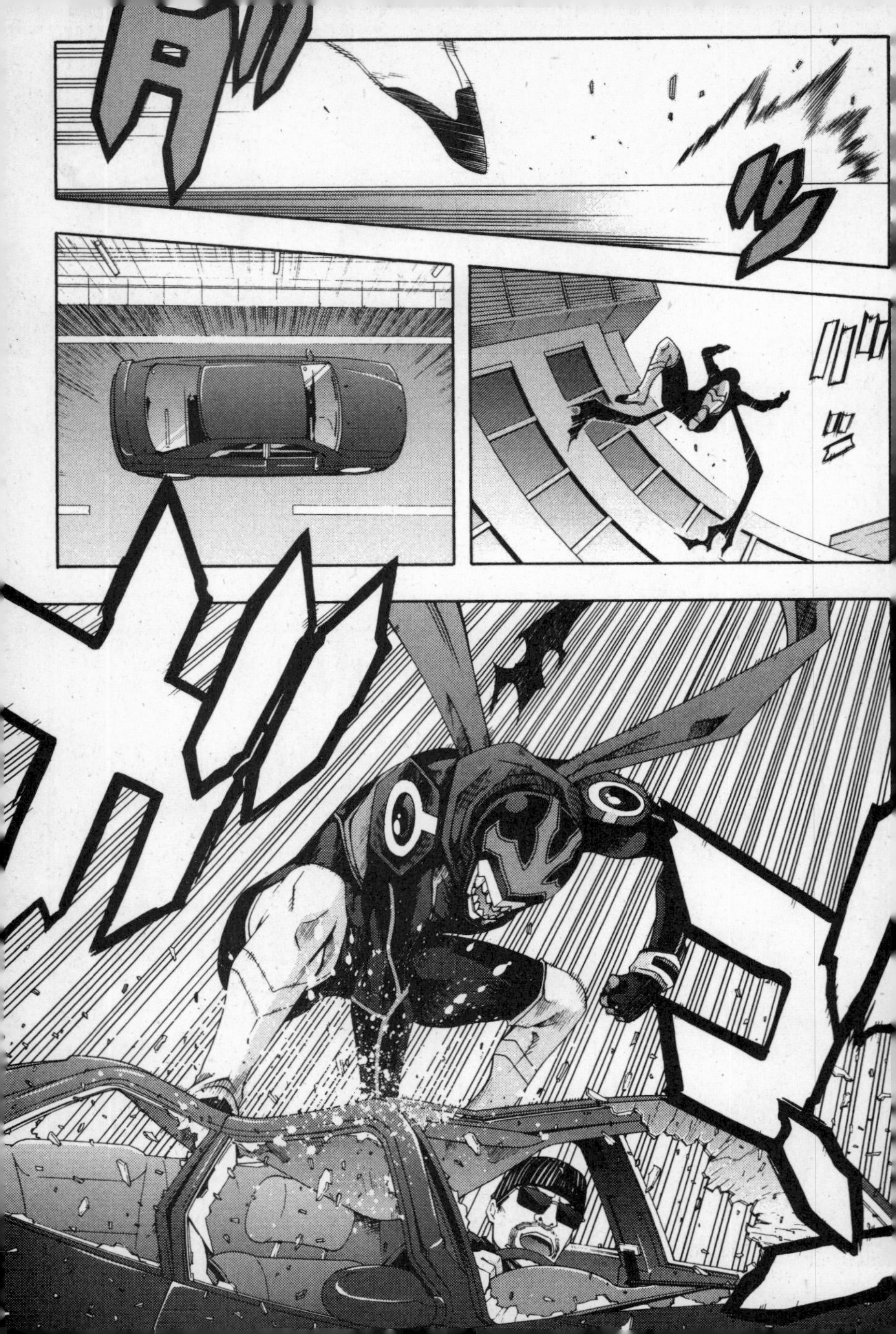
ダッ

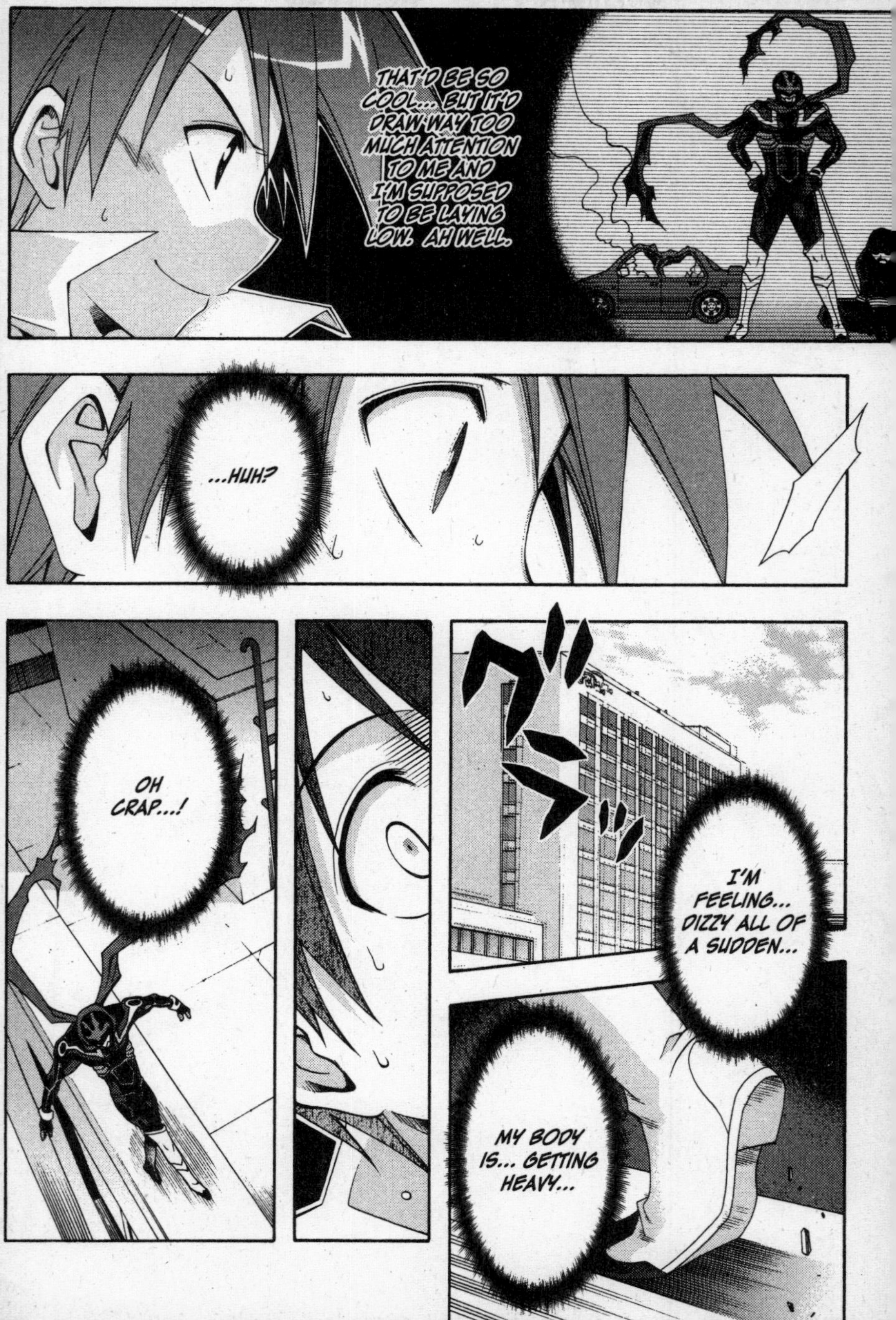
THAT'D BE SO COOL... BUT IT'D DRAW WAY TOO MUCH ATTENTION TO ME AND I'M SUPPOSED TO BE LAYING LOW. AH WELL.
...HUH?
I'M FEELING... DIZZY ALL OF A SUDDEN...
MY BODY IS... GETTING HEAVY...
OH CRAP...!

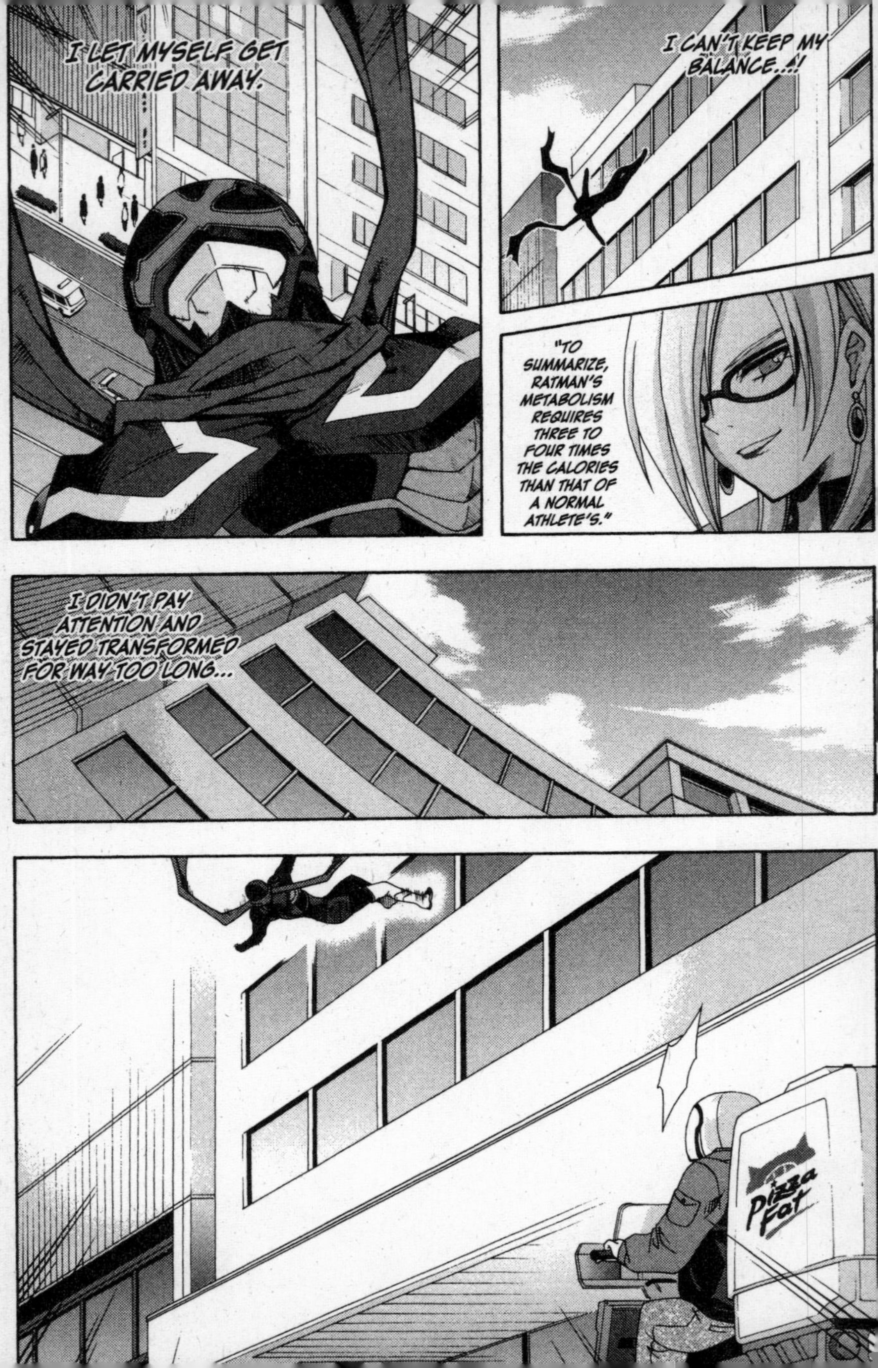
I CAN'T KEEP MY BALANCE...!
"TO SUMMARIZE, RATMAN'S METABOLISM REQUIRES THREE TO FOUR TIMES THE CALORIES THAN THAT OF A NORMAL ATHLETE'S."
I LET MYSELF GET CARRIED AWAY.
I DIDN'T PAY ATTENTION AND STAYED TRANSFORMED FOR WAY TOO LONG...
Pizza Fat

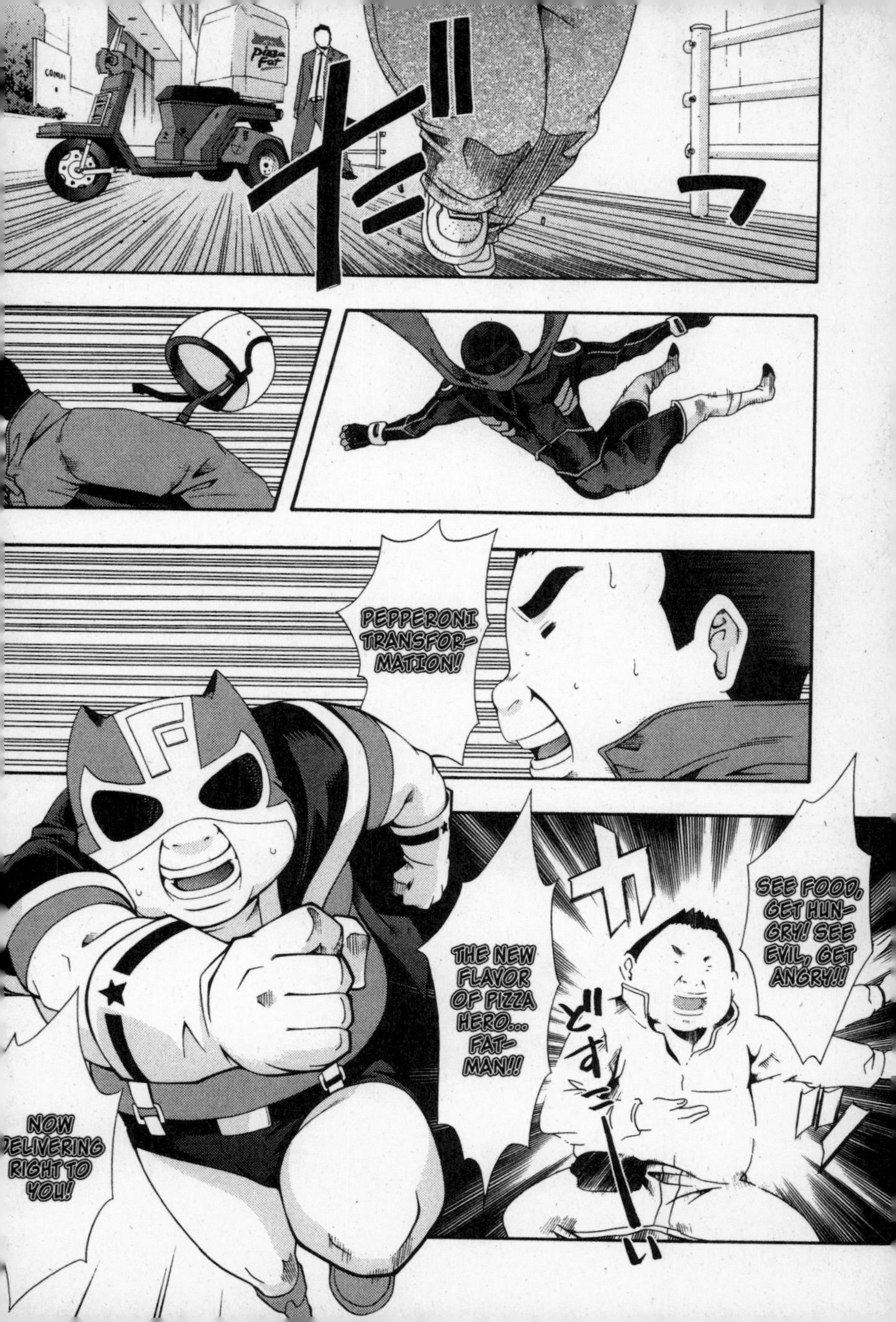
Pizza Fat
PEPPERONI TRANSFOR-MATION!
SEE FOOD, GET HUN-GRY! SEE EVIL, GET ANGRY!!
THE NEW FLAVOR OF PIZZA HERO... FAT-MAN!!
どすーい
NOW DELIVERING RIGHT TO YOU!

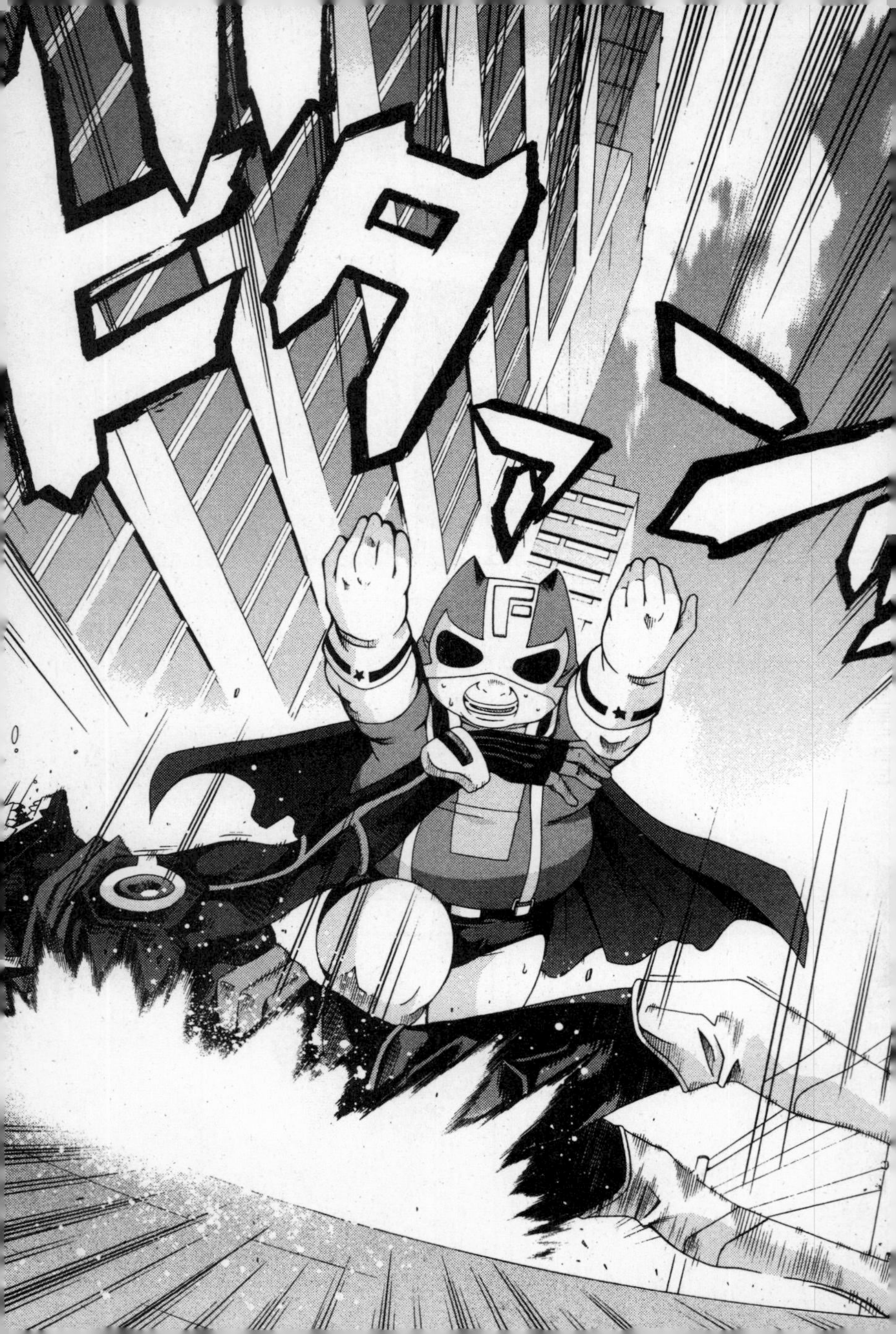

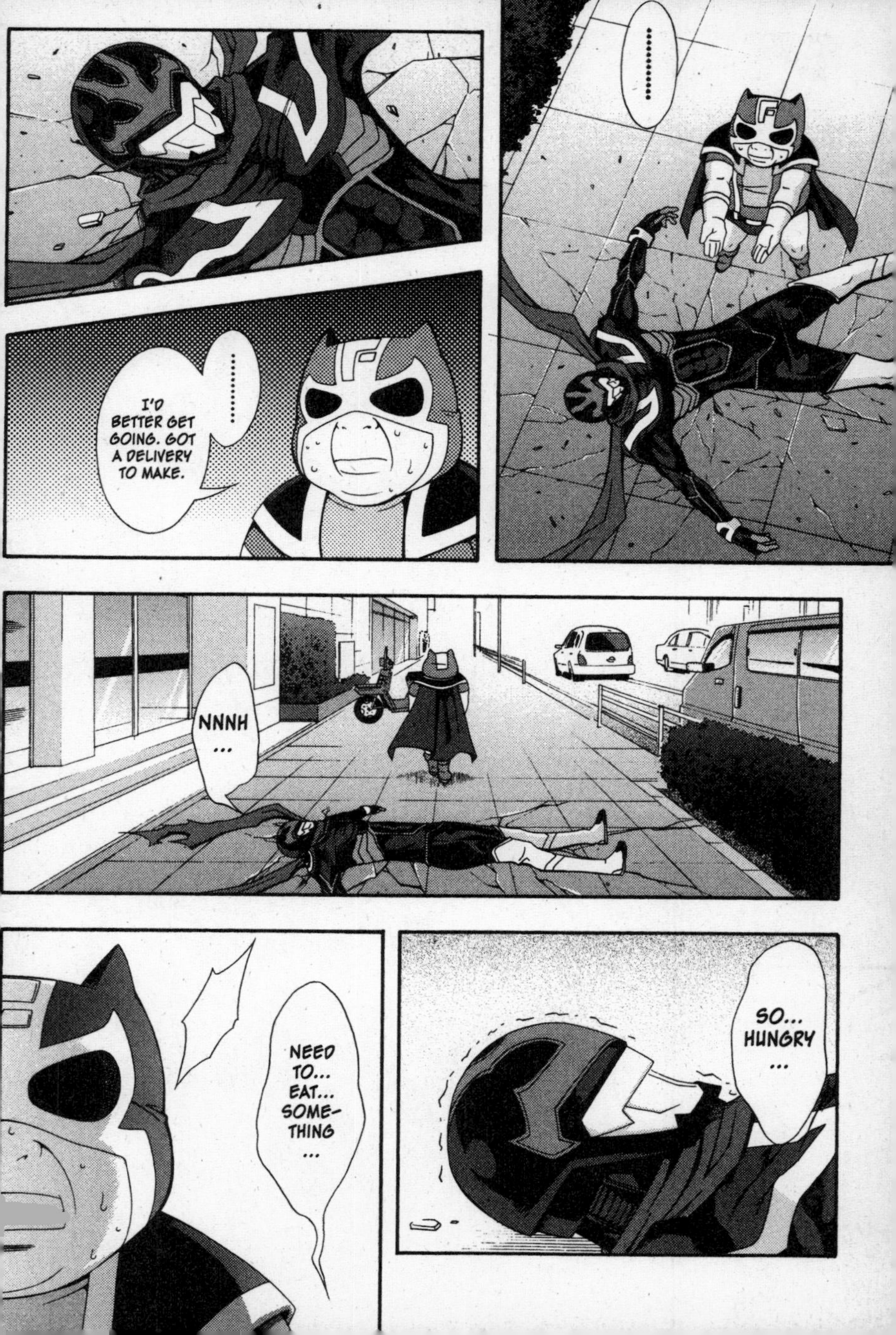
....
......
I'D BETTER GET GOING. GOT A DELIVERY TO MAKE.
NNNH ...
SO... HUNGRY ...
NEED TO... EAT... SOME-THING ...

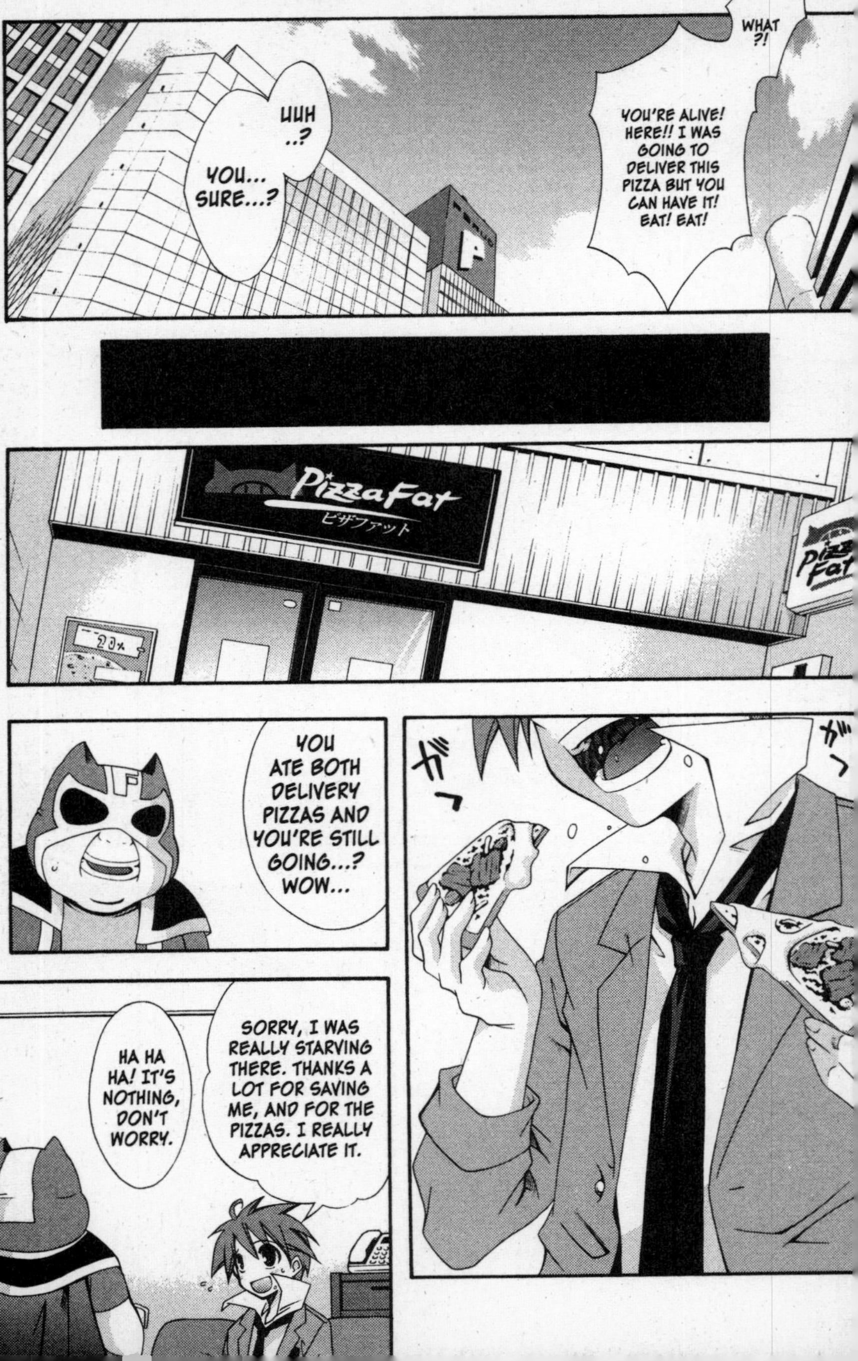
WHAT ?!
YOU'RE ALIVE! HERE!! I WAS GOING TO DELIVER THIS PIZZA BUT YOU CAN HAVE IT! EAT! EAT!
UUH ..? YOU... SURE...?
[redacted]
PizzaFat
ピザファット
20%
ガツ
ガツ
YOU ATE BOTH DELIVERY PIZZAS AND YOU'RE STILL GOING...? WOW...
SORRY, I WAS REALLY STARVING THERE. THANKS A LOT FOR SAVING ME, AND FOR THE PIZZAS. I REALLY APPRECIATE IT.
HA HA HA! IT'S NOTHING, DON'T WORRY.

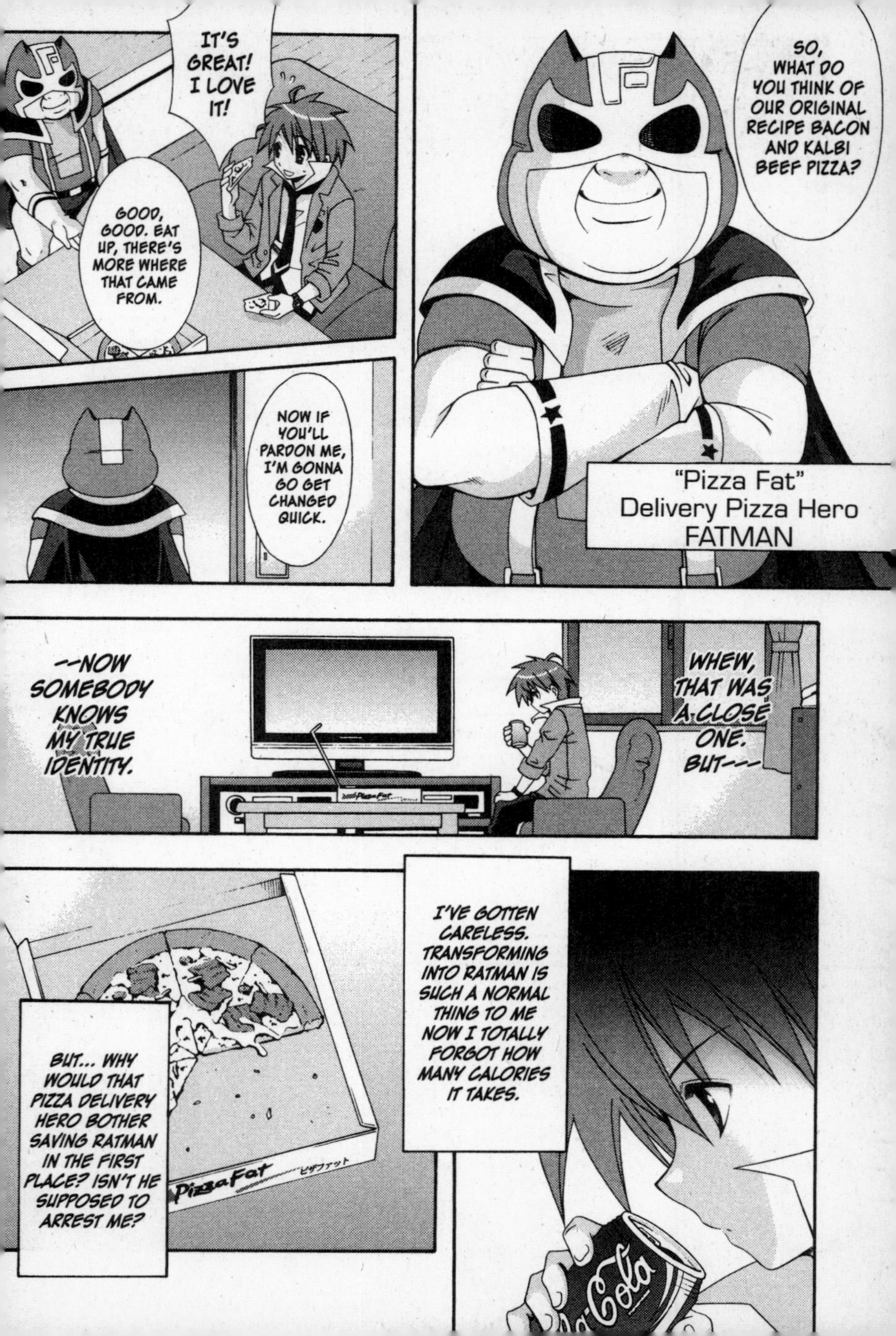
SO, WHAT DO YOU THINK OF OUR ORIGINAL RECIPE BACON AND KALBI BEEF PIZZA?
"Pizza Fat"
Delivery Pizza Hero
FATMAN
IT'S GREAT! I LOVE IT!
GOOD, GOOD. EAT UP, THERE'S MORE WHERE THAT CAME FROM.
NOW IF YOU'LL PARDON ME, I'M GONNA GO GET CHANGED QUICK.
WHEW, THAT WAS A CLOSE ONE. BUT---
--NOW SOMEBODY KNOWS MY TRUE IDENTITY.
I'VE GOTTEN CARELESS. TRANSFORMING INTO RATMAN IS SUCH A NORMAL THING TO ME NOW I TOTALLY FORGOT HOW MANY CALORIES IT TAKES.
BUT... WHY WOULD THAT PIZZA DELIVERY HERO BOTHER SAVING RATMAN IN THE FIRST PLACE? ISN'T HE SUPPOSED TO ARREST ME?
PizzaFat
ピザファット
Coca-Cola

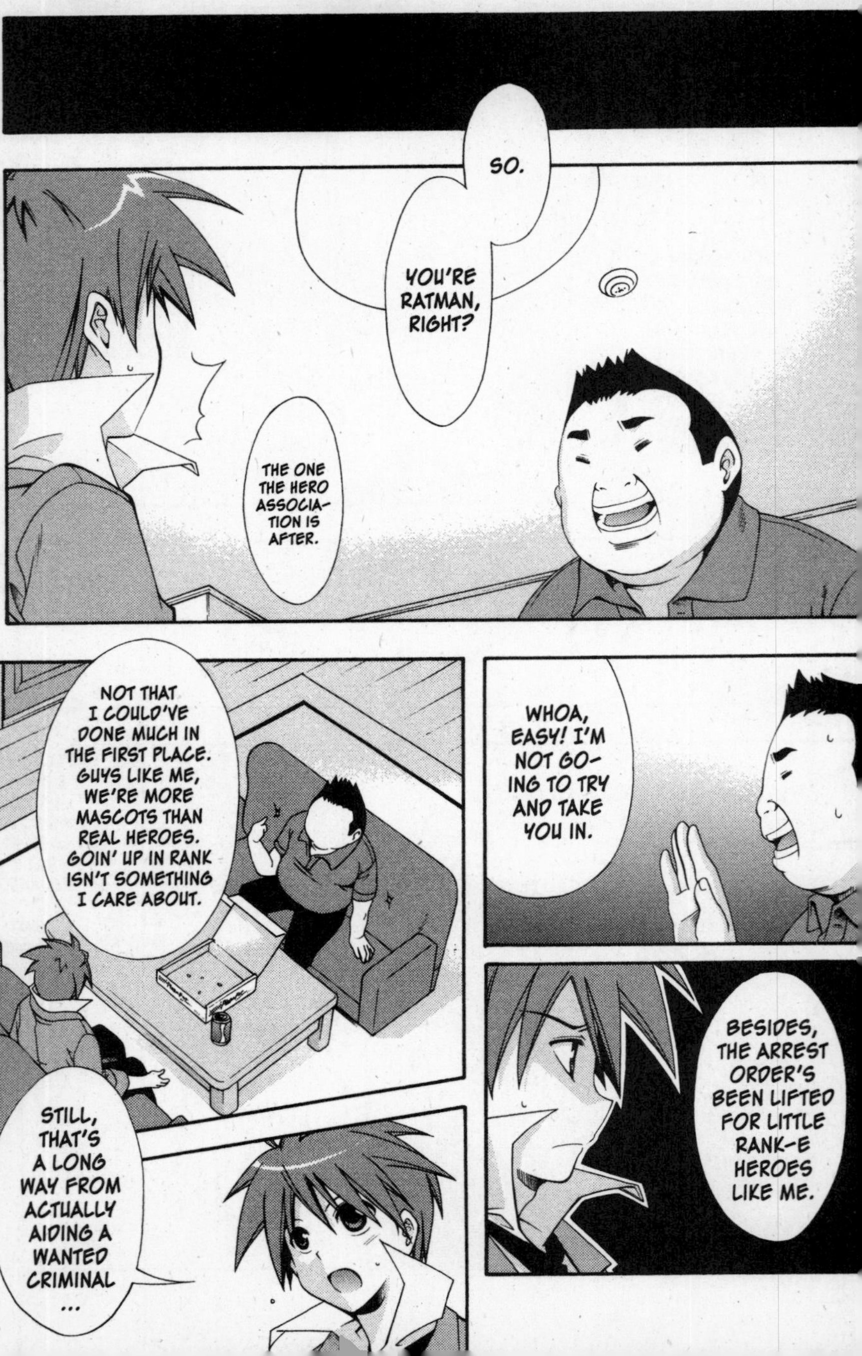
SO.
YOU'RE RATMAN, RIGHT?
THE ONE THE HERO ASSOCIA-TION IS AFTER.
WHOA, EASY! I'M NOT GO-ING TO TRY AND TAKE YOU IN.
NOT THAT I COULD'VE DONE MUCH IN THE FIRST PLACE. GUYS LIKE ME, WE'RE MORE MASCOTS THAN REAL HEROES. GOIN' UP IN RANK ISN'T SOMETHING I CARE ABOUT.
BESIDES, THE ARREST ORDER'S BEEN LIFTED FOR LITTLE RANK-E HEROES LIKE ME.
STILL, THAT'S A LONG WAY FROM ACTUALLY AIDING A WANTED CRIMINAL ...

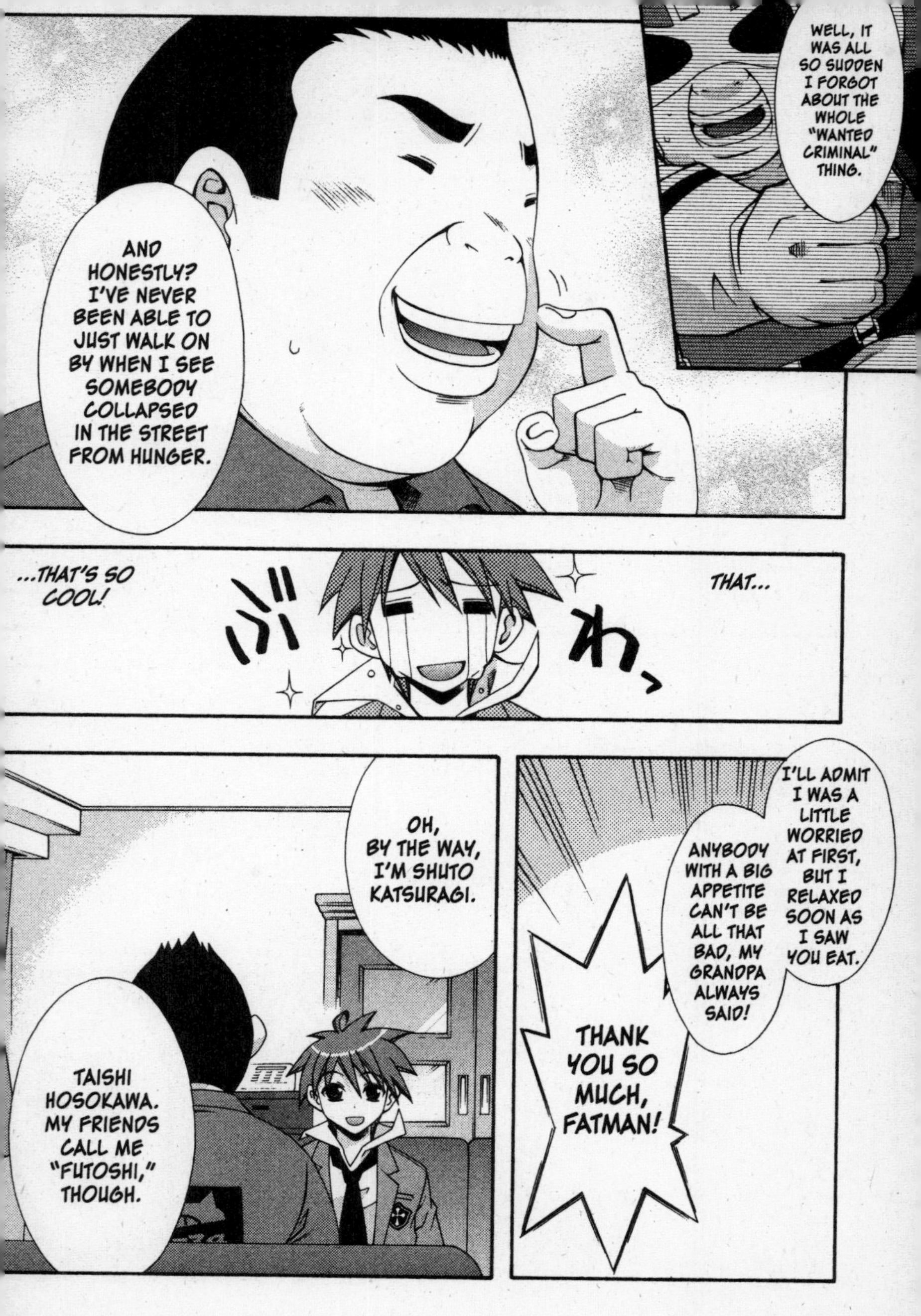
WELL, IT WAS ALL SO SUDDEN I FORGOT ABOUT THE WHOLE "WANTED CRIMINAL" THING.
AND HONESTLY? I'VE NEVER BEEN ABLE TO JUST WALK ON BY WHEN I SEE SOMEBODY COLLAPSED IN THE STREET FROM HUNGER.
THAT...
ぶわっ
...THAT'S SO COOL!
I'LL ADMIT I WAS A LITTLE WORRIED AT FIRST, BUT I RELAXED SOON AS I SAW YOU EAT.
ANYBODY WITH A BIG APPETITE CAN'T BE ALL THAT BAD, MY GRANDPA ALWAYS SAID!
THANK YOU SO MUCH, FATMAN!
OH, BY THE WAY, I'M SHUTO KATSURAGI.
TAISHI HOSOKAWA. MY FRIENDS CALL ME "FUTOSHI," THOUGH.

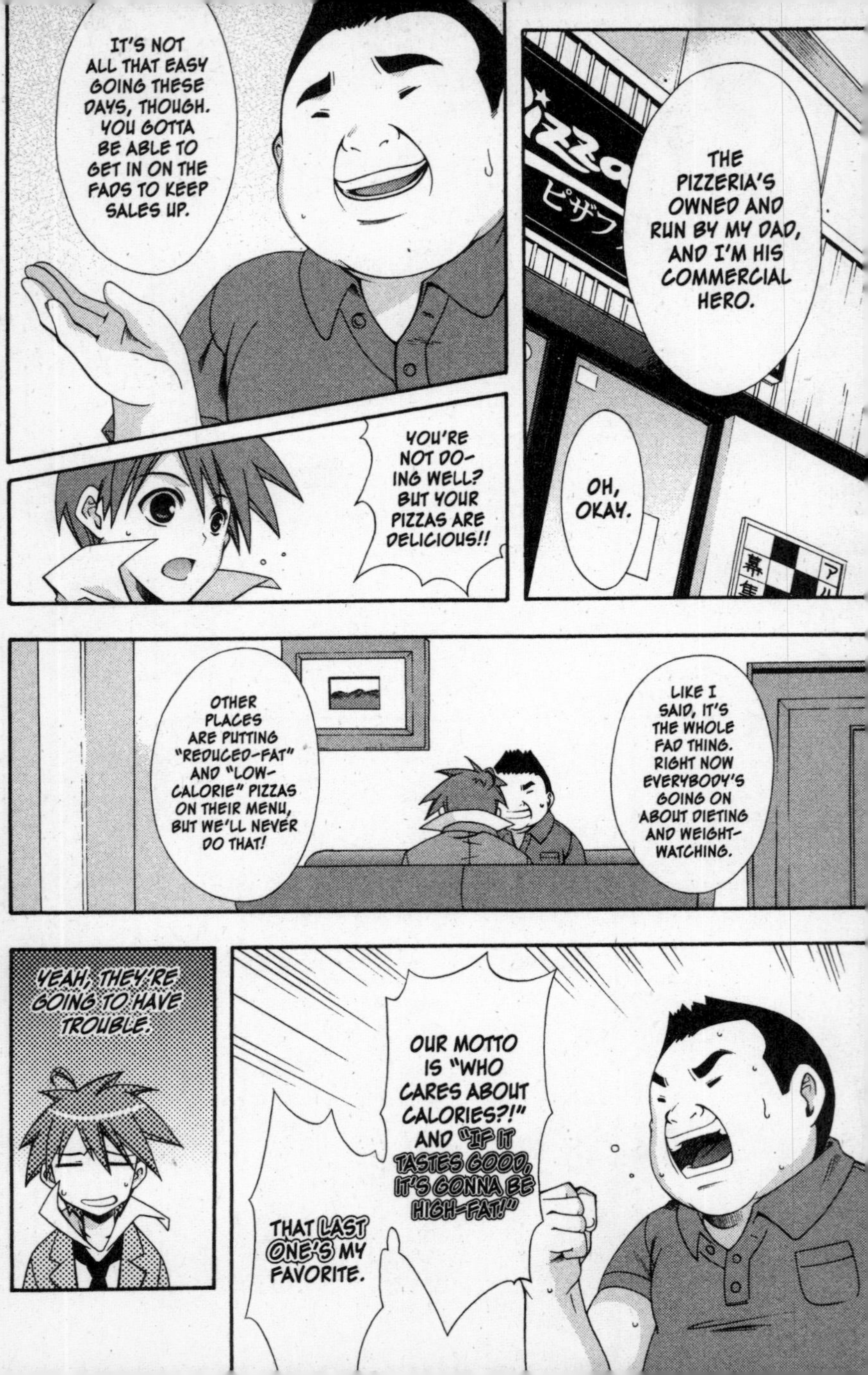
THE PIZZERIA'S OWNED AND RUN BY MY DAD, AND I'M HIS COMMERCIAL HERO.
OH, OKAY.
IT'S NOT ALL THAT EASY GOING THESE DAYS, THOUGH. YOU GOTTA BE ABLE TO GET IN ON THE FADS TO KEEP SALES UP.
YOU'RE NOT DO-ING WELL? BUT YOUR PIZZAS ARE DELICIOUS!!
LIKE I SAID, IT'S THE WHOLE FAD THING. RIGHT NOW EVERYBODY'S GOING ON ABOUT DIETING AND WEIGHT-WATCHING.
OTHER PLACES ARE PUTTING "REDUCED-FAT" AND "LOW-CALORIE" PIZZAS ON THEIR MENU, BUT WE'LL NEVER DO THAT!
OUR MOTTO IS "WHO CARES ABOUT CALORIES?!" AND "IF IT TASTES GOOD, IT'S GONNA BE HIGH-FAT!"
THAT LAST ONE'S MY FAVORITE.
YEAH, THEY'RE GOING TO HAVE TROUBLE.

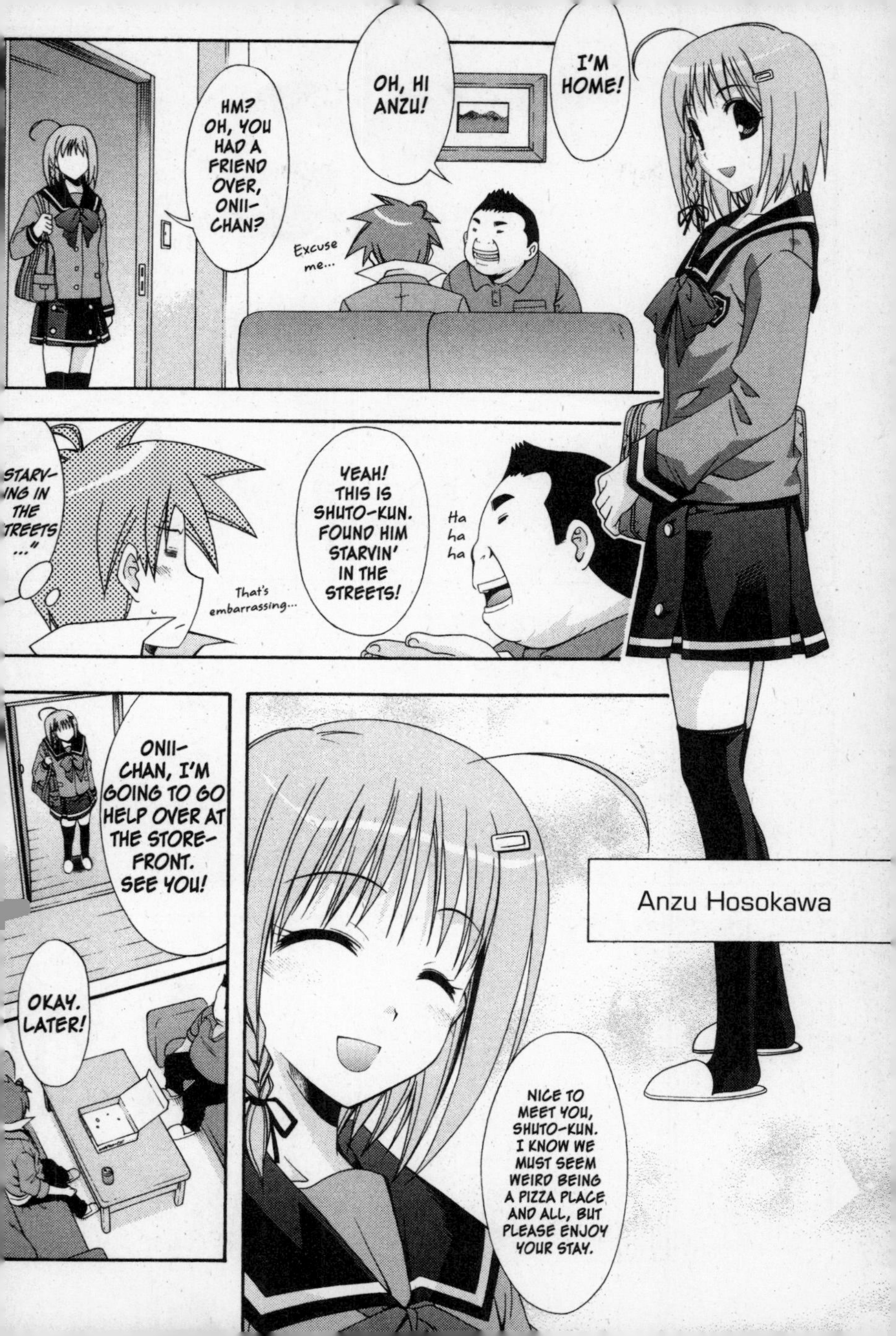

I'M HOME!
OH, HI ANZU!
HM? OH, YOU HAD A FRIEND OVER, ONII-CHAN?
Excuse me...
YEAH! THIS IS SHUTO-KUN. FOUND HIM STARVIN' IN THE STREETS!
Ha ha ha
That's embarrassing...
STARV-ING IN THE TREETS ..."
Anzu Hosokawa
NICE TO MEET YOU, SHUTO-KUN. I KNOW WE MUST SEEM WEIRD BEING A PIZZA PLACE AND ALL, BUT PLEASE ENJOY YOUR STAY.
ONII-CHAN, I'M GOING TO GO HELP OVER AT THE STORE-FRONT. SEE YOU!
OKAY. LATER!

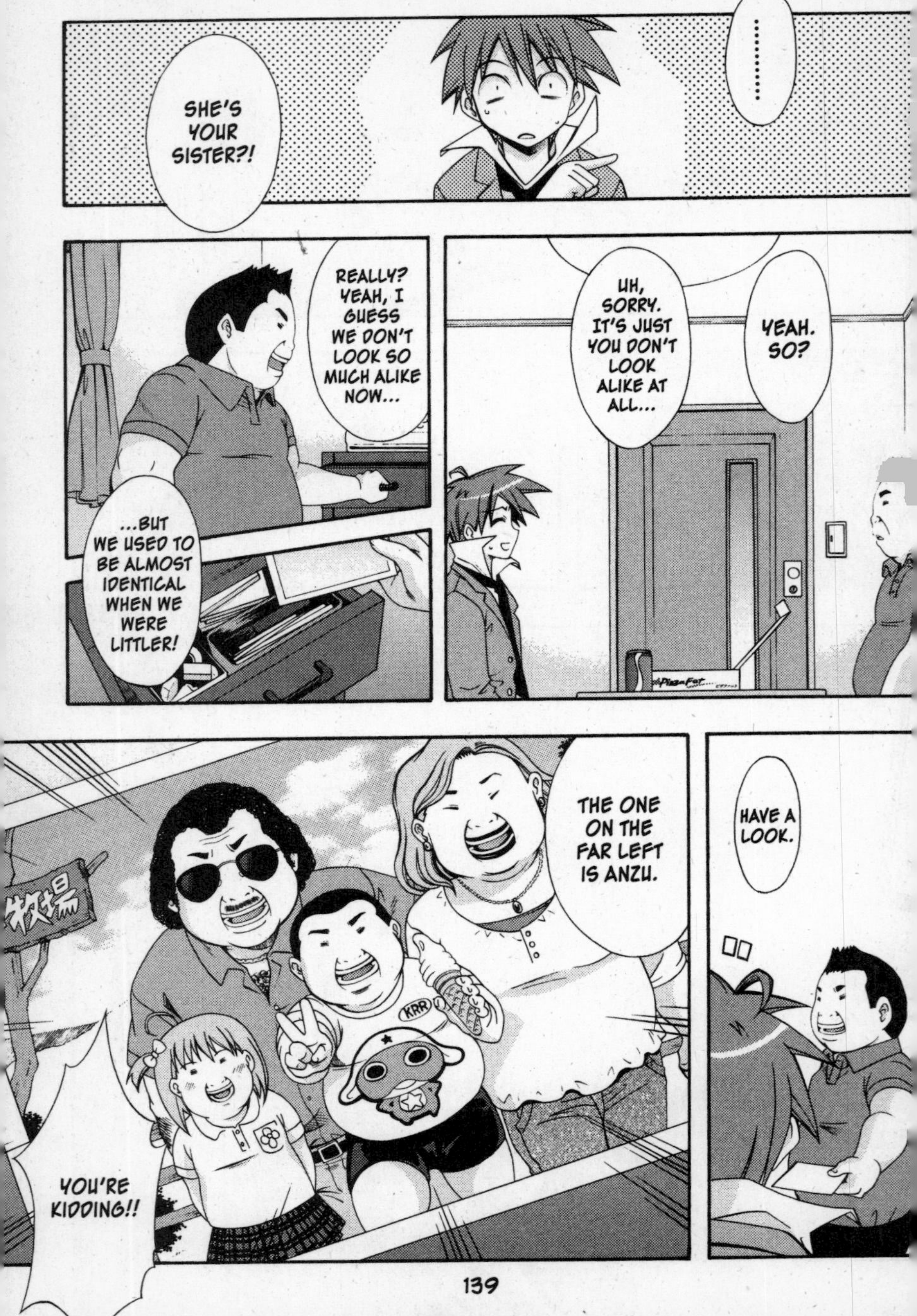
......
SHE'S YOUR SISTER?!
YEAH. SO?
UH, SORRY. IT'S JUST YOU DON'T LOOK ALIKE AT ALL...
REALLY? YEAH, I GUESS WE DON'T LOOK SO MUCH ALIKE NOW...
...BUT WE USED TO BE ALMOST IDENTICAL WHEN WE WERE LITTLER!
HAVE A LOOK.
THE ONE ON THE FAR LEFT IS ANZU.
牧場
YOU'RE KIDDING!!

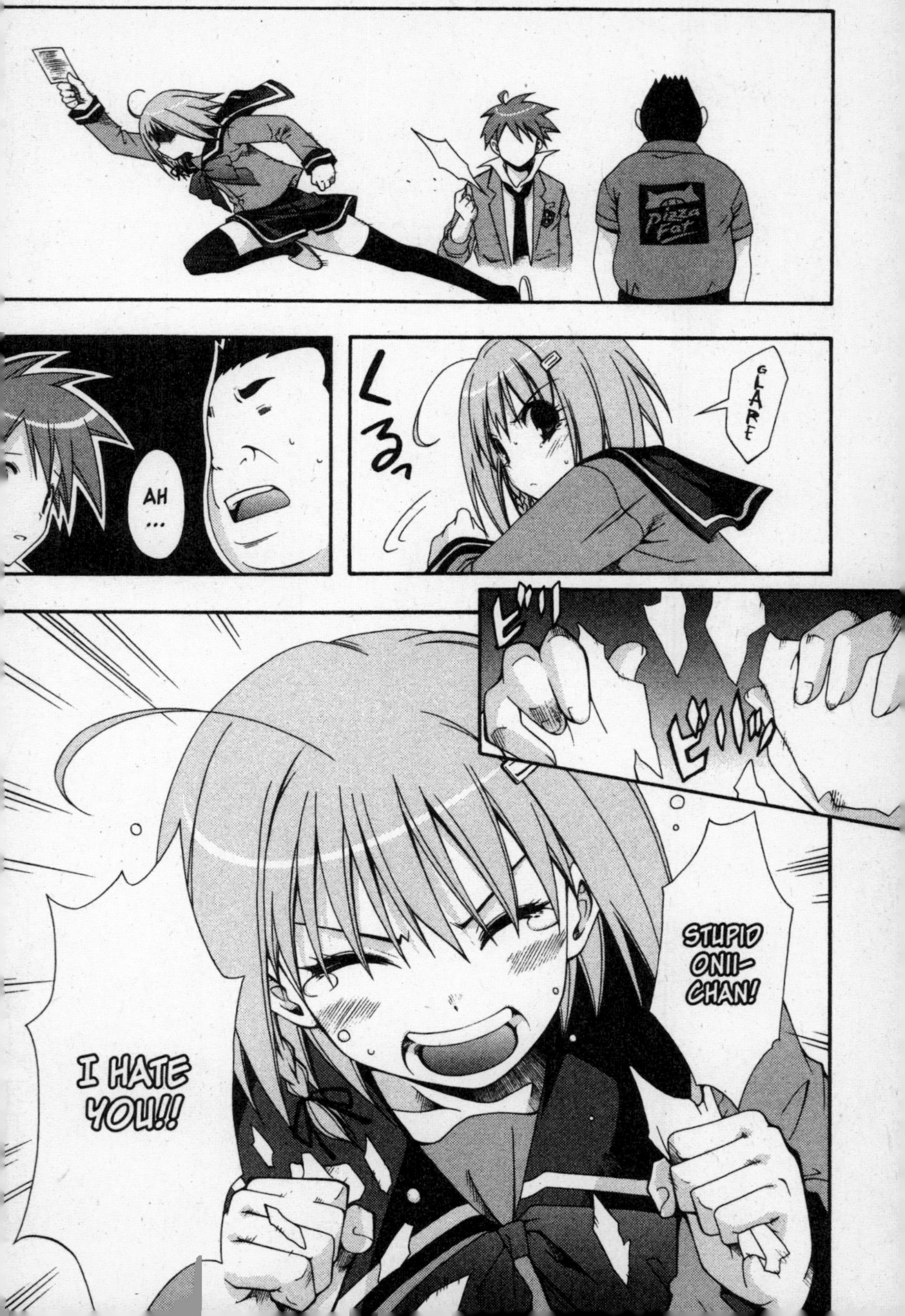
Pizza Fat
GLARE
AH ...
STUPID ONII-CHAN!
I HATE YOU!!

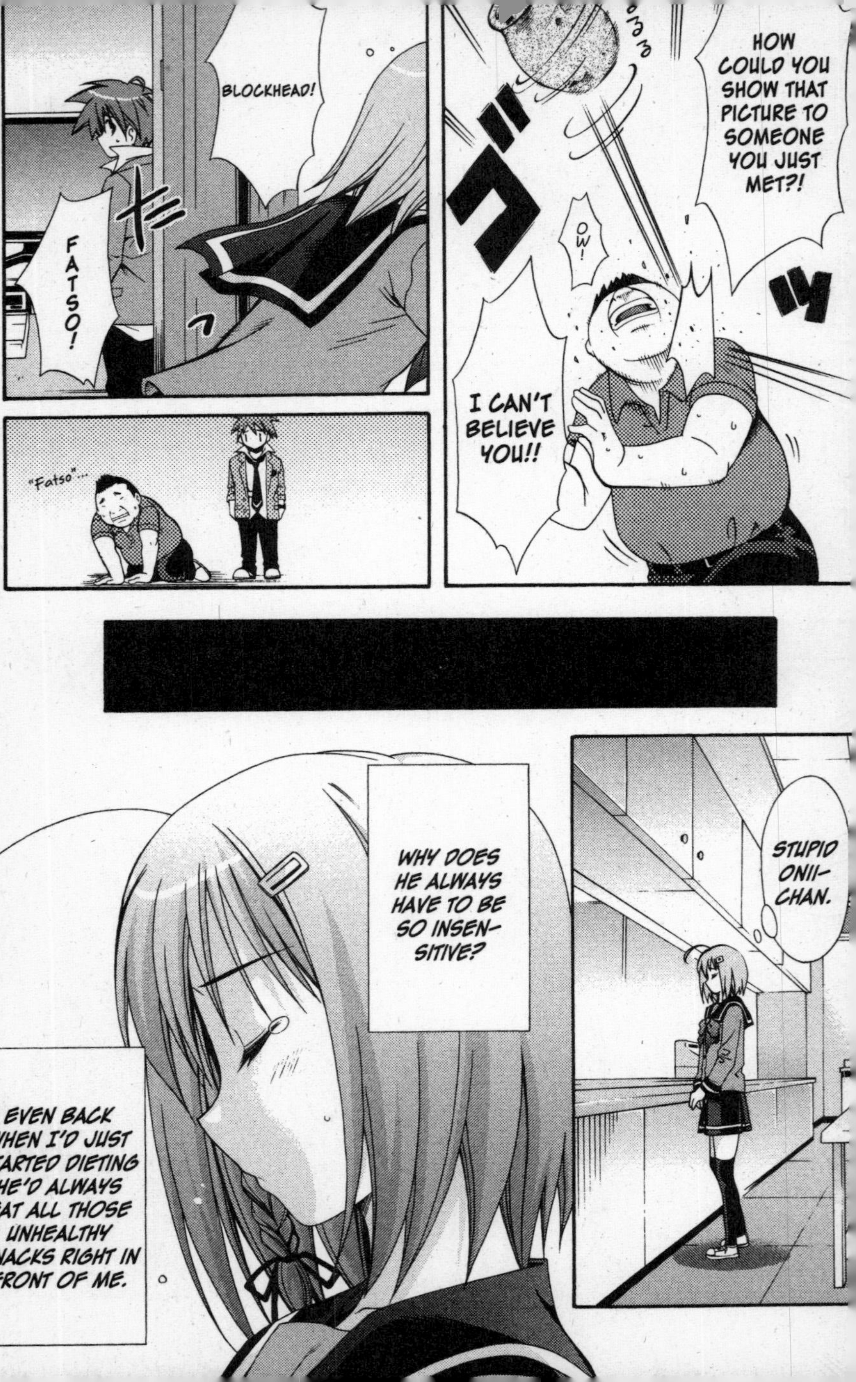
HOW COULD YOU SHOW THAT PICTURE TO SOMEONE YOU JUST MET?!
ゴ
OW!
ッ
I CAN'T BELIEVE YOU!!
BLOCKHEAD!
FATSO!
"Fatso"...
STUPID ONII-CHAN.
WHY DOES HE ALWAYS HAVE TO BE SO INSEN-SITIVE?
EVEN BACK WHEN I'D JUST STARTED DIETING HE'D ALWAYS EAT ALL THOSE UNHEALTHY SNACKS RIGHT IN FRONT OF ME.

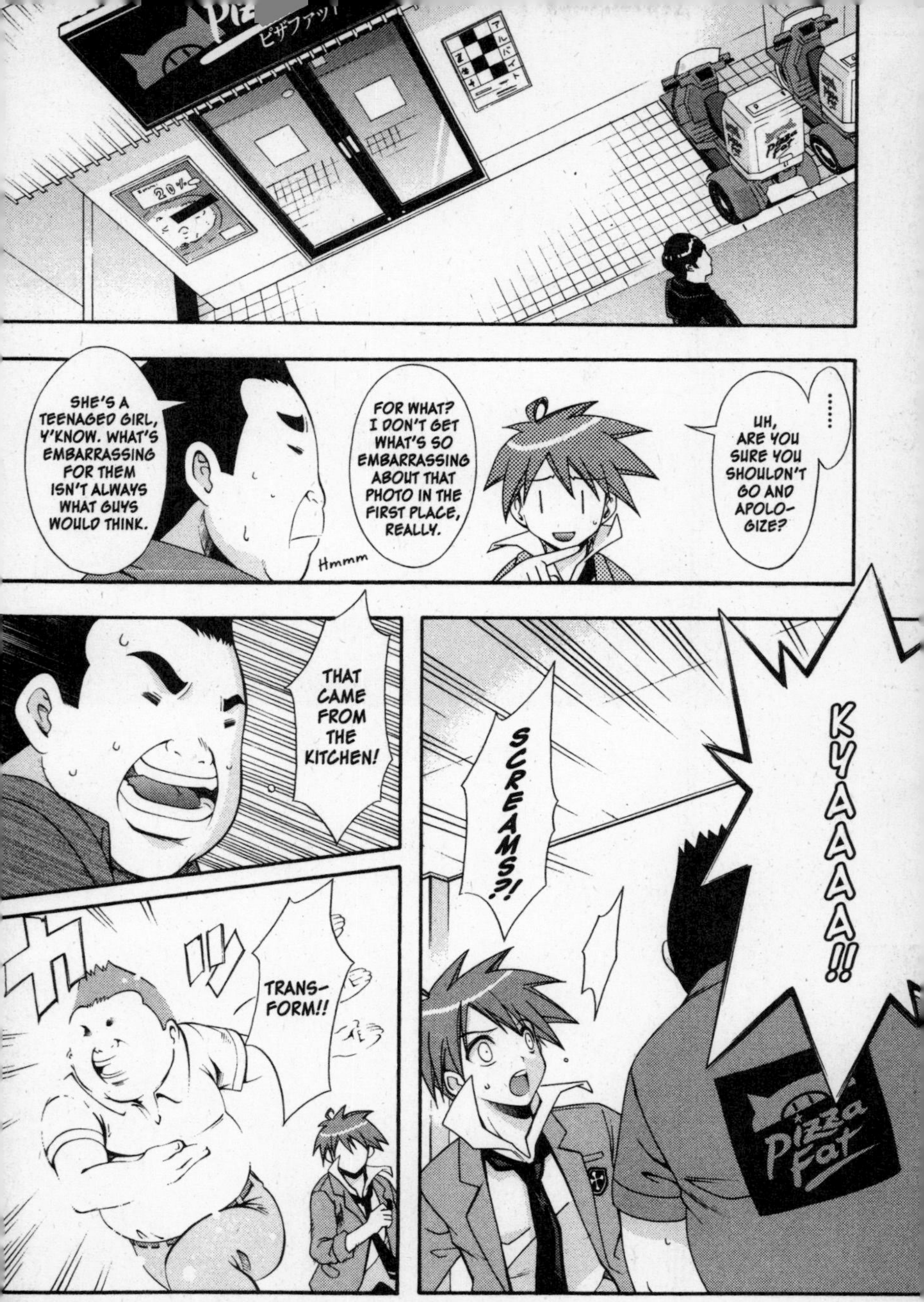

......
UH, ARE YOU SURE YOU SHOULDN'T GO AND APOLOGIZE?
FOR WHAT? I DON'T GET WHAT'S SO EMBARRASSING ABOUT THAT PHOTO IN THE FIRST PLACE, REALLY.
SHE'S A TEENAGED GIRL, Y'KNOW. WHAT'S EMBARRASSING FOR THEM ISN'T ALWAYS WHAT GUYS WOULD THINK.
Hmmm
KYAAAAA!!
SCREAMS?!
Pizza Fat
THAT CAME FROM THE KITCHEN!
TRANS-FORM!!

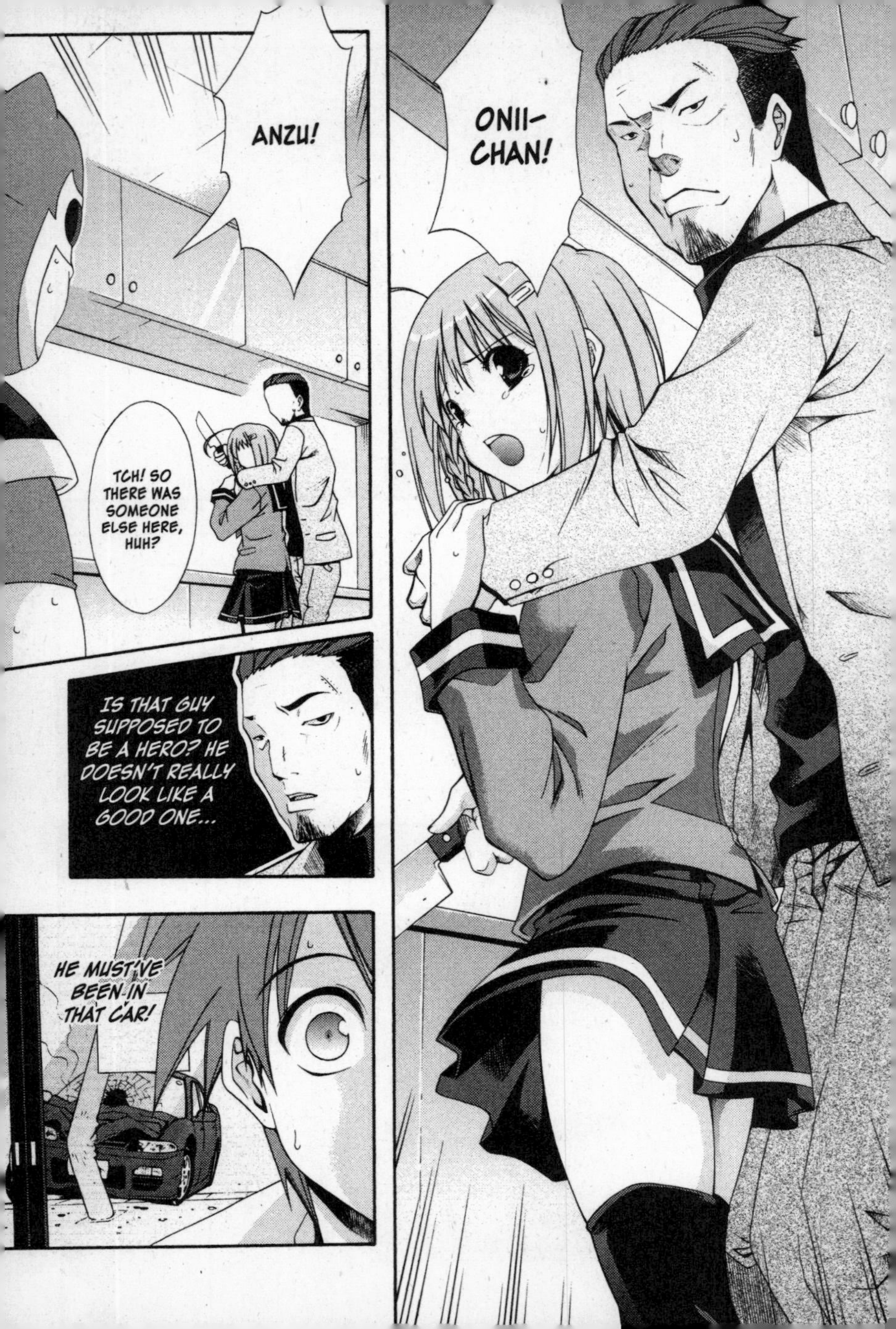

ONII-CHAN!
ANZU!
TCH! SO THERE WAS SOMEONE ELSE HERE, HUH?
IS THAT GUY SUPPOSED TO BE A HERO? HE DOESN'T REALLY LOOK LIKE A GOOD ONE...
HE MUST'VE BEEN IN THAT CAR!

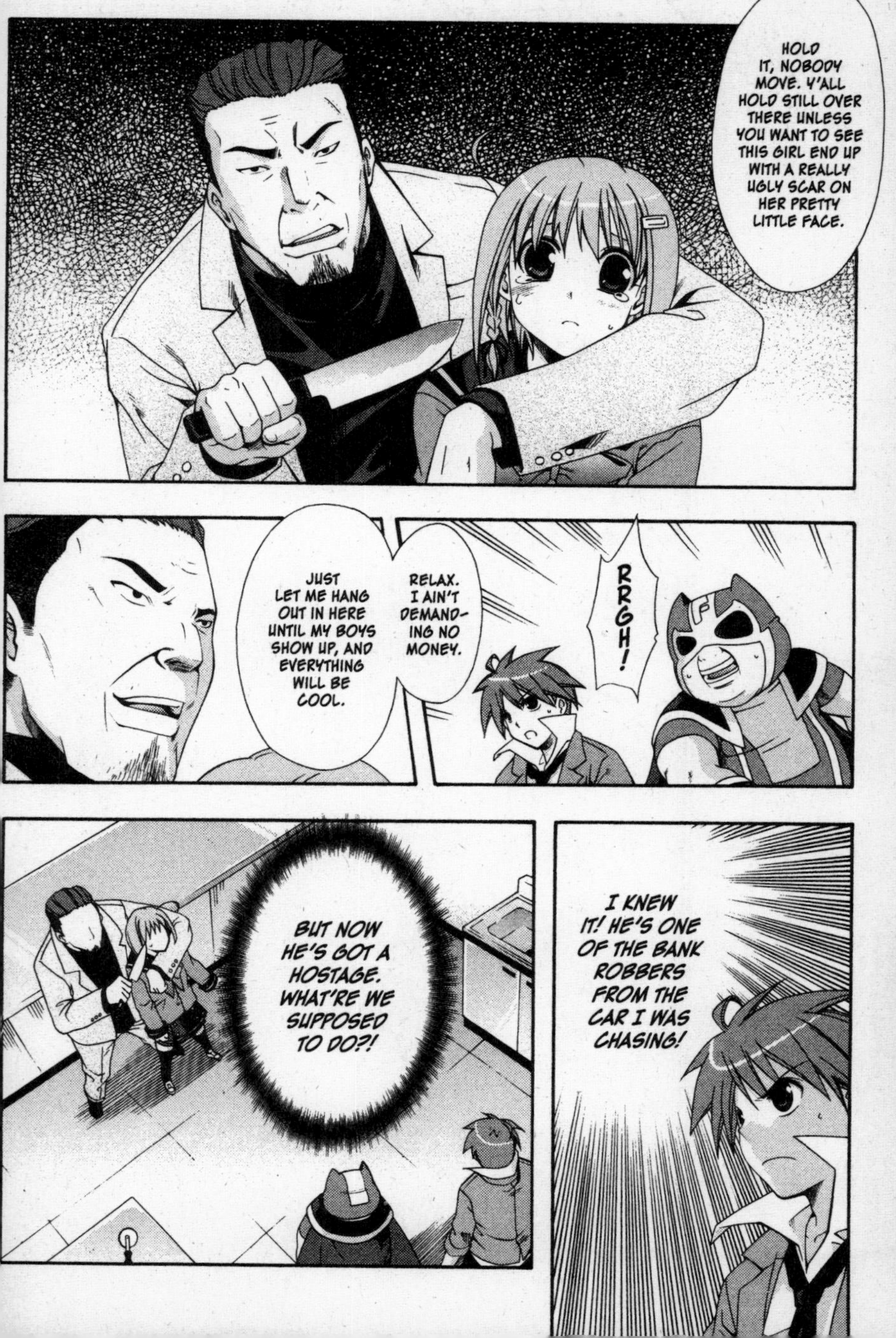
HOLD IT, NOBODY MOVE. Y'ALL HOLD STILL OVER THERE UNLESS YOU WANT TO SEE THIS GIRL END UP WITH A REALLY UGLY SCAR ON HER PRETTY LITTLE FACE.
RRGH!
RELAX. I AIN'T DEMANDING NO MONEY.
JUST LET ME HANG OUT IN HERE UNTIL MY BOYS SHOW UP, AND EVERYTHING WILL BE COOL.
I KNEW IT! HE'S ONE OF THE BANK ROBBERS FROM THE CAR I WAS CHASING!
BUT NOW HE'S GOT A HOSTAGE. WHAT'RE WE SUPPOSED TO DO?!

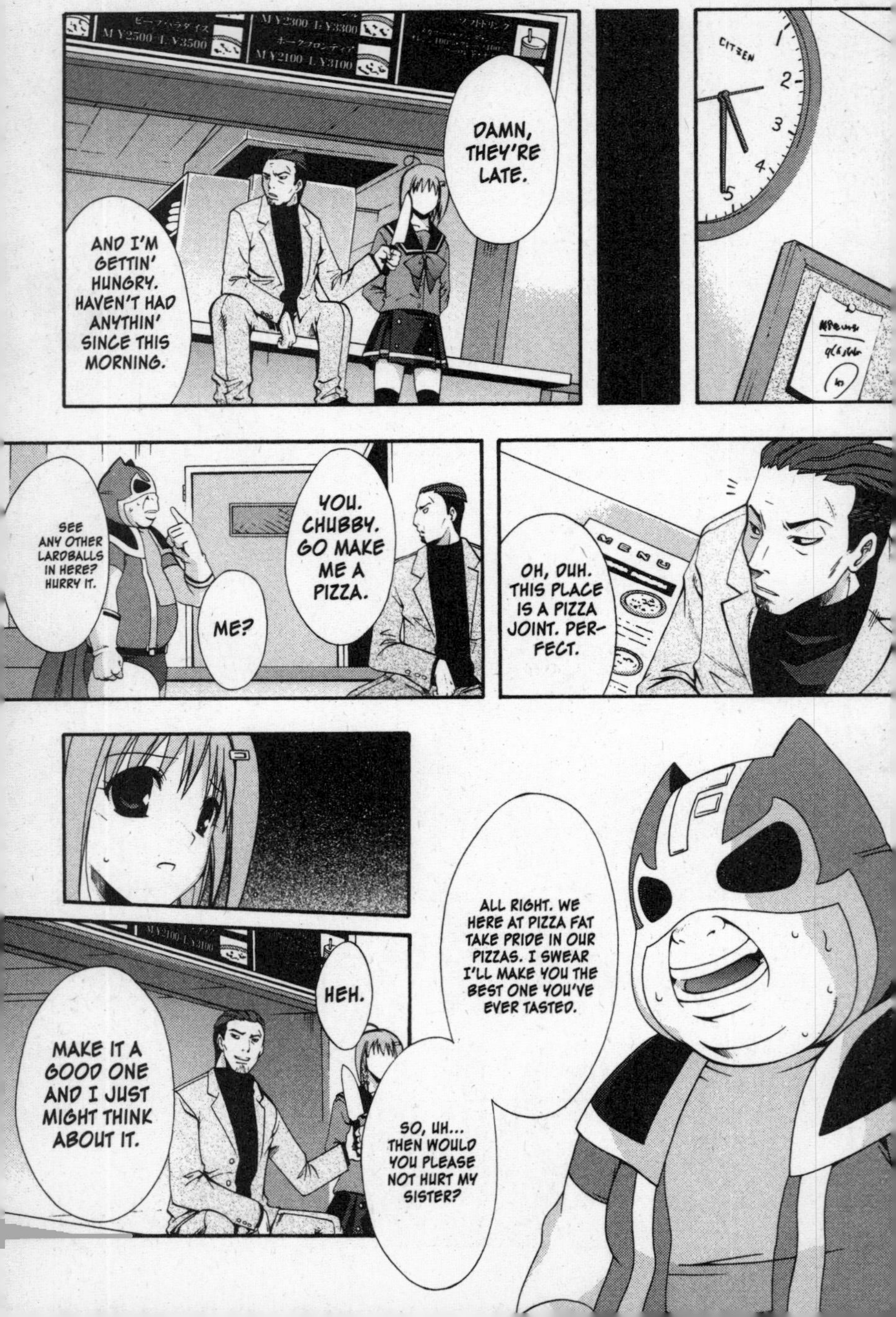

ビーフパラダイス
M ¥2500 L ¥3500
M ¥2300 L ¥3300
ポークフロンティア
M ¥2100 L ¥3100
DAMN, THEY'RE LATE.
AND I'M GETTIN' HUNGRY. HAVEN'T HAD ANYTHIN' SINCE THIS MORNING.
MENU
OH, DUH. THIS PLACE IS A PIZZA JOINT. PER-FECT.
YOU. CHUBBY. GO MAKE ME A PIZZA.
ME?
SEE ANY OTHER LARDBALLS IN HERE? HURRY IT.
ALL RIGHT. WE HERE AT PIZZA FAT TAKE PRIDE IN OUR PIZZAS. I SWEAR I'LL MAKE YOU THE BEST ONE YOU'VE EVER TASTED.
SO, UH... THEN WOULD YOU PLEASE NOT HURT MY SISTER?
M ¥2100 L ¥3100
HEH.
MAKE IT A GOOD ONE AND I JUST MIGHT THINK ABOUT IT.

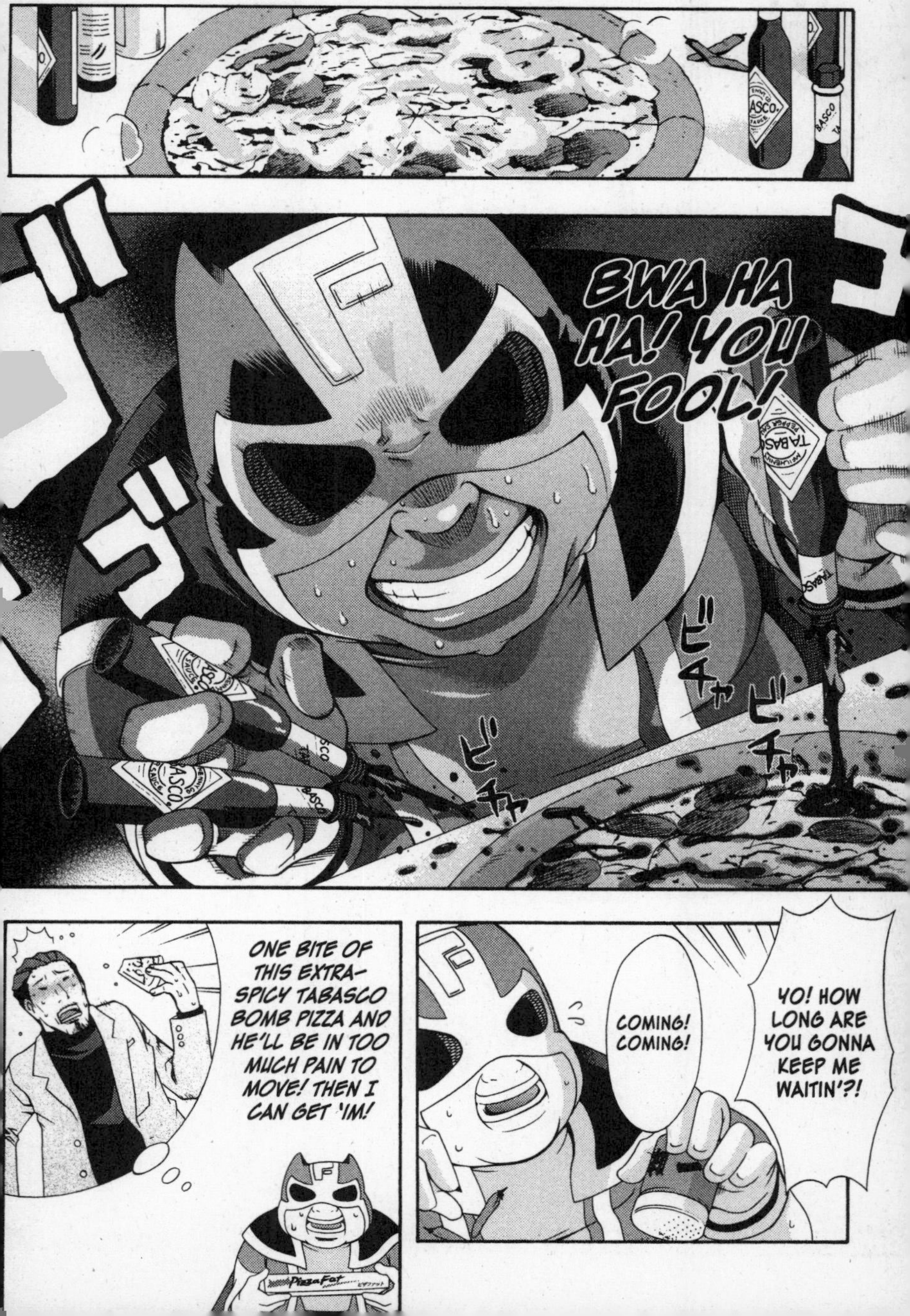
BWA HA HA! YOU FOOL!
ビチャ
ビチャ
ビチャ
YO! HOW LONG ARE YOU GONNA KEEP ME WAITIN'?!
COMING! COMING!
ONE BITE OF THIS EXTRA-SPICY TABASCO BOMB PIZZA AND HE'LL BE IN TOO MUCH PAIN TO MOVE! THEN I CAN GET 'IM!
PizzaFat

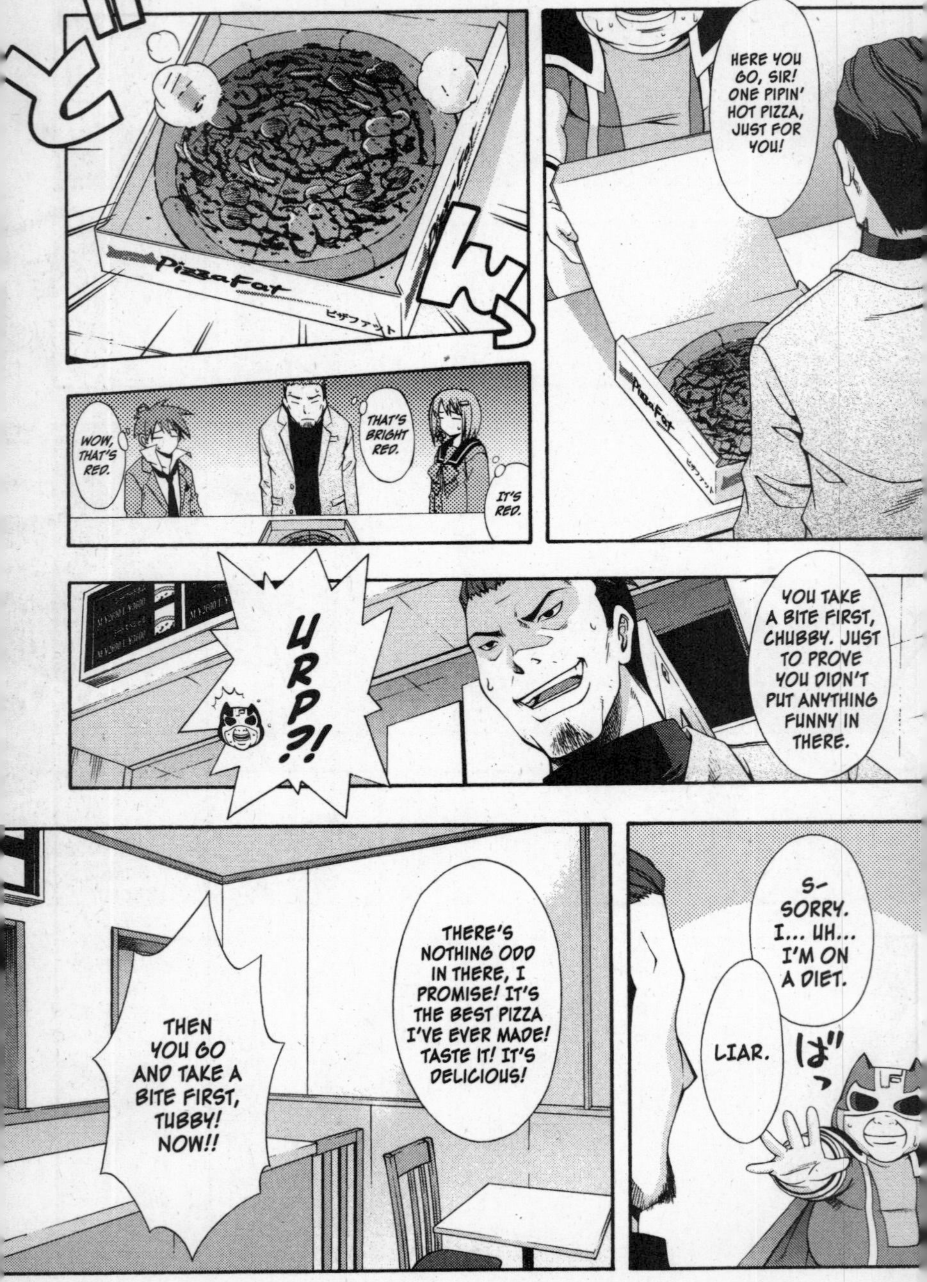
HERE YOU GO, SIR! ONE PIPIN' HOT PIZZA, JUST FOR YOU!
どん
PizzaFat
ピザファット
IT'S RED.
THAT'S BRIGHT RED.
WOW, THAT'S RED.
YOU TAKE A BITE FIRST, CHUBBY. JUST TO PROVE YOU DIDN'T PUT ANYTHING FUNNY IN THERE.
URP?!
S-SORRY. I... UH... I'M ON A DIET.
LIAR.
ばっ
THERE'S NOTHING ODD IN THERE, I PROMISE! IT'S THE BEST PIZZA I'VE EVER MADE! TASTE IT! IT'S DELICIOUS!
THEN YOU GO AND TAKE A BITE FIRST, TUBBY! NOW!!

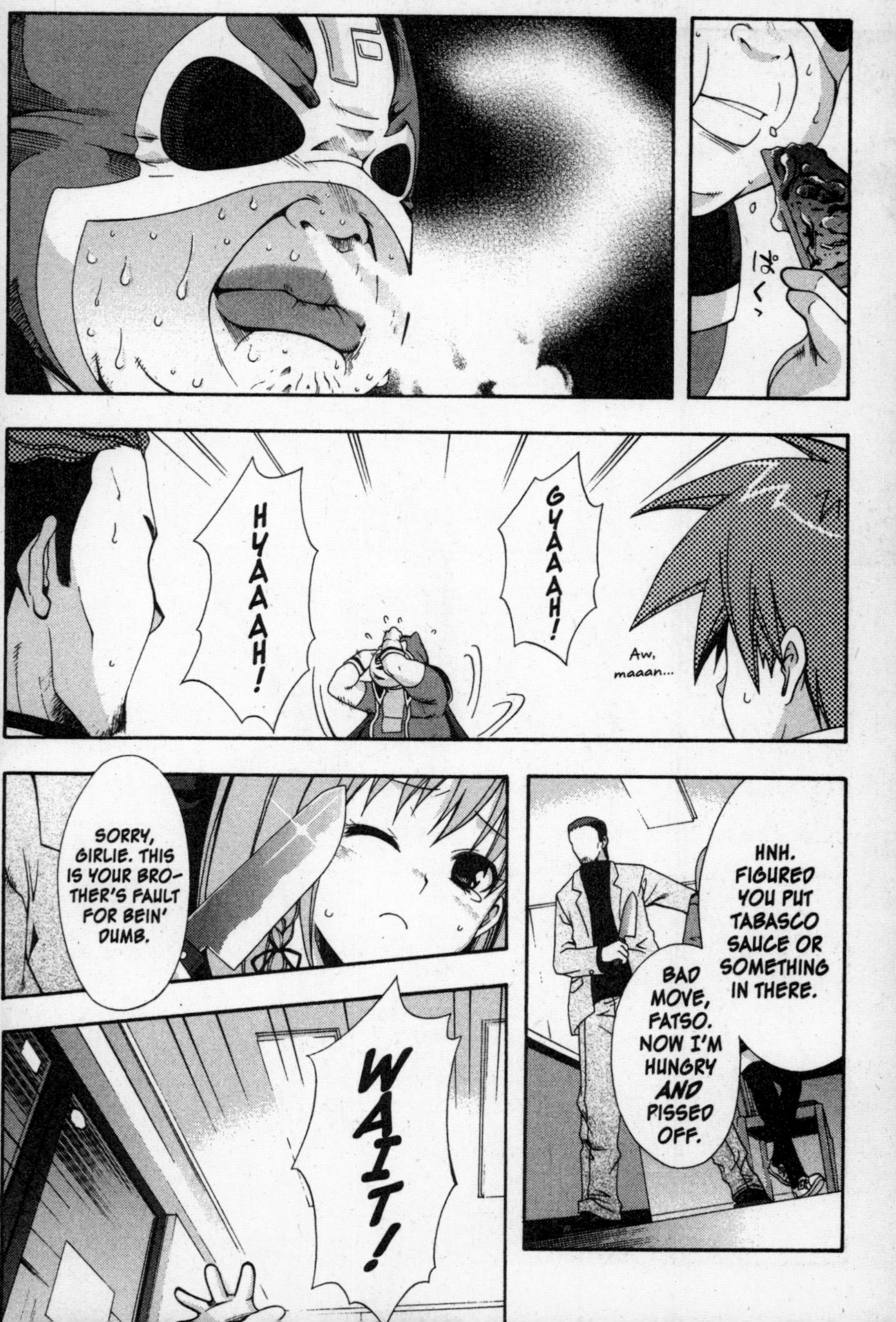
ぱく
Aw, maaan...
GYAAAAH!
HYAAAAH!
HNH. FIGURED YOU PUT TABASCO SAUCE OR SOMETHING IN THERE.
BAD MOVE, FATSO. NOW I'M HUNGRY AND PISSED OFF.
SORRY, GIRLIE. THIS IS YOUR BROTHER'S FAULT FOR BEIN' DUMB.
WAIT!

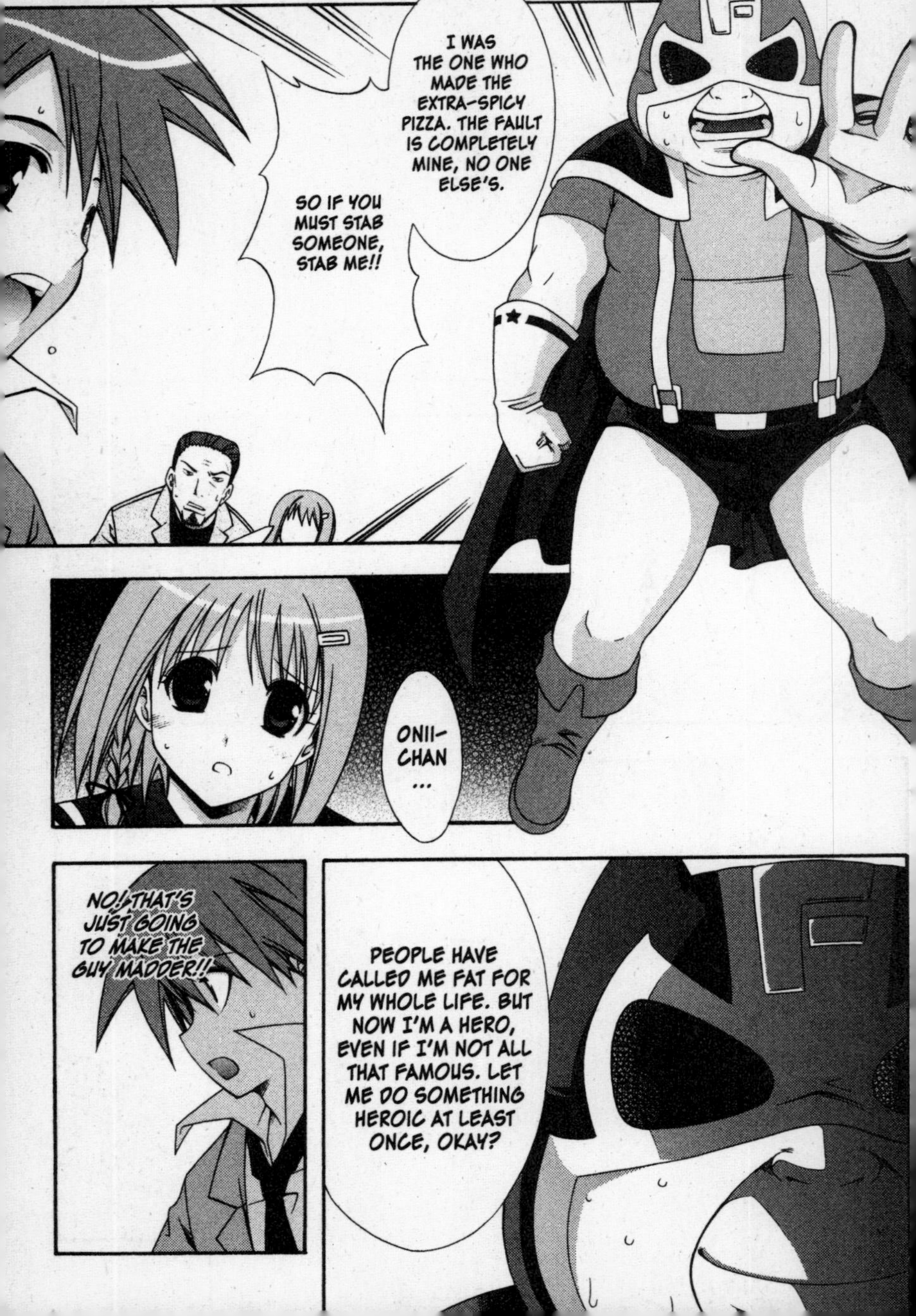
I WAS THE ONE WHO MADE THE EXTRA-SPICY PIZZA. THE FAULT IS COMPLETELY MINE, NO ONE ELSE'S.
SO IF YOU MUST STAB SOMEONE, STAB ME!!
ONII-CHAN ...
PEOPLE HAVE CALLED ME FAT FOR MY WHOLE LIFE. BUT NOW I'M A HERO, EVEN IF I'M NOT ALL THAT FAMOUS. LET ME DO SOMETHING HEROIC AT LEAST ONCE, OKAY?
NO! THAT'S JUST GOING TO MAKE THE GUY MADDER!!

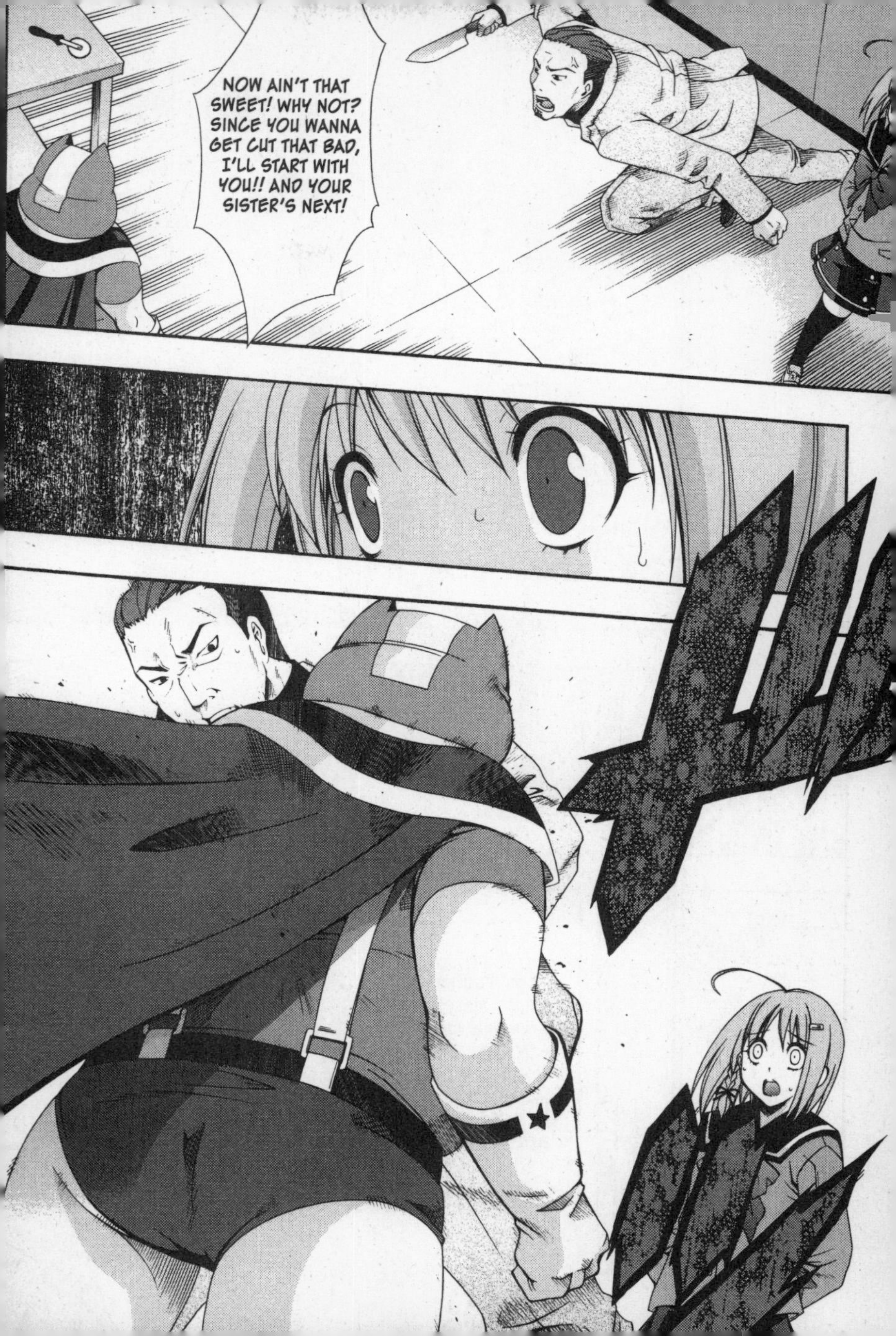
NOW AIN'T THAT SWEET! WHY NOT? SINCE YOU WANNA GET CUT THAT BAD, I'LL START WITH YOU!! AND YOUR SISTER'S NEXT!

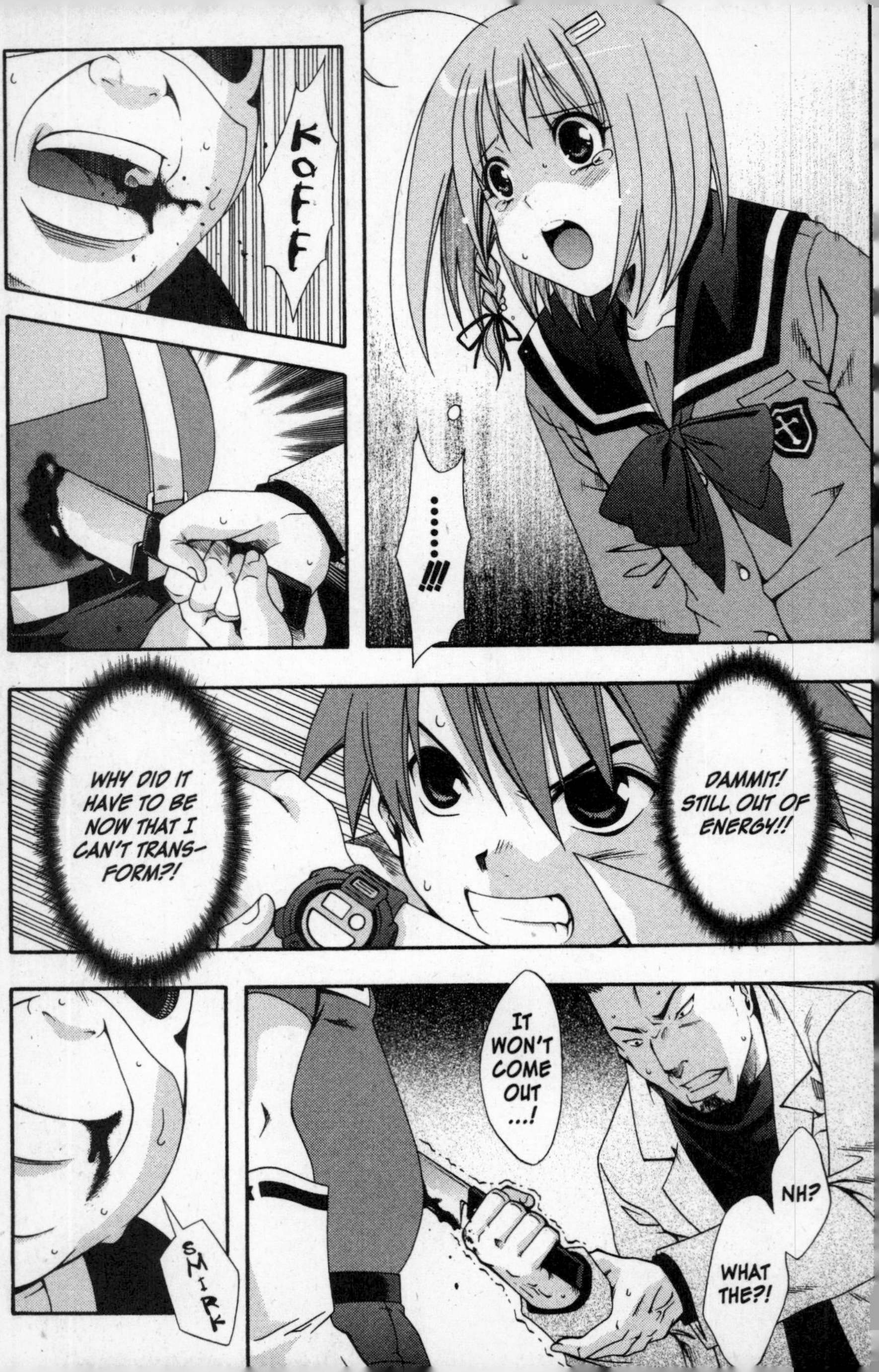
......!!!
KOFF
DAMMIT! STILL OUT OF ENERGY!!
WHY DID IT HAVE TO BE NOW THAT I CAN'T TRANS-FORM?!
IT WON'T COME OUT ...!
NH?
WHAT THE?!
SMIRK

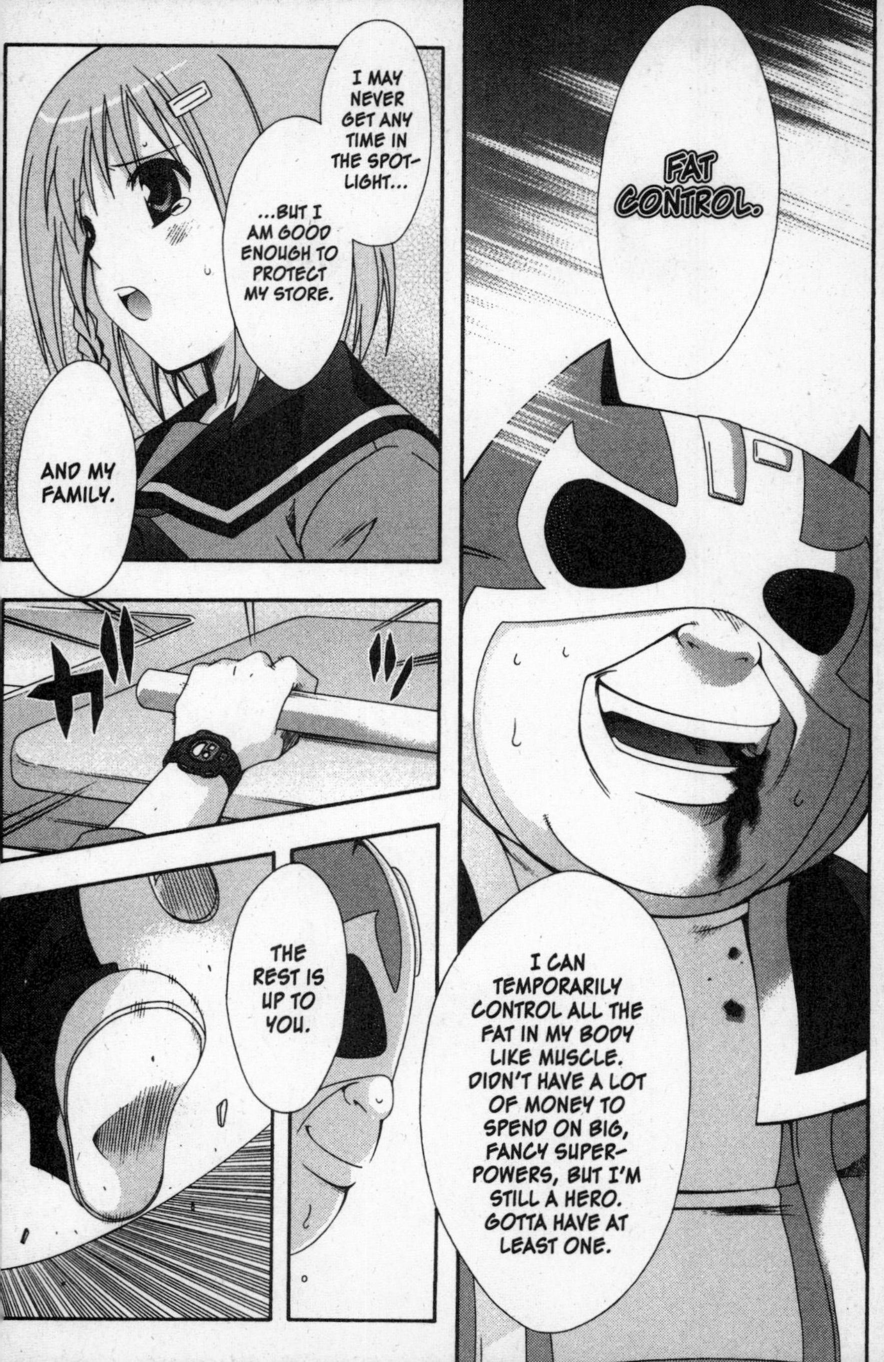
FAT CONTROL.
I CAN TEMPORARILY CONTROL ALL THE FAT IN MY BODY LIKE MUSCLE. DIDN'T HAVE A LOT OF MONEY TO SPEND ON BIG, FANCY SUPER-POWERS, BUT I'M STILL A HERO. GOTTA HAVE AT LEAST ONE.
I MAY NEVER GET ANY TIME IN THE SPOT-LIGHT...
...BUT I AM GOOD ENOUGH TO PROTECT MY STORE.
AND MY FAMILY.
THE REST IS UP TO YOU.

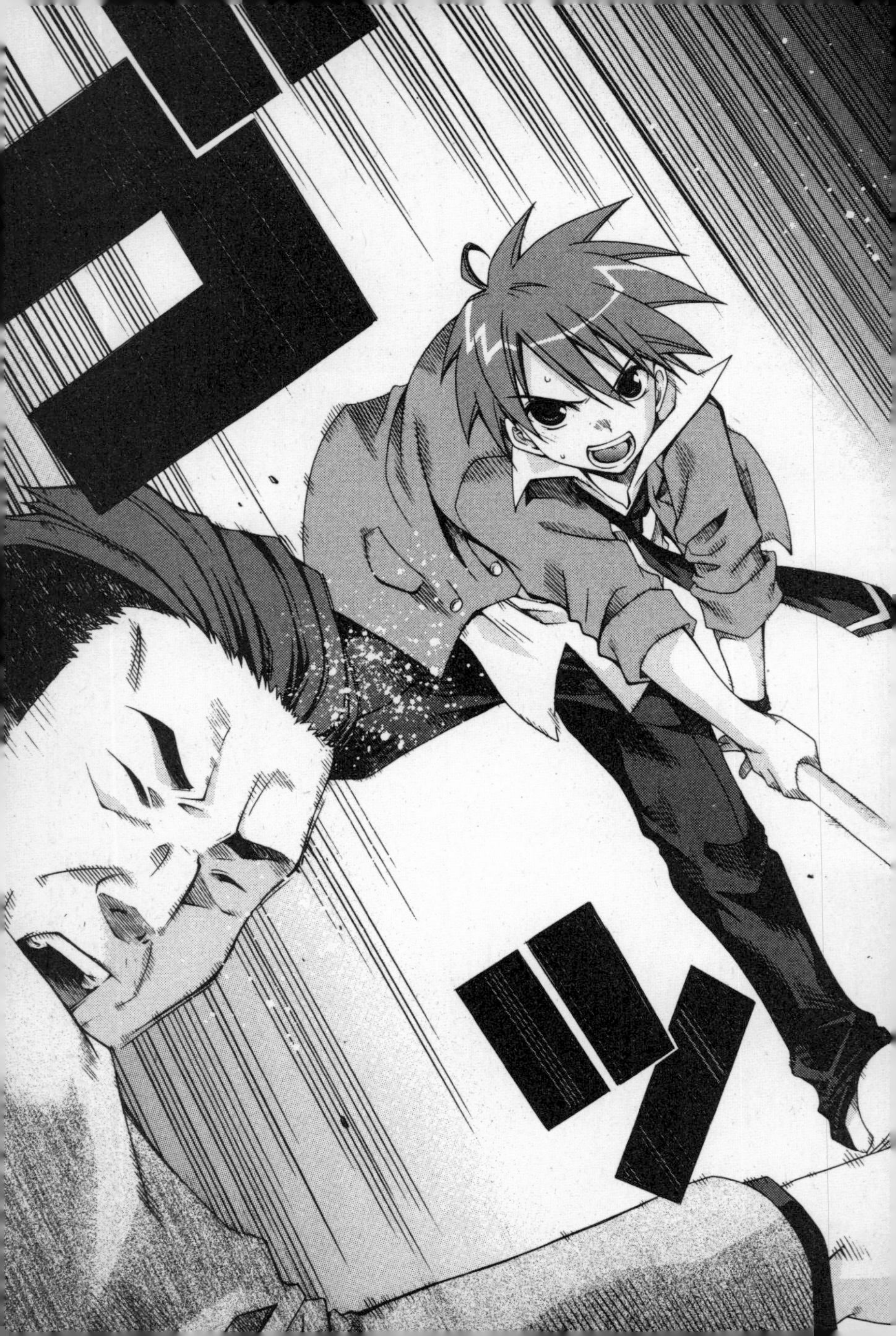
ゴッ

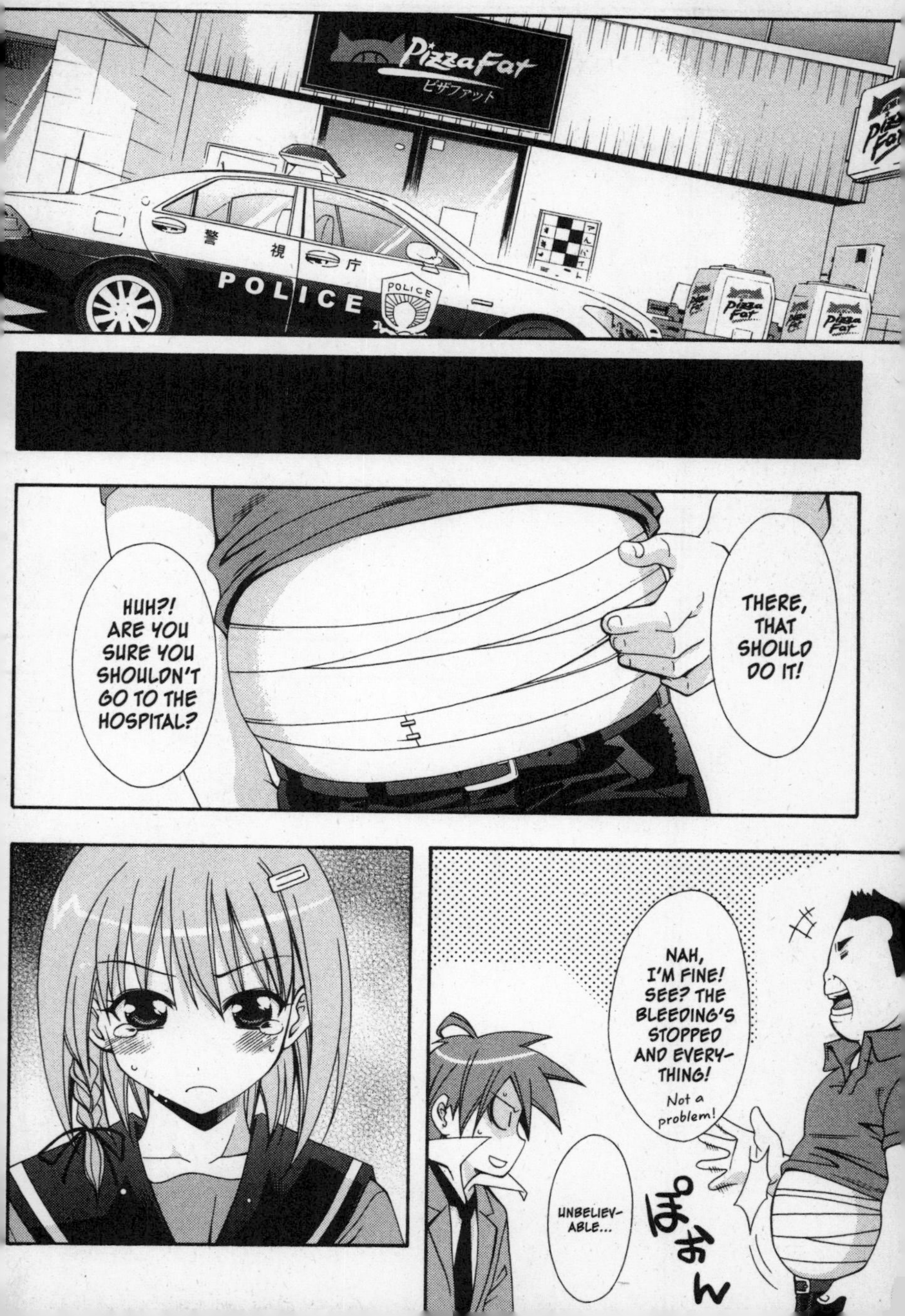
PizzaFat
ピザファット
警視庁
POLICE
POLICE
THERE, THAT SHOULD DO IT!
HUH?! ARE YOU SURE YOU SHOULDN'T GO TO THE HOSPITAL?
NAH, I'M FINE! SEE? THE BLEEDING'S STOPPED AND EVERYTHING!
Not a problem!
ぽおん
UNBELIEVABLE...

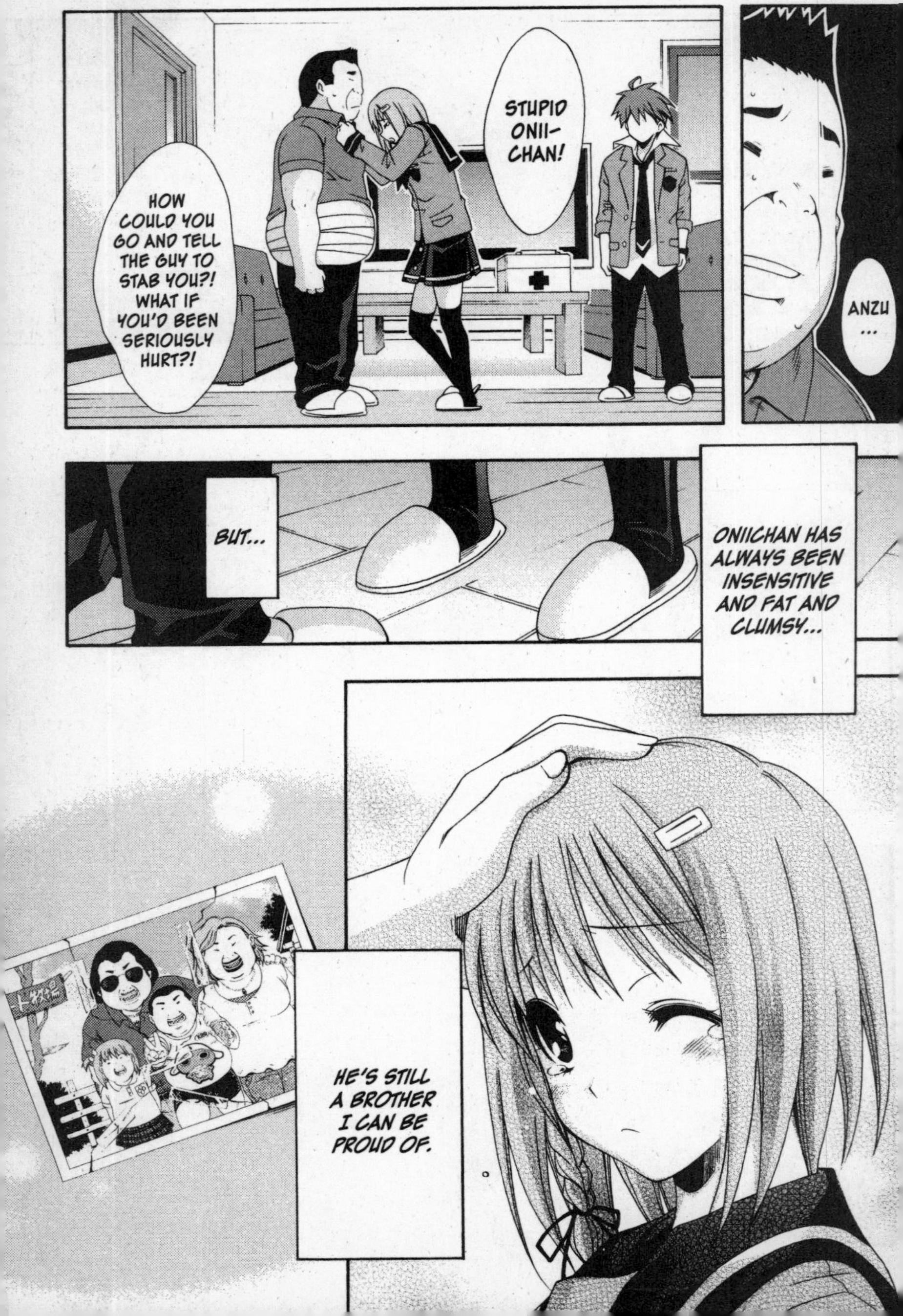
ANZU...
STUPID ONII-CHAN!
HOW COULD YOU GO AND TELL THE GUY TO STAB YOU?! WHAT IF YOU'D BEEN SERIOUSLY HURT?!
ONIICHAN HAS ALWAYS BEEN INSENSITIVE AND FAT AND CLUMSY...
BUT...
HE'S STILL A BROTHER I CAN BE PROUD OF.

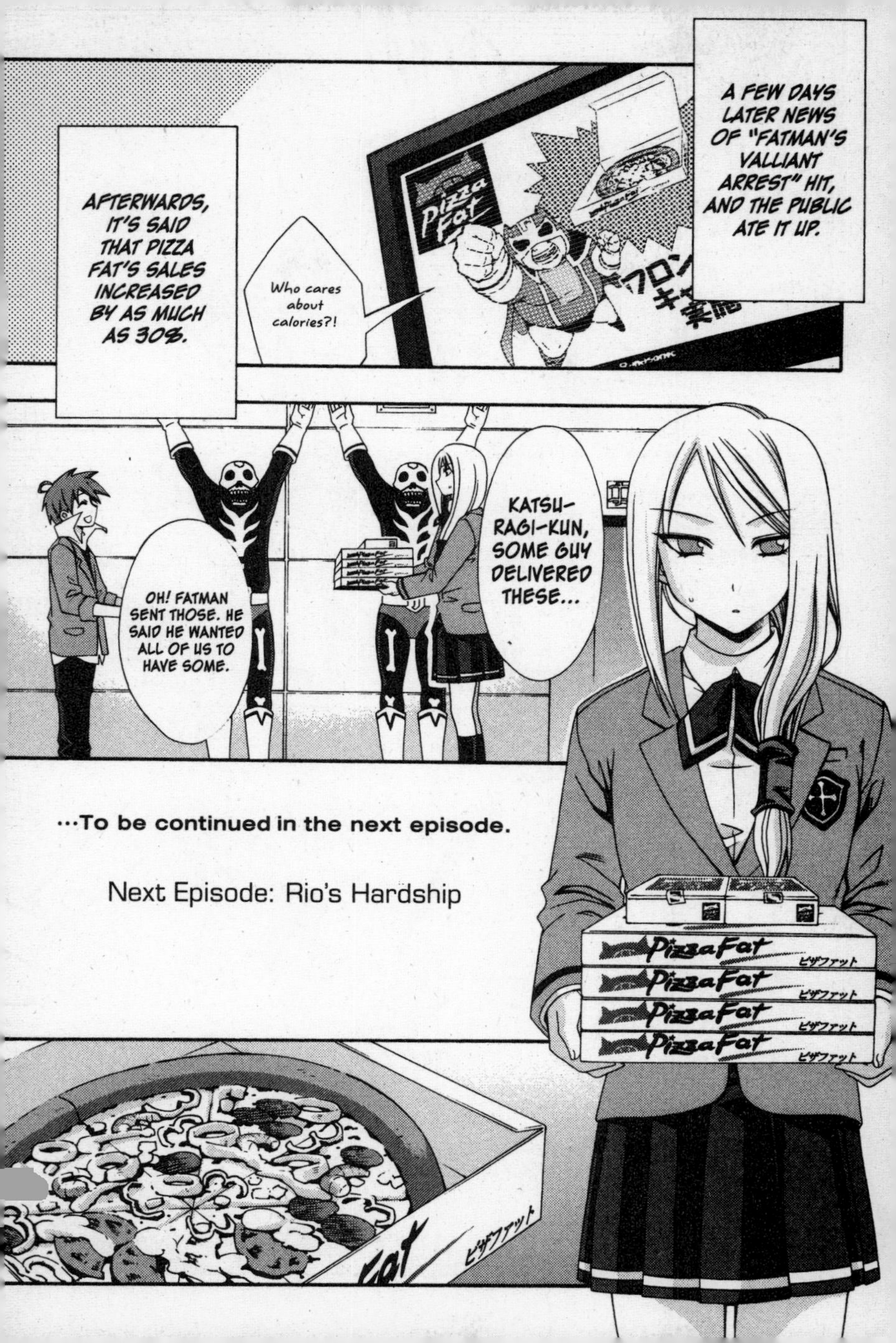
A FEW DAYS LATER NEWS OF "FATMAN'S VALLIANT ARREST" HIT, AND THE PUBLIC ATE IT UP.
Pizza Fat
Who cares about calories?!
AFTERWARDS, IT'S SAID THAT PIZZA FAT'S SALES INCREASED BY AS MUCH AS 30%.
KATSU-RAGI-KUN, SOME GUY DELIVERED THESE...
OH! FATMAN SENT THOSE. HE SAID HE WANTED ALL OF US TO HAVE SOME.
PizzaFat
ピザファット
...To be continued in the next episode.
Next Episode: Rio's Hardship

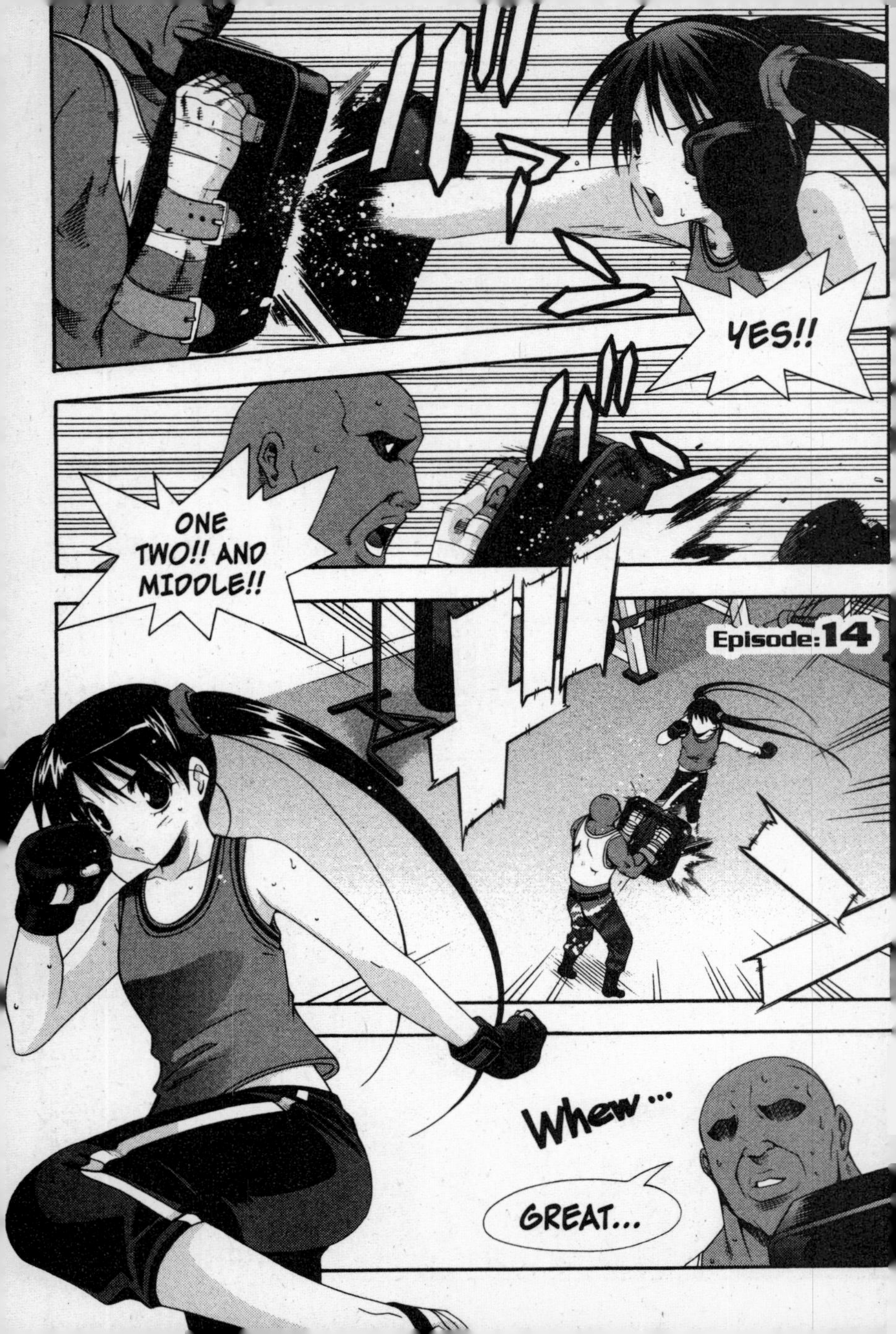
YES!!
ONE TWO!! AND MIDDLE!!
Episode: 14
Whew...
GREAT...

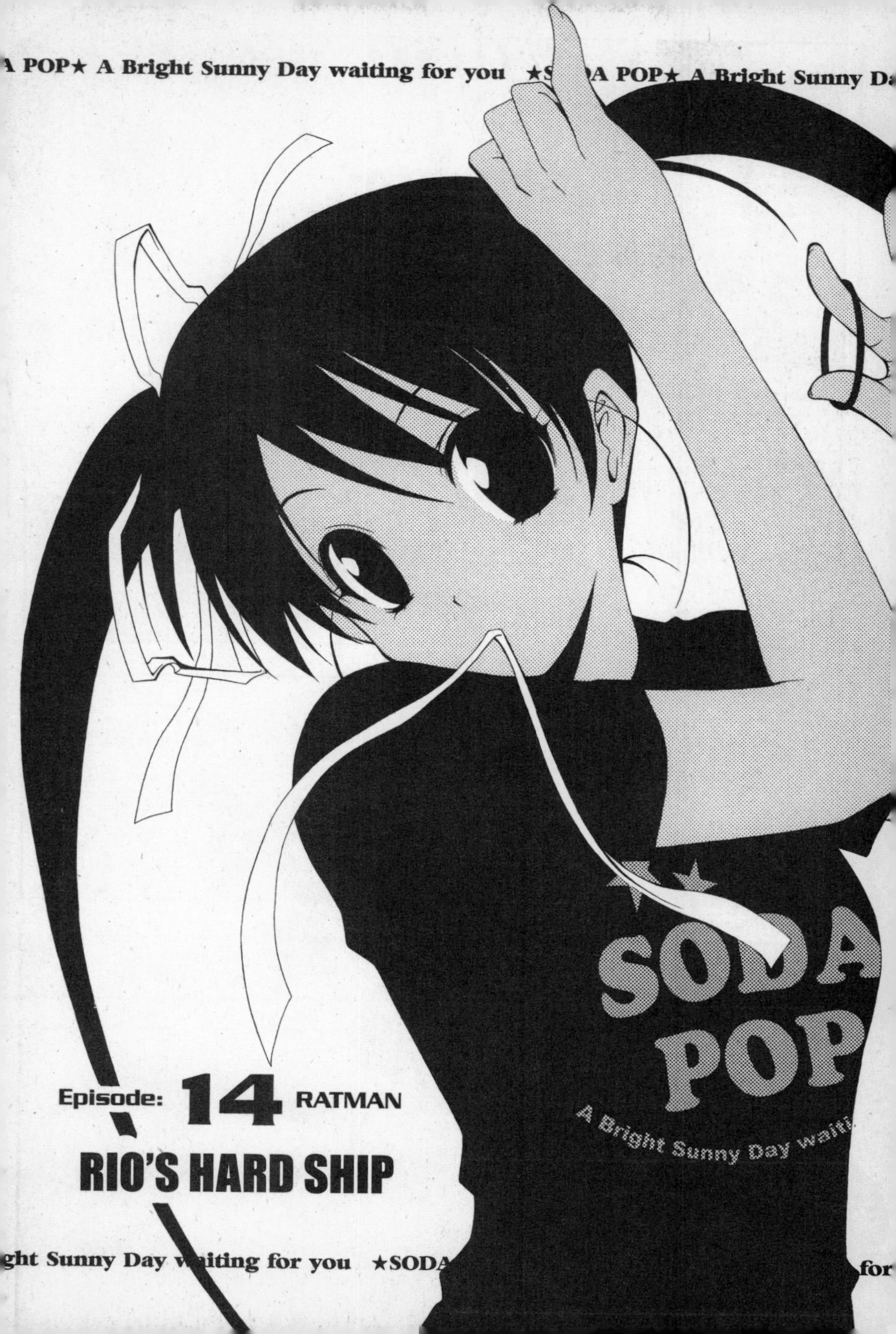
A POP★ A Bright Sunny Day waiting for you ★S DA POP★ A Bright Sunny D
SODA POP
A Bright Sunny Day waiti
Episode: 14 RATMAN
RIO'S HARD SHIP
ght Sunny Day waiting for you ★SODA
for

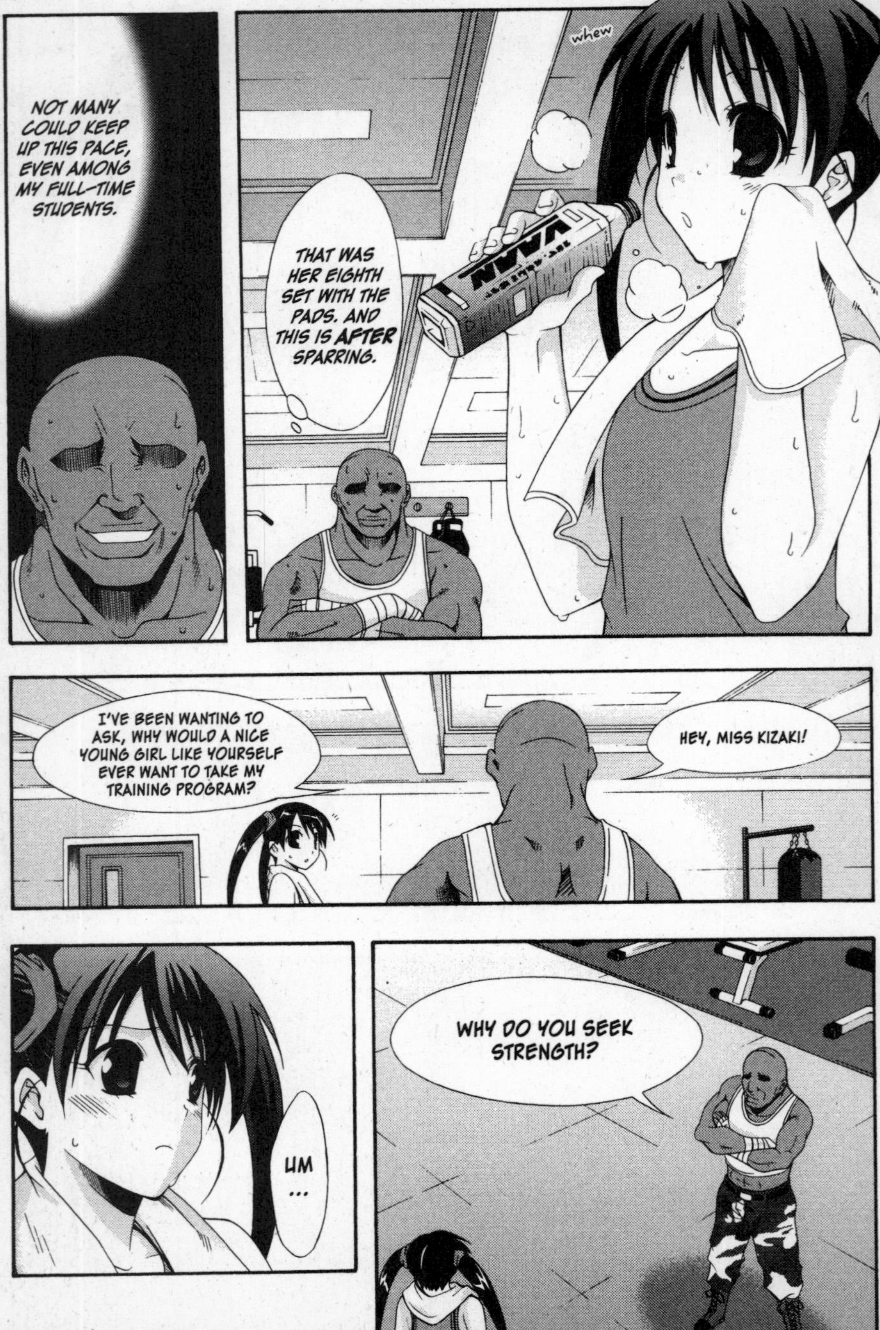
whew
THAT WAS HER EIGHTH SET WITH THE PADS. AND THIS IS AFTER SPARRING.
NOT MANY COULD KEEP UP THIS PACE, EVEN AMONG MY FULL-TIME STUDENTS.
HEY, MISS KIZAKI!
I'VE BEEN WANTING TO ASK, WHY WOULD A NICE YOUNG GIRL LIKE YOURSELF EVER WANT TO TAKE MY TRAINING PROGRAM?
WHY DO YOU SEEK STRENGTH?
UM ...

I WANT TO BECOME A HERO.

...HERO.

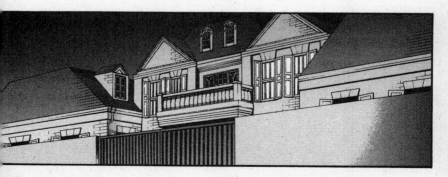

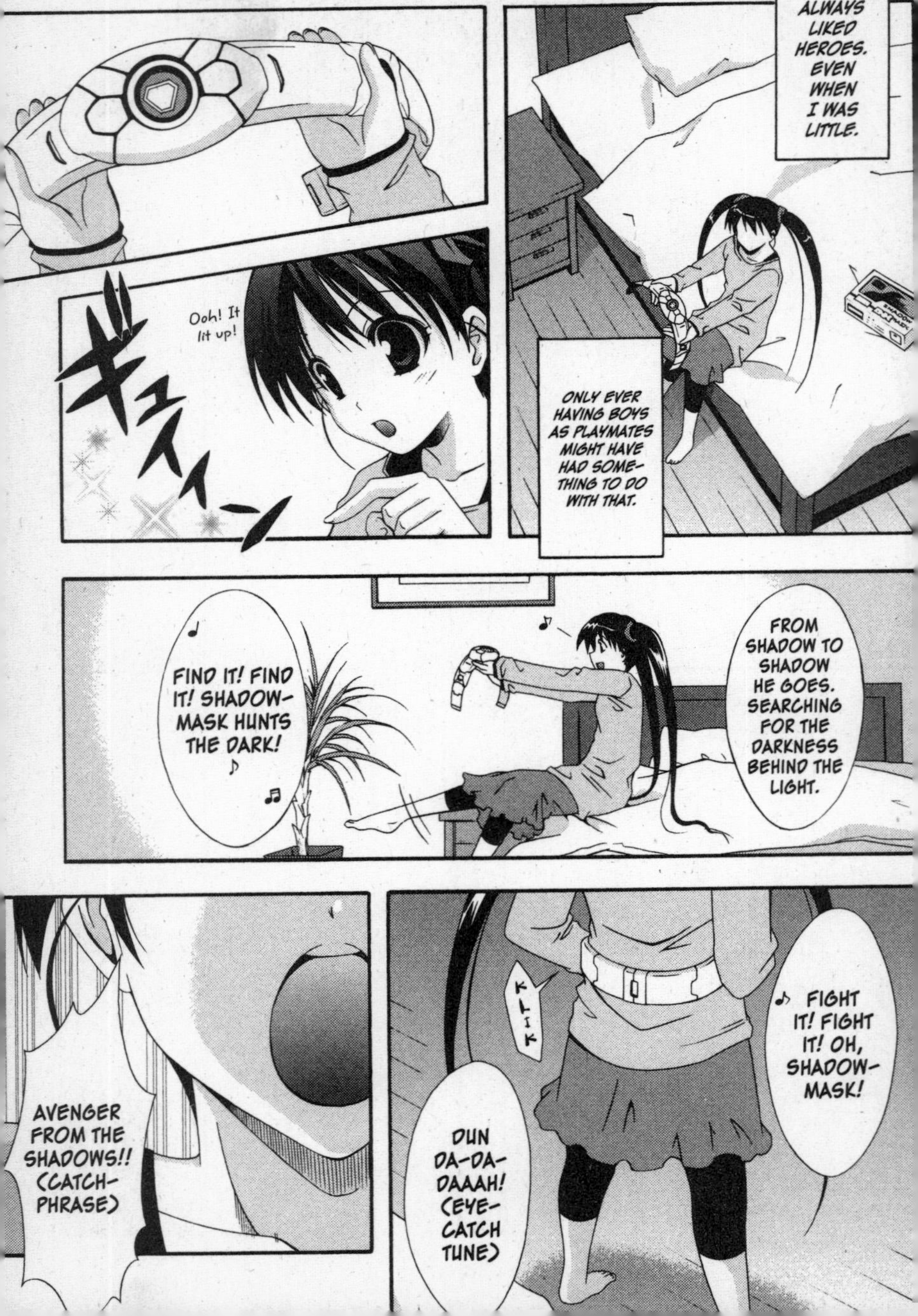
I'VE ALWAYS LIKED HEROES. EVEN WHEN I WAS LITTLE.
ONLY EVER HAVING BOYS AS PLAYMATES MIGHT HAVE HAD SOMETHING TO DO WITH THAT.
Ooh! It lit up!
ギュイイーン
FROM SHADOW TO SHADOW HE GOES. SEARCHING FOR THE DARKNESS BEHIND THE LIGHT.
FIND IT! FIND IT! SHADOW-MASK HUNTS THE DARK!
FIGHT IT! FIGHT IT! OH, SHADOW-MASK!
KLIK
DUN DA-DA-DAAAH! (EYE-CATCH TUNE)
AVENGER FROM THE SHADOWS!! (CATCH-PHRASE)

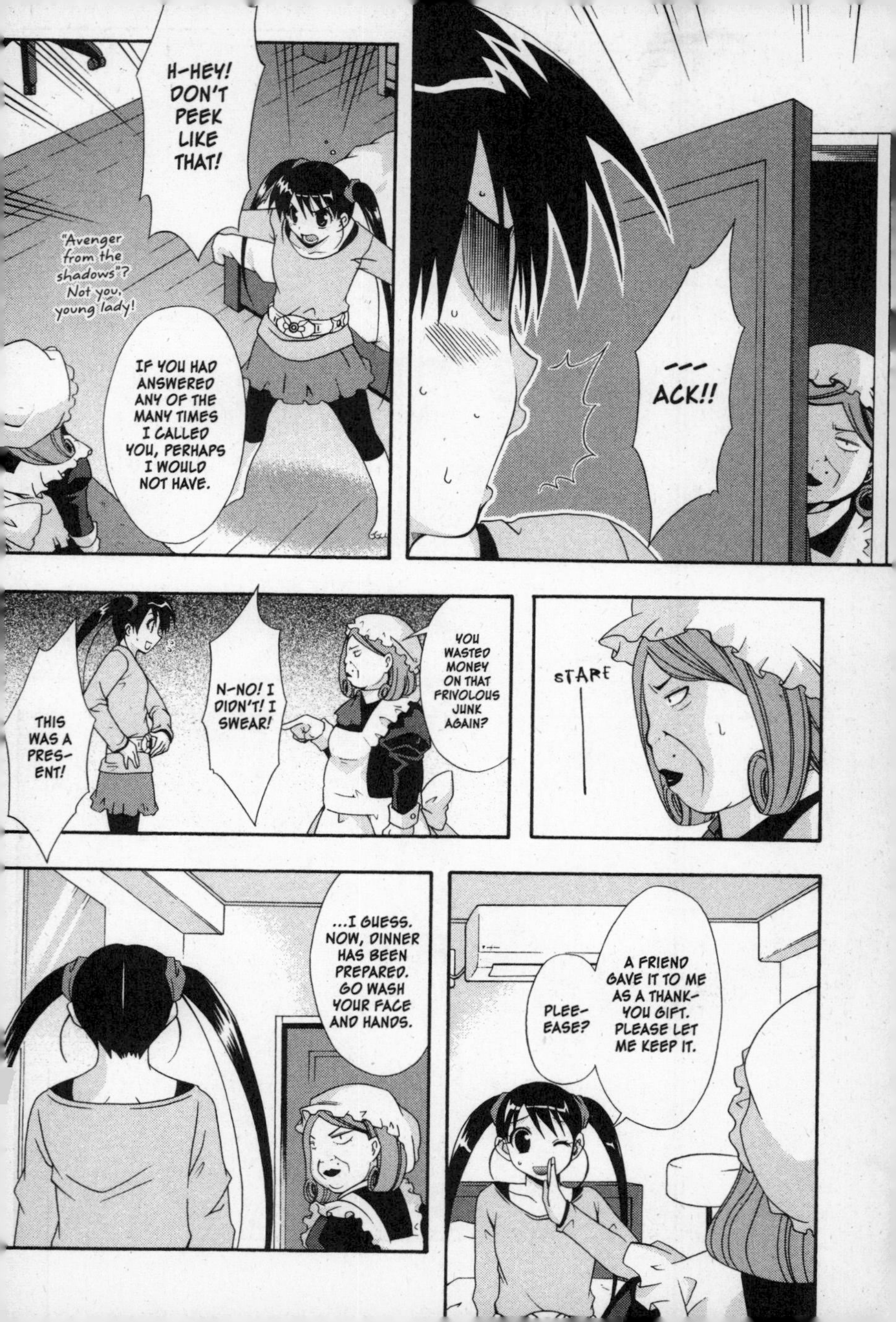

ACK!!
H-HEY! DON'T PEEK LIKE THAT!
IF YOU HAD ANSWERED ANY OF THE MANY TIMES I CALLED YOU, PERHAPS I WOULD NOT HAVE.
"Avenger from the shadows"? Not you, young lady!
STARE
YOU WASTED MONEY ON THAT FRIVOLOUS JUNK AGAIN?
N-NO! I DIDN'T! I SWEAR!
THIS WAS A PRES-ENT!
A FRIEND GAVE IT TO ME AS A THANK-YOU GIFT. PLEASE LET ME KEEP IT.
PLEE-EASE?
...I GUESS. NOW, DINNER HAS BEEN PREPARED. GO WASH YOUR FACE AND HANDS.

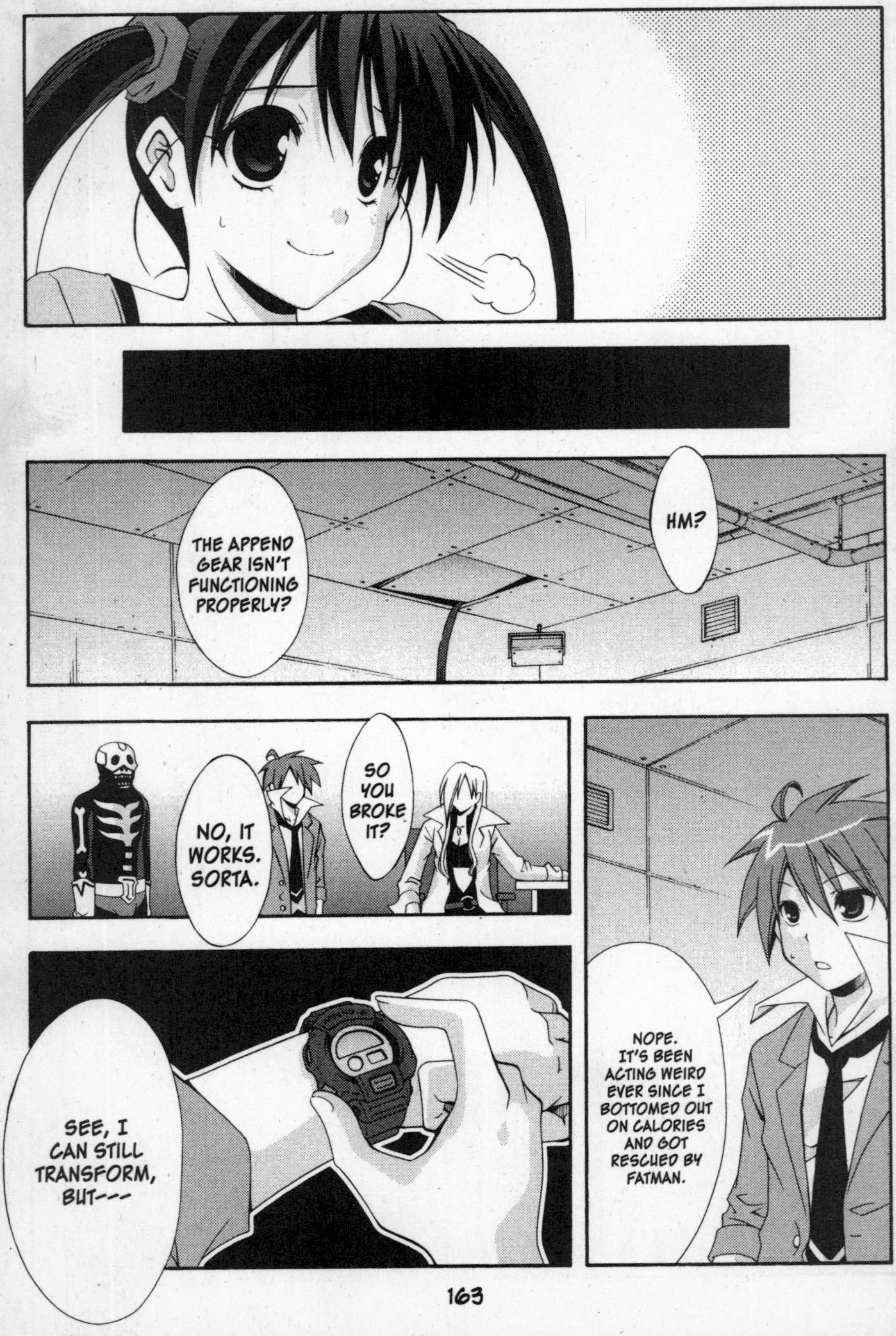
HM?
THE APPEND GEAR ISN'T FUNCTIONING PROPERLY?
NOPE. IT'S BEEN ACTING WEIRD EVER SINCE I BOTTOMED OUT ON CALORIES AND GOT RESCUED BY FATMAN.
SO YOU BROKE IT?
NO, IT WORKS. SORTA.
SEE, I CAN STILL TRANSFORM, BUT---

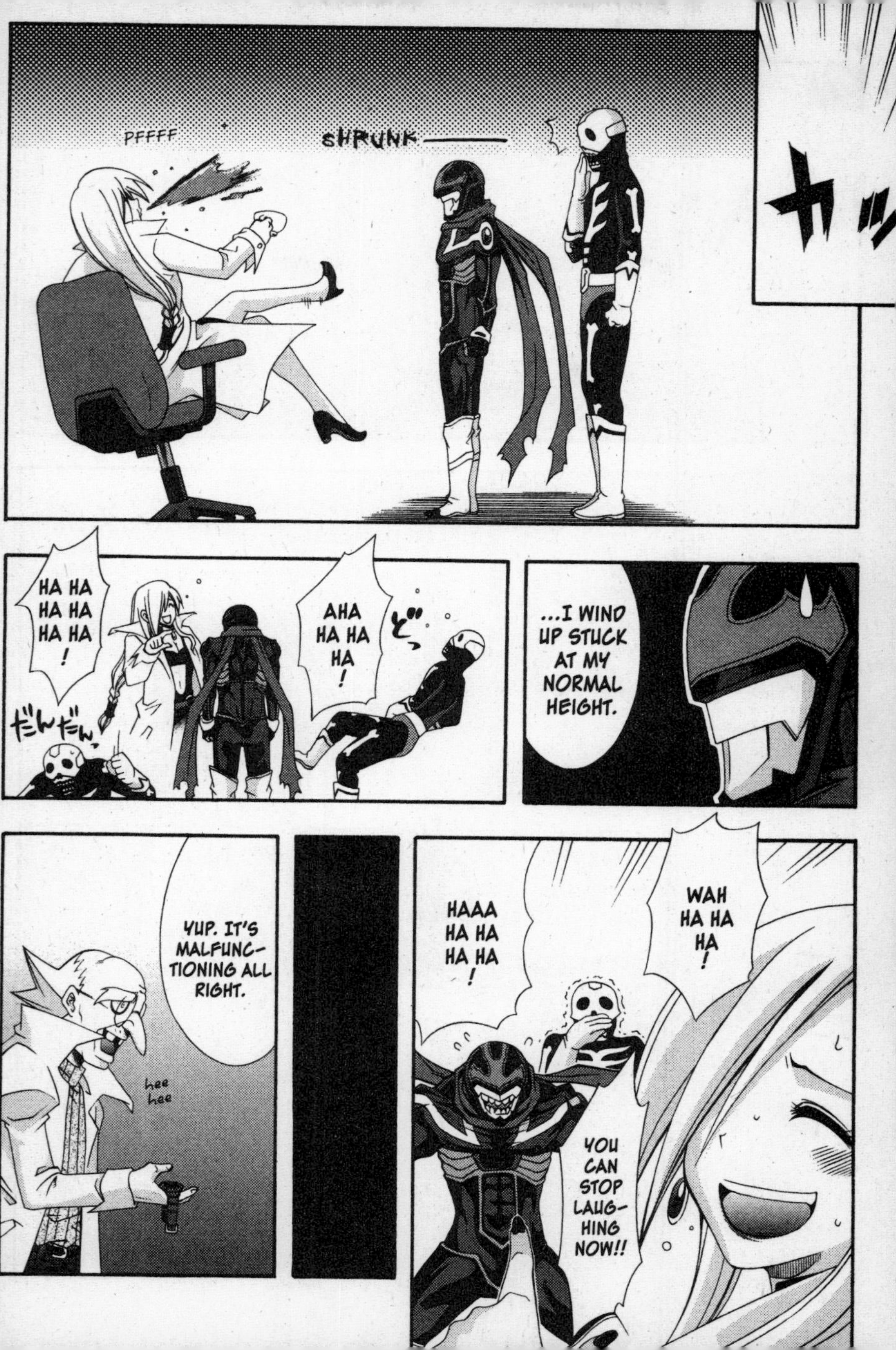
カッ
SHRUNK
PFFFF
...I WIND UP STUCK AT MY NORMAL HEIGHT.
AHA HA HA HA!
どっ
HA HA HA HA HA HA!
だんだん
WAH HA HA HA!
HAAA HA HA HA HA!
YOU CAN STOP LAUGHING NOW!!
YUP. IT'S MALFUNCTIONING ALL RIGHT.
hee hee

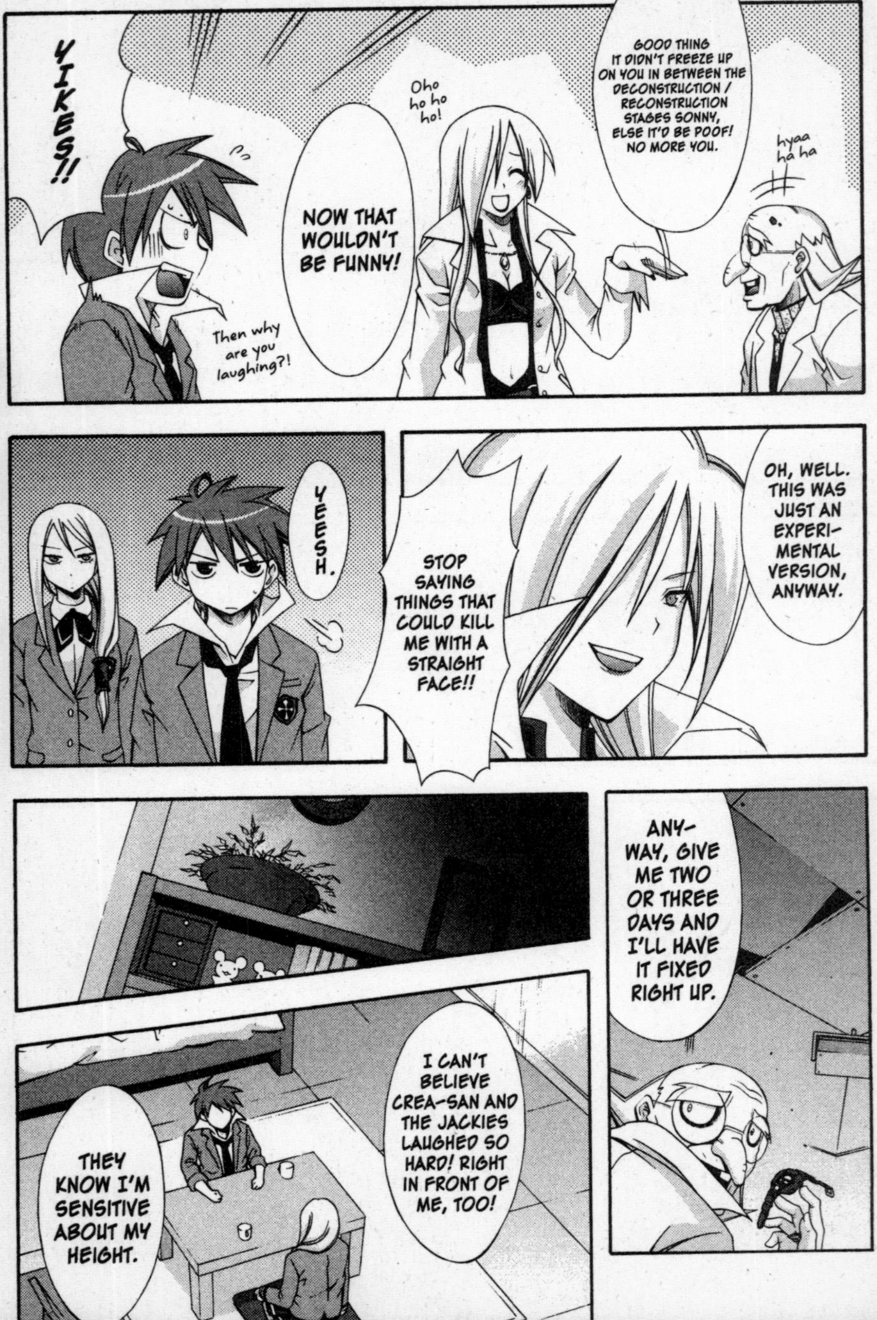
GOOD THING IT DIDN'T FREEZE UP ON YOU IN BETWEEN THE DECONSTRUCTION / RECONSTRUCTION STAGES SONNY, ELSE IT'D BE POOF! NO MORE YOU.
hyaa ha ha
Oho ho ho ho!
NOW THAT WOULDN'T BE FUNNY!
YIKES!!
Then why are you laughing?!
OH, WELL. THIS WAS JUST AN EXPERI-MENTAL VERSION, ANYWAY.
STOP SAYING THINGS THAT COULD KILL ME WITH A STRAIGHT FACE!!
YEESH.
ANY-WAY, GIVE ME TWO OR THREE DAYS AND I'LL HAVE IT FIXED RIGHT UP.
I CAN'T BELIEVE CREA-SAN AND THE JACKIES LAUGHED SO HARD! RIGHT IN FRONT OF ME, TOO!
THEY KNOW I'M SENSITIVE ABOUT MY HEIGHT.

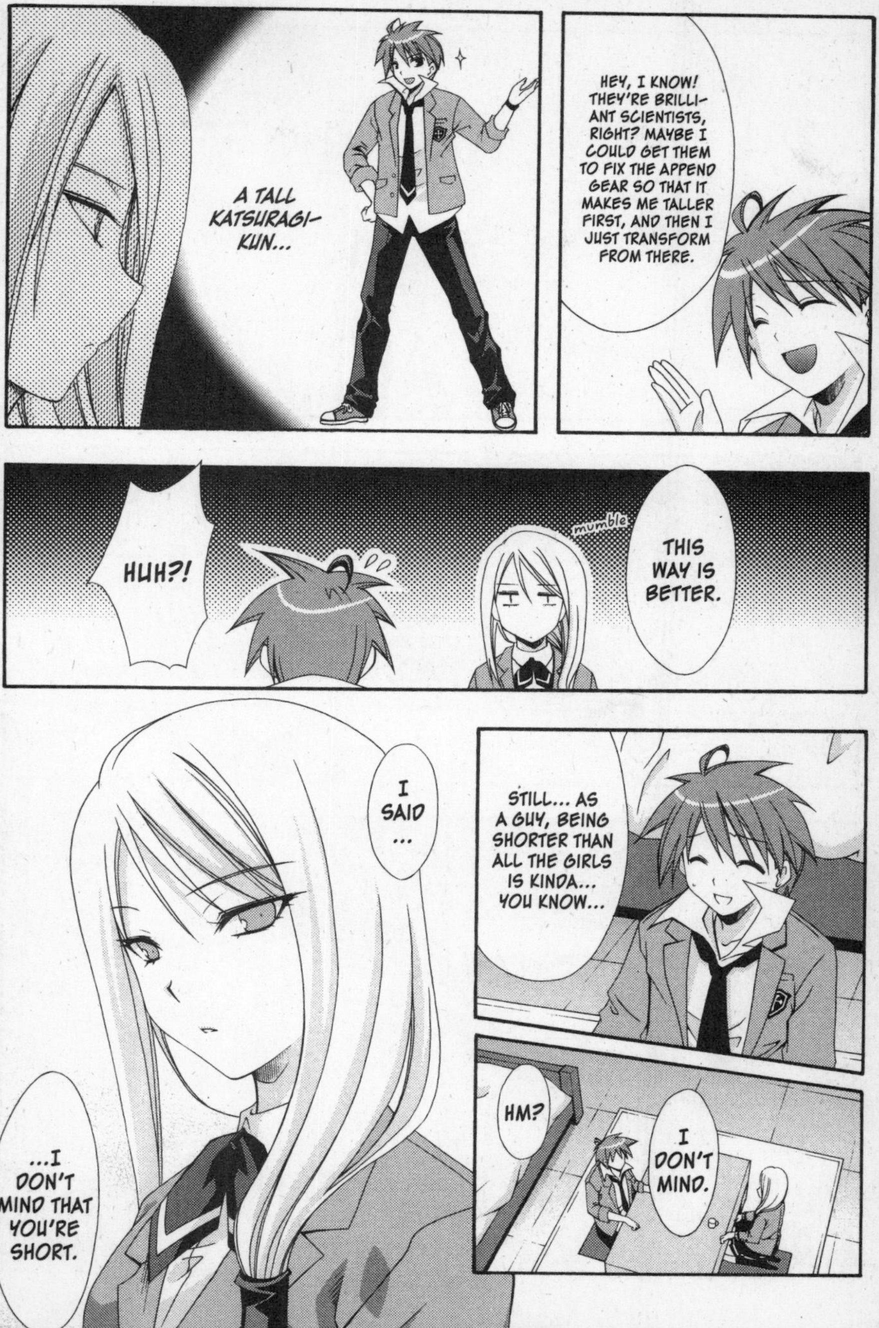
HEY, I KNOW! THEY'RE BRILLI-ANT SCIENTISTS, RIGHT? MAYBE I COULD GET THEM TO FIX THE APPEND GEAR SO THAT IT MAKES ME TALLER FIRST, AND THEN I JUST TRANSFORM FROM THERE.
A TALL KATSURAGI-KUN...
THIS WAY IS BETTER.
mumble
HUH?!
STILL... AS A GUY, BEING SHORTER THAN ALL THE GIRLS IS KINDA... YOU KNOW...
I DON'T MIND.
HM?
I SAID ...
...I DON'T MIND THAT YOU'RE SHORT.

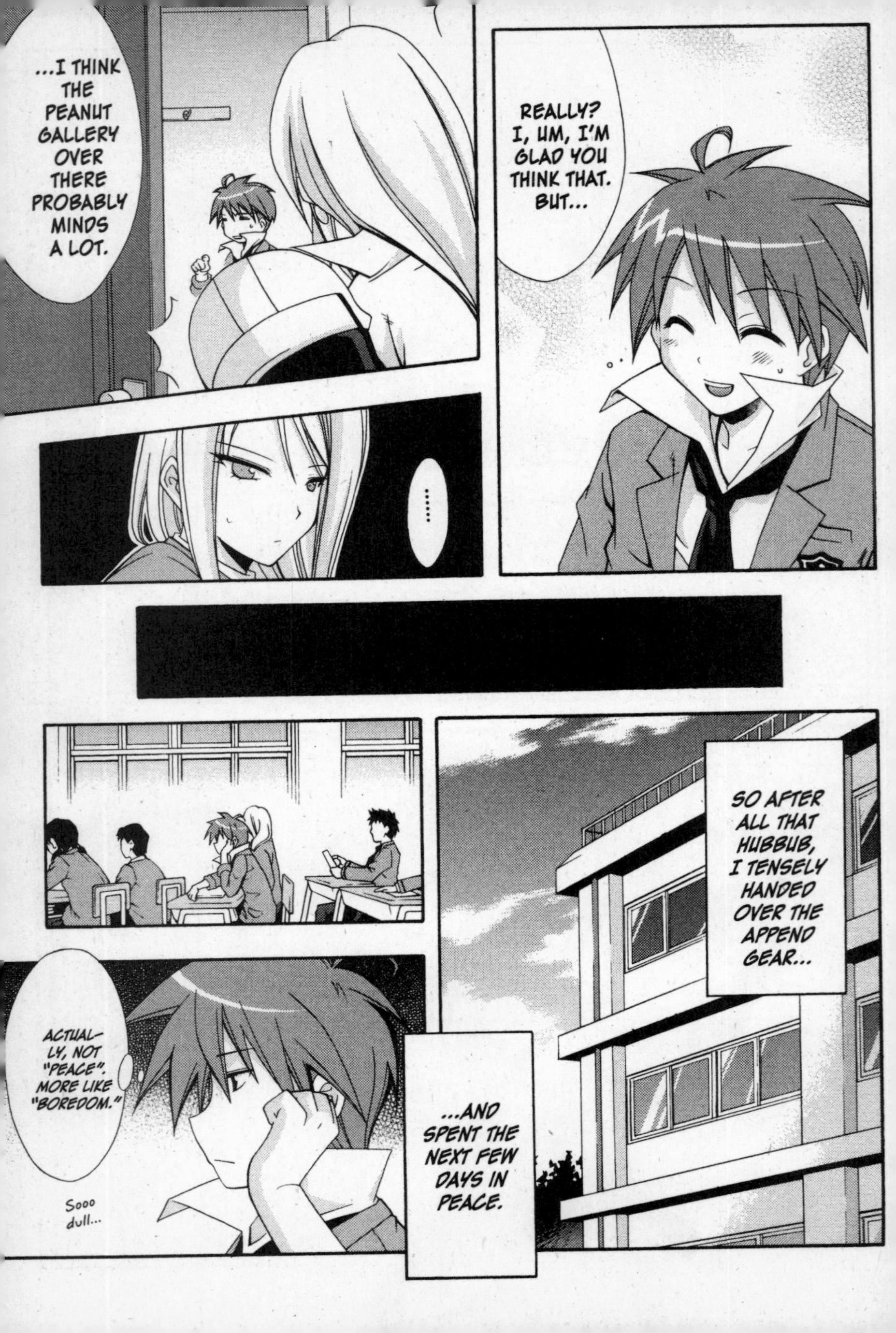
REALLY? I, UM, I'M GLAD YOU THINK THAT. BUT...
...I THINK THE PEANUT GALLERY OVER THERE PROBABLY MINDS A LOT.
......
SO AFTER ALL THAT HUBBUB, I TENSELY HANDED OVER THE APPEND GEAR...
...AND SPENT THE NEXT FEW DAYS IN PEACE.
ACTUAL-LY, NOT "PEACE". MORE LIKE "BOREDOM."
Sooo dull...

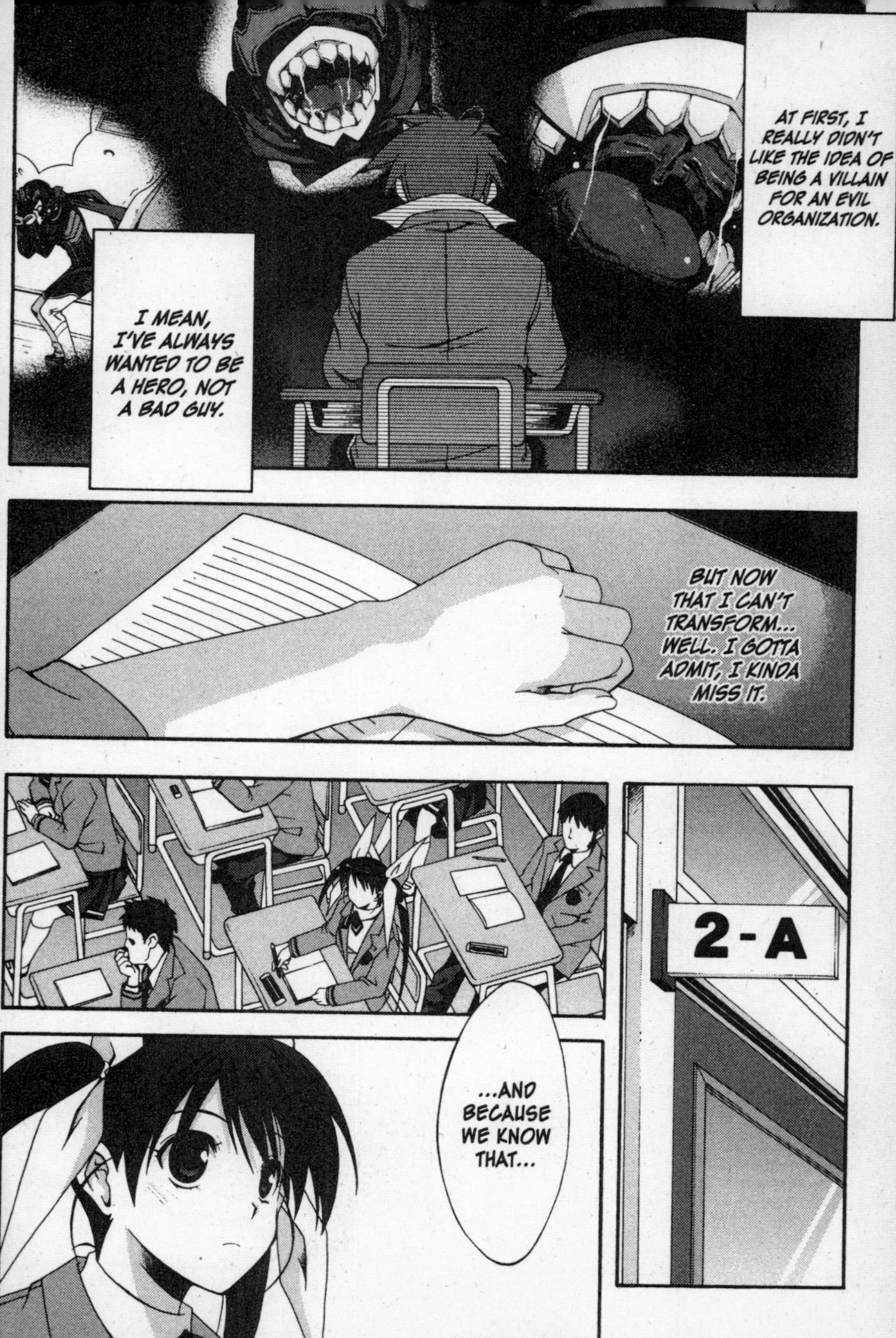
AT FIRST, I REALLY DIDN'T LIKE THE IDEA OF BEING A VILLAIN FOR AN EVIL ORGANIZATION.
I MEAN, I'VE ALWAYS WANTED TO BE A HERO, NOT A BAD GUY.
BUT NOW THAT I CAN'T TRANSFORM... WELL. I GOTTA ADMIT, I KINDA MISS IT.
2-A
...AND BECAUSE WE KNOW THAT...

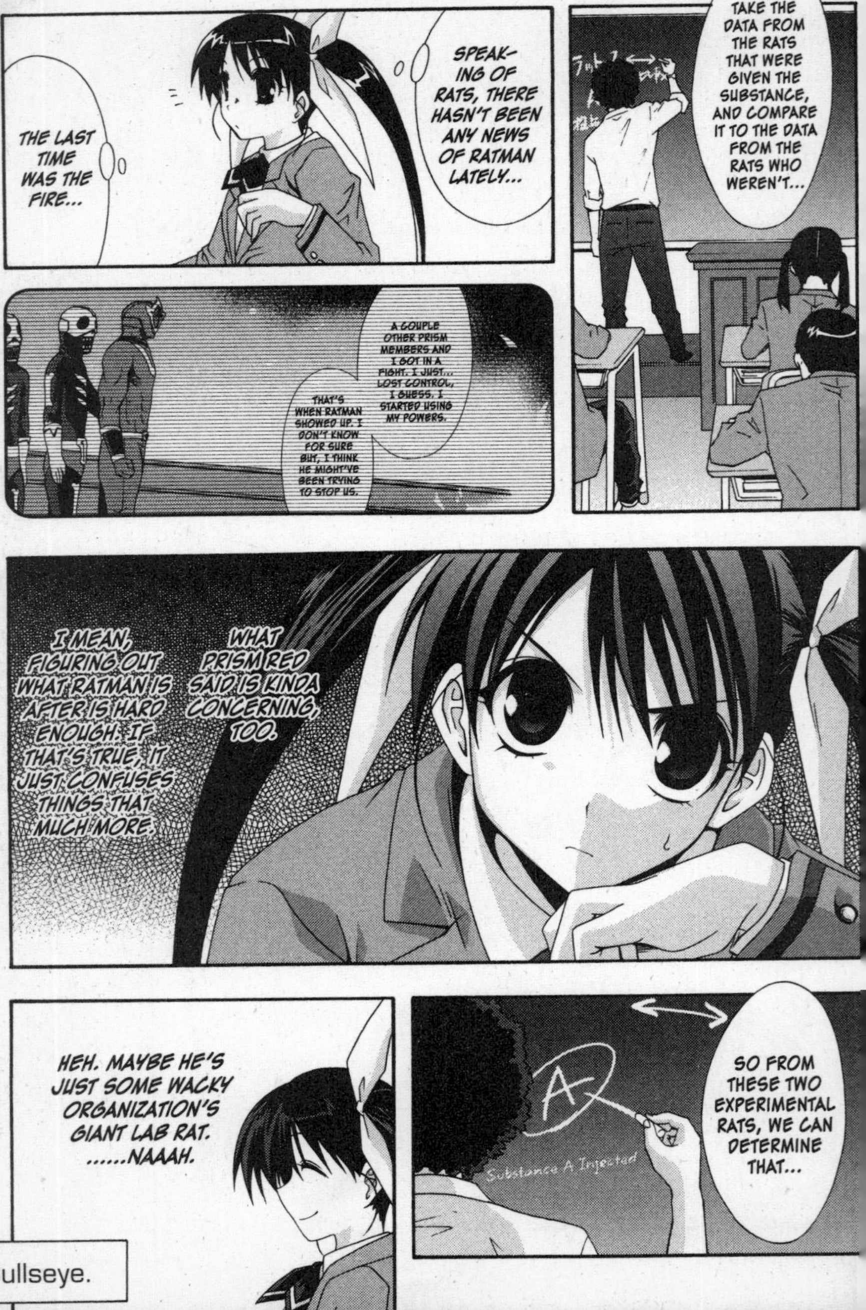
SO WE TAKE THE DATA FROM THE RATS THAT WERE GIVEN THE SUBSTANCE, AND COMPARE IT TO THE DATA FROM THE RATS WHO WEREN'T...
SPEAK-ING OF RATS, THERE HASN'T BEEN ANY NEWS OF RATMAN LATELY...
THE LAST TIME WAS THE FIRE...
A COUPLE OTHER PRISM MEMBERS AND I GOT IN A FIGHT. I JUST... LOST CONTROL, I GUESS. I STARTED USING MY POWERS.
THAT'S WHEN RATMAN SHOWED UP. I DON'T KNOW FOR SURE BUT, I THINK HE MIGHT'VE BEEN TRYING TO STOP US.
WHAT PRISM RED SAID IS KINDA CONCERNING, TOO.
I MEAN, FIGURING OUT WHAT RATMAN IS AFTER IS HARD ENOUGH. IF THAT'S TRUE, IT JUST CONFUSES THINGS THAT MUCH MORE.
SO FROM THESE TWO EXPERIMENTAL RATS, WE CAN DETERMINE THAT...
A
Substance A Injected
HEH. MAYBE HE'S JUST SOME WACKY ORGANIZATION'S GIANT LAB RAT. ......NAAAH.
Bullseye.

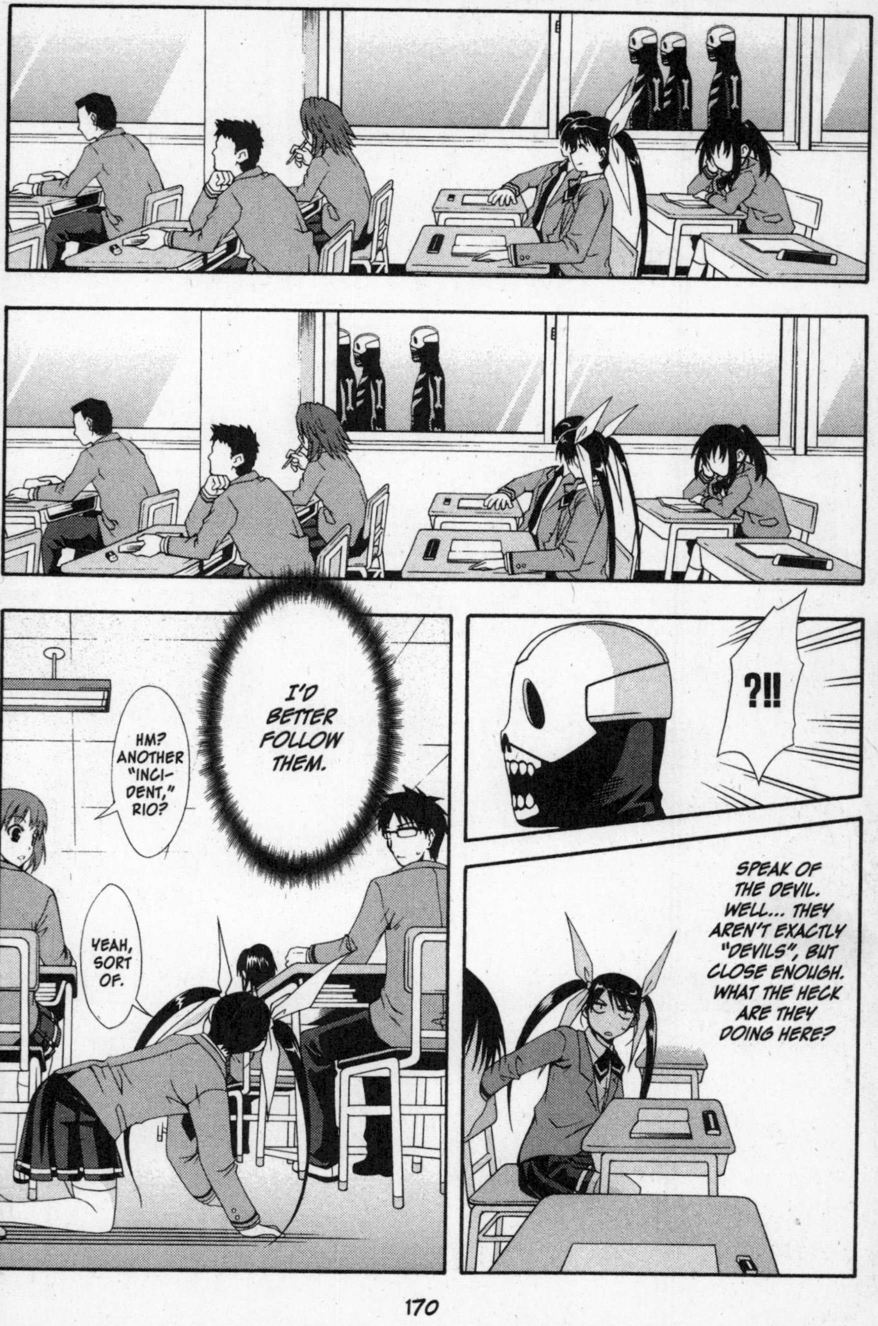
?!!
SPEAK OF THE DEVIL. WELL... THEY AREN'T EXACTLY "DEVILS", BUT CLOSE ENOUGH. WHAT THE HECK ARE THEY DOING HERE?
I'D BETTER FOLLOW THEM.
HM? ANOTHER "INCI-DENT," RIO?
YEAH, SORT OF.

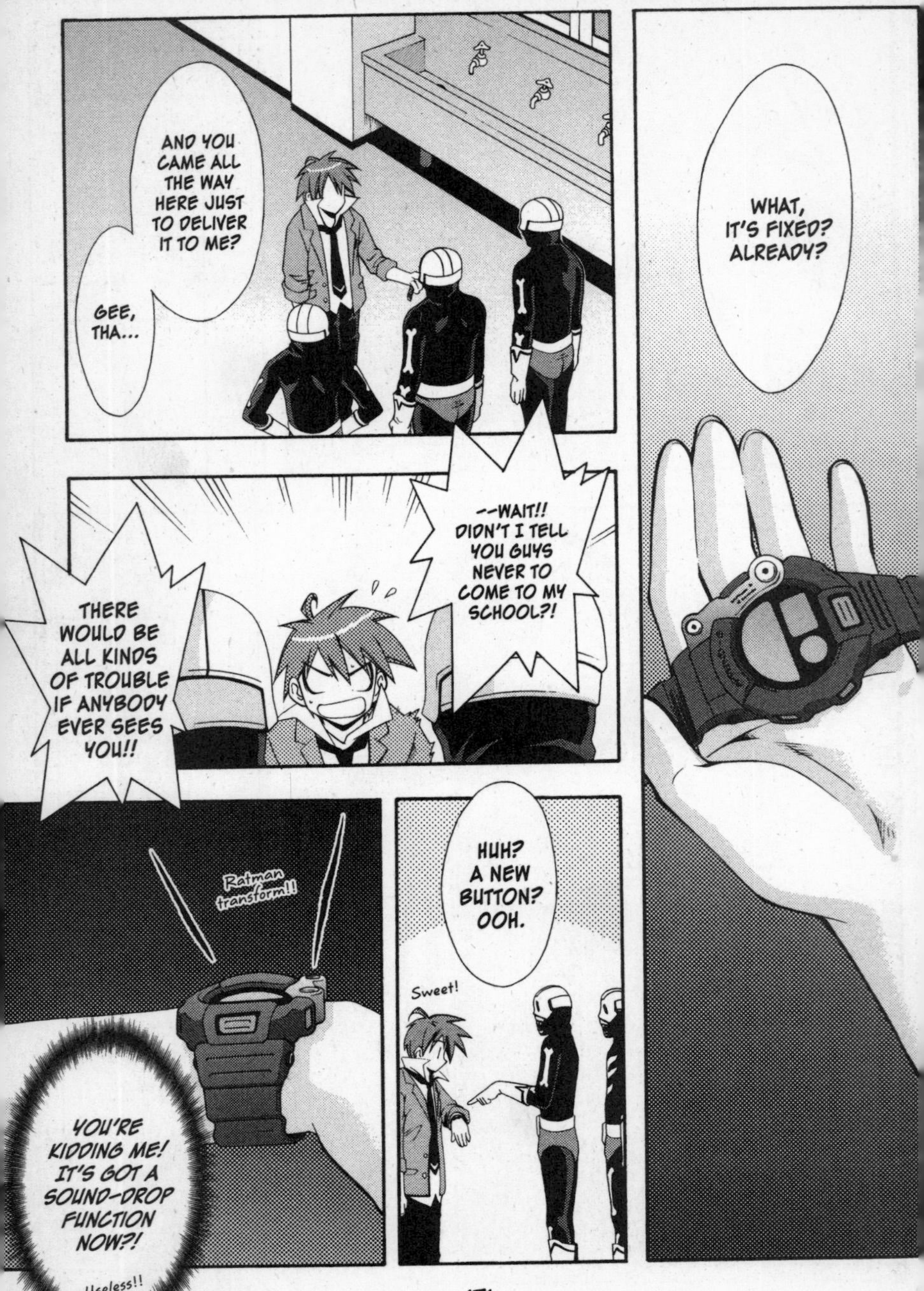
WHAT, IT'S FIXED? ALREADY?
AND YOU CAME ALL THE WAY HERE JUST TO DELIVER IT TO ME?
GEE, THA...
--WAIT!! DIDN'T I TELL YOU GUYS NEVER TO COME TO MY SCHOOL?!
THERE WOULD BE ALL KINDS OF TROUBLE IF ANYBODY EVER SEES YOU!!
HUH? A NEW BUTTON? OOH.
Sweet!
Ratman transform!!
YOU'RE KIDDING ME! IT'S GOT A SOUND-DROP FUNCTION NOW?!
Useless!!

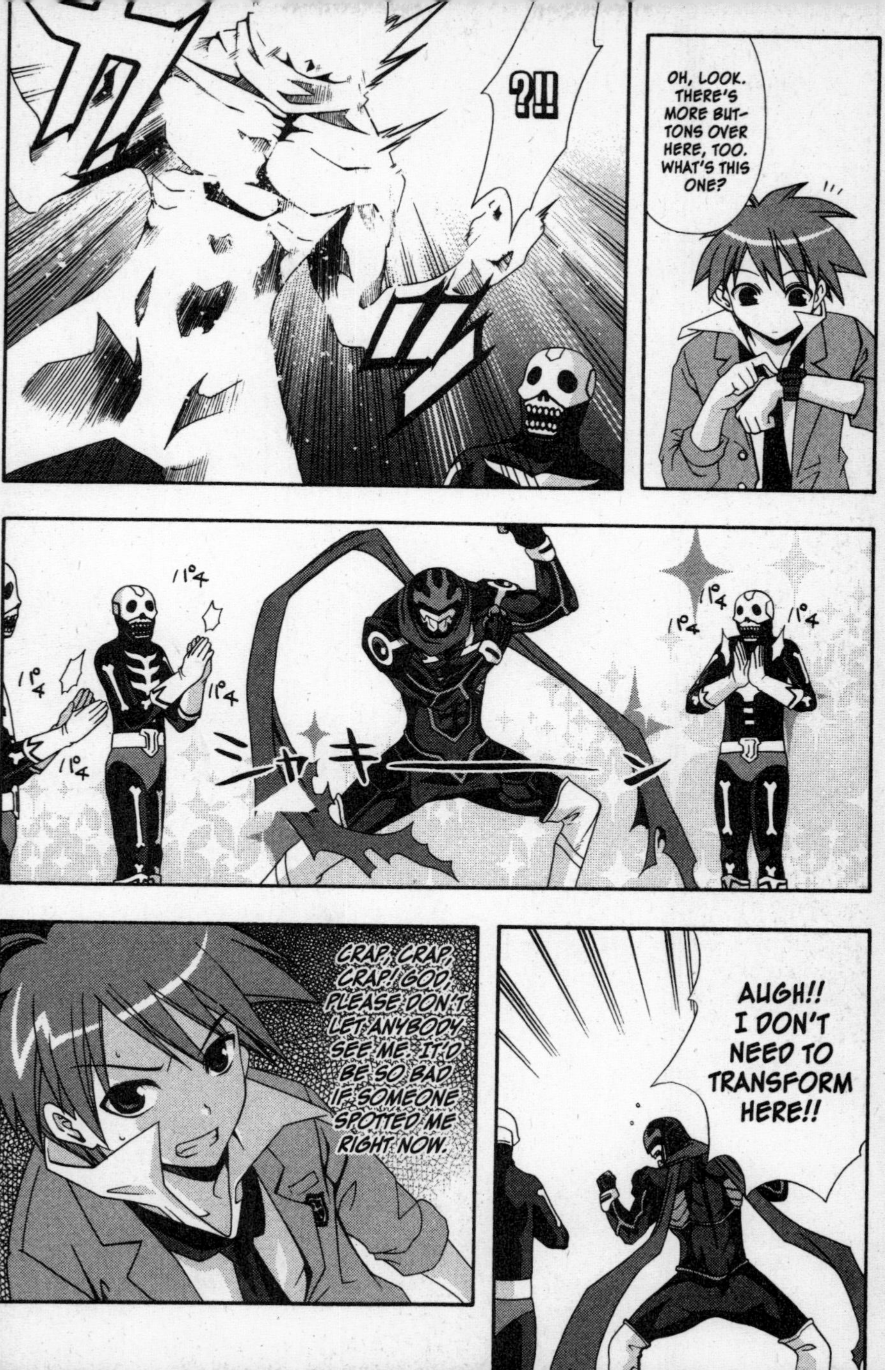
OH, LOOK. THERE'S MORE BUT-TONS OVER HERE, TOO. WHAT'S THIS ONE?
?!!
AUGH!! I DON'T NEED TO TRANSFORM HERE!!
CRAP, CRAP, CRAP! GOD, PLEASE DON'T LET ANYBODY SEE ME. IT'D BE SO BAD IF SOMEONE SPOTTED ME RIGHT NOW.

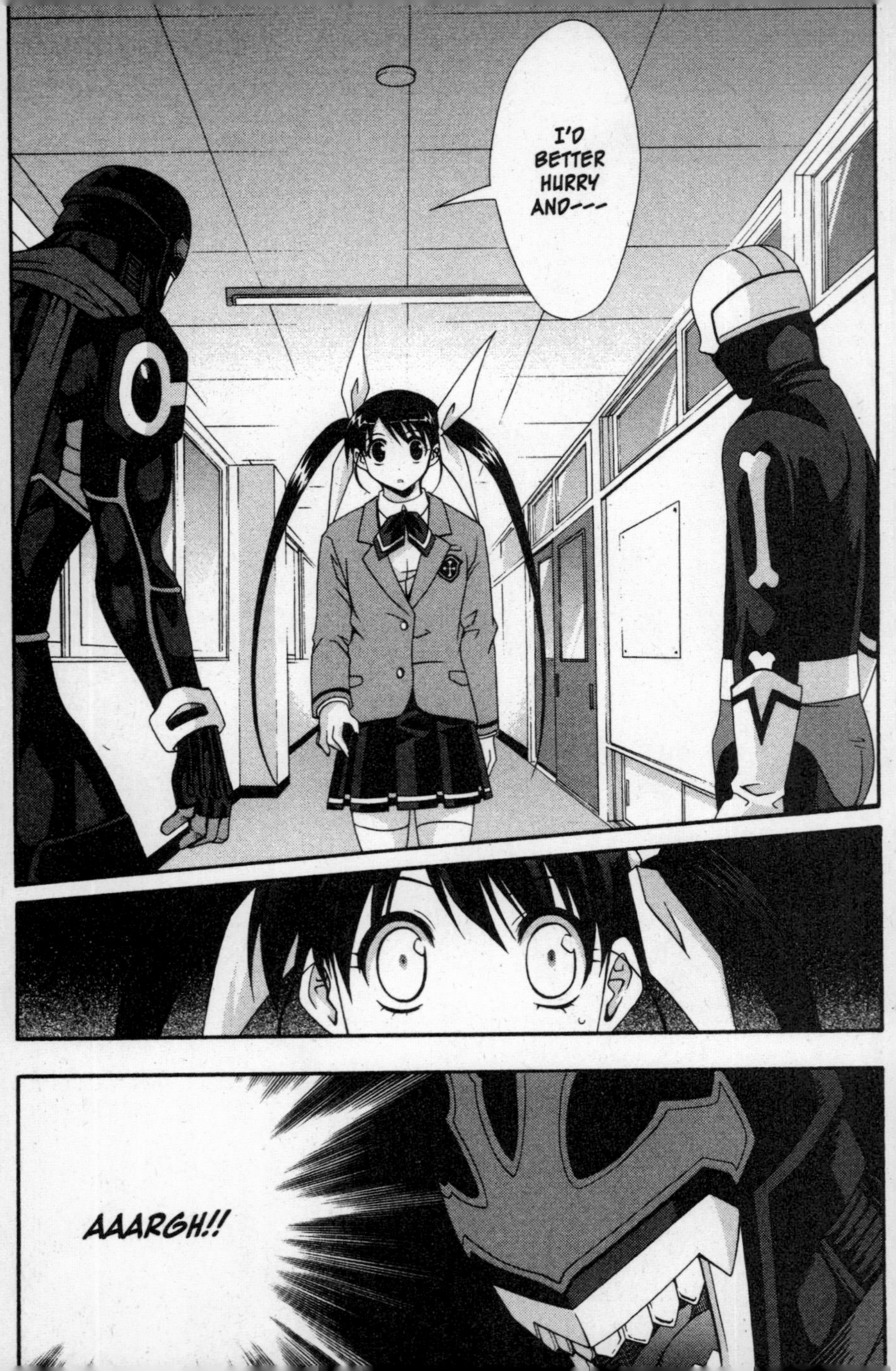
I'D BETTER HURRY AND---
AAARGH!!

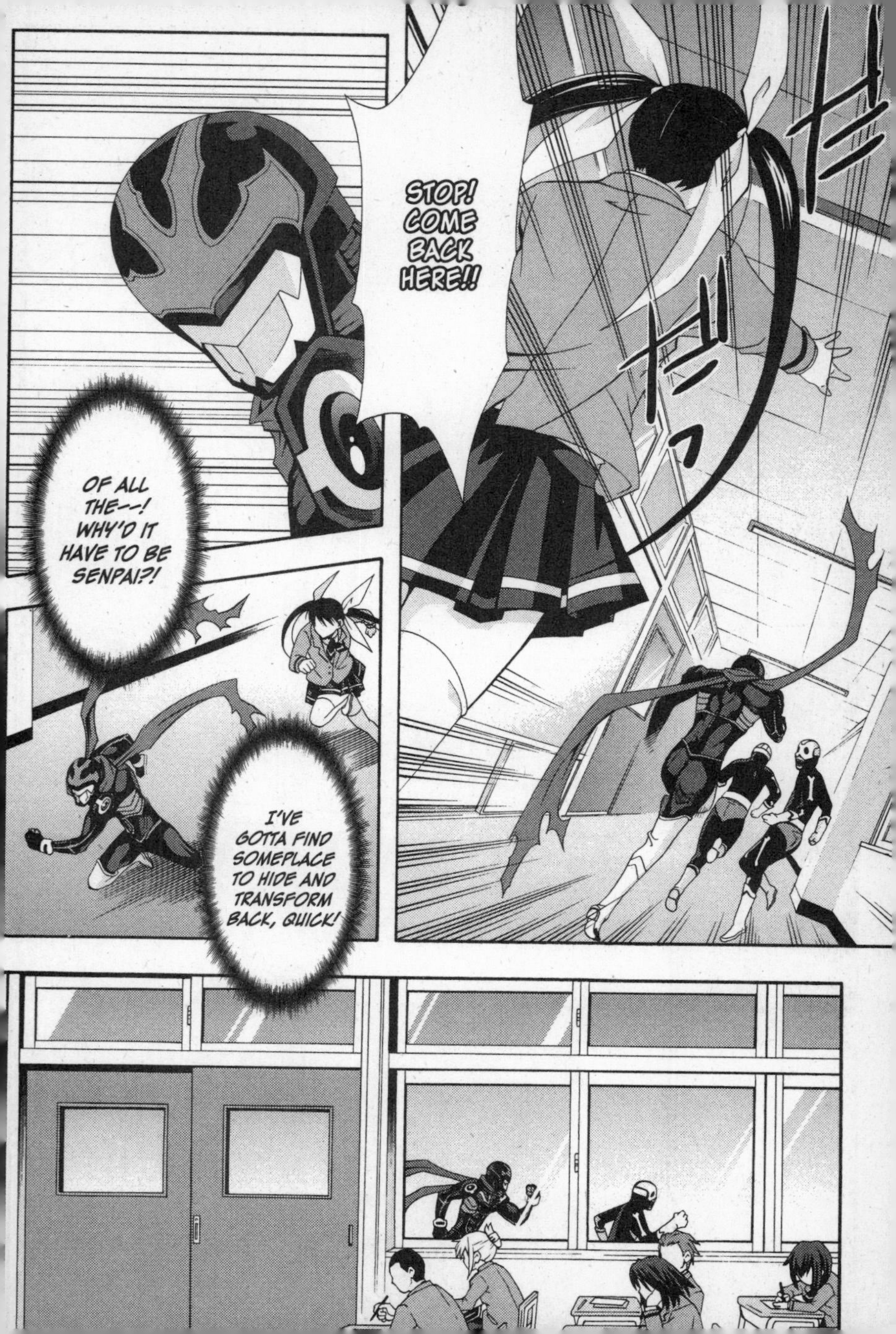

STOP! COME BACK HERE!!
OF ALL THE--! WHY'D IT HAVE TO BE SENPAI?!
I'VE GOTTA FIND SOMEPLACE TO HIDE AND TRANSFORM BACK, QUICK!

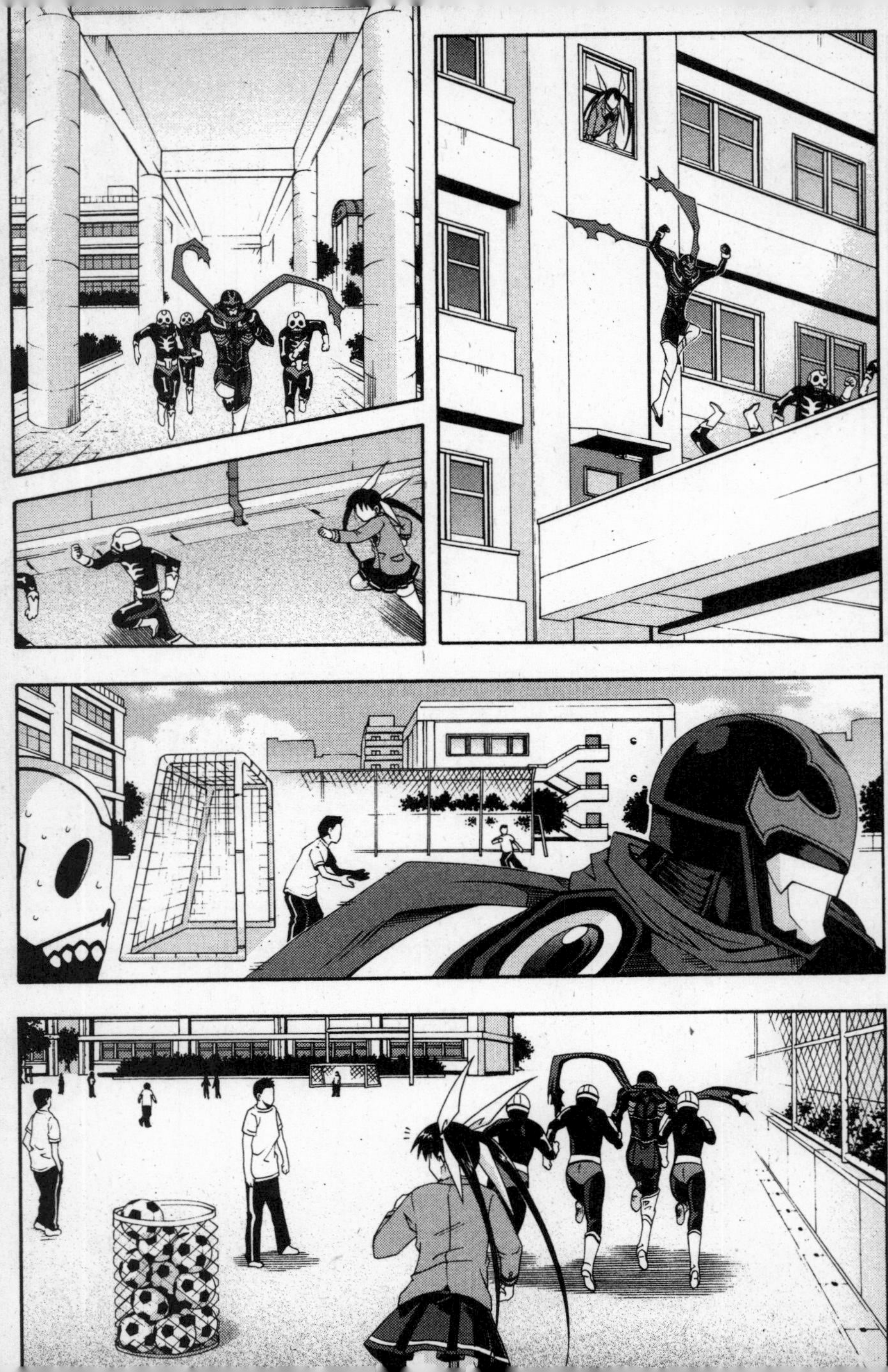

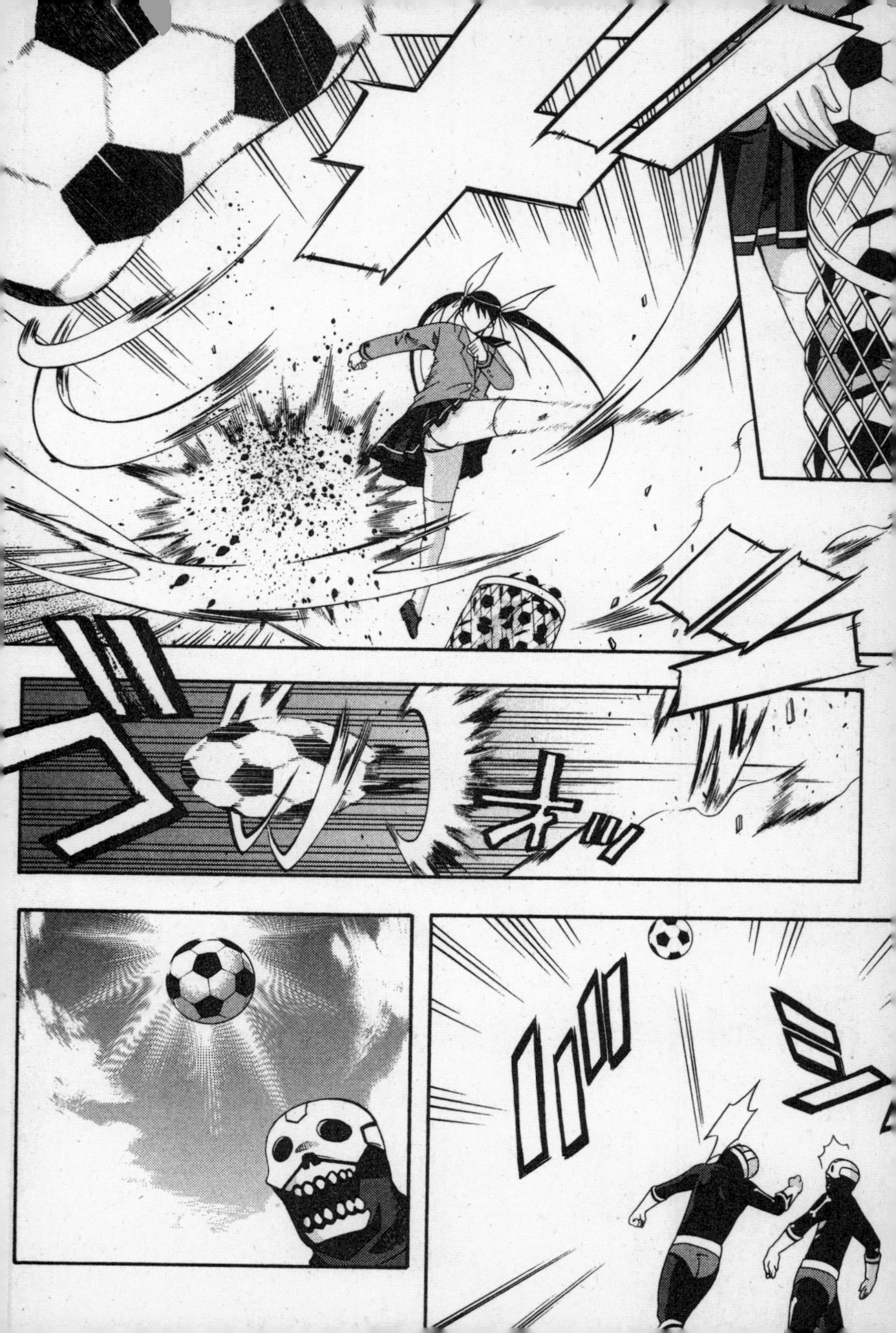

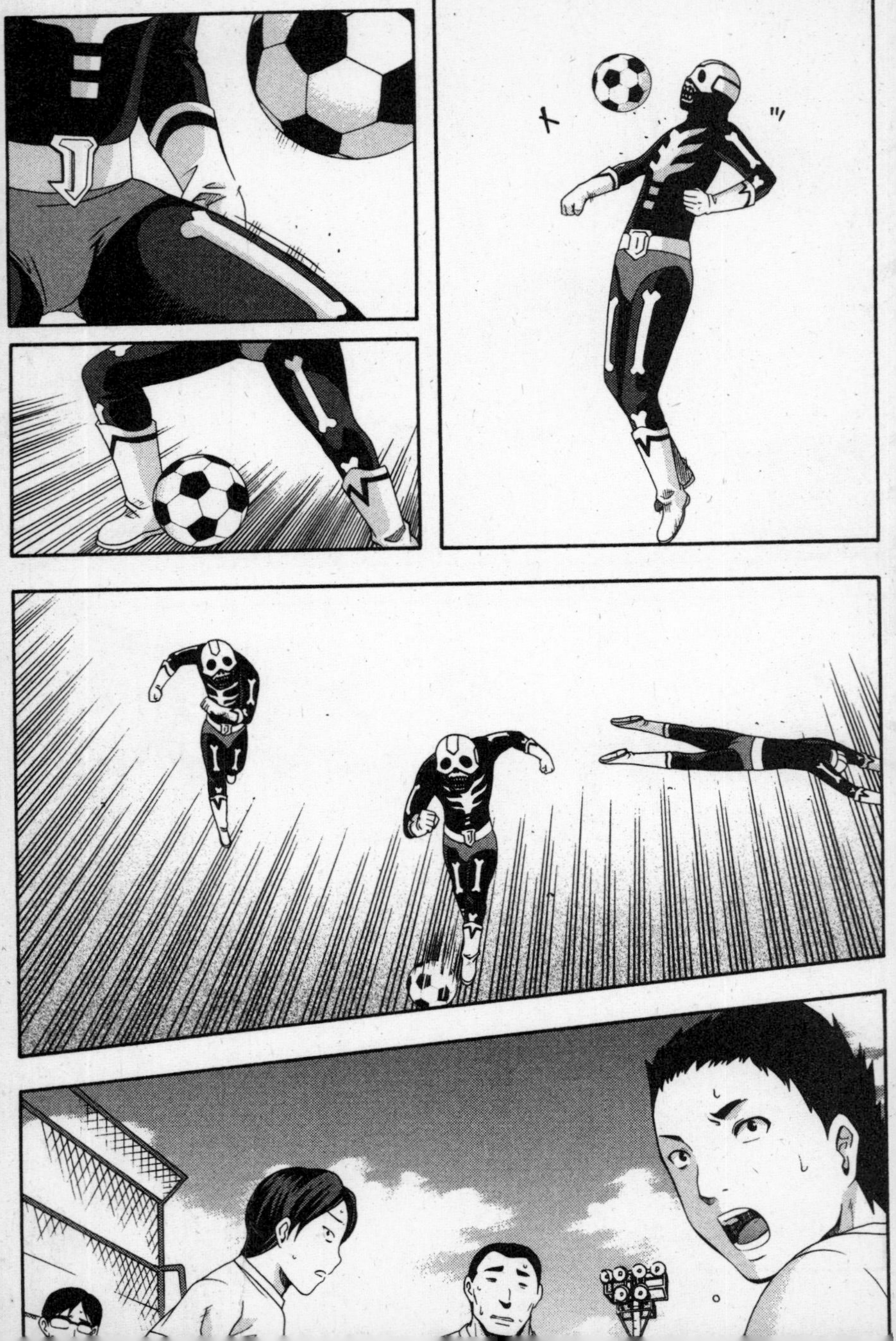

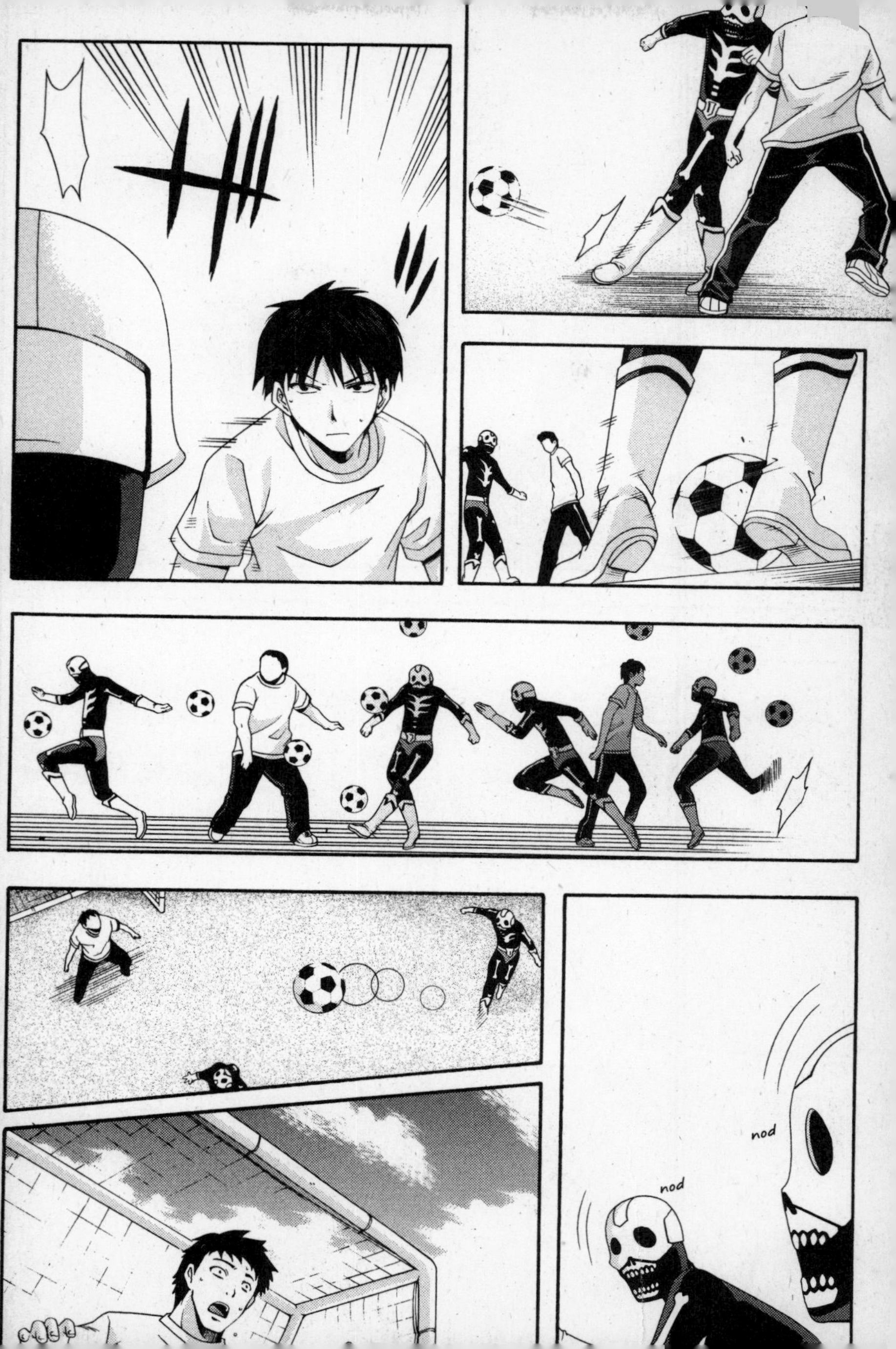
nod
nod

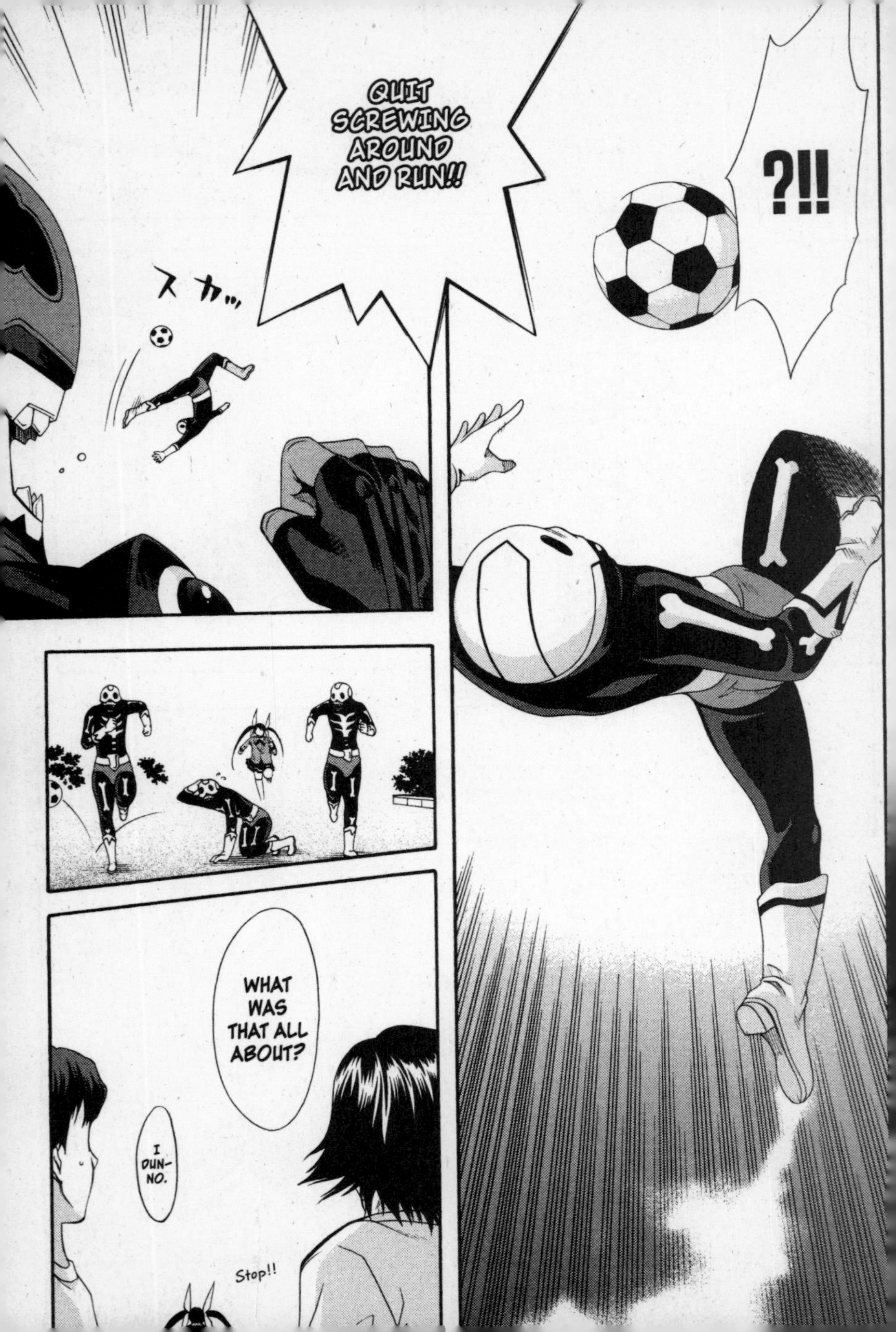
?!!
QUIT SCREWING AROUND AND RUN!!
スカッ
WHAT WAS THAT ALL ABOUT?
I DUN-NO.
Stop!!

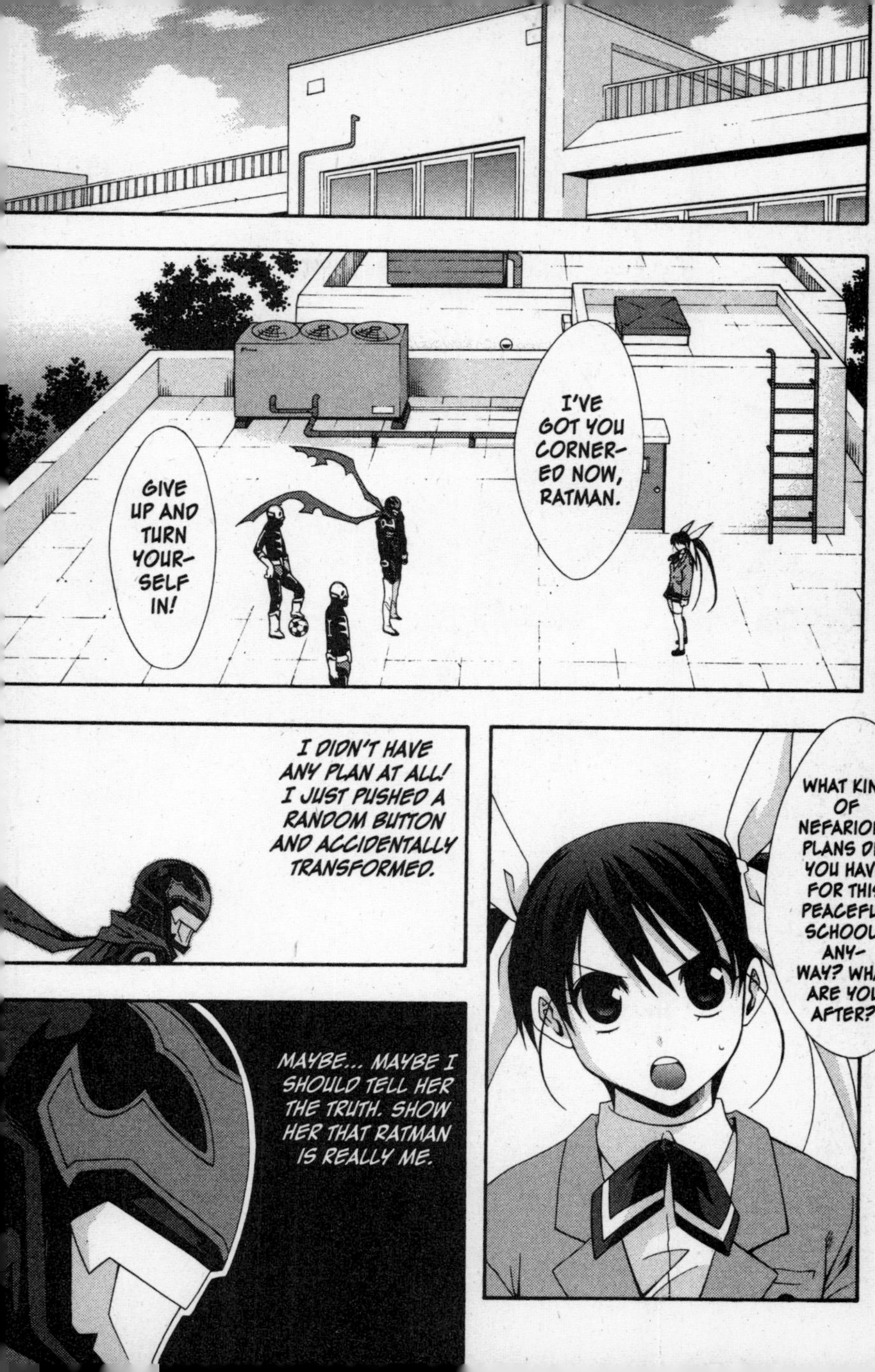
I'VE GOT YOU CORNERED NOW, RATMAN.
GIVE UP AND TURN YOURSELF IN!
WHAT KIND OF NEFARIOUS PLANS DID YOU HAVE FOR THIS PEACEFUL SCHOOL, ANYWAY? WHAT ARE YOU AFTER?
I DIDN'T HAVE ANY PLAN AT ALL! I JUST PUSHED A RANDOM BUTTON AND ACCIDENTALLY TRANSFORMED.
MAYBE... MAYBE I SHOULD TELL HER THE TRUTH. SHOW HER THAT RATMAN IS REALLY ME.

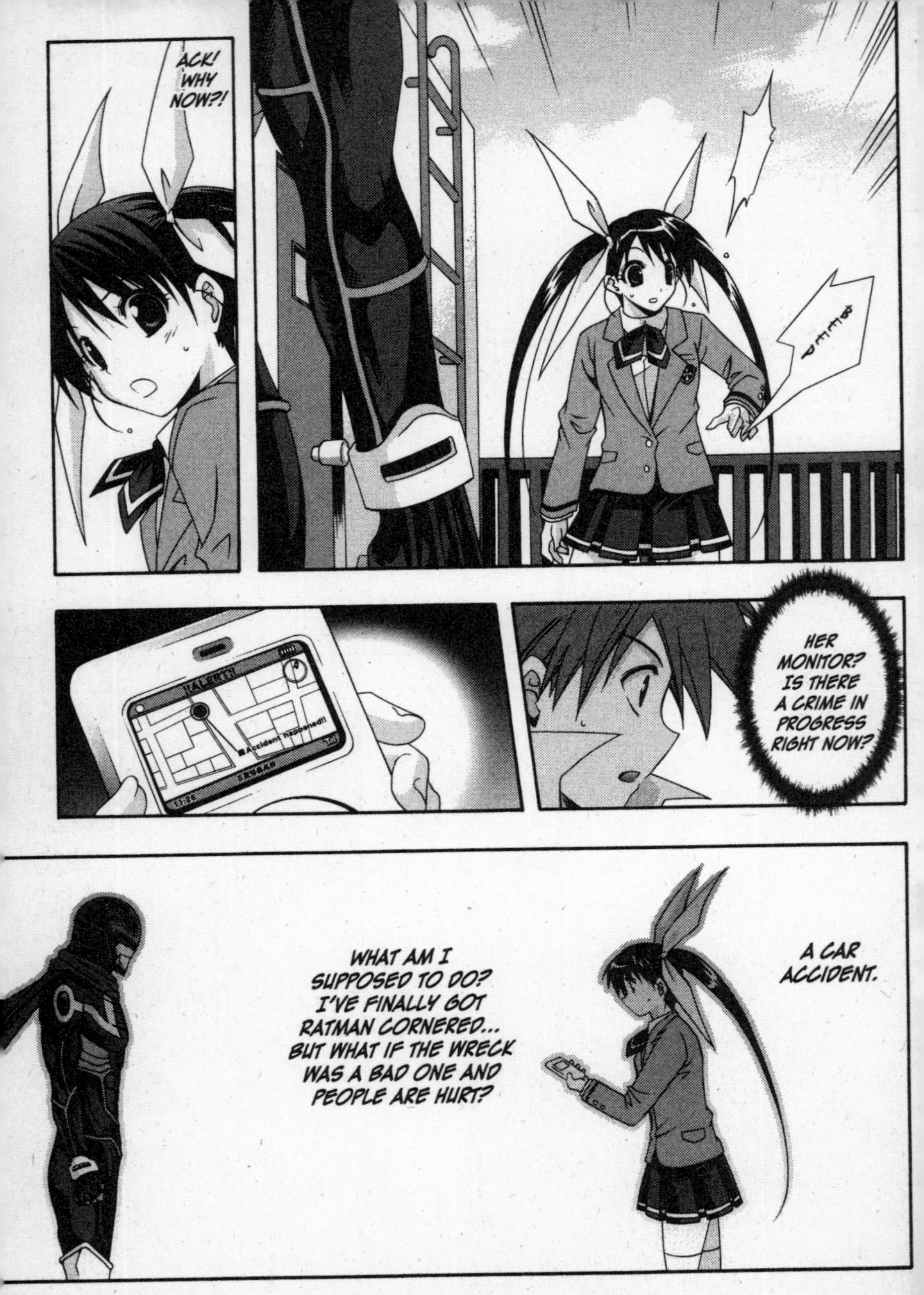
BEEP
ACK! WHY NOW?!
HER MONITOR? IS THERE A CRIME IN PROGRESS RIGHT NOW?
Accident happened!!
A CAR ACCIDENT.
WHAT AM I SUPPOSED TO DO? I'VE FINALLY GOT RATMAN CORNERED... BUT WHAT IF THE WRECK WAS A BAD ONE AND PEOPLE ARE HURT?

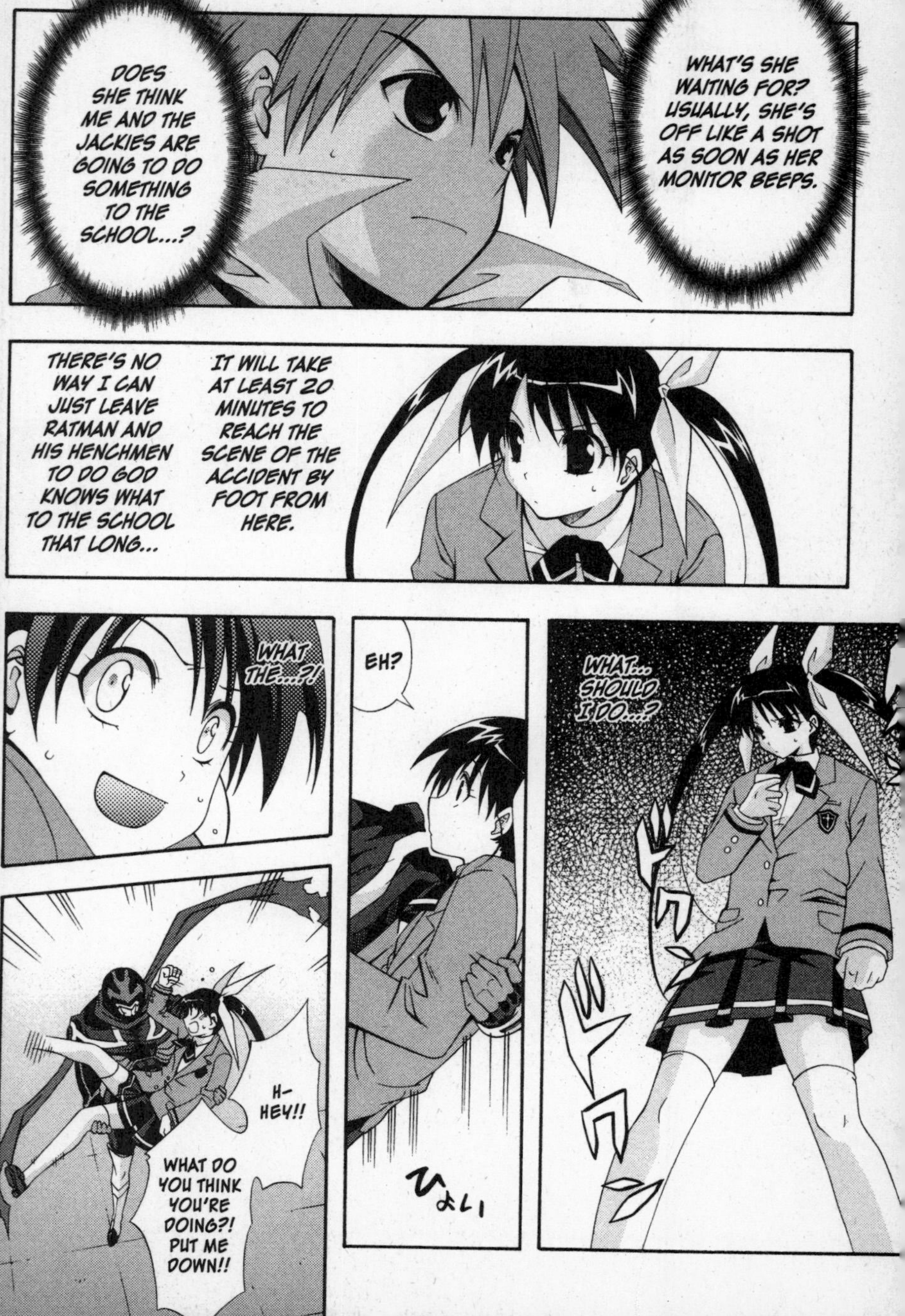
WHAT'S SHE WAITING FOR? USUALLY, SHE'S OFF LIKE A SHOT AS SOON AS HER MONITOR BEEPS.
DOES SHE THINK ME AND THE JACKIES ARE GOING TO DO SOMETHING TO THE SCHOOL...?
IT WILL TAKE AT LEAST 20 MINUTES TO REACH THE SCENE OF THE ACCIDENT BY FOOT FROM HERE.
THERE'S NO WAY I CAN JUST LEAVE RATMAN AND HIS HENCHMEN TO DO GOD KNOWS WHAT TO THE SCHOOL THAT LONG...
WHAT... SHOULD I DO...?
EH?
ひょい
WHAT THE...?!
H-HEY!!
WHAT DO YOU THINK YOU'RE DOING?! PUT ME DOWN!!

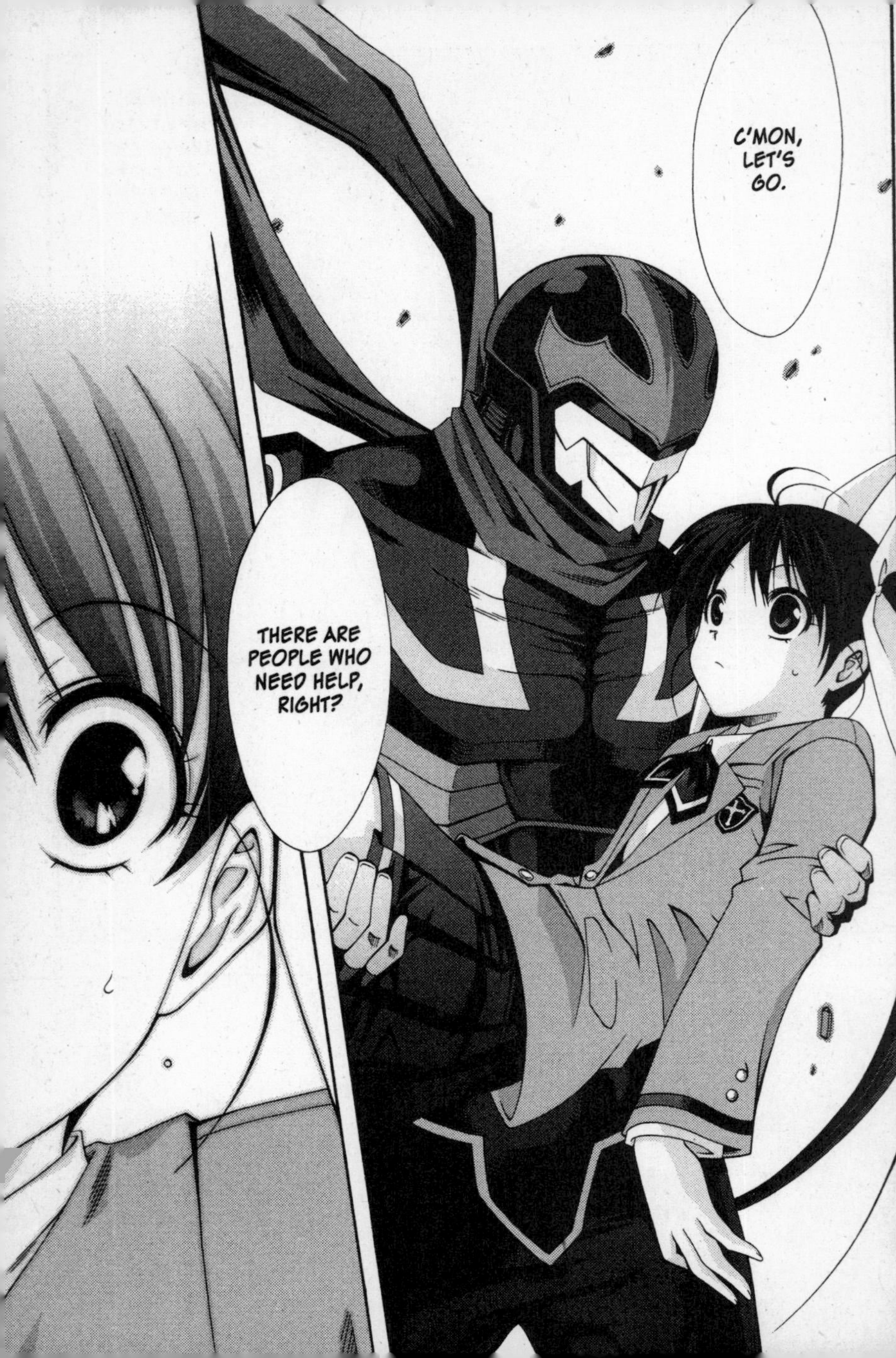
C'MON, LET'S GO.
THERE ARE PEOPLE WHO NEED HELP, RIGHT?

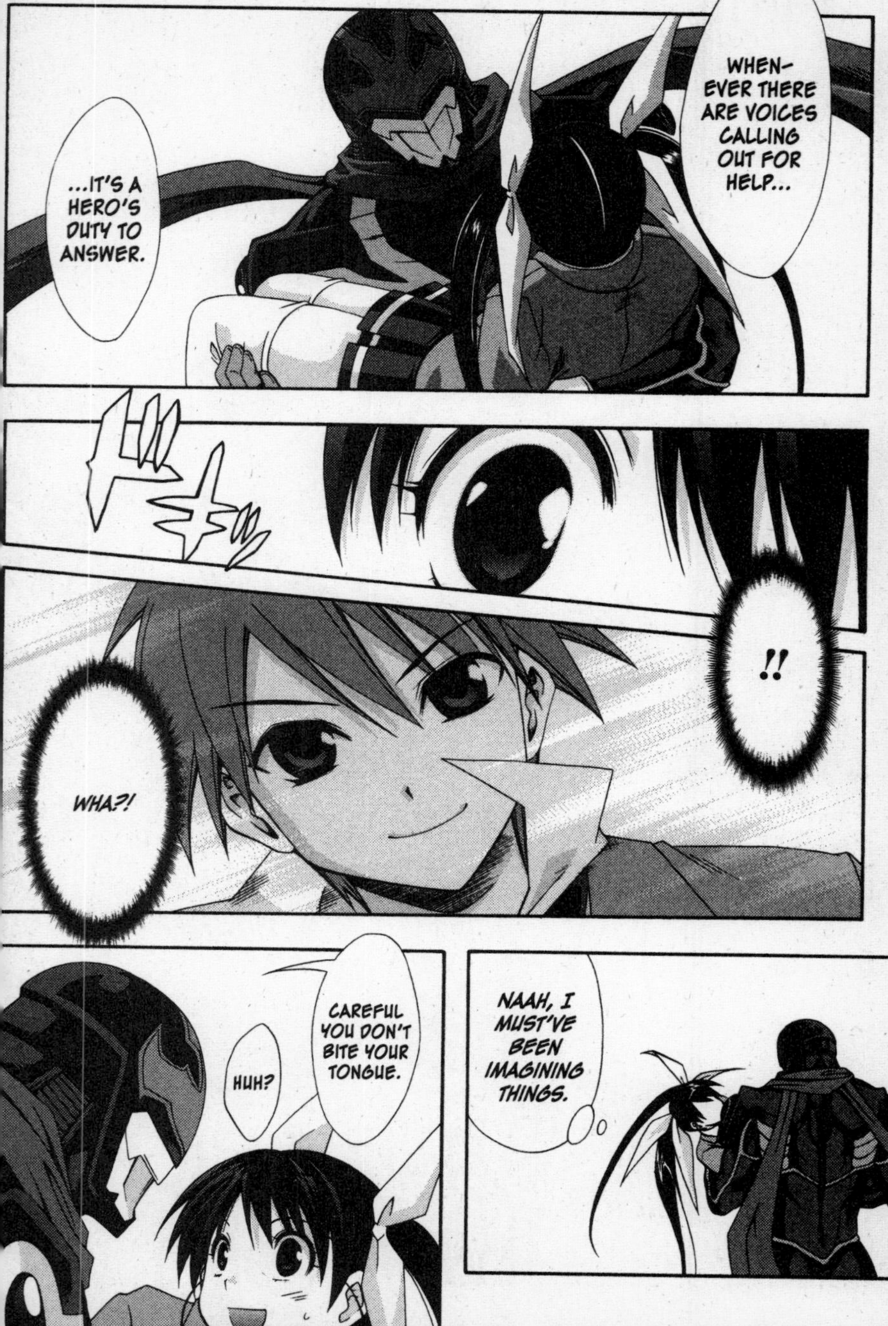
WHEN-EVER THERE ARE VOICES CALLING OUT FOR HELP...
...IT'S A HERO'S DUTY TO ANSWER.
!!
WHA?!
NAAH, I MUST'VE BEEN IMAGINING THINGS.
CAREFUL YOU DON'T BITE YOUR TONGUE.
HUH?

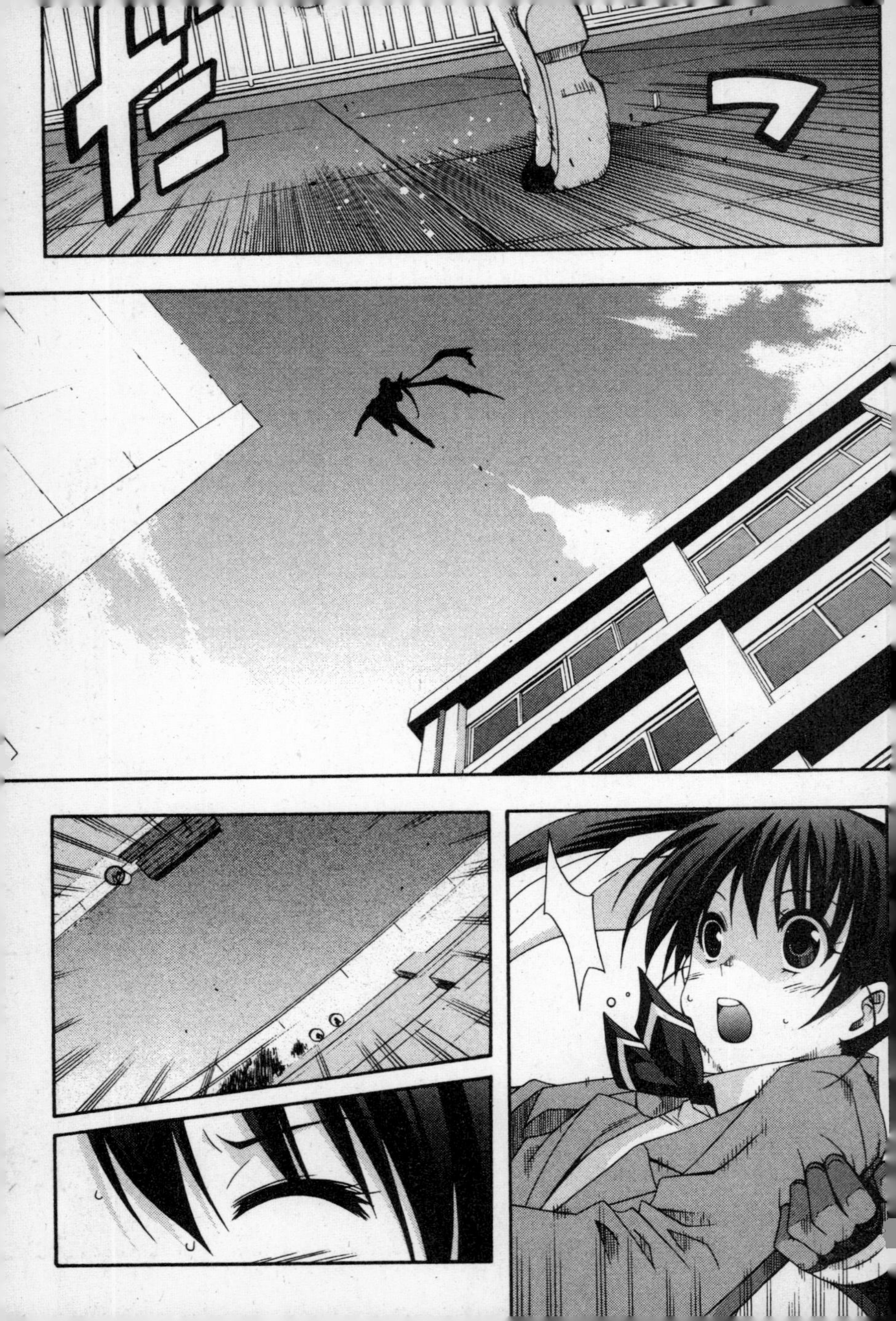

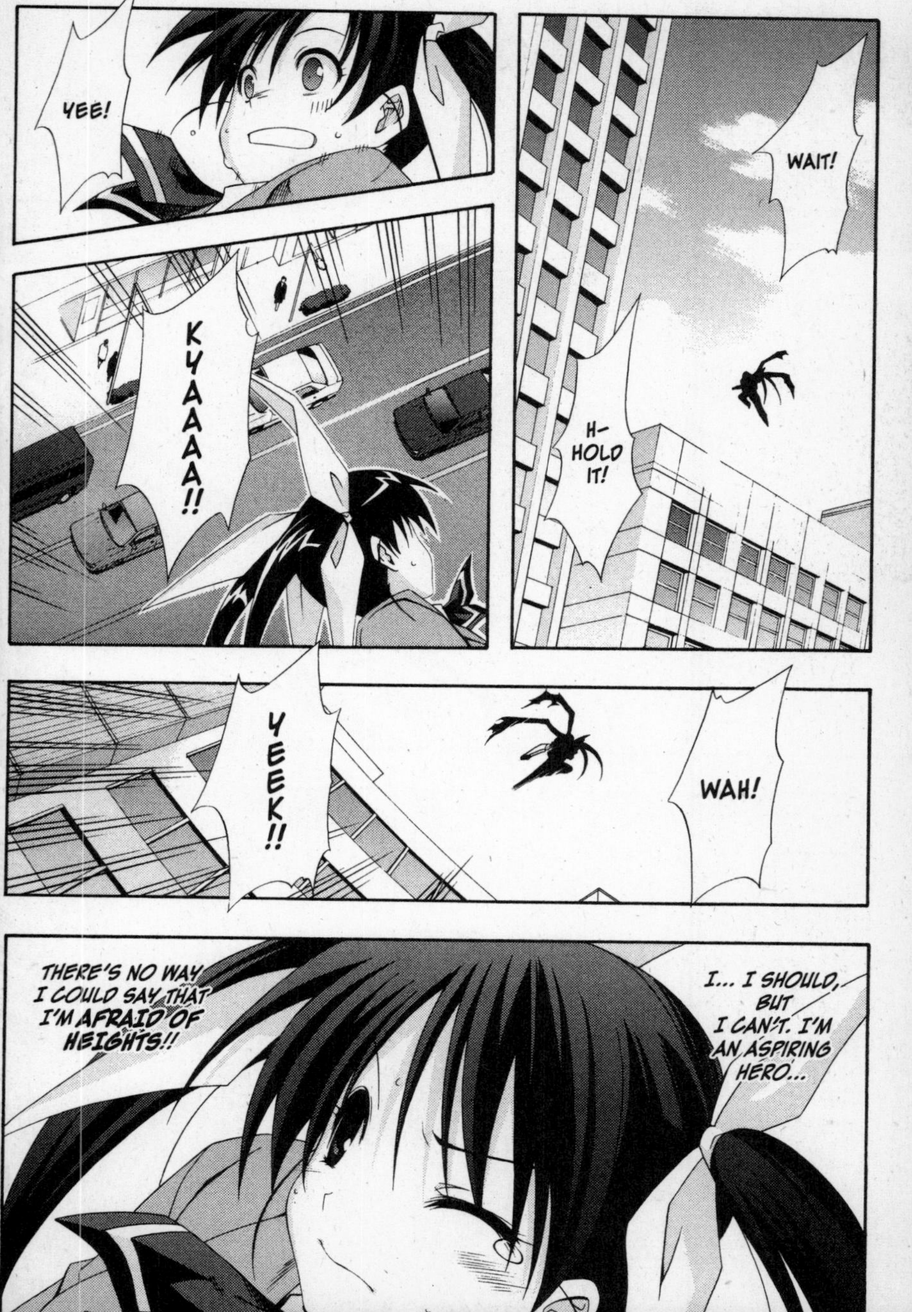
WAIT!
H-HOLD IT!
YEE!
KYAAAAA!!
WAH!
YEEK!!
I... I SHOULD, BUT I CAN'T. I'M AN ASPIRING HERO...
THERE'S NO WAY I COULD SAY THAT I'M AFRAID OF HEIGHTS!!

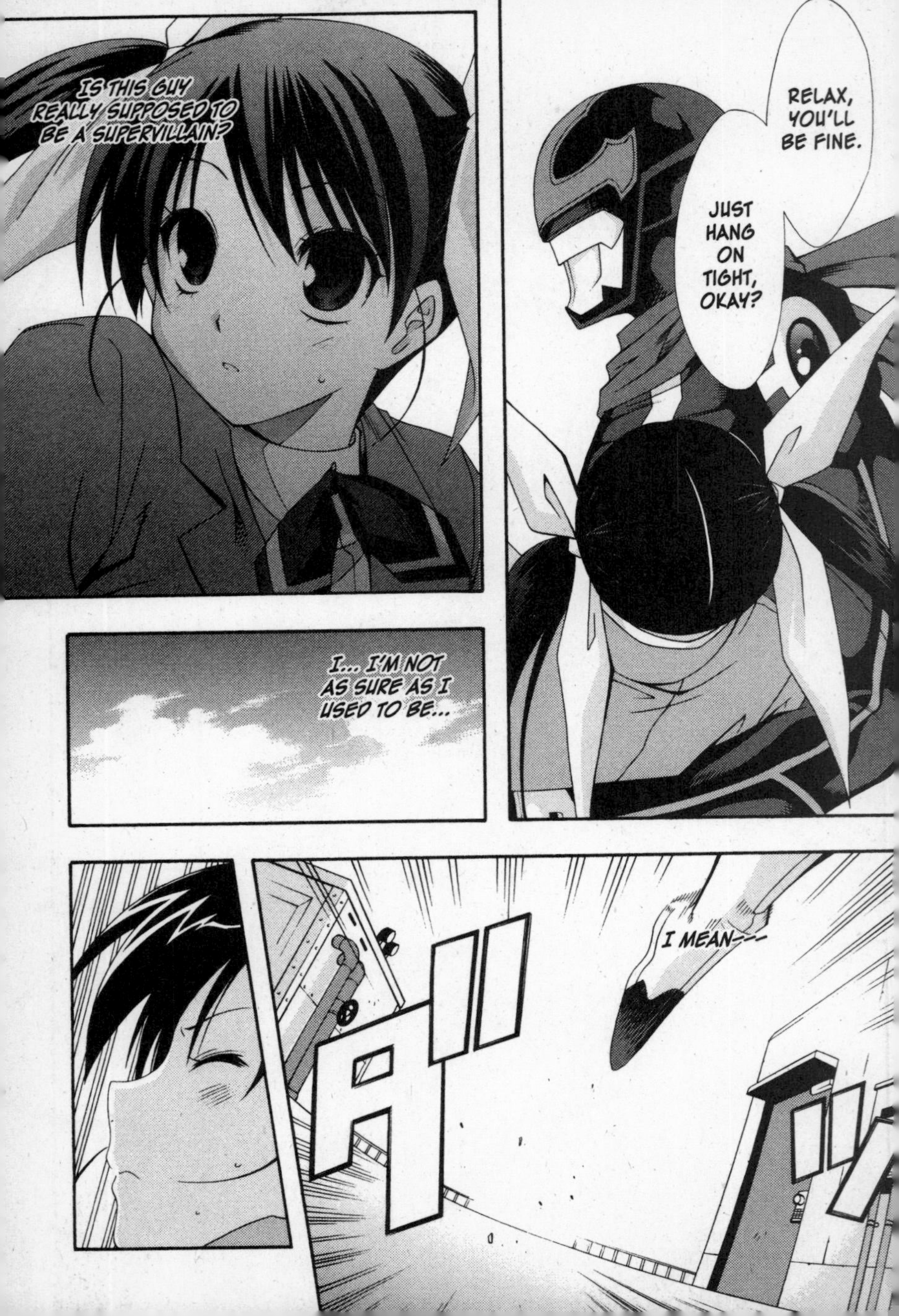
RELAX, YOU'LL BE FINE.
JUST HANG ON TIGHT, OKAY?
IS THIS GUY REALLY SUPPOSED TO BE A SUPERVILLAIN?
I... I'M NOT AS SURE AS I USED TO BE...
I MEAN---

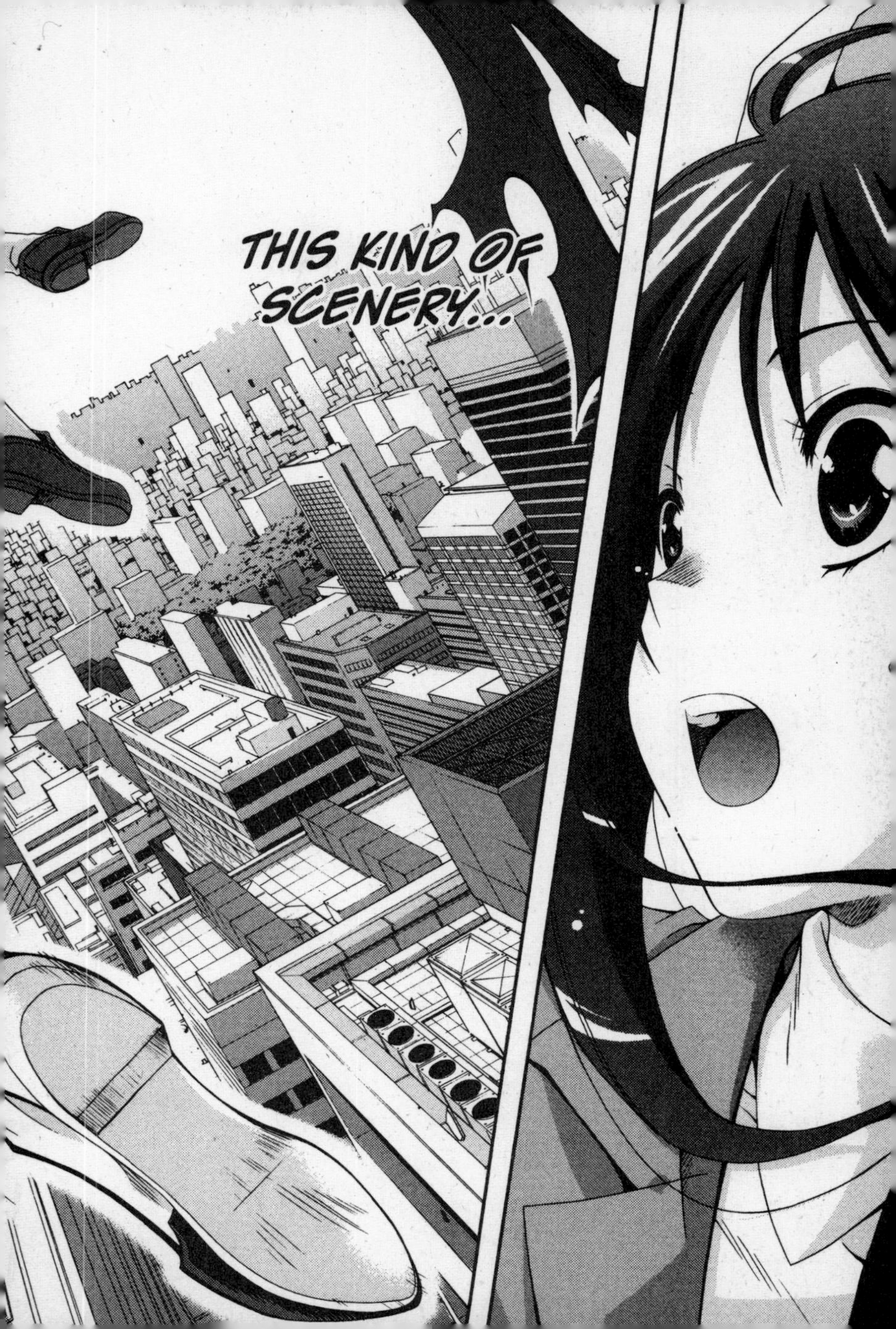
THIS KIND OF SCENERY...

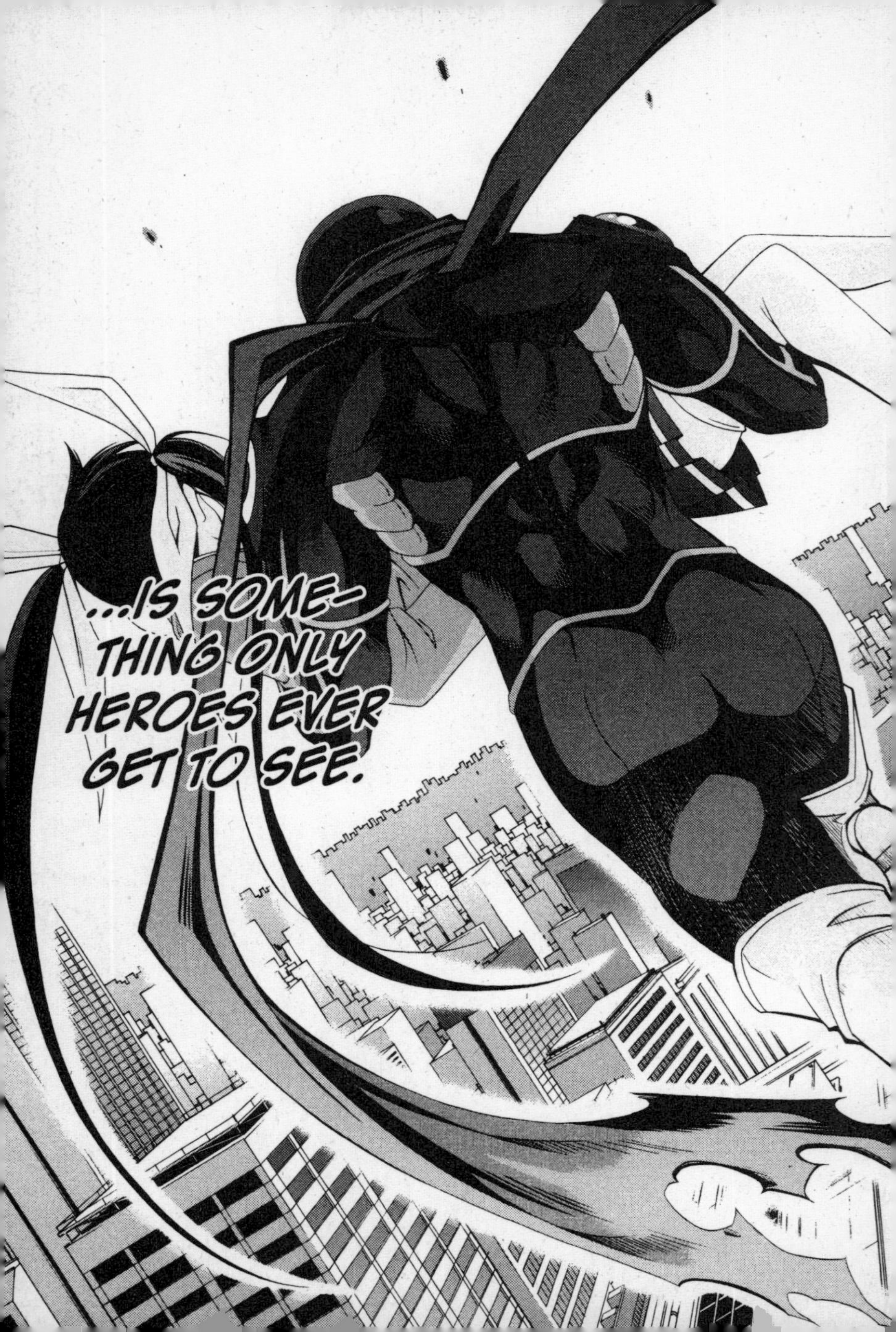
...IS SOME-THING ONLY HEROES EVER GET TO SEE.

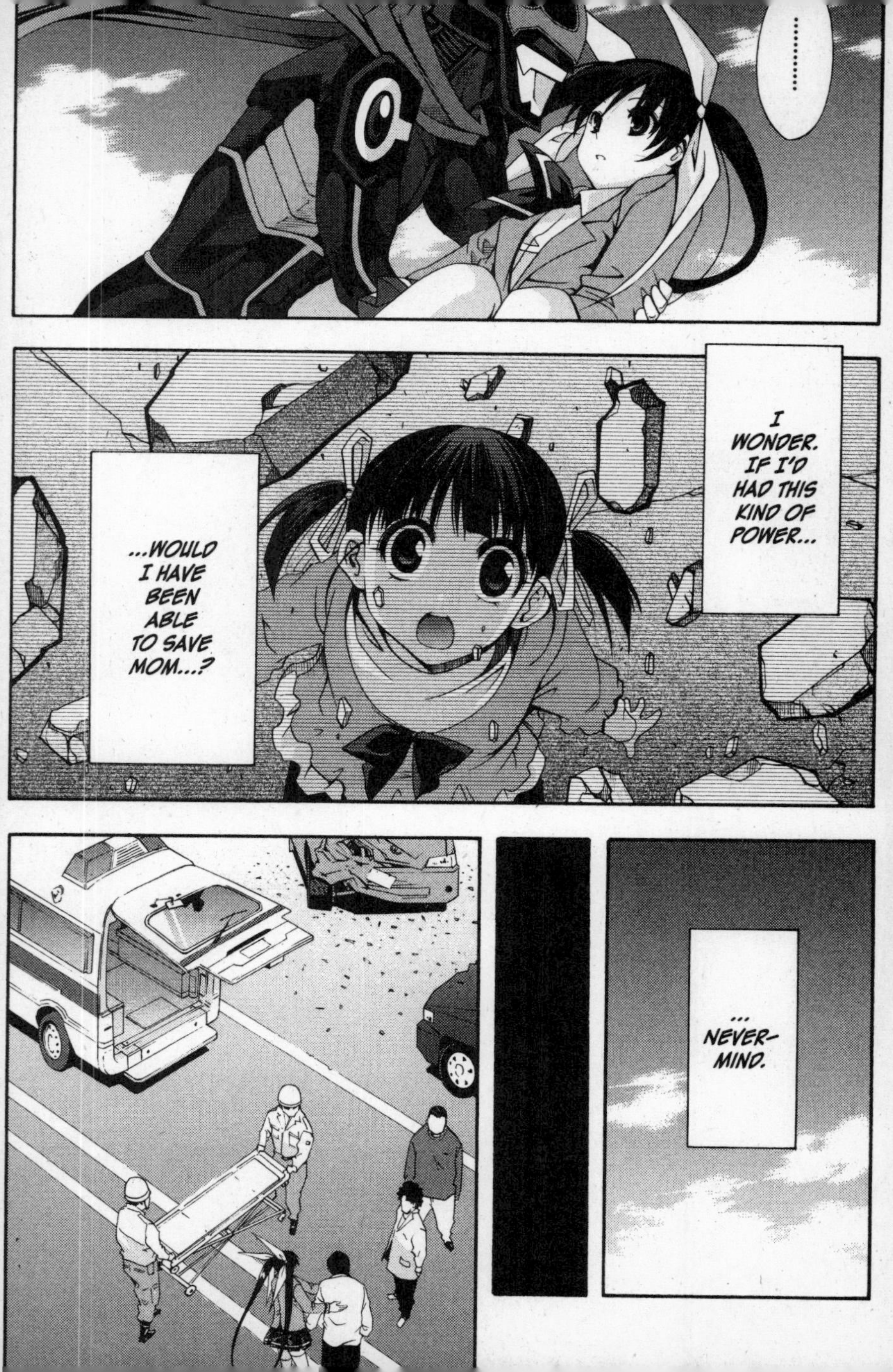
......
I WONDER. IF I'D HAD THIS KIND OF POWER...
...WOULD I HAVE BEEN ABLE TO SAVE MOM...?
... NEVER-MIND.

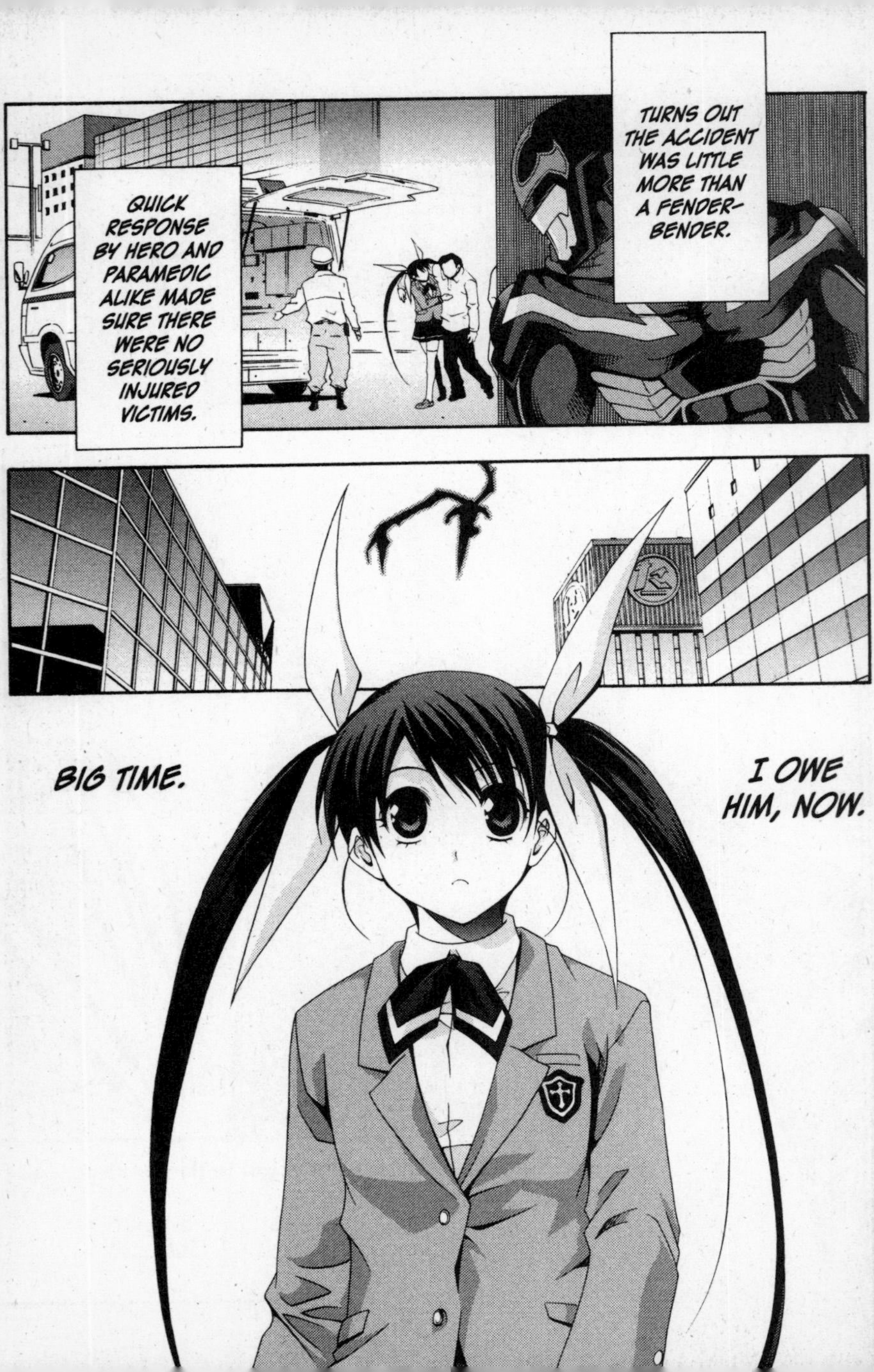
TURNS OUT THE ACCIDENT WAS LITTLE MORE THAN A FENDER-BENDER.
QUICK RESPONSE BY HERO AND PARAMEDIC ALIKE MADE SURE THERE WERE NO SERIOUSLY INJURED VICTIMS.
I OWE HIM, NOW.
BIG TIME.

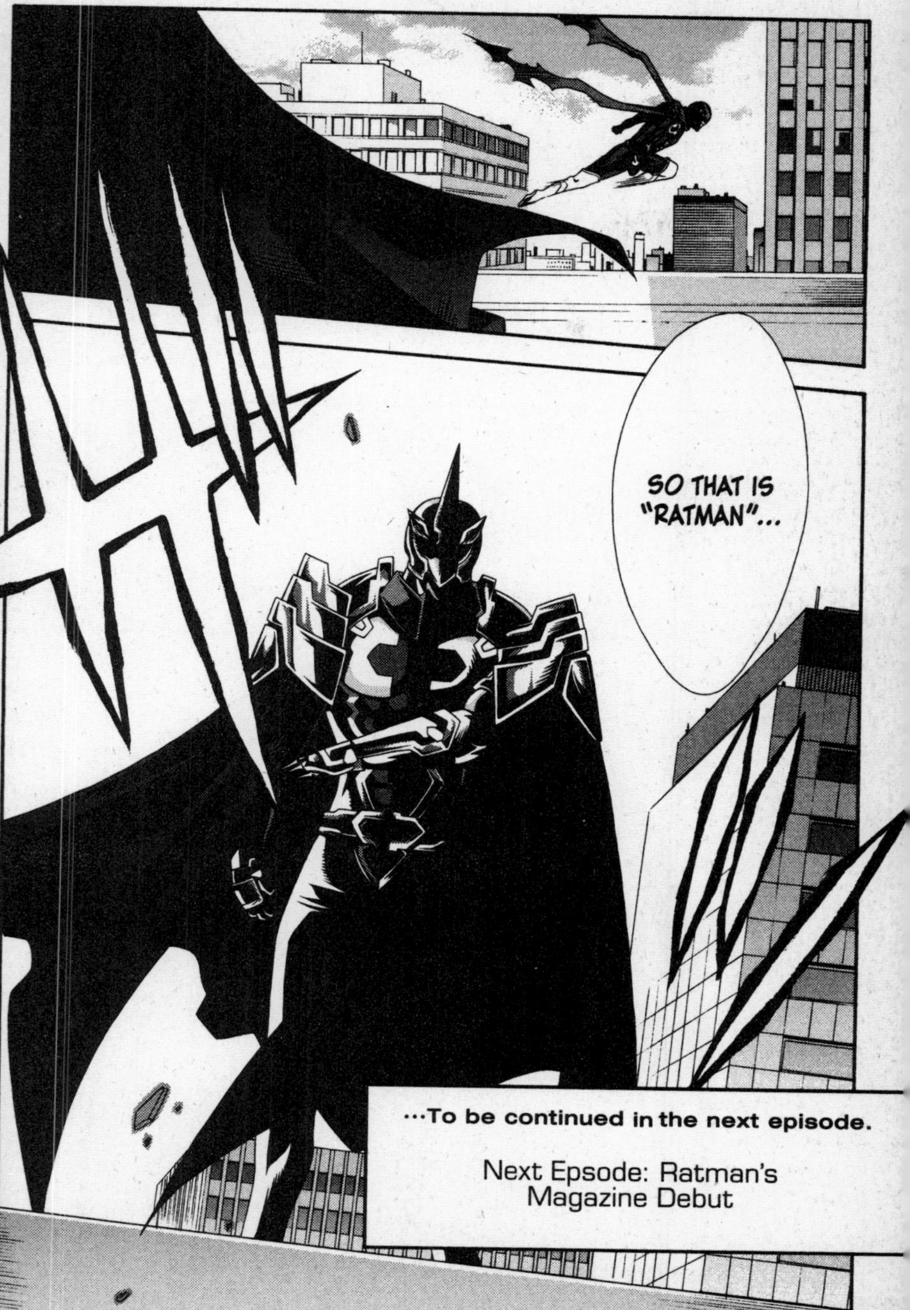
SO THAT IS "RATMAN"...
...To be continued in the next episode.
Next Epsode: Ratman's Magazine Debut

THE SMALLEST HERO!?

RATMAN

ラットマン

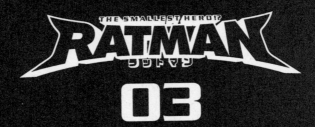

03

Presented by

犬威 赤彦

Inui Sekihiko

Staff

あひる

Ahiru

風川 なぎ

Kazekawa Nagi

神嶋 竜矢

Kamishima Tatsuya

高橋 伸義

Takahashi Nobuyoshi

荒覇吐☆雷矢

Arahabaki Raiya

Graphic Design

沼 利光(D式 グラフヰクス)

Numa Toshimitsu (D式 Graphics)

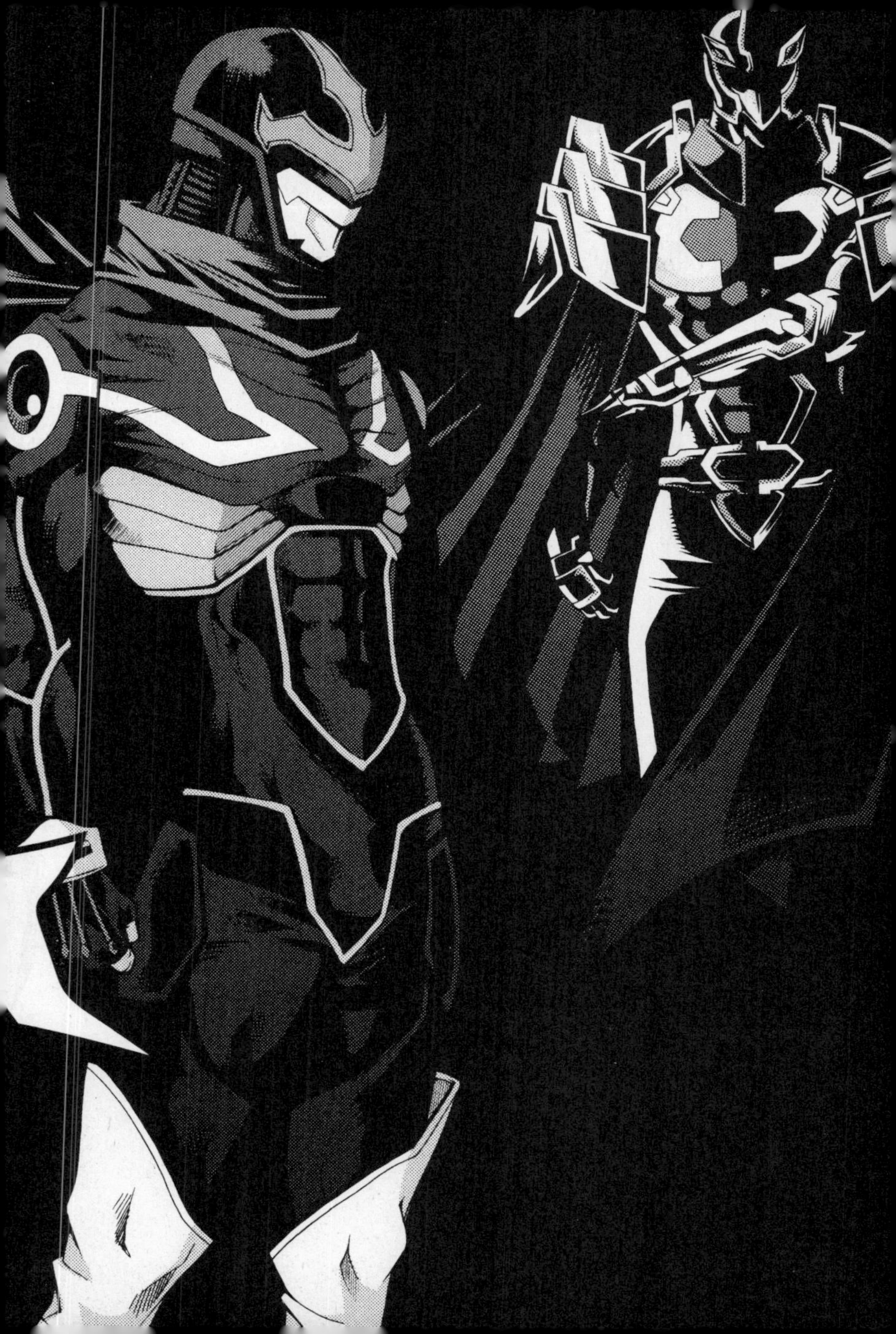

THE JAPAN HERO ASSOCIATION HAS
FINALLY MADE ITS MOVE, SENDING AN
S-RANK HERO AFTER RATMAN. FACED
WITH SUCH ABSOLUTE POWER, WHAT
IS SHUTO GOING TO DO---?!

THE SMALLEST HERO!?

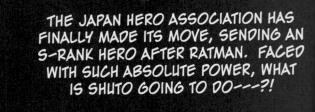

RATMAN
ラットマン
04

★ Fight!! Butterfly Dash Across Edo!! ★

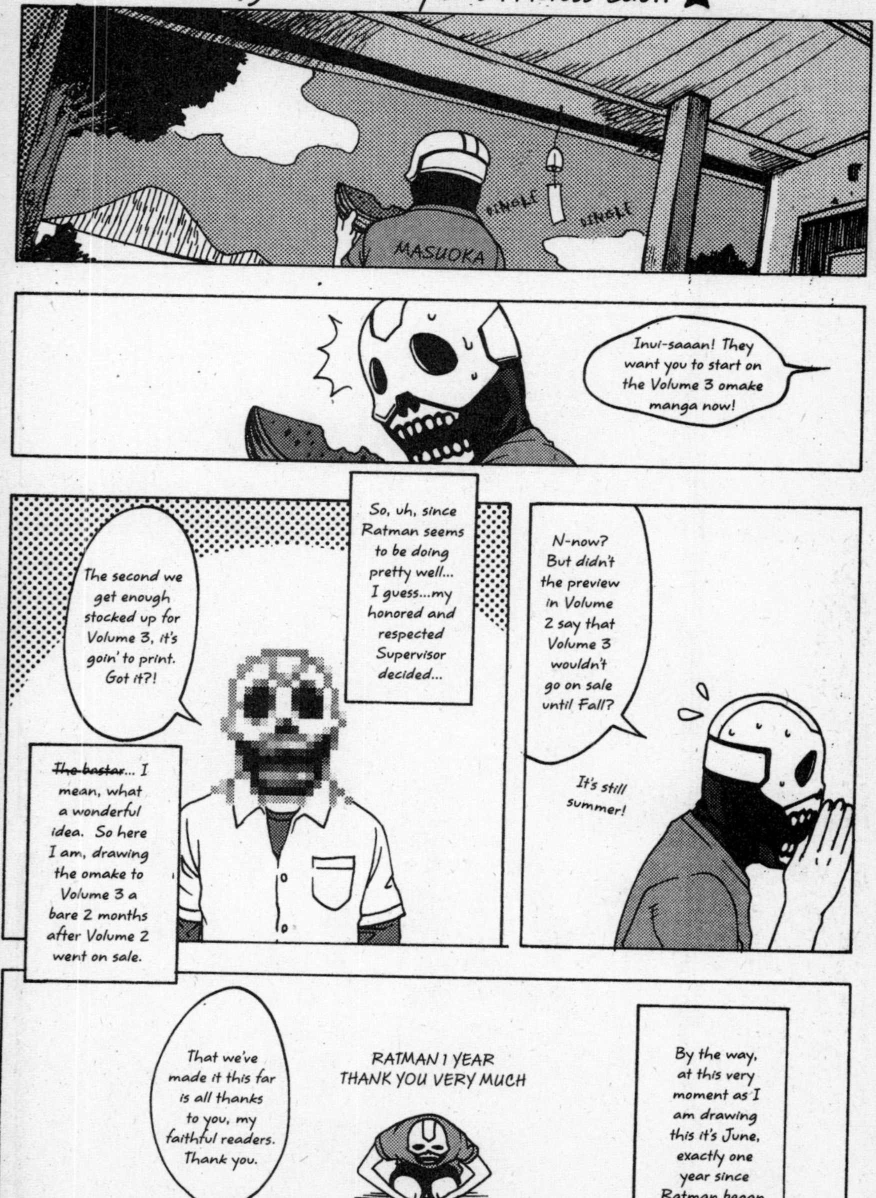
DINGLE
DINGLE
MASUOKA
Inui-saaan! They want you to start on the Volume 3 omake manga now!
N-now? But didn't the preview in Volume 2 say that Volume 3 wouldn't go on sale until Fall?
It's still summer!
So, uh, since Ratman seems to be doing pretty well... I guess...my honored and respected Supervisor decided...
The second we get enough stocked up for Volume 3, it's goin' to print. Got it?!
~~The bastar~~... I mean, what a wonderful idea. So here I am, drawing the omake to Volume 3 a bare 2 months after Volume 2 went on sale.
By the way, at this very moment as I am drawing this it's June, exactly one year since Ratman began.
RATMAN 1 YEAR
THANK YOU VERY MUCH
That we've made it this far is all thanks to you, my faithful readers. Thank you.

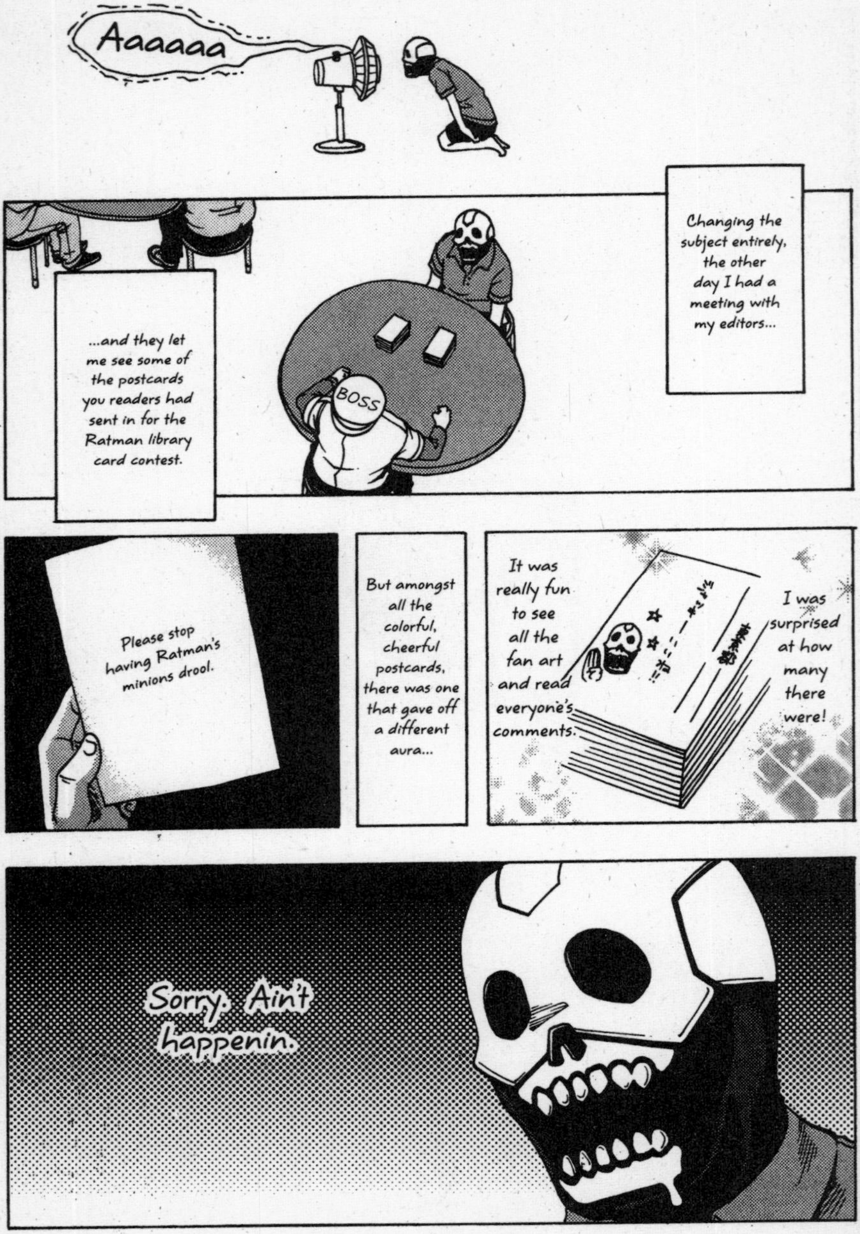
Aaaaaa
Changing the subject entirely, the other day I had a meeting with my editors...
...and they let me see some of the postcards you readers had sent in for the Ratman library card contest.
BOSS
I was surprised at how many there were!
It was really fun to see all the fan art and read everyone's comments.
But amongst all the colorful, cheerful postcards, there was one that gave off a different aura...
Please stop having Ratman's minions drool.
Sorry. Ain't happenin.

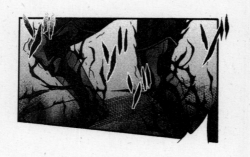

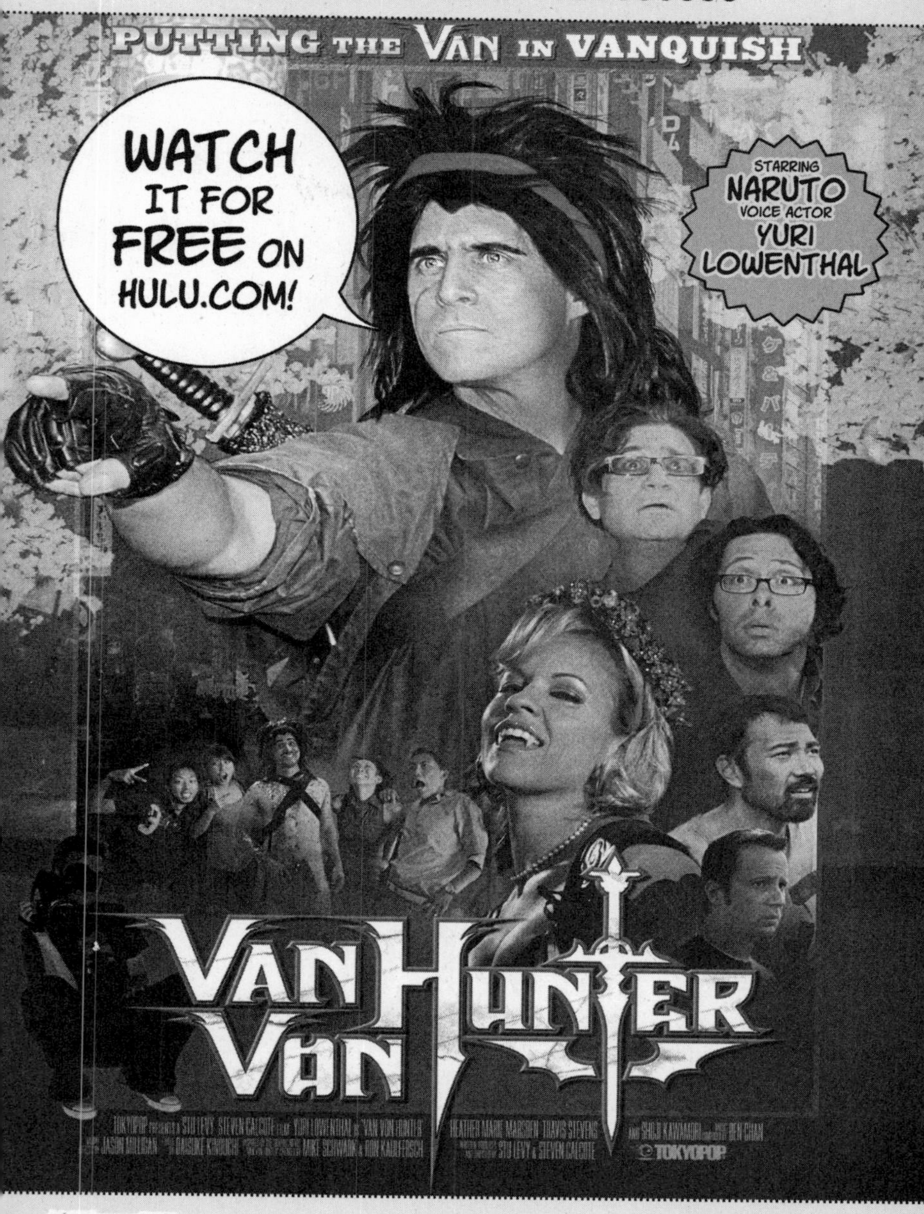

PUTTING THE VAN IN VANQUISH
WATCH IT FOR FREE ON HULU.COM!
STARRING NARUTO VOICE ACTOR YURI LOWENTHAL
VAN VON HUNTER
TOKYOPOP STU LEVY STEVEN CALCOTE YURI LOWENTHAL "VAN VON HUNTER" HEATHER MARIE MARSDEN TRAVIS STEVENS SHOJI KAWAMORI BEN CHAN
JASON MILLIGAN DAISUKE KIKUCHI MIKE SCHWARK RON KAUFERSCH STU LEVY STEVEN CALCOTE
©TOKYOPOP

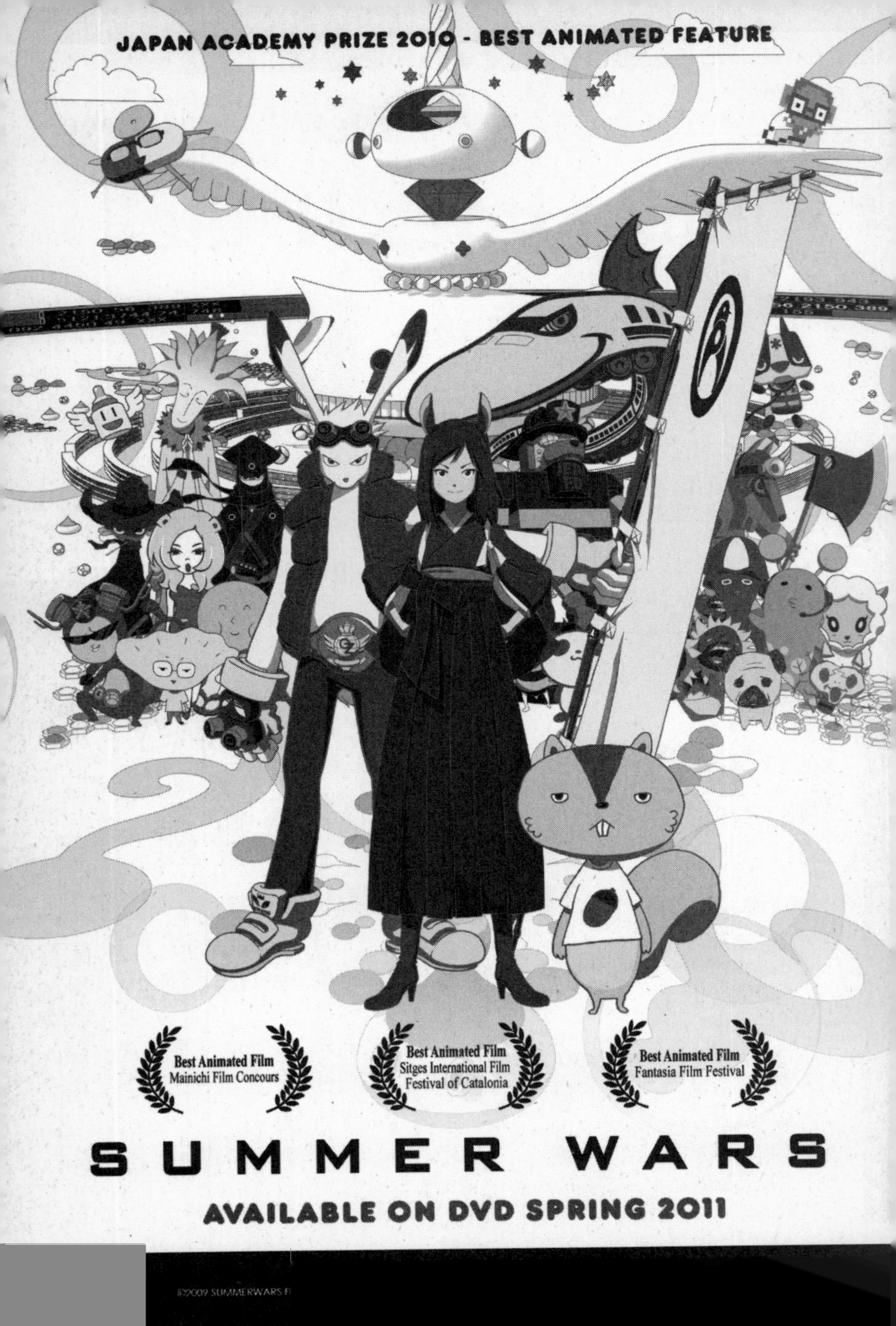

JAPAN ACADEMY PRIZE 2010 - BEST ANIMATED FEATURE
Best Animated Film
Mainichi Film Concours
Best Animated Film
Sitges International Film Festival of Catalonia
Best Animated Film
Fantasia Film Festival
SUMMER WARS
AVAILABLE ON DVD SPRING 2011
©2009 SUMMERWARS F

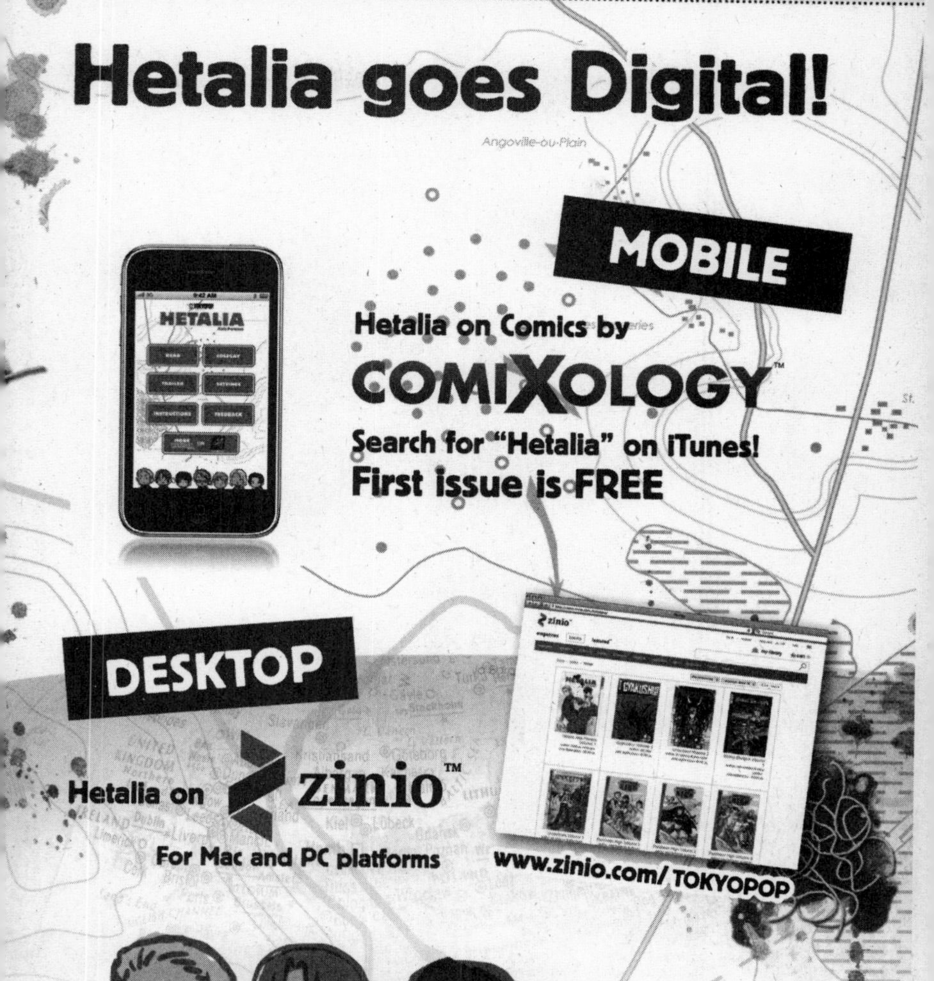
Hetalia goes Digital!
MOBILE
Hetalia on Comics by
COMIXOLOGY™
Search for "Hetalia" on iTunes!
First issue is FREE
DESKTOP
Hetalia on zinio™
For Mac and PC platforms
www.zinio.com/TOKYOPOP
HETALIA
Axis Powers

This is the back of the book.
You wouldn't want to spoil a great ending!

This book is printed "manga-style," in the authentic Japanese right-to-left format. Since none of the artwork has been flipped or altered, readers get to experience the story just as the creator intended. You've been asking for it, so TOKYOPOP® delivered: authentic, hot-off-the-press, and far more fun!

DIRECTIONS

If this is your first time reading manga-style, here's a quick guide to help you understand how it works.

It's easy... just start in the top right panel and follow the numbers. Have fun, and look for more 100% authentic manga from TOKYOPOP®!